THE OLIVIERS

The Oliviers

A BIOGRAPHY BY

Felix Barker

J. B. LIPPINCOTT COMPANY
PHILADELPHIA AND NEW YORK

To My Mother and Father
With Love

Contents

BOOK FOUR

MARRIAGE

BOOK FIVE

IN THEIR OWN THEATRE

Illustrations

Introduction

This is what is called an "authorized" biography, a description which always suggests excessive homage and a great deal of rose-pink lighting. For this reason I should like to say that, while Laurence Olivier and Vivien Leigh have co-operated in the preparation of the book and have given me valuable advice about the completed manuscript, they have not interfered with my interpretation of facts. There has been no censorship of opinions, some of which, for all I know, they may regard as outrageous.

Even had I wanted to, it would have been difficult to write an "Alleluia book" about the Oliviers. They are far too self-critical to be much interested in flattery. In fact, my main problem has been to keep a sense of proportion about their successes because they, themselves, are reluctant to regard much of what they have achieved as important.

Their help has been the best possible guarantee of authenticity, but it is one of the curious tricks of time that while the memory is clear about events of distant childhood it may stumble about something in the unfocused middle-distance of life. So, while Laurence Olivier's memory is excellent (and Vivien Leigh's too, if coaxed), everything in this book has, as far as possible, been checked with other people involved. Diaries, going back to the year when they both met, have been consulted, and I have had access to personal letters.

The Oliviers' friends were badgered and responded gallantly. I fear Vivien Leigh's parents, Mr. and Mrs. Ernest Hartley, were often subjected to a cross-examination which must have seemed rather more searching than that of a prosecuting counsel. To Laurence Olivier's sister Sybille (who wrote a delightful memoir of their childhood) I owe much for valuable information about early years. From America came long letters from many of the Oliviers' innumerable friends—busy people who went to great trouble to answer my questions. At the end of this introduction will be found my thanks to many of them and my acknowledgment of sources of information.

In the world of the theatre and cinema, clashes of temperament are inevitable; they blow up fiercely and die quickly. But a writer, telling his story chronologically, has to convey the emotions of the moment. He cannot anticipate the final outcome. Here and there in this book are accounts of feuds long since forgotten and mention of antagonists who are now close friends. If reconciliations have not always been indicated, I trust that I, and not the Oliviers, will get the blame; for I would repeat that there have been no vetoes and only occasional modifications suggested when they feared that someone other than themselves might be unnecessarily hurt.

It may be of interest to record that much of this book was planned during the run of the Cleopatra plays at the St. James's Theatre two years ago; the first draft prepared while the Oliviers were appearing on Broadway, and revisions completed last autumn while Laurence Olivier was producing and playing in the film of *The Beggar's Opera*. Vivien Leigh and I were still discussing various points and making final decisions about photographs on her return from Ceylon and Hollywood where she had been working on *Elephant Walk*, the film which illness prevented her from completing.

F. B.

Chancery Lane, London
July, 1953

Acknowledgments

It would have been impossible to write this book without the co-operation of all the people in and connected with the theatre and cinema who have given me information and advice. Many of their names occur in the body of the book, and, as they are too numerous to mention individually, I hope they will accept this as an acknowledgment of my gratitude.

I would particularly like to thank Mr. John Marshall, Editor of the London *Evening News*, who sponsored the series of articles which have led to the present volume, and to record the help I have had from a number of people not otherwise mentioned, especially Miss Marie Donaldson, Mr. Jympson Harman, Mr. Geoffrey Lake, Mr. Tom Downes, Mr. David Fairweather and Mr. J. A. Gilbert.

For invaluable material about the Oliviers' early lives I am indebted to Sir Laurence Olivier's sister, Mrs. Gerald Day; his brother, Mr. Gerard Olivier; his stepmother, Mrs. Gerard Olivier; his cousin, Mr. William Olivier (on whose data the family history is largely based); Mr. and Mrs. Ernest Hartley, Mr. Leigh Holman, and the Reverend Geoffrey Heald of St. Stephen's Vicarage, Bournemouth.

Of all the help I have received from the Oliviers' American friends I should like to give special thanks to Mr. Douglas Fairbanks, Mr. and Mrs. Ronald Colman, Mr. William Wyler, Mr. George Cukor and Mrs. Irene Selznick. Mr. Filipo Del Giudice, now living in the United States, has also been most generous in his assistance.

I am grateful to Sir Ralph Richardson, Dr. Dover Wilson, Mr. Tyrone Guthrie, Mr. Stephen Mitchell and Mr. Frank Nortcliffe for permission to quote from their letters; and to the Society of Authors,

13

trustees of the late Mr. Bernard Shaw, for permission to include Mr. Shaw's postcards to Vivien Leigh.

For permission to quote extracts from their papers I wish to thank the Editors of the *Observer*, the *Sunday Times*, *The Times*, the *Daily Telegraph*, the *News Chronicle*, the Manchester *Evening Chronicle*, the *New York Times* and the *Pittsburgh Press*.

For permission to quote extracts from books I have to thank: Victor Gollancz Ltd., Miss Ellen Terry's executors and G. P. Putnam's Sons for the quotation from *Ellen Terry's Memoirs;* Hamish Hamilton Ltd., McGraw-Hill Book Company, Inc. and Mr. John Mason Brown for the review of *Oedipus*, which appears in *Seeing Things;* George G. Harrap and Co. and Crown Publishers, Inc. for the extracts from *Ego 9* (included in *The Later Ego*, New York, 1951) by the late Mr. James Agate; Mr. Donagh MacDonagh for the quotation from *Fading Mansion;* Hamish Hamilton Ltd. and Mr. Alan Dent for the review of *Oedipus* from *Nocturnes and Rhapsodies;* the Oxford University Press and Mr. Christopher Fry for the lines from *Venus Observed;* Macmillan and Co. Ltd., London, and St. Martin's Press, Inc., New York, for the quotation from Professor A. C. Bradley's *Oxford Lectures on Poetry*.

Among many books consulted perhaps the most useful have been *Great Names*, by Thoda Cocroft; *Meeting at the Sphinx*, by Marjorie Deans; *Mr. Rank*, by Alan Wood; *The Film Hamlet*, edited by Brenda Cross; *Old Vic Saga*, by Harcourt Williams; and, of course, those excellent reference books, *Who's Who in the Theatre* and *The Motion Picture Almanac*.

I wish to give special thanks to Mr. P. B. Hepburn, who read the proofs, for his suggestions and criticisms.

For her highly perceptive advice and encouragement; for hours devoted to research; for typing the entire manuscript and vigilantly correcting the proofs; for all this and more I wish to thank my wife. This book owes a great deal to her.

BOOK ONE

Laurence Olivier

CHAPTER 1

The Clergyman's Son
1907-1924

I

IT IS DIFFICULT to shake off the conventional theory that a wide and formidable chasm yawns between the theatre and the church. Prejudice, born of an over-simplified conception of Victorian ethics, casts a lurid glow over the tragedy of a clergyman's son going on the stage. There is an immediate picture of a slammed door, a sorrowing mother, and erasure from the family Bible.

The fact that a number of actors are the sons of clergymen and remain on the best possible terms with their parents does little to unseat the misconception. Imagination insists that for youth to declare for green-room instead of vestry is a family disaster, and it has needed the example of such famous names as Matheson Lang, the Thorndikes, and the Vanbrughs to show that choice of the stage has not always brought sorrow to white clerical heads. But it is still surprising to learn that, after centuries of church tradition, and with a father and grandfather, both of whom were clergymen, Laurence Olivier was not only encouraged by his father to become an actor but, as will be seen, was actually reproved for suggesting an alternative. In his family this departure from historical precedent is all the more conspicuous because, for the previous five generations, only two in the direct line of descent had chosen vocations outside the church. And, however thoroughly the long and widespread

17

branches of the family tree may be searched, there is no other actor to be found.

At the beginning of the sixteenth century the Oliviers or de Oliviers were Huguenots who lived at Nay in Gascony, a small village in the Basses-Pyrénées a few miles south of Pau. There has always been a family tradition that they were among the great number of French Protestants who took refuge in England after the revocation of the Edict of Nantes, but everything points to Laurence Olivier's branch of the family having emigrated first to Holland. From there some went to South Africa, but Laurence's direct ancestor, the Reverend Jourdain Olivier, came to England in 1688 as Chaplain to William of Orange. Eleven years before, and while still residing in Pau where he was born, he had married a woman with the seemingly English name of Anne Day.

Their son, Jerome, who was born in London, also followed into the church, and records exist to show that he served as minister of the French Chapel of the Savoy in 1721. Jerome married a French-woman, and so, too, did his son, Daniel Josias Olivier. Daniel, how-ever, made a break in the clerical line and became an eminent diamond merchant in the City of London. His French wife was Susannah, niece of Jean Baptiste Massé, court painter to Louis XV. Many of his exquisite miniatures are now in the possession of Laurence's cousin, William Olivier.

After being dormant for a generation, the church tradition then re-asserted itself, and the merchant's son, also named Daniel, became rector of Clifton in Bedfordshire during the latter half of the eighteenth century. He married the daughter of a clergyman, but once again the church missed a generation and their second son was an Army man. A justice of the peace and High Sheriff of Wiltshire, Colonel Henry Stephen Olivier had some brief fame for raising "Olivier's Horse," a contingent of mounted volunteers who helped to suppress the Rick Riots and agrarian revolts in the southern counties prior to the Reform Bill. All three of his sons were clergymen, and one of his two daughters married a clergyman. The eldest son, the Reverend Henry Arnold Olivier, became the rector of Poulshot in Wiltshire during the middle of the last century, and had a large family of six daughters and four sons. His youngest child, Gerard Kerr Olivier, was Laurence's father.

The family of this Wiltshire rector was a remarkable one, and although Laurence did not see a great deal of his uncles and aunts when he was a boy, he was to have particular reason to remember his Uncle Sydney who was, perhaps, the most eminent. An early Fabian, a friend of Bernard Shaw and the Webbs, and for some years Governor of Jamaica, he became Lord Olivier and was Secretary for India during Ramsay MacDonald's administration. Laurence met him once a few months before he went to the Central School to study for the stage, and having heard of his friendship with Shaw eagerly asked him if he went to the theatre much. His answer was disconcerting. "No," said Uncle Sydney, "I prefer the cinema. Makes less tax on the intelligence!" Besides Uncle Sydney, there were Uncle Henry, an Army colonel, and Uncle Herbert, a portrait painter who has only recently died, but who as long ago as 1935 held what he called a Premature Posthumous Exhibition of his work.

There was always a certain amount of money in the Olivier family, perhaps an inheritance from old Daniel, the wealthy diamond merchant, but it was not to be expected that Olivier's father, as the youngest son, would see much of it. He was, in fact, left only some family cutlery and a Canaletto painting of the Rialto. Yet even though the Reverend Gerard Kerr Olivier was to be poor throughout most of his life, he was given a liberal and unusual upbringing. At sixteen, while he was a schoolboy at Winchester, he was taken by his parents on a tour of France, and he spent several holidays in Italy where his father, skilfully combining duty and pleasure, would take on the incumbency of the Church of England in Alassio while the regular chaplain was away for the summer. It was during one of these holidays that objection by a clergyman to his son contemplating the idea of going on the stage was shown in the most abrupt and traditional manner. Gerard had been encouraged to take singing lessons and was discovered to have a potentially fine voice. It was so good that a then famous tenor, Signor Lamberti, who heard him, offered to train him for opera. Gerard came home in great excitement with the news, but it was met very coldly. His mother even went to the lengths of handing him a lira, presumably in lieu of the more customary shilling, and threatened that it was all the money he would ever receive from her if he adopted "that monstrous profession."

Once again the church presented the obvious choice for an Olivier, and when he made his decision to become a parson his father was delighted and sent him to Merton College, Oxford. His university career was hardly a dazzling one, and Laurence, who heard little about it until he was grown up, often wished he could have been told more when he was a boy. It would certainly have helped him to regard his father as far more of a human being and less of a martinet if he had known the truth about his life as an undergraduate. For at Oxford Gerard did all those things of which a boy imagines his father incapable. He lived above his income and ran into debt; he joined the Oxford University Dramatic Society; he read Plato and so completely lost his faith that he decided to give up the church; finally, so the story went, he was sent down. The incident which caused him to come home in disgrace is cloaked in a certain amount of mystery, but it was his dinner-time boast to his family that it was for driving a coach-and-four down the High. Later, Laurence formed the private opinion that he was not sent down by the University at all but was withdrawn by his parents because of his debts. From Oxford he was sent to Durham University and there completed his studies and took his degree.

He was a good cricketer and had once played for Hampshire, and this made the question of an alternative career to the church extremely easy. A degree and a county cap were the exact qualifications for schoolmastering, and he slipped into the unexciting routine of an assistant master at Boxgrove, a preparatory school in Guildford. At Boxgrove he met the girl who was to become his wife and Laurence's mother. Her name was Agnes Crookenden and she was the sister of the headmaster's wife. She was a pretty, brown-eyed girl with a strong sense of humour, and, in the unpredictable manner of these things, it was one sunny afternoon during a winter term—as he saw her pouring out tea for the boys—that the young assistant master fell in love with her and decided to ask her to marry him.

She must have needed all her sense of humour for she and Gerard Olivier were engaged for four years while they patiently saved enough money on which to marry and buy a small school of their own. At last they were able to start their married life at Tower House, Dorking, with just enough pupils during the first term to cover the household expenses. The school flourished, but they were not to be there for long. Three years after the birth of their first child, which was a girl, and while their second, a boy, was still a baby, Gerard Olivier rediscovered the religious faith which he had lost in his early days as an undergraduate. In his mid-thirties, and to his wife's considerable disquiet, he decided to take Holy Orders. Agnes had always vowed she would never marry a parson, partly because of the inevitable poverty it entailed, but principally because she simply did not fancy the idea of becoming a parson's wife. Now, with two young children, her whole life was to be revolutionized. With zealous enthusiasm for his new vocation Gerard insisted that the school must be sold. All the domestic staff with the exception of the children's nurse were dismissed, and Agnes decided to learn to cook and do housework. It was a wise precaution, for her husband's first clerical appointment as an assistant at St. Martin's, Dorking, was not a remunerative one.

II

The Oliviers moved to Wathen Road just off Dorking High Street, and it was here, at No. 26 in a row of semi-detached Victorian villas, that their third child was born at five o'clock in the morning of May 22nd, 1907. He was christened at St. Martin's, and the name given him was Laurence, after Laurent Olivier, his sixteenth-century French ancestor and the earliest recorded name on the family tree. The small red-brick house with the slate roof in Wathen Road was far from imposing, and Laurence does not remember it; before he was three the family had moved to a larger, far more pleasant house which stood on the edge of a common known as the Cotmandene. They named it East Dene, and, in the long narrow garden behind the house with its view which stretched to Box Hill, Laurence, sitting in his pram and wearing a large sailor hat, whiled away the hours in the indolent bliss of early childhood.

The house which looked down on the then unspoilt country town of Dorking would have been a happy place in which to grow up and make friends, but none of the Olivier children was to enjoy any sense of permanency during their upbringing. Throughout their early life, it seemed to them, they were no sooner settled comfortably in one house and getting to know the countryside and their neighbours, than they were told they were moving again. Tears and protests were useless; father had been given a new appointment and the decision was unalterable. Shortly after Laurence's third

birthday the family left Dorking for London, a hateful change for
the three children. The move took place at about the same time
as the phrasing of his first complete sentence. His mother had
pricked her finger with a needle and her reaction provoked curiosity.
"Why you say damn for, Mummy?" came an inquiry from the
pram.

The frequent transfers from one parish to another were not, perhaps, entirely accidental. Laurence's father had all the enthusiasm
and sense of mission peculiar to the late convert, and some of his
low church congregations found his methods a little unorthodox.
It was a period when high Anglican trends in the Church of England generally found less favour than they do to-day, and while
most people liked him there were a few complaints which probably
got back to the bishop. He liked to be known as "Father" Olivier,
practised a good deal of ritual, and burnt incense; to the low church-
man it was an ominous combination. He was also a vivid and dramatic preacher, another suspect quality, and those who saw him in
the pulpit at the time have said it was quite obvious from whom his
son inherited his acting ability. Doubts were murmured about
whether such histrionics were compatible with sincerity, and this
was a sentiment that was to be shared by the next vicar to whom
he became an assistant.

The move from Dorking was to Notting Hill, and there Gerard
Olivier was attached to St. James's Church, but his real duties were
as curate in charge of a small mission hut with a tin roof in Notting
Dale. The family had a house in Elgin Crescent from the nursery
of which the children could just see the lights of the White City
Exhibition. Laurence's father stayed there a year, a year of increasing friction which ended in open conflict. From the start there had
been objections because he walked about the streets in his cassock
and black shovel-hat to match like a Roman Catholic priest. Then
there was the question of incense. Quite apart from burning it in
his little mission church, he had taught the local slum boys to swing
the censers. Such corruption of youth caused the vicar to ask him
to resign. He replied that he loved his church and congregation,
and he refused point blank. The vicar said this left him no alternative but to dismiss him.

Father Olivier reported the interview in detailed and dramatic
terms to his family over lunch on the day that it took place. It

was not quickly forgotten by the children who knew that they would soon be packing their toys again. "Imagine," he concluded in a voice of thunder. "Sacked. Dismissed. Disgraced. And all for a matter of principle!" Laurence's mother tried to look sympathetic, but faced the prospect of moving again without enthusiasm.

During the summer of heat-waves in 1912 there followed a series of moves for the Olivier family from one seaside town to another, at each of which Father Olivier acted as a "locum" while the resident vicar was on holiday. In the meanwhile he was searching for a fresh and more permanent appointment. By Christmas he had found one. He was made first assistant priest at St. Saviour's, Pimlico, and, much relieved after months of uncertainty, the family moved into No. 22 Lupus Street.

By then Laurence was five, and it was in the tall narrow house in Lupus Street that he was to spend the next six years of his life. Here, using the eiderdown for vestments and solemnly copying the ritual he saw his father performing on Sundays, he played at being a clergyman in front of a toy altar. These services were conducted in his bedroom on the door of which was pinned, perhaps prematurely, a notice which read, "S. Laurence's Shrine." Children in the neighbourhood were dragged in to serve as his congregation. There was also less religious play-acting. With his brother Dickie, he would form chairs in rows to represent a train and on to this he would jump like a guard and emit the piercing whistle of the engine. This was a game which never lost its fascination and the train was never left behind when they went on holidays. With its varied noises and whistle it would appear, to the deep dissatisfaction of innumerable landladies, on wet afternoons in seaside lodgings.

At the age of seven Laurence made his first stage. Alone, and without any help from his brother, he dragged a heavy wooden box, used for storing the family baby clothes, in front of the window in the nursery and draped some blue curtains round it. With his father's help this was further improved by placing a row of candles, shielded by half cocoa tins, in front as footlights. On this stage he would act and sing and dance for hours and to his heart's content. His sister recalls that if he could persuade Dickie to act with him that was fine; if not, he was quite content to take not only the leads but the subsidiary parts as well. An audience composed of the family was a welcome but by no means essential feature of the performances. The plays were nameless charades, created on the whim of the moment, shouted and postured in the nursery air, their plots and characters now lost for ever.

The year in which he built his first stage acquired a wider significance. It was 1914, but for Laurence this was not so much the year war broke out as the year he first went to school. The year before, when he was only six, he had been sent as a boarder to a little school at Blackheath, but he had cried so much at being separated from his parents that they had taken him away. Now a day school was found in Graham Terrace, much nearer his home, where a friend of the family named Miss Sheppard was a teacher. This was the Francis Holland Church of England School for Girls, which, like many girls' schools, had a junior class for small boys. If it did not cause tears like Blackheath, it did not seem to create much of an impression on Laurence who, in a bid for independence, soon invented an ingenious way of playing truant. He would ask permission to leave school in the morning an hour before the other pupils were let out; he had to meet a Miss Finlayson on Eccleston Bridge and have lunch with her. His mother was sorry, he told Miss Sheppard, that she hadn't had time to write a note. Permission granted for him to make this mythical rendezvous, he would then walk home at his leisure, eating sweets bought with the money for his bus fare. If he arrived home earlier than his mother expected he would meet her surprise with the bland assurance, "Oh, we were let out earlier to-day." Boredom at school tempted Laurence to try this trick rather too often, and Miss Sheppard wrote to his mother to complain of these frequent luncheon arrangements. Truancy ended with the slipper.

III

It was while they were living in Pimlico that the Oliviers started what was to become a long association with the church of All Saints in Margaret Street, near Oxford Circus, and the small choir school attached to it. The number of boys was always maintained at fourteen, and it produced one of the best choirs in England. Sybille, Laurence's sister, was confirmed at the church when she was ten and Dickie was sent to the school as a pupil and chorister when he was nine. In 1916 Laurence joined him.

As well as ordinary school work, there were long practices for the church choir, and as it was not practicable for them to go home each night both he and Dickie became boarders. It was not a school that would have been popular with most boys because holidays, too, were subject to the exacting training and were shorter than those of most schools. To make up for this in some measure, a week's sea-side camp was arranged in the summer and there were various treats during term-time. At Christmas the Duke of Newcastle, a patron and churchwarden of All Saints, always took a block of seats in the dress circle at Drury Lane so that the boys, their relatives, and even their friends could see the pantomime. It was at Drury Lane that, dressed in an Eton jacket and with a white tie and waistcoat, Laurence leaned eagerly forward as the lights dimmed and the cur-tain went up on the first performance he had seen in a real theatre. The pantomime was *Babes in the Wood* with Stanley Lupino and Will Evans, and the delight of the boys knew no bounds when Lupino in a cross-talk gag with Will Evans made a reference to the choirboys in the dress circle. Afterwards the Duke of Newcastle took the boys back-stage, and, when he was ushered in to meet the comedian, Laurence entered a theatrical dressing-room for the first time in his life.

Education at the choir school was by no means exclusively spirit-ual. Dancing lessons had their place in the curriculum, and a young actress named Fabia Drake who, at thirteen, was already appearing in the West End, came in to take the rather clumsy and uncertain young choirboys through the steps of the polka and the waltz. Great interest was also shown in drama. The vicar, H. F. B. Mackay, and Geoffrey Heald, the precentor, who were, themselves, excellent amateur actors, frequently put on plays, and early during the time Laurence was there a harlequinade was staged in which he was cast for the policeman. He wrote home for some props and received a papier-mâché policeman's helmet. With this he gave an impromptu comic impression at one rehearsal and Geoffrey Heald was pleased to note that it was not just a wild, silly burlesque. It seemed to him that the boy must have studied his subject carefully. When he came to produce *Julius Cæsar* at the end of the Christmas term in 1917, Heald chose Laurence for the part of First Citizen, but he proved so good during early rehearsals that, although he was the smallest boy in the cast, he was switched to Brutus. Thick-set, with a large head, wide mouth and grave eyes, Laurence seemed ideal for Brutus, and he had no hesitation in taking the part away from a slightly older boy named Ralph Forbes. Forbes, who was to become a film star and whom Laurence was to meet years later in Hollywood when Forbes was married to Ruth Chatterton, was cast for Cassius. Dickie played Cæsar. Rehearsals sometimes took place during air raids through which Laurence, curled up on a rug in the crypt of the church, went on learning his lines oblivious of the noise. Heald thought he had never come across any boy who so quickly picked up the points of diction and deportment, and when the play was produced he gave a remarkable performance.

It must also have been a remarkable production to attract to the little school hall an audience which included Ellen Terry, Lady Tree, and Sybil Thorndike. Ellen Terry enjoyed it so much that she asked to be allowed to come again on the second night. At the end of the play she was taken up on to the stage by Geoffrey Heald and introduced to the cast. The boys shook hands politely with the white-haired lady of seventy, only conscious of her fame through the reverent whispers of their elders. She had a special embrace for the somewhat embarrassed Laurence whom she startled by asking: "Oh, don't you love it—don't you love the words?" Before he could answer she had switched to a more matter-of-fact tone of voice and requested him to help her down the steps from the stage. "I've got me best boots on," she confided by way of explanation. The subsequent comments on Laurence's performance which she recorded in her diary were charged with prophecy. "The small boy who played Brutus," she wrote, "is already a great actor."

Lady Tree added her praise, and Bishop Temple, who also seems to have been among the unexpectedly distinguished audience, said he was so moved that he had cried. Sir Johnston Forbes-Robertson, who saw a performance of the play when it was revived nine months later, was equally enthusiastic. Taking Laurence's father on one side he said, "My dear man, your son *is* Brutus." He followed this up by a personal letter to Heald in which he commented: "Brutus delivered his oration to the citizens with a pathetic air of fatalism which was poignantly suggestive—remarkable in one so young."

Allowances must probably be made. All this praise seems a little too generous and may have been the result of famous players, determined not to appear superior, ending by being fulsome. Even so, it is clear that this first serious stage performance at the age of ten and a half was an outstanding one. It was followed by Maria in *Twelfth Night* the next Christmas, and then, just before his voice broke and in what must have been the most effective of all Geoffrey Heald's productions, as Katharina in *The Taming of the Shrew.*

Once again the play seems to have attracted the theatrically famous into the little school hall in Marylebone which held an audience of only a hundred. Ellen Terry attended one of the four performances and so, too, did Fred Terry and Julia Neilson, Kate Terry, and Balliol Holloway. For lack of anyone sufficiently experienced among his fourteen pupils, Geoffrey Heald played Petruccio as well as producing. In a dark wig, earrings, and a large striped hat, Laurence, if not the prettiest Kate in Christendom, made a strikingly handsome girl. He brought so much fire to the part that Heald, for all his greater age and experience, found that he had to pull out all stops to prevent himself being acted off the stage.

IV

In the following September Laurence, who was now fourteen, was sent to a public school, and his father chose St. Edward's, Oxford, as suitable for a boy whose future career seemed likely to be in the ministry. He had been there only two terms when he was given the chance to repeat his success as Kate—this time not in a small school hall, but at the Shakespeare Memorial Theatre at Stratford-on-Avon.

The production at All Saints had been sufficiently good for the Governors of the Memorial Theatre to invite the school to bring it down during the Birthday Week of 1922. Fortunately this came in the Easter holidays, so that Heald could arrange for Laurence to take his old part again.

The day before the performance the choir school took part in a ceremonial procession from the theatre to Stratford Parish Church, and, as an old boy of All Saints with the added prestige of being at a public school, Laurence carried the wreath. As they walked up the aisle and took their places in the choir near the spot where Shakespeare lies buried in a grave seventeen feet below the grey flagstones, the boys sang "De Profundis" and "Fear no more the heat o' the sun" from *Cymbeline*, specially set to music by their own choir master and organist.

On the morning before the performance Heald took the boys to the theatre to give them a chance of a short run-through, and so that the little church hall production could be adapted to the vast stage. They found a rehearsal in progress with James Hackett, the American actor, playing Othello and Balliol Holloway as Iago. A little impatiently but filled with interest, the boys sat in the darkness at the back of the stalls, watching the rehearsal until Hackett suddenly became aware of their presence. He asked who they were, and, on being told, immediately cleared the stage for them with an apology for keeping them waiting. Heald, who was now certain in his own mind that Laurence was destined to become an actor, noted with interest his excitement when he walked for the first time across the stage of a real theatre. His theory that the boy had the makings of an actor was confirmed when, as the time came for the actual performance, Laurence's excitement turned to a quite professional calmness.

Heald had his own ideas about the reason for this absence of nerves and the complete lack of self-consciousness shown, not only by Laurence, but by all the small boys in this unusual company. He believed it owed much to their discipline and because they had daily taken part in the religious ritual of All Saints Church as a matter of course. Throughout rehearsals he had concentrated on the way they delivered their lines, and his call from the back of the hall at the first suggestion of mumbling had been, "Words! Words!" As choristers who sang the masses of Palestrina and other great masters of church music, the boys were familiar with fine cadences and trained to enunciate subtle and difficult rhythms. He was therefore pleased but not at all surprised when, at the end of the Stratford performance, his pupils were complimented on their speaking voices, and *The Times* expressed "wonder at lines so well and clearly spoken."

For Laurence the following morning there was to be another first experience, that of reading his press notices. The papers were to spoil him with praise right from the start. "The boy who took the part of Kate," said the critic of *The Daily Telegraph*, "made a fine bold, black-eyed hussy, badly in need of training, and I cannot remember any actress in the part who looked better." *The Times*, referring to his Katharina, said that it called neither for reservation

on account of age nor for patronising indulgence; it was a performance which had "fire of its own."

But whatever Geoffrey Heald might think about his future
chances as an actor, to Laurence Stratford in the Easter holidays was
only a temporary interlude in the more formidable undertaking of
making a success at a public school. He was shrewd enough to know
that popularity at St. Edward's would not lie in boasting that he had
acted the part of a girl in a prep. school play during the holidays.
So he kept very quiet about the press cuttings, which secretly burnt
a hole in his wallet, when he returned for the summer term to the
school on the Woodstock Road where he was to spend the next
two years.

V

Few people enjoy things they do badly, and Laurence was no
exception. During the comparatively short time he spent at St.
Edward's, he cut an indifferent figure, and he disliked school. It
takes a special sort of talent to be popular and successful at a public
school—a chameleon quality of identifying oneself with one's background and a friendliness which makes it possible to accept people
easily and uncritically. To be different from the crowd is fatal. At
this time Laurence was a boy of fitful moods. One moment he was
animated to the point of giggling excitement; the next, surly and
introspective. He had an eccentricity not calculated to endear him
particularly to other boys. To be "pi," let alone deeply religious,
was an inexplicable and suspect deviation from the normal. A chap
who actually *enjoyed* chapel was really beyond the pale!

In the constant moves during his childhood he had not made any
friends or developed any talent for friendship. He was happiest
when he was alone, and found little in the mass activities of school
to interest him. He was far from popular, and his three years at St.
Edward's were aimless and extremely boring.

Without much enthusiasm, he attempted to concentrate on his
books and cricket. But in those days not even Shakespeare held any
pleasure. In "Eng. Lit." texts, befuddled with footnotes, the plays
were as dull to him as cricket. Being bad at cricket worried him
most. What little esteem he had from his companions rested largely
on the fact that his father, even if he were a clergyman, had played
for Hampshire. Laurence tried desperately hard to live up to his

father's reputation, and finally keenness rather than ability won him
a place in his house team. But even this ended in catastrophe. Not
only did he drop two catches, but when the house needed only eight
runs to win, L. K. Olivier, last man in, buckled on his pads, scored
three, and then was clean bowled.

The theatre still tugged at his imagination, and the urge to play
truant was as strong as when he was at the little preparatory school
in London. Once, risking serious punishment, he visited the New
Theatre, Oxford, when a touring company arrived with *Lilac Time*.
At St. Edward's they have built up the comfortable legend that a
master actually saw him slipping into the theatre, but, with tolerance
and perspicacity, decided not to stop or report him. Later it was
to be a matter of satisfaction to someone signing himself R.C.M. in
the school magazine, that he had encouraged the career of a pupil
destined to become one of the school's most famous old boys. In
an account of the 1923 Christmas term production of *A Midsummer
Night's Dream*, he spotted the performance of Olivier who played
Puck, as "by far the most notable." A little too robust, thought
R.C.M., but he seemed to have more "go" in him than the others.
Not the least of Olivier's original touches in this part was the wearing of two green lights shining from his breast and attached to a
battery in his pocket. But he had no misapprehension about his
popularity, and certainly none about his abilities, for in his diary he
wrote: "Played Puck very well—much to everybody's disgust."

It was on this faintly disillusioned note that he came home for the
Christmas holidays. By this time the Oliviers had moved from Pimlico to Letchworth, where Laurence's father had accepted the living
of St. Michael's and All Saints at the end of the war. For some
while the family had lived in a large Queen Anne house, but in the
March of 1920 Laurence's mother had died with tragic suddenness,
and the Reverend Gerard Olivier had taken his three children to a
smaller house near the centre of the Garden City which was more
convenient for the church. It was from this rectory that, in January,
1924, Laurence's brother, Dickie, left for India to take a job on a
plantation.

Laurence and his father accompanied him as far as Fenchurch
Street Station on the day of his departure, and then returned to a
house which, in the few hours they had been away, seemed to have
become unnaturally deserted. The hall looked quite empty now that

it was no longer piled with suitcases and tin trunks, boldly marked "Not Wanted on Voyage." After a Christmas holiday during which there had been a constant uproar of preparation the whole rectory was dismally quiet. Laurence went upstairs to find only one bed turned down in the room which he had shared so long with his brother. That suddenly brought home to him with an ache of despair that he wouldn't see Dickie again for four years, and as he got into his bath he began to plan a wild scheme to go out to India too.

When his father came upstairs to the bathroom and sat down on the edge of the bath, Laurence told him that when he had finished at school he would like to go out to join his brother. The Reverend Gerard Olivier's reply was unexpected. It was so different from anything he had even hinted at before that Laurence looked up at him in surprise, and for a moment was unable to take it in.

"Don't you be a fool, Kim," said his father, using the nickname by which Laurence was known to his family. "You are going on the stage."

That remark, coming as it did out of the blue, has never ceased to puzzle Laurence Olivier. Looking back, it has somehow seemed almost too neat and to have the false ring of a highly theatrical curtain line. His surprise was largely due to the fact that he had never realized until then that his father had given any thought to his future. He himself had never thought about a career very seriously. His ideas had veered at different times between the Merchant Service and forestry, and he'd always had the vague notion that his father expected and wanted him to go into the church. But if that had been the clergyman's secret wish he had been forced to abandon it when Laurence's reports from school had shown that he could never hope to win the scholarship which would have made the university and theological college possible.

Laurence had a long and open talk with his father that night. It was as if his shyness and his father's usual aloofness were broken down by their mutual sense of loneliness following Dickie's departure. They exchanged more confidences than they had during the whole of the three years since Laurence's mother had died. And he learned that he had always been mistaken in assuming that his father lacked interest in him, and that really the matter of his future had been given a great deal of thought. The mention of the stage was not just a sudden whim; even details had been worked out in the Reverend Gerard Olivier's careful, calculating way.

"You will leave St. Edward's at the end of the next summer term," his father told him, and said that he would arrange with his housemaster for him to come up to London for an interview with Miss Fogerty. She was the principal of the dramatic school where Sybille, his sister, had been a student. If he were lucky he might get some sort of grant, and there were often small parts to be obtained in repertory or touring companies during the holidays, so that he could earn a little money to help keep himself. After that, his father continued, he was sure Canon Thorndike's daughter would have some advice. If he played his cards right her husband, Lewis Casson, might even give him a start.

CHAPTER 2

His Finger on the Bell
1924-1926

I

ONE DAY IN JUNE during his last term at St. Edward's Laurence Olivier came up to London from Oxford. It was an occasion marked with all the nervous excitement which, when one is at school, is associated with anything to do with the outside world. It was a visit heavy with portents and a good deal more glamorous than similar visits made by other boys. He had to go, as he explained to his housemaster and his companions, for "an audition." It was a word which sounded unfamiliar and colourful at school, where boys rarely went away in the middle of the term for anything more exciting than a university *viva voce* or Foreign Office interview. His English master, who vaguely supposed he was responsible, asked him if he had something "worked up," and what he was going to do. The master who had produced the play at the end of the Christmas term offered to hear him say his set Shakespeare speech. Both knew that for once they were sending a boy out beyond their academic walls into a world about which they were extraordinarily ignorant, the bizarre world of the theatre. St. Edward's really did not have much to do with that sort of thing.

Olivier was going to the Central School of Speech Training and Dramatic Art to be given an audition by the redoubtable Elsie Fogerty. To Elsie Fogerty must go much of the credit that the

London stage has had for fine speaking, for, in the dramatic school which she had founded in 1906 and of which she was principal, speech training was given pride of place. Her ideas of acting were, perhaps, a little out of date, but her methods of voice production were not. Her school had its dingy, lofty classrooms and little theatre in the Albert Hall, curiously situated off the circular corridor which runs right round the building on the same level as the balcony of the auditorium. Up the long flight of stone stairs to the Central School climbed not only young actors to learn their job, but a great many experienced ones as well. Sybil Thorndike and John Gielgud were among the many established actors who constantly returned to her for "speech therapy" when their voices became tired.

Elsie Fogerty was a remarkable character and long before her death in 1945 had become part of theatrical legend. With her large brimmed hats and inevitable brown tippet, she seemed to belong to a different era, but her faintly old-world appearance was offset by enormous vitality and a caustic tongue. She was a mass of contradictions. She was absent-minded and as keen-eyed as a hawk; she had a manner of regal dignity and yet was quite capable of appearing in odd shoes and with a slip showing beneath her long skirt; she hated the slovenly in her students, but would herself conduct rehearsals waving an apple or a half-eaten sandwich. Munching loudly while some nervous pupil went through a speech she would breach any hesitation with an impatient, "Go on, dear, go on!" Short and plump though she was, her bearing always made her seem quite tall. Her age was a closely guarded secret and consequently a matter of much speculation among her students, many of whom assumed she possessed witch-like longevity. Once she let it slip out that, as a child, she had been patted on the head by Garibaldi, and this led to a rush to reference books, to discover the date he was in England in the hope of a clue. The mystery gave rise, of course, to the idea that her age was fabulous, and it came almost as a disappointment to learn at her death that she was only in her eightieth year.

It was to this teacher, at once forbidding and amiable, that Olivier, just seventeen, came to give his audition. He had the "Seven Ages of Man" speech all ready; he had rehearsed it over and over again as he had walked alone, well away from white flannels, round the playing fields of the school. He wasn't wired for light, as during the Christmas play, but he had worked out some wonderful gestures. The best of these involved fighting a shadow duel on the lines:

> "*Then the soldier*
> *Full of strange oaths and bearded like the pard*
> *Jealous in honour and quick to quarrel . . .*"

But before he had parried the air more than once he heard a cool, not entirely unamused voice saying: "I don't think we need *that!*"

One of Miss Fogerty's characteristics was an uncompromising directness about her pupils' physical defects. A claw-like hand would dart out to correct sitting or standing postures, and those who studied under her say she possessed extraordinary insight into the capacity of those she was teaching. Olivier was to catch a glimpse of that insight on the very first day he met her, for at the end of the audition Miss Fogerty did a strange thing. She went up to him, as he stood there on the stage, a nervous schoolboy with untidy hair and ill-cut clothes, and placed her forefinger vertically in the middle of his forehead. "You have a weakness there," she said.

Olivier, given to frowning and eye-rolling, knew that she spoke the truth—that he was, in fact, badly self-conscious about that part of his face. His hair at that time came far forward; his eyebrows, thick and long, almost met; the whole effect was of a small, lowering brow. He soon shaved the eyebrows and time looked after the widow's peak, but he has never been quite sure whether his much-remarked addiction to false noses is not an attempt to conceal a weakness in the centre of his face of which he is subconsciously afraid.

Whatever she may have felt about his forehead and his gestures, Elsie Fogerty gave him not only a scholarship of a year's free tuition, but a bursary of £50 a year. It seemed very generous and very complimentary until he discovered that the school was desperately short of men, and that for six young actors there were over seventy women. Then his bursary began to look suspiciously like stud fees.

With few regrets, Olivier left St. Edward's at the end of the summer term of 1924 and came to live in London. He took some very cheap digs in the attic of a house in Castellain Road, Paddington, near Warwick Avenue tube station, and there, with a fierce burst of independence, tried to live without any allowance. But even by spending only 4d. on lunches he found it almost impossible and had to accept an additional £1 a month from his father.

However lonely he felt in London, Olivier considered it preferable to living at home and coming up to town from Letchworth each day; for a change had taken place at the rectory which had badly upset him. His father had married again. It had happened very suddenly following a voyage which Gerard Olivier had made earlier in the year to Jamaica, and, charming as Olivier found his stepmother, he could not adjust himself to the idea.

His father was little over fifty, but to adolescence this seemed an age long past marriage, and particularly inconsistent with the views his father had expressed ever since the death of his mother; frequently and strongly he had condemned marriage for Anglo-Catholic clergy.

A lurid splash of publicity had not made it any easier to accept. Just before he married, the Reverend Gerard Olivier had been offered the living of St. Paul's, Brighton, but the congregation who largely subscribed to his salary declined to have a married vicar. The popular papers had seized on the story, and for several weeks a sensitive and worried boy saw his father in the pillory under such headlines as "Should Vicars Wed?" and "Cupid v. Congregations." For a while his father stood out against the decision of the congregation, but eventually he had to give in, and took his new wife to the delightful, but ill-paid, parish of Addington in Buckinghamshire.

Olivier was pleased to be able to bury his thoughts in his new and all-engrossing work at the Central School. Under the strict supervision of Elsie Fogerty, he was cramming all the rudiments of a theatrical training, from deportment to fencing, into a year's study. Back in his digs, he spent hours in front of his mirror practising make-up, and, in the guise of everything from Mr. Wu to Old English, went down to the basement for the critical inspection of a fellow-lodger. Except for plays demanded by the course he read little, and his allowance would not run to many theatres. When he did go it was to see Gerald du Maurier or Leon M. Lion from the gallery, and he accepted the productions uncritically and with little regard for standards. Taste and judgment had yet to form; any appreciation of the theatre as an art was still quite beyond him. Pitch-forked from rectory to school and then into dramatic school when he was only just seventeen, he was, as he and his friends now recall, very ingenuous. There was, for example, a first night of the revival of Granville-Barker's *The Madras House* at the Ambassadors, an occasion when his poverty and unworldliness were mixed to an almost pathetic degree. He had planned, as usual, to go in the gallery, and seeing a man with stools, had taken one apparently under the impression that it would cost him nothing. Money was not asked for in advance, but just before the doors opened the stool man came round to collect. Olivier, appalled, ran through his pockets and found that he had not enough to pay. In embarrassed confusion he told the man he would go and get the money, and this he did, leaving the queue and actually going all the way to Castellain Road to raise the sum he needed. When he got back to the theatre the first act of the play was already over, but this annoyed and surprised him less than the fact that the stool man was nowhere to be seen. That he should not have waited all that time for 6d. seemed to Olivier incomprehensible; "After all, I *said* I was coming back," he thought to himself as he hurried up the stone stairs to see what was left of the play.

If his approach to life was unformed, so, too, was his acting during the first few months at the Central School. To one of his teachers, Henry Oscar, it seemed almost impossible that he would ever overcome his lack of grace and untidy appearance sufficiently to make much of an actor. He always gave the impression of being surrounded by what Oscar described as "an invisible wall of discomfort," and his teacher could only assume that his success in school plays had been achieved before he was overcome by the shy embarrassment of later adolescence. The problem was discussed with Elsie Fogerty and she, either seriously or with her renowned and caustic humour, is reported to have said that he would really be much better off on a farm. Whatever his rural potentialities, however, his loss would mean one fewer in the small and gallant band of young men who circulated rapidly from class to class acting with the girls who so out-numbered them. Henry Oscar never got over his idea that Olivier lacked inner fire during his year as a student, but others among his teachers and contemporaries were more impressed. He might be rather young in his manner and inclined to play the fool during classes, but once it came to an actual performance it seemed to them that Olivier immediately showed that he had a flair. One afternoon Athene Seyler was invited by Elsie Fogerty to come to the school and judge the best students in a scene from *The Merchant of Venice*, and she was immediately struck by Olivier's performance as Shylock. His facial expressions were a trifle difficult to discern, it was true; for, what with his beard, hair which started half an inch above his eyebrows, and eyebrows themselves which almost met in the middle, there was very little of his face to be seen. It did not seem to Athene Seyler that he gave any great character performance, but she was quickly conscious of intelligence behind the words, a concentration of purpose, and a quality of latent power that she found difficult to define. This young Shylock, she noted, did not hand you his whole performance on a plate; he left it to you to discover *him*. She had no hesitation in awarding her marks equally between him and a girl student, Peggy Ashcroft, who, also heavily bearded, read the clerk's speech in the court scene with special distinction.

During his second term Olivier's performances showed considerable improvement, and he succeeded in winning one of the Dawson Millward Cups awarded annually to the two best students, male and female, in a modern one-act play or excerpt. Peggy Ashcroft won the cup for the girls, and later she and Olivier appeared together in a short play as two allegedly comic characters called Mr. and Mrs. Inkpen.

II

The year at the Central School provided acting experience not entirely confined to the classroom. In his very first term he "walked on" in three Sunday night charity shows, and during the Christmas holidays he heard that Edith Craig, Ellen Terry's daughter, was producing a play by Algernon Blackwood called *Through the Crack*, and there was work to be had at a salary of £4 a week. By a coincidence it was to be put on at Letchworth. Olivier went to see her, but was disappointed to hear that the play was completely cast. If, however, he cared to understudy seven of the male parts and help back-stage, he could join the company. So it was that his first professional engagement was not even noted on the programme—or wouldn't have been had he not been quick to get a printed label stuck on the bottom bearing the information: "Asst. Stage Manager . . . Laurence Olivier."

The subtleties of this function rather baffled the Oliviers' old housekeeper who was still living at Letchworth and was naturally keen to see him. "But tell me, Master Laurence," she demanded before she set out for the theatre, "what do you *do?*" Master Laurence even then could build up a part. He looked at her steadily and said: "When you are having tea during the interval and you hear a bell summoning you back to your seat, *you'll know that my finger is on that bell!*"

She was to have a chance, however, of really seeing him act, for in the following Easter holidays he went back to Letchworth to appear as Lennox in Norman V. Norman and Beatrice Wilson's production of *Macbeth* (and to continue as A.S.M.). This was his first professional stage appearance, but as the St. Christopher Theatre in Letchworth Broadway was little more than a glorified church hall, Olivier considered his first real part to be one which he played at the Brighton Hippodrome in the summer of the same year, 1925 and immediately after completing his final term at the Central School. It was a small part in a curtain-raiser before a touring production of *The Ghost Train*, and meant the chance of acting with Ruby Miller. One of the stipulations of the management was that actors should provide their own clothes, and Olivier, who at the age of eighteen still had no dinner jacket, had to borrow £6 from his stepmother so that he could buy one. His first entrance was almost in the Mack Sennett tradition. In those days doors in scenery had wide wooden bars across their bases—from force of habit some old-time actors still lift their feet to walk over them whenever they make an entrance—and Olivier was warned about this. He was warned by everyone from the producer to the stage manager. And then, when he came to make his entrance, he forgot. He tripped on the bar and sprawled into the footlights. "Mr. Laurence Olivier makes a good deal out of a rather small part," commented the local paper acidly.

III

When the tour of *The Ghost Train* (in which he walked on as a policeman and, inevitably, was again A.S.M.) came to an end, Olivier returned to London no longer safely cushioned between parts by terms at the Central School. A cold wind was starting to blow down Castellain Road; now he was on his own. He had to face the climb up innumerable stairs to dingy offices above Shaftes-

bury Avenue where agents said they were sorry but there was nothing to-day, and in whom, Olivier soon learned, the news that he was
the winner of the Dawson Millward Cup evoked extraordinarily
little interest. For a while he was to know the suspense of watching for the post, and schooled himself to sound casual whenever he
got back to his digs and asked his landlady, "Any calls for me while
I've been out?" But he did not have to wait as long as many young
actors. At the beginning of October a telegram came for him which
read: CALL CENTURY THEATRE PART TO OFFER LENA ASHWELL PLAYERS.

Lena Ashwell, then middle-aged and with many years of distinguished service behind her as an actress and producer, was one of
those gallant optimists which the theatre breeds expressly, it seems,
in order to separate them from their money. It certainly needed a
brave woman to try and bestow the benefits of Shakespeare on
Notting Hill Gate (at the little Century Theatre in Westbourne
Park Road), and then insist on taking him into the suburbs even as
far as Deptford Baths. Outer London could never complain to Lena
Ashwell that they had no chance to see Shakespeare. On Monday
nights her little company went to Fulham Town Hall, on Tuesdays
to Battersea Town Hall, Fridays to Shoreditch and Saturdays to
Camberwell. Deptford and Camberwell Baths were also on the cir-
cuit. In cultural addition, there were special performances for
schools, and it was, as far as Olivier can remember, at a matinée for
a girls' school at Englefield Green in Surrey that an incident occurred during a performance of *Julius Cæsar* which cost him his job
and his precarious living of £2 10s. a week. This was one of the
Shakespeare productions which he found rather silly, and few in
the cast, which included Basil Radford and Mackenzie Ward, took
them as seriously as Lena Ashwell intended. Indeed, it was Olivier's
feckless ambition each night to pull down the improvised curtain
which served as a back-cloth, an action which, he knew, would
reveal a flash of pink confusion among the girls changing behind it.
He never succeeded, but there were always other diversions. That
afternoon at Englefield Green during the very first act Philip Leaver,
who was playing one of the Tribunes, lost his trousers or whatever
passes for trousers under a toga. At that time Olivier had very little
self-control, and the occurrence was enough to send him into fits
of laughter from which he was unable to recover. He was playing
Flavius, and he simply could not stand on the stage listening to

Leaver trying to complete the "Knew you not Pompey?" speech; there was nothing for it but to leave the streets of Rome as quickly as possible. Still shaking with laughter he slipped into the wings.

When Lena Ashwell heard she was furious, and promptly dropped him. There might have been another lean period had not Sybil Thorndike and Lewis Casson been there to pick him up. Casson may have felt some responsibility for Olivier going on the stage for, as well as being friendly with his father, it had been to him that Olivier had come for advice before he started on his career. Casson had growled all the proper warnings, but like his wife had thought him a born actor ever since he had seen him in the school productions. Perhaps, too, he may have heard a word from the vicar of All Saints, who, by chance, had one day met Olivier in the street and been seriously worried to see how thin he looked, and had rightly guessed he was not getting enough to eat. Anyway, early in December Olivier received a letter from Bronson Albery, Lewis Casson's partner in a venture to put on a spectacular production of *Henry VIII*. It offered him £3 a week to walk on, understudy if required and, with Matthew Forsyth, to be an assistant stage manager.

Henry VIII was the last straight play at the old Empire Theatre, Leicester Square, before its conversion into a cinema and before it was redecorated, with elaborate regard for Renaissance detail, by Metro-Goldwyn-Mayer. The play, which had Norman V. Norman, E. Lyall Swete and Angela Baddeley, in addition to Sybil Thorndike and Lewis Casson, in the cast, must have been the first, as well as the last, Shakespeare production in the forty years' existence of a theatre which had been generally devoted to lighter matters. Olivier found that his job was principally to keep people quiet during rehearsals. Quietness while people are acting became a fetish which was to remain with him all his life, and he undertook his job so zealously that on one occasion he shushed two men who were talking together in the wings. Neither Tom Kealy, Sybil Thorndike's business manager, nor Bronson Albery took the reproof kindly.

The play opened two days before Christmas, 1925, and once during the run the over-anxious assistant stage manager rang down the curtain at the wrong time, but denied that this had anything to do with his emotional preoccupation with Angela Baddeley, who was playing Anne Boleyn. Olivier was not alone in being in love with her, but as he was on the programme as First Serving Man while his rival, Carol Reed, was just lumped among the ranks of "Bishops, Lords, Ladies, Officers, Guard, Scribes, etc." he was not afraid of the competition. He was also apparently unperturbed by the fact that Angela Baddeley was happily married.

At this period Olivier was constantly falling in love in a romantic, entirely innocent way. The next actress to attract him was an exquisite girl called Muriel Hewitt, whom he met the following spring during rehearsals of a play called *The Marvellous History of St. Bernard* which Barry Jackson was putting on in London. She, too, had a husband somewhere in the background, though Olivier was not to meet him until later in the year. Whether his rôle as her husband prejudiced him is uncertain, but he remembers that (as a prelude to a friendship which has been unbroken ever since) he began by disliking Ralph Richardson very much indeed.

IV

In the middle 'twenties Barry Jackson was frequently surprising London with unusual productions. He had started his management of the Kingsway Theatre with modern-dress Shakespeare, a production which still lives in public memory as "Hamlet in Plus-fours"; and *The Marvellous History* was his own translation of a play which he had found in strange circumstances.

While on holiday in Switzerland he had read in a local paper of a French Mystery play which was being put on to celebrate the thousandth anniversary of either the birth or death of St. Bernard of Menthon. This was the sort of thing that had an irresistible fascination for Barry Jackson. With considerable difficulty he discovered that the production was in the grounds of the Château de Menthon near Annecy. He drove there, fell in love with the play, and almost then and there acquired the translation rights. To add to the romance of his discovery, he learnt that, until then, the play had existed only in a fifteenth-century manuscript which had been for generations in the Menthon family's possession.

He was to say later that the play gave him more pleasure than anything he had hitherto done in the theatre, and he lavished a great deal of care on its casting and production. Olivier went to see him at the Kingsway and found him to be a large, untheatrical man with intellectual, almost clerical features, and they began then an association which was to last for more than two years and which was to have an incalculable influence on Olivier's career.

Olivier had gone to the audition for the part of St. Bernard. He read extracts for Barry Jackson and the producer, A. E. Filmer, and also some Shakespeare; but he lost the part to Robert Harris, who was several years older, had considerably more experience, and had been at Barry Jackson's repertory theatre in Birmingham only a month previously. Olivier was given instead the part of a minstrel, and was told to understudy Robert Harris. Eventually, however, Denys Blakelock became the understudy and he was informed that he was to be *second* understudy. It took him several days to work out exactly what had brought about this decline in his fortunes, and only slowly did it occur to him that perhaps the reason was that the producer had not cared for the familiar way in which he had called the leading lady by her Christian name. That Filmer should be fond of Valerie Taylor, Olivier found easily understandable, but he was still young enough to be dismayed that such a thing should cause discrimination. He decided to ask the producer point-blank why he had been displaced. If he expected a confession he was disappointed; Filmer turned aside his question very quickly. "Well," he said, "you seemed self-conscious in the religious bits." As Olivier was deeply religious at this period, it was a criticism which he strongly resented.

The play was on for only two months, and was interrupted by the General Strike in May, 1926, during which Olivier shouted himself hoarse for two days calling out names of stations as a guard on an underground train. Barry Jackson was sufficiently impressed with Olivier's work to want to keep him, and that summer during the run of a comedy he was trying out at Clacton called *The Barber and the Cow*, he sent him there to take over one of the parts from another actor. This was Olivier's first encounter with one of the great figures of the Birmingham Repertory Company, Cedric Hardwicke. It was also his first meeting with Muriel Hewitt's husband and the two men immediately and mutually disliked each other. Olivier, who was four years younger, found Richardson ponderous and very superior; Richardson considered Olivier gauche and extremely naïve. Because of this antipathy, the week at Clacton turned out to be a miserable one for Olivier, who, unaware that junior members of a company are often ignored, began to imagine that he was being slighted not only by Richardson but by the whole cast.

It came as a considerable relief when he heard that the play was doing such bad business that Barry Jackson did not intend to keep it on any longer. Clacton had declined to be amused by the farce which centred round the doping of a cow, and Olivier did not blame them. The second act curtain came down after two lines of dialogue which have haunted him ever since:

One character: The cow has fallen into a coma.
Another character: That wasn't a coma; it was a full stop.

Few plays, he considered, could survive those lines; *The Barber and the Cow* wasn't one of them.

Chapter 3

The Birmingham "Rep."
1926-1928

I

THERE ARE CITIES which, when one is starting upon a career, are as clearly indicated as those at the departure platforms of a railway terminus. A singer wishes to study in Milan; an artist to paint in Paris; the architect needs the inspiration of Rome; and there are many journalists who will swear that the road to Fleet Street starts in Manchester. For an English actor, between the two wars, Birmingham was the place. Not that Birmingham, even with a population of a million, was particularly theatre-minded; in fact Barry Jackson lost £100,000 during the twenty-one years in which he ran the small but comfortable theatre in Station Street. It was a loss for which countless talented actors could be very thankful. The Birmingham "Rep." put on them the stamp of success.

Here was the nursery of such players as Cedric Hardwicke, Gwen Ffrangcon-Davies, Felix Aylmer and Leslie Banks, directed by a man who, careless of London values, put on plays by Chekov and Ibsen and was not afraid of the *avant-garde* playwrights like Kaiser and Pirandello. Barry Jackson indulged his own taste and judgment with complete disregard for the usual commercial plays which were staged by most provincial repertories in imitation of the West End of London. It was for this reason that, in 1913, he built this theatre in his native city; as he was a rich man he was able to keep the doors open even if the plays he presented did not appeal to the mass of his public. But philanthropy and high artistic ideals were not proof against continual disillusionment, and three years before Olivier joined the company Jackson had nearly closed down the theatre. He began to look towards London, where he could enjoy some measure of appreciation, but although he threatened Birmingham that he would close, he never did. His fortune with more popular plays like *The Farmer's Wife*, which he was able to send out on innumerable tours (at one time he had three companies on the road playing it simultaneously), could always help to balance the budget. Eden Phillpotts and, to a lesser degree, Drinkwater, were the good fairies of Andreyev and Molnar. The queues at the Court Theatre in London, where *The Farmer's Wife* ran for three years, made up for empty seats in Birmingham.

It was in one of the money-spinning tours of *The Farmer's Wife* that Olivier spent the larger part of the summer and autumn of 1926 after his unproductive visit to Clacton, and before he actually went to Birmingham to join the repertory company. For six months he toured the country from Woolwich to Edinburgh, playing Richard Coaker, the love-sick suitor of Sibley Sweetland. Unfortunately it is not really possible to assess his performance as the local papers never dared anything but praise, and judgment can only be based on "capital" (Wimbledon), "excellent acting" (Clifton), "brought the house down" (Glasgow), "clever study" (Southend) and, most perplexing of all, "artistically acted" (Edinburgh).

Trailing these inconclusive epithets, Olivier arrived in Birmingham with the play early in December, and was asked to remain there as juvenile lead for the second half of the 1926–1927 winter season. He was not yet twenty, and this was to be his real grounding in the theatre. He was more fortunate than actors in weekly repertory, but had to play one part and be learning another every two or three weeks, and had to vary his performances from Chekov to modern-dress Shakespeare. If he was conscious of any honour in joining a company with such traditions and high standards, his performance gave no indication of it in the very first play in which he appeared. A piece of fooling one night might easily have ended his career in Birmingham as abruptly as it had sixteen months before with Lena Ashwell.

The play was a new comedy written by Eden Phillpotts and was

set in a Tudor manor house where a group of young men is surprised by the arrival of a burglar. The burglar, played by Melville
Cooper, asks them who they are, to which, according to the script,
the Hon. Guy Sidney, a monocled "dude" played by Olivier, gives
the haughty reply, "We are Conservatives." Throughout rehearsals
and during the short run Olivier supplied that reading and then, on
the last night, decided to improve on the author. The burglar
snarled his question, and up piped the Hon. Guy: "We're Free-
masons, frothblowers, and gugnuncs!" It was juvenile and not very
funny, but Olivier had the satisfaction of hearing the whole house
roar. He came off-stage feeling very pleased with himself, but his
pride was quickly shattered. He was given a severe dressing-down
by W. G. Fay, the producer, who must have thought that "gagging"
by a young actor playing his first part with a new company was unforgivable.

The Birmingham season had not run many weeks before it was
obvious that the company had a very useful actor in Olivier. He
brought intelligence and subtlety to all his parts, which varied from
the roaring and romping Tony Lumpkin to that incarnation of
futility, Uncle Vanya. No part seemed outside his range, and Barry
Jackson's small but faithful audience began to watch for his performances with increasing interest. The fifth play in which he appeared
was another experiment in putting Shakespeare into modern dress,
and this time *All's Well That Ends Well* had been chosen. Olivier
had been given the part of Monsieur Parolles, which is normally
played as a boasting braggart of a soldier; he chose to interpret him
more subtly as a well-dressed and pleasant young man, a departure
from tradition that was apparently remarkably effective. Some people thought that he even succeeded in stealing the play from Eileen
Beldon, who was Helena; and as he came off on the first night he
had the satisfaction of learning that Bernard Shaw, who had been
out in front, had particularly enjoyed his handling of the scene in
which the blindfold Parolles believes himself at the mercy of the
enemy.

For the opening of the autumn season that year Barry Jackson had
a new play by his old friend John Drinkwater. Drinkwater had
started his career as an actor and producer in Birmingham, and his
play *Abraham Lincoln* had been a great success there in 1918. This
was not such stern stuff; it was a pleasant little domestic comedy

called *Bird in Hand*. For Olivier the play had an added interest because Peggy Ashcroft, with whom he had acted at the Central
School, came up to Birmingham to play Joan Greenleaf. In rehearsal
this rather moral homily of a squire's son who falls in love with an
innkeeper's daughter showed few signs of the sparkle that might be
expected of a play that was to become one of the most popular post-
war comedies, and was to be acted up and down the country by
repertories, touring companies and amateurs.

II

One of the principal objections that most young actors have to
repertory work is that it may mean provincial oblivion. But this did
not apply to Birmingham, as Olivier was soon to see. Barry Jackson might have a Midland contempt for London standards, but he
would have been inhuman if he had not wanted to show London
the mettle of which Birmingham was made. With this in mind he
took a short lease of the little Court Theatre in Sloane Square in
January, 1928. His idea was to put on five plays, to run a month
each, failure or success. He had done this three years before, and
once again he wanted London to see the sort of plays Birmingham
had been enjoying for years. One, which he could be certain would
cause a rattle of shocked tea trays if it were presented at a Haymarket matinée, was Elmer Rice's expressionistic play, *The Adding
Machine*. He had staged it in Birmingham the previous October,
and although Olivier had had only a small part, Barry Jackson invited him to join his company at the Court.

London was to be offered an exciting season. He would follow
The Adding Machine with a modern-dress version of *Macbeth;* then,
Jackson decided, his southern audiences would be sufficiently broken
in to cope with Shaw's *Back to Methuselah*. This was a revival of
his own original production, for he had first presented it in Birmingham in 1923, in defiance of a warning from Shaw, which read, "Mr.
Jackson, are your wife and children provided for?" It was Barry
Jackson's custom to defy. He did so with the fourth play in his
repertory. Because he thought Tennyson's long verse drama *Harold*
contained some lovely lyrical poetry, he ignored the verdict reached
by Henry Irving years before that it was "quite impossible" for the

stage. And what more suitable for the climax to a defiant season than yet another modern-dress Shakespeare that could be guaranteed to upset the purists? He settled on *The Taming of the Shrew.*

Then, as now, Olivier was meticulously careful about accents. He had been forced to assume a rough-and-ready "Stage American" in *The Adding Machine* for Birmingham, but for his first London part he was determined that his accent should be absolutely authentic. How was this to be done? Elsie Fogerty, superb as she was at ironing out exotic accents to her own highly-disciplined stage English, was hardly able to school him in American. Then one day he went to see *The Silver Cord* at the St. Martin's for which Clare Eames had come over from New York. Playing the part of her son was Denys Blakelock, with whom Olivier had become friendly during the run of *The Marvellous History of St. Bernard.* After the performance he went round to see Blakelock, told him his problem, and asked to be introduced to Clare Eames. Blakelock may have had private doubts of how a famous American leading lady would respond to the request to teach her native accent to a young actor; but he was too loyal to refuse, and took Olivier to her dressing-room. If Clare Eames thought it an impertinence, when she also saw how genuinely keen he was she agreed to help him. She was extremely thorough, and took him through his part over and over again until he had perfected a New York East Side accent. Unfortunately W. G. Fay, the producer, wasn't impressed at rehearsals. Perhaps the spurious sounded more authentic than the real thing. "Whatever's the matter with you?" he demanded. "You played the part all right in Birmingham. Now you're terrible!" Olivier quietly persisted in carrying on as Clare Eames had told him, and when the play was produced stole all the notices. To Fay's amazement it was Olivier (among a cast whose accents were much criticized) who was said to have "by far and away the best Americanese."

Olivier has always believed it was because of a notice in *The Observer* by St. John Ervine that, instead of having to return to Birmingham after the month in *The Adding Machine,* he was invited to stay on for the rest of the season. In those days Mr. Ervine spread himself amply over several columns each Sunday, and he found space at the end of a long and despairing dissertation on expressionism in the theatre to say that Laurence Olivier had given a very good performance indeed, the best, he thought, in the play. "He had little to do, but he *acted*," said Mr. Ervine.

So, instead of returning to the smoke of Birmingham, Olivier assumed a silk dressing-gown and a double-breasted grey flannel suit as Malcolm in the modern *Macbeth*. This was not to count among the Birmingham Repertory Company's successes. Perhaps it was a mistake to cast Eric Maturin, essentially a realistic actor with no background of Shakespeare, for Macbeth; because the clothes were modern it did not mean that the play could shed its poetry without grave loss. Maturin, it was said, had never seen Macbeth before, and he tried to level the poetry down to the realism of modern prose. More wisely Olivier sought a compromise. Malcolm has few big speeches calling for full-throated delivery, and while making the long speeches conversational and sincere, he did not lose the poetry.

Olivier had little sympathy with the production and was inclined to agree with those who saw the khaki uniforms, the machine-gun fire, the champagne and *pêches Melba* at the banquet, and young Macduff in an Eton collar as a stunt. If, as the programme note stated, the aim of modern dress was to help the audience "concentrate on the grandeur or gaiety of the story," he was sure that it had failed. For perhaps the first time in history the witches, who had become charladies, failed to be theatrically effective; comic melodrama was always perilously close round the corner. Barry Jackson was too shrewd not to sense it himself, and when he said in his first night curtain speech that "experiments have their failures" it was clearly an admission and an apology. He was to have far more success with *The Taming of the Shrew* at the end of the season.

When the casting for the next production, *Back to Methuselah*, was announced, Olivier noted with some misgivings that Ralph Richardson, to whom he had developed so immediate an antagonism at Clacton, was in the cast. Would he still find him unbending and rather formidably superior? Would Richardson continue to regard him as frivolous and immature, and retain a veiled dislike simply because Olivier had developed a hopeless passion for his wife? At the early rehearsals they both remained frigidly polite. Then one day Olivier could bear the strain no longer. When the break came for lunch, and as they gathered up their prompt copies, he went over and asked Richardson if he felt like a drink. Richardson was a little surprised, but nodded, and together they went into the refreshment room which was then over Sloane Square underground station. A joke was made, and the tension eased. Richardson said that he and his wife sometimes motored on the Sussex Downs of a Sunday and perhaps one weekend Olivier would like to come along. Olivier said he would—very much indeed—and what about having the other half. The ice was broken, and then and there a friendship started which was to become deeper and closer in the years to follow and which has continued ever since.

If after their drink together anything was needed to help Olivier forget his inferiority complex and any slight he might have suffered at Clacton, it came when the cast list went up for Tennyson's play *Harold*. On the notice-board just inside the stage door it announced that Laurence Olivier was to play Harold. Richardson was to have the smaller part of his younger brother. A month before his twenty-first birthday, and with little over two years' professional experience, he had been given his first leading part in London. His year of varied work in Birmingham and especially his handling of the part of Malcolm convinced Barry Jackson and his stage director, H. K. Ayliff, that they could take a chance on him. It was a more than usual responsibility for a young actor for he had to create the part. This was the first performance of the play ever put on, and as he and everyone else saw at rehearsals, it was not going to be a light burden. It was very soon clear why Irving (who produced both Tennyson's *Becket* and *Queen Mary*) had fought shy of it. The verse was of the blanker sort quarried from the type of archaic vocabulary which delighted in such phrases as "thyself was wont to love the chase."

Olivier, making up on the first night, was suddenly struck by the fact that his long flaxen wig gave him the general appearance of Mercia in *The Sign of the Cross*, but he survived this purely personal reflection. He also overcame the difficulty of having to play the older brother of two actors—Robert Speaight and Ralph Richardson—who were his seniors by several years. The critics were kind to him and, after devoting most of their space to trouncing Tennyson, were obviously happy to find someone whom they could sincerely praise. They suggested that the part of Harold really required a combination of Martin Harvey, Henry Ainley, and several other romantic actors all rolled into one, but said that Olivier's performance was remarkable for so young a man. What he lacked in authority he made up for in his speaking of the verse. "Sincerity," the word so much used of his Malcolm, was widely applied to his Harold. It was a word destined to have a considerable influence on his career.

CHAPTER 4

London and New York
1928-1930

I

THE ASSISTANT PRODUCER ran a critical eye over the company
assembled for the dress parade. Up on the stage the actors,
many of whom had improvised their own costumes, hoped
that they would be passed as suitable. After all, there were few
precedents for what should be worn in a modern-dress *Taming of
the Shrew*.

Laurence Olivier, who was to play the lord in the Christopher
Sly prologue, wore a dinner jacket, and the assistant producer noted
that the actor who had been clean-shaven, almost baby-faced for
Harold had now grown a moustache. It was the sort to be identified
for a generation as a Ronald Colman moustache. The assistant producer smiled to himself.

"Ah well," he commented to no one in particular, "we all know
Basil Dean is looking for a Beau Geste!"

Olivier heard him, and the shot went home. The assistant producer, who was Matthew Forsyth, had obviously heard the latest
theatrical gossip. Basil Dean had bought the stage rights of P. C.
Wren's novel, *Beau Geste*, had adapted it for the stage, and was now
hunting for a romantic hero. He had confided to Hannen Swaffer
that manly young actors were rare, and Swaffer, writing of this,
had added his own observation that the stage seemed recruited from

the ranks of those who would make good male mannequins. He was immediately inundated with letters from amateur actors, grocers' assistants, waiters and mothers' only sons who enclosed photographs and assured him that they neither lisped nor minced. These letters were sent on to Dean, but they brought little comfort to his office in Adam Street.

Young actors, aware that the search was on, began to prepare themselves; the West End came out in a small rash of Ronald Colman moustaches; the whisper of "Dean's out front!" was enough to make leading men change their characterizations into line with the swaggering bravado for which they imagined Dean was looking. The search continued for a long time, and Olivier was determined that his moustache should be right up in the front of the queue. He knew that to be starred in a Basil Dean production would mean that he was made.

The Taming of the Shrew was far more successful than Barry Jackson's previous exercises in modernized Shakespeare because, as a knock-about comedy with little poetry, it could be accepted, on the level of a boisterous college rag, for what it was. Olivier's part as the lord was short, but he was in front of the audience throughout the evening. In a box on stage-right he played attentive host to the drunken Christopher Sly of Frank Pettingell during the whole action of the play. It was not, however, until some time later, when the season at the Court was over that he had a chance of impressing Basil Dean with his abilities.

The five months at the Court, which he had so much enjoyed and which had given him a definite reputation in London, ended in May, and the following month Barry Jackson asked him to take over the part of Gerald Arnwood in *Bird in Hand* at the Royalty. One evening he heard that Basil Dean was in the stalls and gave the part everything he possessed in the way of light romantic charm. He would have been badly deflated could he have heard Dean's comments to his friend, Aubrey Mather, as he left the theatre. "That beetly-browed boy's no good at all," he said.

Despite this criticism Dean asked Olivier to come to see him a few months later, and, previously warned by Mather that his appearance was against him, Olivier was careful to pluck his eyebrows and brush his hair well back off his forehead before the interview. It was a very encouraging interview, for it lasted half an hour and

Dean was full of searching questions about his work, and made careful notes about all he had done and the parts he had played. It was not, however, until nearly the end of the year that Olivier was actually asked to attend a reading, and even then nothing was settled; Dean merely said that he would like another chance of seeing him act.

Bird in Hand had settled down to a run which was to last only just short of a year, and Olivier, in the part which he had created in Birmingham, was at the Royalty for seven months. It was a run destined to have a considerable influence on his life, for in the cast was a slender, dark-haired girl, a year younger than himself, who was then acting under the name of Jill Esmond Moore. As her name suggested to an older generation of theatregoers, she was the daughter of parents both famous in the theatre. Her mother was Eva Moore, the actress, and her father H. V. Esmond, the playwright and actor-manager. Educated at Bedales and later a student at the Royal Academy of Dramatic Art, she was already a highly accomplished young actress with six years' experience on the stage when she took the part of Joan Greenleaf and was first confronted with the eager, rather unkempt-looking Olivier who, she was informed, was to be her new leading man. On the stage he was very assured, and not above trying to steal some of her best scenes; off it, he was attentive and clearly highly romantic. She invited him down to her home at Hurley, near Maidenhead, to meet her mother, who quickly decided that it was a shame for him to stay in his stuffy digs in Paddington through the summer months. Surely it would be far more pleasant for Jill and him to come down after the show at night and then spend the days together by the river? Olivier thanked Mrs. Esmond for her kindness and accepted. For several weeks on end he stayed at Hurley, and the romantic disposition which Jill Esmond had noticed from the first soon took definite form. Within three weeks of their meeting he proposed to her. It was very precipitous, and perhaps seemed rather more like a determination to be "settled" and a longing to get married than the expression of a deep passion. Gently she suggested that they should get to know each other better before becoming engaged, and it was to be two years before the decision to be married was finally made.

In the November of the year in which they met, and while they were both still in *Bird in Hand*, Olivier was asked by the Stage

Society to appear in a special matinée of a war play. With his eyes still fixed on what seemed the infinitely more glittering alternative of *Beau Geste*, he accepted without much enthusiasm. The play was by an unknown amateur actor whose theatrical experience was limited to the dramatic section of his local rowing club, and who had had his manuscript returned by nearly every management in London. His name was Robert Sherriff, and the play was *Journey's End*.

Olivier's first reaction as he read it was that there seemed an awful lot of meals in it; and, like a great many people, he considered that a war play without any women would be doomed commercially. As he thumbed through the typescript marking the part of Stanhope he had no idea that it was a great play, or even a particularly good one. His main concern was that if Basil Dean came to see him he should not consider that an actor who was good as Stanhope would be impossible as Beau Geste.

In rehearsal he soon discovered that the part of the young infantry captain, sensitive and afraid of being a coward, was a good one. He was able to sink himself into the character very deeply, for the play gave him the chance of doing something on the stage he had wanted to do in real life. As a schoolboy he had always been upset that he was not old enough to go to France.

Great moments in the theatre are rarely born on Monday afternoons, but at the Apollo Theatre on that afternoon of December 10th, 1928, R. C. Sherriff's play took its place in the history of the stage as a modern masterpiece. Perhaps it was even more than that; it was not difficult to see it as the theatre's most sincere memorial to a generation which had died in Flanders. Here was a war play free from false heroics and sentimentality. Ten years after the armistice it was at last possible to say that everyone in khaki was not automatically a hero and that there was nothing dishonourable in the admission that in the trenches men were very frightened indeed. It arrived at precisely the right moment, in the van of a disillusionment that was to be voiced by Edmund Blunden, Robert Graves and Siegfried Sassoon.

Although he had got fine notices, Olivier regarded the play as little more than a bait for Basil Dean, and by the time it was put on for a Sunday night and a Monday afternoon performance at the old Prince of Wales Theatre, the decision for the lead in *Beau Geste* lay between himself and Maurice Evans, who was playing the young second-lieutenant, Raleigh. As they made up side by side in the same dressing-room that Sunday evening they both knew that Basil Dean was to be in the audience and that before the night was out one or the other would be chosen.

As at the Apollo, the performance was a great success. Once again the dug-out at St. Quentin in March, 1918, came alive on the stage with its painful glimpse of a handful of young men in khaki who, typical of thousands, were to die in the futile battle that was impending. Among them was Stanhope, the young company commander drinking himself away from fear, and Raleigh, the even younger subaltern, fresh from England and the public school where Stanhope had been his hero. At the climax of the play Raleigh, shot in the back during the attack, was brought down to die in Stanhope's arms. Never was any climax played by two actors with more sense of what was at stake.

At the end there were several curtain calls before Olivier and Evans went up to their dressing-room. Then, as they started to take off their make-up, there was a knock at the door. It was Basil Dean. He was obviously embarrassed to find them together, and asked if it would be possible to have a word with Olivier. There was a moment's pause. Then Maurice Evans, knowing exactly what this meant, got up, and, with perfect tact and good grace, left them alone.

By this time Maurice Browne had decided to give *Journey's End* a trial in the West End. As the play was to be put on with great economy for £200—James Whale, the producer, even painted the set—it was not too extravagant a venture. The critics might rave, but in the saloon bars where men with loud, knowing voices discuss "show business" the verdict was that *Journey's End* didn't stand an earthly; just not box-office. It never for one moment occurred to Olivier, offered £30 a week and his first starring part in *Beau Geste*, that he was doing the wrong thing in handing over Stanhope to Colin Clive. He saw himself leaving a gloomy failure for a spectacular success. He was going into a production at His Majesty's at the head of a cast of forty with Marie Löhr and Madeleine Carroll.

Only after rehearsals started did he suspect that *Beau Geste* was a very bad play. All the flag-waving, battles on the stage, the hosts of Legionnaires, Spahis, Arabs and ex-public-schoolboys with stiff

upper lips, could not disguise its weaknesses. He found Basil Dean
a terrifying producer. After a few days under his fierce, almost
military discipline, he began to believe all the stories he had heard
of young actors fainting and dissolving into tears under his criticism.
To make matters worse, *Journey's End* opened at the Savoy with
enormous success. Combing a matinée idol's moustache and select-
ing a deep tan make-up, Olivier realized too late that he had made
a mistake.

II

There were material compensations for his loss. One was the great
hoarding outside His Majesty's with his name in large letters which
he saw each day as he walked down the Haymarket on his way to
rehearsal. He could certainly feel that his start to the New Year
of 1929 was promising. At twenty-one he was, if not a star, a leading juvenile in London. It was impossible to believe that the drab
digs in Castellain Road and the 4d. lunches at the Central School
had been part of his life only four years before. As soon as the play
opened there would be £30 a week coming into his bank; he could
afford that essential livery of a successful actor, a belted, camel-hair
coat; Paddington was now exchanged for Notting Hill Gate, and his
attic for a room in a large pleasant house in Pembridge Villas.

In the theatre a new dignity was assumed, and it was difficult not
to feel a little smug. Now he had a dresser, and the first-night telegrams round the make-up mirror were not only from his family and
close friends. People whom a year before he had known only by
sight and at a respectful distance sent their good wishes and signed
their christian names.

If only the play had matched these mounting honours! *Beau
Geste* turned out to be even worse than Olivier had feared. On the
first night the audience escaped into the street only a few minutes
before midnight, after an assault on their emotions—to say nothing
of their eyes and nostrils—that has rarely been equalled in the history
of the theatre. They had been subjected to four hours of old-fashioned melodrama, spectacular effects, and heroic flourishes that left
them absolutely limp. They had endured an attempt to tell on the
stage a story that really needed the facilities of the cinema. Olivier,
all dash and fire, irresistibly reminded them of Douglas Fairbanks
and Ronald Colman, but it was quite impossible to take him seriously

in this part of a young Englishman who, to save a woman's honour, forsook his dinner jacket and the comforts of the baronial hall at Brandon Abbas for the dusty barrack room of Sidi-bel-Abbes.

With a straight face he suffered the nickname of "stout fellah" and a plot in which young men were continually slapping one another on the back and exhorting each other to "stick it." A man went mad on the stage; Foreign Legionnaires were crucified with much flowing of artificial blood; a bully was killed in a fight. And after the battle scene in which the whole theatre was filled with asphyxiating smoke, a frightened fireman back-stage rang down the safety curtain in alarm. Coughing threatened to drown the tepid applause.

It was all much too heady to last. Certainly it was a mistake to have opened after the end of the school holidays. Olivier himself got good notices, but the show fizzled out after a month, and he began to wonder where he should look for his next job. However, there was no need for him to worry. Apparently unconcerned about the failure, Basil Dean had another play up his sleeve. In those days the man who had given London *Hassan* and *The Constant Nymph*, and shocked audiences with *Rain* and *Young Woodley*, was seldom missing from the West End. No sooner had the notices gone up for *Beau Geste* than he offered Olivier a leading part in *The Circle of Chalk*. This was a play "from the ancient Chinese" and was another unfortunate mixture of incompatibles. It had to reconcile the beautiful and the tedious, artistic good taste and a bad error of showmanship.

With the passion he was already beginning to develop for complicated make-ups, Olivier tried every trick in his box to achieve the almond eyes and high forehead and cheekbones of a character called Prince Pao. The part also required him to sing, and while he had never become a singer of great ability at All Saints, his choir training had equipped him with a sufficiently true, light baritone voice for him to agree to try a solo. Unfortunately a week before the play opened he developed laryngitis, and not only was he forbidden to sing, but was not allowed to rehearse lines even in a whisper. In desperation he went to see a doctor for the most extreme and risky antidote an actor can try. Just before the first night he had nitrate of silver dropped down his vocal chords. It helped a little, but when he tried to make his entrance singing:

*"I'm as weak as any woman
When I hear a tender song ..."*

his voice, high pitched and uncertain, made the words comically appropriate.

It was an embarrassing incident, but it was not Olivier's voice that caused the real trouble in *The Circle of Chalk*. Anna May Wong had been brought over from America to play the part of the Chinese girl sold into slavery and loved by the prince. She looked as exquisite as she had on the silent screen, but to an English audience the illusion of the Orient faded when she spoke. "Her face is a lotus-flower of Pekin; her voice is the nasal pipe of Broadway," was the comment of one critic, and this disturbing opinion was echoed by many of them. It might have been expected that after *Beau Geste*, Basil Dean would have fussed over his next play with scissors and a stop-watch. But that did not seem to be the way of Mr. Dean. He had employed Aubrey Hammond to design lovely sets and Ernest Irving to arrange the music. With enormous effort he had achieved a riot of beauty and was completely intoxicated by it. So, like *Beau Geste*, he allowed it to go on too long, and also like *Beau Geste*, it came off too quickly. Within a month Olivier found himself out of work again.

III

The year which began with big billing and such high hopes dissolved in disappointments. By the middle of it Olivier looked back not on the great personal successes for which he had hoped, with a starring part in a long run, but on a succession of failures. It was as if, by throwing away his chances in a play of importance, he was to be denied easy success in trivialities. His run of ill-luck was sufficiently marked for the papers to comment on it, and for tactful friends to assure him that it was better to play a number of different parts in a short time than to be stuck in a long run. After *The Circle of Chalk* he had gone into *Paris Bound*, a domestic comedy with Herbert Marshall and Edna Best, and this was quickly followed by *The Stranger Within*, a lurid drama set in the Middle West of America with Olga Lindo, which closed after only a short run at the Garrick.

Then, just when he was wondering how to change his luck, he

was offered a part in a play which promised to be a certain success and which gave him his first chance of going to America. He had always wanted to act on Broadway, and a visit to New York had an added attraction just then because Jill Esmond was playing there in *Bird in Hand*.

At least three British plays with British casts, including Ernest Milton in *Rope*, were doing well on Broadway, and, in the theatrical boom before the Wall Street crash, there were English actors playing in many of the seventy-four theatres open in New York. There seemed an excellent chance for Frank Vosper's *Murder on the Second Floor*, in which the author was having a great success at the Lyric. The play was cast and rehearsed in London by William Mollison, and with the company, which included Phyllis Konstam, O. B. Clarence and Viola Lyel, Olivier sailed in the *Aquitania* towards the end of August. He devoted most of the voyage to a largely unsuccessful attempt to learn bridge under the tuition of Richard Bird, who was also bound for Broadway with his wife Joyce Barbour. As they had been to New York before, the Birds also appointed themselves as guides on the first bewildering taxi ride. Olivier had booked a room at the Algonquin, a small, unpretentious hotel much frequented by actors and already acquiring a legendary reputation from the former patronage of Alexander Woollcott and the literary wits of the Round Table. It was on West Forty-Fourth Street, and all the way in the yellow cab which streaked at an alarming pace from the Cunard dock on the Hudson he was eagerly peering out and so constantly demanding to be told which was Broadway that the Birds grew a little impatient. "There you are, Larry!" they cried. "Look! That's Broadway over there!" Then a few blocks further on they repeated the routine. "Ah! There it is again! Quick! You can just see it down that street!" Every street became the Great White Way; he was shown no mercy.

IV

Until the play opened there was little time to get to know New York, and once it had opened there were only five weeks before it closed. On the very first night at the Eltinge Theatre the whole cast of *Murder on the Second Floor* were given clear and emphatic indication that Broadway did not want them. They discovered that, unlike the long-suffering English, members of an American audience are not inclined to nurse their boredom through a long evening for the satisfaction of booing at the final curtain; they just get up and go. On the first night Frank Vosper's play was punctuated by a fatal, intermittent percussion more deadly to actors than machine-gun fire. It was the noise of seats banging up. And in the morning the critics damned it with faint praise. It was dismissed as "a harmless little English importation." In fierce competition with so many other theatres and the increasingly popular temples of the talkies, it didn't stand a chance.

The first person Olivier had looked up on his arrival in New York had been Jill Esmond, who was playing at the Ethel Barrymore Theatre. She had no reason to regard American audiences as unsympathetic, for *Bird in Hand* was already in its seventh month. During the mornings and on days when neither had matinées they explored the city, and the five weeks passed very quickly. There was hardly enough time to see all the conventional sights, go to the theatres, to visit "Tony's" and "21" and sample the doubtful iniquities of the basement speakeasies which served bootlegged liquor. By the time he had heard the saying that there was a broken heart for every light on Broadway, the Eltinge was in darkness and Olivier had to pack for home. It was impossible for him to remain in New York, for American Equity, fighting a fierce battle with unemployment, would not allow an English actor to play more than one part in six months. There was hope at one moment of a film, and a reminder of missed opportunity when James Whale arrived in America to cast the film of *Journey's End*. Olivier made a test with Derek Williams, who was then playing Raleigh on Broadway, but was told soon afterwards that once again the part had gone to Colin Clive. Clive had now become completely identified with Stanhope in the minds of the public.

During the time they had been together in New York, drawn closer as old friends are in a foreign city, Olivier had again pressed Jill Esmond to marry him. They had been friendly too long, he insisted, for further delay to be necessary; he thought that either they should marry or else end the friendship. This time Jill Esmond accepted. When the run of her play was over and she was back in England—it would be sometime in the following year—they would be married.

With this to comfort him, Olivier was more able to face a London where *Journey's End* was still playing at the Savoy after eleven months, and where people were politely surprised to see him back so soon. Fortunately he did not have to wait long before he was offered a part, that of a nerve-wrecked airman, in *The Last Enemy*, and this opened at the Fortune Theatre in the middle of December. It was the only part of any real quality which Olivier had in the whole of that disappointing year, but he had still to shake off the jinx that seemed to have settled on him. The play itself, symbolic, and uncomfortably poised between heaven and Hampstead, proved too bleak as entertainment round Christmas-time. It came off very quickly and there followed a long and depressing period of little work. For eight months he did nothing except an unpaid Sunday night play with Elissa Landi at the Arts and four days' shooting on a very unfunny "quickie" called *Too Many Crooks*. As the date which had been fixed for his marriage drew near he had the un-pleasant suspicion that Jill Esmond, after her long run in New York, almost certainly had more money in the bank than he had. They were to be married at All Saints, St. Marylebone, on July 25th, 1930 and Olivier was seriously worried about where he would find enough money to start a home.

Then one day, providentially, the phone rang. It was his agent, to say that Noël Coward, who had seen him in *Paris Bound* the year before, would like him to call. A play of his own, the agent be-lieved; he was putting it on with C. B. Cochran. Coward was at that time living in Ebury Street, and so Olivier found himself walking towards Chelsea through the Pimlico streets he had once known so well. It was their first meeting, and after a short talk Coward handed him a manuscript which he said he would like him to glance through. On the cover was the title *Private Lives*. There was a cast of only five. "Have a look at the part of Victor, if you will," Coward said.

It did not take Olivier long to see that *Private Lives* was virtually a duet—that only Amanda, to be played by Gertrude Lawrence, and Elyot, which Coward was taking himself, were in the least worth while. The part of Victor, a deserted prig of a husband, was thin and unexciting. It would have been easy to have been overawed by Coward, who was eight years his senior and who, after several big successes as a playwright and an actor, was already famous. Most young actors would have been flattered into immediate acceptance, but Olivier all but turned the chance down. He said he was sorry, but he did not see himself as Victor and was sure he would not be right for it. Coward saw through this, but was accustomed to getting his own way.

"Look, young man," he said dryly, "you'd better be in a success for a change!"

It was a telling, conclusive argument, and when Coward added that the part would be worth £50 a week, Olivier, who was due to marry a few weeks later, changed his mind and accepted.

Practically everything that has to be said about *Private Lives* has already been written. The three main participants have all published their memoirs. Coward has told how he conceived the idea for the play in the middle of the night in the Imperial Hotel, Tokyo; wrote it recovering from influenza in Shanghai, and spent £40 cabling Gertrude Lawrence in New York asking her to play in it. Gertrude Lawrence has explained how, after reading the manuscript, she came to send him a cable which read: PLAY DELIGHTFUL STOP NOTHING WRONG THAT CAN'T BE FIXED, a cable which Coward (knowing nothing of a previous commitment she had with Charlot) took as a criticism of the play. Cochran, the man of business, has blown the financial gaff and told how each of them put up £1,000, and how Coward drew a salary as leading actor, a huge royalty as author, and over £300 a week as his share of the profits. In only one respect does Olivier's recollection differ from Coward's. In *Present Indicative* Coward said that the preliminary tour was "swathed in luxury" and that the cast all thoroughly enjoyed themselves. This was not, perhaps, entirely true of Olivier, for during the week the play was in Manchester he gave a newspaper interview full of Chekovian gloom.

Interviews in dressing-rooms are not to be taken as clinical and exact records of the mental state of an actor, but this one is interesting because it is the first of any length that Olivier gave during his career. Clearly he did not assume any false gaiety, for to the man from the Manchester *Evening Chronicle* he appeared "unusually pessimistic—almost cynical."

"Only fools are happy," he is reported as saying. "I suppose it is because they don't really know what they want in life, and so every little pleasure that comes along they regard as a paradise of happiness. I somehow can't get away with that. I always examine things so very closely that immediate pleasures are dwarfed by my insistence on ultimate benefits. I want events to go my way; I don't want to be driven by events."

He knew that for the next few months he had no alternative but to be "driven by events." As he had suspected when he first read *Private Lives*, he and Adrianne Allen were condemned to play muted second fiddles to the stars. Even Coward, who had persuaded him to accept the part of Victor, confessed himself "conscience-stricken" at rehearsals because it was so thin. He had constantly tried to encourage him by saying that he was bringing the wooden, humourless Victor to life, but Olivier was still fretting. London and an important first night lay ahead, and he had the inevitable fear of an ambitious young actor that the audience would identify him with the boorish character he was playing.

v

It was one of those first nights which are always called "brilliant." A new Coward play with Coward and Gertrude Lawrence as its stars would in itself have caused interest, but the event was given added importance because it was also the opening of a new theatre. From the moment the posters had gone up for *Private Lives*, the Phoenix, which had just been completed in the Charing Cross Road, was on the theatrical map. The box-office was besieged, and for the first night stalls sold for £2 4s. 6d., a price which in 1930 verged on the fabulous. It was a night for flash-bulbs in the new foyer, a rippling sense of anticipation before the curtain went up, and sporadic bursts of applause from the gallery as the celebrities took their seats. It was a night for the gossip-writers, one of whom, nimbly adopting the style of the author, wrote: "Was ever a première so crashingly *soigné*?" Every adjective that had ever been applied to Coward was used to describe the play. Sophisticated, gay, cynical, amoral, flippant, chic, dazzling, scintillating, impertinent, outrageous . . . the critics ran the whole gamut of Roget's *Thesaurus*. They found space, too, for sympathetic and considerate regard for the plight of the almost neglected Olivier, who for the first time in his life had the experience of being in a success and the one play in London which everyone wanted to see. Coward had lived up to his promise about that.

Private Lives could have run a year, but, ignoring the dark forebodings of people who said it was unlucky to fly in the face of fortune, Coward closed it after three months. He was a writer first, he said, and an actor second, and already his mind was flying ahead from the little five-handed comedy to a spectacular play, a sort of nostalgic cavalcade of England's history during the previous forty years. He would work on it, he promised Cochran, in New York during the three months he would be acting in *Private Lives* on Broadway.

Early in the new year the play moved out of the Phoenix, sailed across the Atlantic, and opened with an even greater acclaim at the Times Square Theatre. Adrianne Allen was unable to go to New York, so Coward asked Olivier if Jill Esmond would consider the part. She was delighted, as it would mean that she and Olivier would not have to be separated after only six months of marriage. They would be acting together again after two and a half years and for the first time since the play in which they had met.

During the New York run, while Coward was poring over old numbers of the *Illustrated London News* for background for *Cavalcade*, Olivier and Jill Esmond were also busy. Like a great many British actors they were looking West. A new Gold Rush in the form of talkies was booming (and sending silent stars toppling every time they opened their mouths); Hollywood was scouting for actors who could act *and* talk. At the Lambs Club, where actors foregathered in New York, Olivier had to suffer the caustic comments of American actors who, talking in a hideous parody of English accents, said they supposed an English accent was now the only way to stardom. When both he and Jill Esmond were signed up it looked as though their tormentors were right. They had made a number of tests in the studios which all the major Hollywood companies maintained near New York, and R.K.O. had made a dazzling offer. As soon as the three months' run of *Private Lives* had ended they would leave for Hollywood.

CHAPTER 5

Depression over Hollywood
1930-1933

I

To ANYONE who has not been there Hollywood always sounds romantic. The most highly-geared publicity set-up in the world has not failed in its task of persuading the uninitiated that the city which exports glamour is in itself glamorous. Cynics have been able to make only a few dents in this beautiful conception. By weight of numbers the publicists have drowned the realists, and until he went there Olivier was caught up in the highly-coloured day-dream. He knew, of course, that serious actors laughed at the place, but he thought Hollywood must have some secret fascination if it could make actors like Clive Brook and George Arliss forsake the theatre to work under its spell. As the train travelled westwards across the plains of Kansas, through the deserts of New Mexico, and over the Rockies into Southern California, he awaited the realization of his day-dream with a good deal of curiosity and anticipation. R.K.O. had telegraphed that he was wanted urgently, and this had meant that he had to go by himself, for Jill Esmond, who was recovering from appendicitis, could not leave New York for several days.

Like everyone else who arrives there for the first time, he was surprised to find the world's film capital so little of an entity that it did not even possess a railway station. On arrival from New York on the Santa Fe "Chief," passengers for Hollywood had to get out at either Pasadena or Los Angeles and then take a car. The car awaiting him had been arranged with inflexible studio efficiency by R.K.O., and like all cars in Hollywood was low and sleek and very fast. It was so fast that on the way to the Beverly Hills Hotel at the end of Sunset Boulevard he had only a confused image of a city of wide streets, lined with palm trees and buildings which gave the curious impression of all being two storeys high. That was until the car began to climb into the lush residential quarter. Here uniformity was thrown to the Pacific breezes, and he found himself passing huge private houses in a bewildering variety of styles from English Tudor to Spanish Colonial. Olivier was to learn that he must be prepared for such contrasts. In the business part of Hollywood he was to see a cheap eating-house next to the imposing façade of a huge bank. The film magazines which had extolled the beauties of Pickfair had been strangely silent about the garish advertisements and the innumerable drug-stores. They had not done justice to that masterpiece of whimsy, a restaurant in the shape of a bowler hat, or perhaps the crowning architectural folly, a cinema in oriental rococo. They had not explained that it was possible to travel quite a distance along the straight sunbaked sidewalks without encountering Clara Bow.

For the first few months it was all new and quite enjoyable. To be a good-looking young man who could learn lines and not mutilate the English tongue when you spoke was to be wanted; and, after New York, Hollywood was an island of escape from people who talked about the Depression. While the rest of America staggered under the impact of the Wall Street Crash, Hollywood in 1931 was still a comparatively peaceful oasis. Apparently the public still wanted the cinema. Banks might fail and families be impoverished, but there still seemed to be enough money at the box-office. The studio where Olivier and Jill Esmond were to work had broken all records with *Cimarron*, and *City Lights* and *Min and Bill* brought dollars rolling in to Chaplin and M.G.M. It had even been possible to tempt the public with more serious films like *Street Scene*, and *Five Star Final*. The movies were the cheapest entertainment available, and the fact that they now talked proved to be something more than a temporary novelty.

These were the conditions in which Olivier settled down to make his first Hollywood film, a steaming tropical affair with Adolph

Menjou, called *Friends and Lovers*. R.K.O., noting his moustache and the slight resemblance that had already caused comment in London, let it be known that they had a new Ronald Colman up their sleeve. If they were disappointed that, unlike Colman, he was not to be coaxed into flannels and represented as a typical cricket-playing Englishman, they soon got another idea. He was a regular guy who played baseball! To prove it the publicity stills department provided the fan magazines with hundreds of glossy photographs of him looking grimly determined in a catcher's mask and swinging a baseball bat.

Friends and Lovers was not a very good film, and Olivier was little happier about *The Yellow Ticket* with Elissa Landi, for which he was loaned to Fox later in the year. But between films there was plenty of fun to be had outside the studio. He was making a lot of new friends. He met Anthony Bushell who, like himself, had been acting on the American stage and had gravitated to Hollywood. Bushell was to become a close friend, and so, too, was an American actor who, although he was two years younger than Olivier, had already been in films for ten years. Douglas Fairbanks was then firmly Douglas Fairbanks *Junior*, and one of Olivier's earliest meetings with him was when he was with his father at the United Artists Studio. They found they had mutual friends in Robert Montgomery and Raymond Massey, and took an immediate liking to one another. Fairbanks was particularly attracted by the unpredictable sense of humour which Olivier hid behind a rather serious demeanour. This was combined with a slight unworldliness, and, as Fairbanks and Robert Montgomery were to find out, made him an ideal butt for practical jokes.

At one period, quite early in their friendship, Olivier and Fairbanks, who was then married to Joan Crawford, both ran simultaneously into domestic troubles which seemed, in the perspective of young men in their twenties, to be of appalling gravity. According to Fairbanks, there was only one antidote for husbands in such circumstances, and that was to visit Hollywood's Russian club, where vodka, Russian songs and the balalaika proved the perfect accompaniments to the sort of pleasure which is faintly tinged with the melancholy of unhappy love. They learned some of the songs, and after a very short time found their personal troubles reduced to infinitesimal proportions compared to those of the White Russian refugees who ran the club. With them they sat up well into the morning plotting the overthrow of the Soviet and a world-wide counter-revolution. Enthusiasm sometimes carried them to the point of putting on Russian blouses and toasting the memory of the Czar and his family.

II

It was only a matter of time before the Depression caught up with the movies and Hollywood was no longer privileged to remain one of the few cities in the United States which were free from bank failures. In 1932 several of the banks closed and suddenly there was a sense of panic in the air as stories spread of stars and executives who had lost all their savings, of suicides, and of studios which were threatened with bankruptcy. Shooting on several films in which Olivier was to play had barely started before mysterious men, vaguely designated as "the front office," suddenly announced cancellations. Economies were being made throughout the studios, but like Paramount and Fox, R.K.O. was soon to go bankrupt. It was revealed that it had been losing money steadily for some years, and this was blamed largely on the story department.

As in political crises, there was a search for a "strong man" to stop the rot. He was found in David O. Selznick, a young man of thirty, who had made a big reputation for himself during his previous four years as an associate producer with Paramount. He was appointed Vice-President in charge of Production at R.K.O., and one of his first moves was to set up a "story cabinet," each member of which was responsible for finding stories suitable for different sections of the public. One supervised stories with an appeal for women, another stories for young people, while a third had to search for stage plays that could be adapted to the films. Into which category *Westward Passage* came is uncertain, but it was a slight improvement on Olivier's previous films. In the part of a temperamental young author he had one very roguish scene with a two-year-old baby, in which he fell into the child's bath, but despite this piece of slapstick he enjoyed the film more than the other two he made for R.K.O. One reason was that Ann Harding, whom he found the complete antithesis of the usual Hollywood star, so helped him during the making of the film that "angelic" was the only adequate description he could find for her in a letter he sent to his family about this time. He told them how, during the shooting of a scene, she would turn slightly so that he would be photographed to greater advantage, and sometimes even insisted on completely reversing positions so that his face should be to the camera instead of hers. "It is unbelievable for a star of her reputation to be so good," he wrote enthusiastically.

Partly due, perhaps, to Ann Harding's thoughtfulness, Olivier received some excellent press notices for his performance in *Westward Passage*, and, beyond anything he could visualize at the time, the film was to have an important effect on his career. It was to be the direct cause of his making a second journey to Hollywood only a year after he had left.

When the film was a few days from completion Douglas Fairbanks suggested that in the two weeks' holiday Olivier would have before he had to return to the studios for "retakes," he should come on a fishing holiday off the Mexican coast. Robert Montgomery, who was sometimes their companion at the Russian club, would be a third member of the party. Olivier said he thought it was a wonderful idea and on the night before they were to sail they met to make final arrangements. These were complicated because at the last minute Olivier had to do some additional work on the film before he could leave Hollywood. He said he would fly down to join them in a few days.

It was an evening of high spirits and even more vodka than usual. The small balalaika orchestra seemed especially suited to their mood, and they decided hazily but quite firmly at one stage that the orchestra must come with them on the yacht in the dual rôle of sailors and musicians. Before they left for home extravagant offers must have been made, for next morning when they arrived at the dock, Fairbanks and Montgomery were horrified to find the Russians, complete with balalaikas, all in smiling eagerness to start. It seemed impossible to explain that the suggestion of the night before had not been entirely serious, and that really the very last thing wanted on a Mexican fishing holiday was a Russian orchestra. The men were so pathetically keen to come that they hadn't the heart to refuse. By good fortune, just out of harbour they hit a heavy sea, and the musicians proved to be such bad sailors that they had to be put ashore.

As soon as the shooting of his film was finished Olivier caught a plane to join his friends. It had been arranged that they would sail about two hundred miles down the coast to Todos Santos Bay, where they would come ashore and meet him off the plane at Ensenada. But when he arrived at the airfield neither Fairbanks nor Montgomery was there to meet him. Instead he was greeted by two Mexican policemen who promptly arrested him. His demands for an explanation were met with an incomprehensible flow of Spanish accompanied by dumb show which suggested that, because he was English, his passport and papers were not in order. He was taken to the local gaol and there faced by an official who frowned heavily over his passport and demanded 1,000 pesos. This was about £100, an impossible sum for Olivier to pay as he had left all the money arrangements to Douglas Fairbanks. When he explained he had only twenty dollars on him the official merely shrugged implacably and indicated the cells. Half an hour of frantic argument in the boiling mid-day heat followed, at the end of which, and just when he was on the point of cabling the British Consul in Mexico City, Fairbanks and Montgomery appeared. In a surprisingly short time they had secured his release, but suspicion only dawned when they got into the car and Olivier caught them exchanging a secret smile. They hardly bothered to put up any pretence; yes, they admitted, they'd arranged the whole thing. They had tipped the police, who really spoke English, to make the arrest, and had squared the official. What an excellent actor he'd been! Olivier listened to them patiently and then told them that their joke might easily have meant the end of their holiday. "You see," he explained, "my papers *aren't* in order; I haven't got a visa!"

When the fishing trip was over he returned to Hollywood to complete all the retakes necessary on the film with Ann Harding. Then he was faced with a period of inactivity and frustration. Studio plans seemed to be in a melting pot; one day he would be growing a beard to make a test for a Jewish part and the next he would be climbing into a grotesque uniform at the R.K.O.-Pathé studios to see if he were suitable for Pola Negri's leading man in *Queen Draga.* Like many other ideas these came to nothing, and after several months he was completely disenchanted. The films he had made were mediocre and he had no wish to remain in Hollywood waiting indefinitely for more rôles as the conventional leading man. He was all for packing and going back to London, particularly as he knew that Gloria Swanson was soon to start a film, *The Perfect*

Understanding, in England and wanted him for her leading man. But here he was faced with a difficult decision. Jill Esmond, who had also made three films, was suddenly presented by Selznick with what seemed to be her big chance in a starring part. The "story cabinet" had bought Clemence Dane's *A Bill of Divorcement* in which John Barrymore was to play the father, and they wanted her for the part of the daughter. Because of studio economy, Selznick said, he would have to ask her to take a half cut in salary; but in exchange she should have a wonderful part and a star billing. It was a great temptation, but Olivier was suspicious about the offer, especially when in the middle of negotiations he learnt that R.K.O. were about to bring an unknown "discovery" from New York and that she was to be paid $500 a week more than his wife. In view of this it seemed to him extremely unlikely that she would ever get the part.

For several days they argued about it. Jill Esmond wanted to stay, and for the first time Olivier saw how difficult it was to combine marriage and a career successfully. At last, and feeling on the whole rather mean, he said that whatever Jill decided to do, he proposed to go home. He longed to get out of Hollywood and back to England. Once he had made the film with Gloria Swanson he would have enough money to be able to forget the studios for a while and return to the more important business of acting on the stage. Reluctantly Jill Esmond said good-bye to her part and they left for home in July. To coincide with their departure, R.K.O. came out in a blaze of publicity for the girl who was to star in *A Bill of Divorcement.* She was a New York stage discovery with high cheekbones and a deep, rather grating voice, and her name was Katharine Hepburn.

III

When he left Hollywood, Olivier was full of good resolutions never to return. He went back to England with the pious air of a convert who, having tasted worldly things, has finally put temptation behind him. After *The Perfect Understanding* which, he confidently believed, was the worst film ever made, he eagerly accepted the part offered him by Gladys Cooper in *The Rats of Norway* at the Playhouse. Although he was only in a supporting rôle to Raymond Massey and Gladys Cooper, his part as a young assistant master in Keith Winter's play was a good one. He got excellent notices and felt himself properly re-established in the theatre. He told Jill Esmond that they must really look round for a nice house, preferably in Chelsea, and he was very pleased when they were ofered Whistler's house in Cheyne Walk. It was then, just as the play was settling down to a run at the Playhouse and he had signed his new lease, that Hollywood once again put out its tentacles.

It all started with a Western Union cable which was delivered at his flat in Roland Gardens towards the end of May. It was from his agent in Hollywood, Frank Joyce, and said that M.G.M. wanted him to sign a contract with them for a year. It would mean forty weeks' work at $1,000 a week. He sent back a reply that he was not interested in any contract for a long period, and two days later he received another cable which was far more calculated to excite him:

HAVE ONE PICTURE PROPOSITION LEADING MAN OPPOSITE GARBO GREAT PART STARTING IN TWO WEEKS ANSWER IMMEDIATELY REGARDS.

This was something that could not be ignored, but as he did not know if *The Rats of Norway* was going to run, or whether Gladys Cooper would consider releasing him, he replied on June 6th:

DEAR FRANK WILL CABLE DEFINITELY TOMORROW OR NEXT DAY REGARDS.

He was forced, however, to stall until June 12th, when he cabled from his new home in Chelsea:

THEATRE BUSINESS UNCERTAIN PROBABLY ABLE TO SAIL IN TWO WEEKS STOP CHANGED ADDRESS 74 CHEYNE WALK LONDON REGARDS.

By return Joyce came back with:

IF YOU CAN SAIL IN TWO WEEKS AND BE HERE JULY SEVENTH CAN DEFINITELY MAKE DEAL ANSWER IMMEDIATELY REGARDS.

That night, June 13th, Olivier was able to send a decision:

CAN SAIL IN TWO WEEKS WANT NOT LESS THAN FIFTEEN HUNDRED DOLLARS WEEKLY STARTING ARRIVAL FIRST CLASS RETURN TRANSPORTATION STOP CABLE CONFIRMATION IMMEDIATELY STATING

WHAT CLOTHES IF MOUSTACHE IS REQUIRED AND HOW LONG PIC-
TURE LIKELY TO LAST ALSO LOOK OUT FOR PICTURE FOR JILL WHO
MAY ACCOMPANY ME REGARDS.

Joyce's next cable on June 16th was rather less satisfactory:

FOUR WEEKS GUARANTEE FIFTEEN HUNDRED DOLLARS WEEKLY
TRANSPORTATION BOTH WAYS FOR LEAD OPPOSITE GARBO STOP
SHOULD THE PICTURE NOT BE MADE METRO WILL GIVE YOU LEAD
IN ANOTHER IMPORTANT PICTURE WHICH YOU HAVE RIGHT TO
TURN DOWN SHOULD YOU DESIRE TO DO SO REGARDS.

Already old in the ways of Hollywood, Olivier could see the obvious snags in such an arrangement. He replied on June 17th:

CANNOT ACCEPT PROPOSITION AS CABLED BUT WILLING TAKE TERMS
FOR GARBO PROVIDED SALARY STARTS FROM DATE ARRIVAL STOP ALSO
WILLING TO DO SUBSTITUTE PICTURE SUBJECT APPROVING SCRIPT
ONLY IF GARBO CANCELLED BUT IN CASE REJECT SUBSTITUTE MY
MINIMUM MUST STILL BE PAID BY COMPANY FURTHERMORE IM-
POSSIBLE TO WAIT IN HOLLYWOOD MORE THAN FOUR WEEKS BE-
FORE COMMENCING SHOOTING BECAUSE OF AUTUMN ENGAGEMENTS
REGARDS.

This did the trick and three days later Joyce cabled "METRO HAS
AGREED" and followed this up with another asking him to be in
Hollywood not later than July 17th. But Olivier was not to be
hurried. His next cable read:

IMPOSSIBLE ARRIVE HOLLYWOOD BEFORE JULY 24 STOP RELY ON
YOU PROTECT ME BILLING ETC REGARDS.

and only after two further cables and on June 27th, nearly a month
after the start of the exchange, did he ask:

WHAT WILL THE PICTURE BE ABOUT AND ABOUT WHEN WILL IT
FINISH REGARDS.

For an actor to want to know the film he was being asked to travel
5,000 miles to appear in must have seemed a supremely irrelevant,
almost frivolous question to the agent, for he ignored it and only
replied (June 28th):

GARBO ENGAGEMENT SHOULD CLOSE APPROXIMATELY SEPT 8 RE-
GARDS.

The next cable was from Olivier on July 4th:

IMPERATIVE BOOK PASSAGE IMMEDIATELY IN ORDER ARRIVE 24TH
STOP CABLE TRANSPORTATION MONEY TODAY REGARDS.

From Frank Joyce, July 5th:

PLEASE CONTACT SAM ECKMAN LONDON MGM MANAGER WHO HAS
BEEN INSTRUCTED TO PAY TRANSPORTATION TO YOU REGARDS.

This was followed on July 7th by:

IMPORTANT YOU CABLE US AT ONCE YOUR MEASUREMENTS AS MGM
MUST PREPARE YOUR WARDROBE STOP ALSO LET YOUR MUSTACHE
GROW IN CASE THEY DESIRE TO USE IT REGARDS.

From Olivier, July 8th:

MEASUREMENTS FOR COSTUME HEIGHT FIVE FOOT TEN STOP NAPE
TO WAIST SEVENTEEN AND A HALF STOP FULL LENGTH JACKET
TWENTY EIGHT AND A HALF STOP WIDTH BACK EIGHT AND HALF
STOP ELBOW TWENTY TWO STOP FULL SLEEVE THIRTY TWO AND
HALF STOP CHEST THIRTY EIGHT STOP WAIST THIRTY STOP HIPS
THIRTY EIGHT STOP MOUSTACHE BEING WORKED ON SAILING EUROPA
SATURDAY FIFTEENTH REGARDS.

From Frank Joyce, July 9th:

MGM ADVISES MEASUREMENTS NOT SUFFICIENT REQUEST YOU
CABLE DETAILED TAILORING MEASUREMENTS URGENT REGARDS.

From Olivier, July 11th:

REFER TO PESTERRE BEVERLY HILLS OR RKO WARDROBE FOR FULL
MEASUREMENTS STOP ENGLISH TAILORS DO NOT TAKE MORE THAN
I CABLED REGARDS.

This completed the supplication of the gods, the prayer to Melpomene. Satisfied with the auspices, Olivier handed over his part of the schoolmaster to Louis Hayward and started to pack. He had at last learnt that the film in which he was to appear was based on the life of Queen Christina, whose history Garbo had been studying during a holiday which she had just spent in Sweden. His part was to be that of Don Antonio, a Spanish emissary with whom Christina falls in love while he is at the Swedish court to ask for her hand on behalf of the King of Spain. The Press, on whom the name of Garbo has never ceased to have a magical effect, leapt on the story that Olivier was to be her new leading man. If he had been chosen to become consort of a queen he could hardly have received greater publicity than he did for going to play opposite an actress who was to portray one. That an English actor should be given the part was treated almost as a national honour, and at Waterloo Station on the morning of his departure, he was surrounded by reporters. No, he had not met Miss Garbo before. Yes, this would be the first time. Indeed, he was looking forward to it. Yes, it would be a great experience to act with her. Certainly they could take his photograph if they liked. Where? Looking out of the train window. A most original suggestion.

Not until he arrived in Hollywood did he hear exactly how he had come to be chosen. Under the terms of a new contract which Garbo had just been given by M.G.M. she was permitted to choose her leading man, and there had been a long search for an actor suitable for Don Antonio. Garbo had seen the tests of a number of actors but had not been pleased with any of them. Then, some old films with likely leading men in them had been run through for her privately. *Westward Passage* had been one, and immediately, or so Olivier was told, she had decided that he was the ideal choice.

Apparently the problem of Anglo-American tailors' measurements had been overcome, for when he arrived at the M.G.M. studios in Culver City he found his costumes ready for him in his dressing-room. There seemed to be a certain amount of urgency for him to put them on, and it was hinted that he had already kept Miss Garbo waiting long enough. Rouben Mamoulian, the Russian director, told him that it had been decided to start with one of the most important scenes in the film, and this, in itself, seemed unusual to Olivier. However, comforting himself with the thought that anything was possible in films, he listened while Mamoulian explained that it was a love scene set in the bedroom of an inn outside Stockholm where Don Antonio first meets the Queen. They would be rehearsing and testing it the next morning.

The following day when he arrived on the set he was introduced to Greta Garbo for the first time. She was wearing dark glasses and smoking a cigarette, and it seemed to Olivier that he was not greeted with any particular warmth. Few words were wasted, and he formed the immediate impression that, as everyone had warned him, Garbo was inordinately shy. Introductions over, Mamoulian told them what he wanted for the scene they were going to shoot. Don Antonio would take the Queen in his arms and she would slowly respond to what Mamoulian called "awakening passion." The very first time that they rehearsed the scene it seemed to Olivier that the response was a good deal slower than the director could possibly have wanted. He was not conscious of any passion awakening at all; in fact, so unresponsive was Garbo that he found it quite impossible to give a good performance. He tried to explain this to himself by saying that perhaps Garbo was purposely making this a difficult test for him. But after they had tried it several times and there was still no change in her attitude or improvement in his acting he became a little worried.

He was prepared for Garbo to be rather remote, and made allowances for her shyness, but he considered that as a leading man, summoned all the way from England, he deserved to be treated with rather less formality, and as the days went by the whole business assumed an atmosphere of total unreality. It was quite unlike any relationship he had ever known between an actress and a leading man, and there seemed no chance of breaking down the invisible but quite definite barrier between them. If he couldn't establish some sort of friendliness off the set, he was certain that any harmony would be quite impossible when they were acting together. Somehow he must get through her reserve.

His chance came one day when he found her sitting quite alone on a trunk in one corner of the sound stage. It was during a break while the cameras were being set up, and he began to talk to her. It was the stilted, one-sided conversation of a young man meeting a girl for the first time and making a desperate attempt to please. He found himself talking in very nearly a gabble about acting, about Sweden, about costume, about history—about anything he could think of. Garbo's replies were non-commital; she hardly turned to look at him as he spoke; and only when his flow of talk finally petered out did she look round and, with a rather sad smile curling up the edges of her mouth, make one of those disconcerting remarks which have so helped to promote the Garbo Legend. "Life's a pain anyway!" she observed.

A few days later Olivier was summoned by Walter Wanger, the

producer, and the conversation opened ominously with the words: "We want you to know we're crazy about you here at Metro, Larry, but . . ." It ended, as far as he could remember, with an explanation that they were afraid Miss Garbo found him not quite tall enough. Now, Wanger went on, they were just about to start filming *Romeo and Juliet* with Norma Shearer, and they would like to try him as Romeo if . . . but at that point Olivier, hurt pride, resentment, and disappointment all welling up, interrupted. He told Wanger rather coldly that he did not believe in Shakespeare on the screen.

The next day he heard that he had been replaced by John Gilbert, who had been Garbo's leading man in the silent days. It was news which caused a Hollywood sensation, and it seemed an extraordinary choice, for Gilbert, who was nearing forty, and whose broad Utah accent clashed badly with his appearance as "The Great Lover," had been one of the many actors killed by the talkies. It had been Gilbert who had given Garbo her first chance in *Flesh and the Devil* when she came, an unknown actress named Greta Gustafsen, from Sweden. All the papers played the event up as the come-back of the man Garbo had secretly always loved, but as Olivier heard later, there was part of Gilbert's story which they never mentioned. It was a story which quickly made him forget any resentment he might have felt against either Gilbert or Garbo. It was really a gesture of extraordinary loyalty on Garbo's part to a man who had been leading a wretched existence for several years. Gilbert had tried very hard to train his voice, but without success, and as he had slipped more and more out of the limelight, his position with M.G.M. had become increasingly difficult. But stubbornly and in the face of every humiliation he had refused to let the studio break his spirit. He had been given bad parts and worked under conditions which were highly unsympathetic, but had never given the studio one technical fault that could be translated as a breach of contract.

Now his waiting and patience had been rewarded, and Olivier, grasping at a chance to save his face, told friends and curious journalists that he believed Garbo had wanted Gilbert the whole time. One fan magazine graphically related how John Gilbert had climbed into Olivier's discarded costume and how Olivier, watching the same scene behind the camera had seen Gilbert bring warmth and love into Garbo's eyes—"eyes," he said, "which I found only veiled and cold." It was completely fictitious, but at the time provided a convenient escape from his own secret suspicion that he had lost the part for the simple reason that he hadn't been good enough.*

To escape from polite condolences Olivier and his wife took refuge in Honolulu, and there, to add injury to insult, he broke a toe surf-riding. Sitting in the brilliant sunshine on the veranda of the Royal Hawaiian Hotel one day early in September, he was brought a cable by a page-boy. Olivier put down the script of *The Green Bay Tree*, in which he and his wife were to appear on Broadway the following month, and opened it. It was from his agent in Hollywood.

WOULD YOU BE INTERESTED IN METRO CONTRACT FIFTEEN HUNDRED FORTY WEEKS IN ONE YEAR GUARANTEE REGARDS.

He passed it over to Jill Esmond with a smile.
"No answer," he told the boy.

* Quite recently Olivier heard through George Cukor, who is a close friend, that Garbo had told him that she was rather upset by the whole affair and very sorry for the way he had been treated. He asked Cukor to give Garbo a message next time he saw her, that she had been absolutely right.

CHAPTER 6

With Gielgud in "Romeo"
1933-1936

I

THE EXPERIENCE with Garbo was probably salutary. At the age of twenty-five it would have been all too easy to have accepted the salary of $60,000 a year M.G.M. would have paid him to work in Hollywood. Once under contract he would have been lost to the stage in a succession of parts over which he had no choice. As it was, he shunned Hollywood for the next five years, and at a vital point in his career had the good sense not to be diverted from doing what he wanted by the offer of big money.

But however clearly he was able to see this later, at the time his pride was hurt by the fiasco of *Queen Christina*. As he had visions of the reporters who had seen him off at Waterloo now grimly demanding a post-mortem, he was pleased to be able to delay his return to London for several months. The run of *The Green Bay Tree* in New York would help to cushion the blow. It was a production put on by Jed Harris, who for some years had been rather in eclipse, but who was determined that his come-back as a Broadway impresario should be a success. He had cast Olivier for Julian, the part which had been played in the London production by Hugh Williams, and Jill Esmond as Leonora, the practical young woman who tries to get him away from his guardian. James Dale had the Frank Vosper part of the middle-aged sybarite whose affection for

81

the boy he had adopted is rather more than paternal. Rehearsals in New York during the autumn were far from pleasant, for Harris proved to be a ruthless, exacting producer who would lash his actors with sarcasm and keep them rehearsing for twelve hours at a stretch. Even with Basil Dean at his most acid, Olivier had never been worked up into such a temper. Never was he so near to losing all self-control and walking out of the theatre as he was with Jed Harris. But although he was ruthless, Harris obtained results, and when the play opened at the Cort Theatre on 48th Street, Olivier won almost consistent praise for a performance in which he managed to suggest both the moral weakness and epicene charm of Julian.

The New York critic of the *Pittsburgh Press* sent back a very vivid account of his performance to her paper, and for once acting was not dismissed in a token adjective at the tail-end of a notice.

"I cannot remember ever having been more impressed with a young man's *immersion* in a role," wrote Florence Fisher Parry. "Julian does more than spring to life—we feel that he has grown upon us over the period of a lifetime.

"His entrances seem not to be made from the wings of a stage— but from an adjacent room where he has been conducting his life as vividly as upon the visible stage. And in the horrifying scene where he is beaten into slavish submission by his benefactor's abnormal attraction for him, his acting becomes not *acting*, but an exhibition of emotional collapse so painful to witness that the eyes of the audience are torn away; the spectacle of his ignominy actually becomes too terrible to bear."

The play ran for five months, and as the run drew towards its end during March, 1934, both Olivier and Jill Esmond began to think longingly of England. He wrote to his sister Sybille that he was homesick and relieved that the play was not doing too well. "It's a terrible thing for an actor to say, isn't it?" he confessed, "but honestly I've never hated playing any part so much before . . ."

In his letter he added that Noël Coward was coming over to New York, and this visit was to prove fortunate, for it put an end to any worries he might have had about prospects when he got back to London. Coward had come to see John C. Wilson about a plan to present Ina Claire in London in *Biography*, the play by S. N. Behrman in which she had been starring for nearly a year on Broadway. One night, at a party at the Waldorf, Coward, who was sitting on a settee with Ina Claire, called Olivier over to talk to them. "How would you like to play with Ina in London?" he asked; and so, with hardly any more formalities, it came about that when, after nearly a year's absence, Olivier sailed for home in March, he had a contract to appear as her leading man.

II

Biography was not a success. As someone remarked, a play by Coward was expected to be champagne; the same test must be applied to one he produced, and the best that could be said for *Biography* was that it came from the champagne district. Ina Claire, back in London after twenty years, did not have the triumph she had enjoyed with the part in the States. Coward had encouraged her to underplay, and the result was a performance of great subtlety but one which somehow failed to inspire enthusiastic notices. Olivier gave a good performance in the unsympathetic part of a self-righteous, occasionally ranting prig, although he was accused by one critic of bad gestures. Luke-warm first-night notices did the play damage from which it could not recover. By the end of the first week the cast had been asked to go on half salary, and four weeks later the play closed. For Olivier it was an inauspicious return to London after a year abroad.

As soon as the notices went up he began to look round for work, and found it almost immediately in an unexpected way. His friend Ralph Richardson had been rehearsing as Bothwell in Gordon Daviot's play *Queen of Scots*, but was finding it extremely difficult to make anything colourful out of what should have been a very showy part. Finally he asked John Gielgud, who was producing, if he would release him, and although there was little more than a week before the first night, Gielgud, who could see that he was unhappy, agreed. Bronson Albery who was presenting the play with Howard Wyndham, then asked Olivier if he would like the part. With only eight days to learn it there was little time for shades of character or great subtlety, and Olivier was content to play Bothwell for the swaggering, attractive philanderer that he was—a performance considered by some to be "more Hollywood than Holyrood."

Queen of Scots did not have the success of the same author's *Richard of Bordeaux*, but it was a play which Olivier was to remember long after many more successful ones had been forgotten because it started so many friendships. It was his first professional introduction to the highly-strung and sensitive Gielgud, and also to a young actor named Glen Byam Shaw. The friendship with Byam Shaw started on a note of sarcasm. Remarking that Olivier had worn a different suit every day to rehearsals, Byam Shaw commented one morning: "How wonderful it must be to go to Hollywood and be rich!" "Not at all," Olivier had said quickly. "Each of these suits is a relic of a different flop!" The reply immediately endeared him to Byam Shaw, and with Campbell Gullan, the Scottish actor, they became so friendly during the run that they formed themselves into an exclusive, exuberant club of three.

The club was called the Bothwell Club, had a tie and a very clearly defined function. The tie, which Olivier designed to incorporate all the symbolic colours of youth, had stripes of blood red, passionate purple, murky black, whisky yellow and venturesome green. The principal nightly activity of the club was drinking, and this was carried out with ceremony and rigid formality. A strict rule insisted that no drop should be touched until after the show, but this was tolerantly interpreted to mean after the actual performance of each of the three members. Thus, at the end of Act II when William Maitland (Gullan) disappeared from the play it was his duty to assemble glasses and bottle in Olivier's dressing-room; the moment Darnley (Byam Shaw) was killed at the end of the first scene in Act III he would pour the drinks out; but not until Bothwell (Olivier) finally came off stage during the second scene and had reached his dressing-room, would the three raise their glasses and declare the club open for the night. The play had a short run but the club was destined to survive, and even after Campbell Gullan's death in 1939, Byam Shaw and Olivier were to continue the custom of always wearing the club tie on the day before each other's first nights.

When it became clear that *Queen of Scots* was not going to survive the doldrums of August in the West End, Olivier received an offer from Noël Coward which he did not find particularly flattering. Coward was producing a tornado of a play by Edna Ferber and George Kaufman called *Theatre Royal*, with Marie Tempest.

It was a full-blooded satire on that "royal family of Broadway," the Barrymores, and he wanted Olivier to play Tony Cavendish, a thinly-disguised portrait of the eccentric John Barrymore. Unfortunately he only wanted him as a stop-gap to take the part on tour for two weeks and then hand over to Brian Aherne when the play came to the West End. It meant a good salary of £100 a week, but this was hardly sufficient compensation for being what amounted to a provincial understudy. Olivier's first reaction was to turn the offer down, but then he read the play and had an idea. It was the sort of part any actor dreams about. Every entrance was theatrically superb, every line of dialogue crackled. So, with dissimulating modesty, he agreed to play Glasgow and Edinburgh and flung himself into the part. Recalling everything he could of Barrymore, whom he had met in Hollywood, he twirled his moustache at the ends, made an entrance with two Borzoi, fought a duel on the stage, leapt over a balcony and gave a gusty, eye-blazing performance which invariably brought the house down. There is a story of a music-hall comic who, after taking several curtain calls and with the audience still yelling for him, remarked pleasantly to the next act who was waiting in the wings, "Follow that!" Olivier was virtually saying this to Brian Aherne, and Aherne suddenly began to wonder if an offer of Mercutio in New York was possibly a more interesting alternative.

By the time the play reached Manchester, it seems safe to assume, Aherne was wondering no longer, for Coward took Olivier on one side. "Suppose," he said, "just suppose Brian Aherne was not available, would you be prepared to play the part in London?" This was Olivier's moment. He shook his head sadly. He had just bought the rights of a new play by Keith Winter and preparations were pretty far forward. He was afraid . . . Coward became very persuasive, however, and a week later his name went up in lights in the same size as that of Marie Tempest and of Madge Titheradge outside the Lyric in Shaftesbury Avenue.

When the play opened he received magnificent notices and at least one critic said his performance was the best thing he had ever done. For two months he played the part up to the hilt, and then one night went even further. He misjudged his leap from the balcony in the second act and broke his ankle. In great pain he had to be helped to his dressing-room while his understudy, Valentine

Dyall, hastily put on his make-up and finished the performance. A doctor insisted that he should go straight home to bed, without waiting even to take the make-up out of his hair. This caused some consternation to the maid the following morning. "Oh, madam," she said sympathetically to Jill Esmond after she had taken up the breakfast, "the master must be bad. His hair's gone all white in the night."

The excuse he had given to Coward at Manchester that he had bought a play by Keith Winter was quite genuine. It was called *The Ringmaster*, and, like *Rats of Norway* and *The Shining Hour*, had the eternal triangle for a plot and a neurotic for its leading character. Here he was a soured cripple in a wheel chair who dominated the world of a Devonshire guest house and the lives of at least six people who were involved in complicated love affairs. The play was produced soon after his accident, and it was difficult to believe that Olivier had not persuaded Gilbert Miller to put it on precisely because he was a temporary invalid and was, like the hero of the play, confined to a chair. But in fact, by the time the play came to the Shaftesbury, he had completely recovered. Without any pain whatsoever he was able to get to his feet from the chair and go through the agonized contortions with which he brought down the final curtain. Those contortions, following a performance of considerable power, had enough sheer theatrical bravura about them to ensure that the audience were cheering at the end. Unfortunately their numbers did not match their enthusiasm, and before the end of the first week receipts fell so low that it was decided to take the play off.

On the Saturday night, at the end of the eighth and last performance, the applause produced six curtain calls and Olivier for the first time in his career had, as the leading actor, to respond with a speech.

"We as characters have unfortunately died to-night," he said. "We hope that, brief though our appearances have been, we will live in your memories."

There was a shout of "Don't take it off!" to which Olivier could only shrug and watch the curtain come down for the last time on the shortest run in which he had ever been in the West End.

III

It was a failure which he could well afford to forget. Not only was he now firmly established as an actor, but he had become that less easily defined thing, a personality in the world of the London theatre. He was on more than nodding terms with the famous. Cochran invited him to lunch to meet James Barrie; he was a welcome guest in Cannon Place, Hampstead, for drinks with Sir Gerald du Maurier; at the Central School he was so much the honoured old-boy that Elsie Fogerty invited him to judge the passing-out exams.

In the spring of the Jubilee year of 1935 his prospects seemed limitless. Alexander Korda, a fabulous Hungarian who was spending a fortune in building great studios on the new by-pass near Denham village, offered him a film contract which he decided to accept as the work would not encroach too seriously on his acting in the theatre. But apart from films the question was, what next? What new fields were there for him to conquer?

A telephone call from Maurice Browne supplied the answer. Browne, who had made a fortune out of *Journey's End*, had just bought a comedy which he thought would give Olivier a good part and also, if he cared, the chance to produce. *Golden Arrow* had been written by the novelist, Sylvia Thompson, in collaboration with Victor Cunard. It was moderately "daring" in the circumscribed West End sense that it showed a man living with a girl who was not his wife; it was sprinkled with a certain amount of wit; and it was probably the only play ever written with a scene set in the Ladies Gallery of the House of Commons. The play's shortcoming, which was soon to be clear to Olivier, was slowness in the development of the plot, and lack of action. But he was prepared to ignore this in his enthusiasm for his new job.

He and Maurice Browne started casting and, when they could not get Carol Goodner for the part of the American girl who embarrasses a foreign secretary when she arrives at an international conference, Olivier decided to take a chance on an auburn-haired Irish girl who had been engaged as an understudy. Her name was Greer Garson, she had had a good grounding in Birmingham, and, rather surprisingly for an actress, she also held an honours degree from London University.

For a long time Olivier had been developing a theory for production which he was anxious to try in practice. It was a theory born largely from a dissatisfaction he had often felt as an actor. He considered that during early rehearsals many producers tended to devote too much time to getting inflexions exactly right, and trying out different moves experimentally. As an actor, groping with a part in its early stages, he had always found such hold-ups and indecision infuriating. So, with Helen Haye, Cecil Parker, Denys Blakelock and the rest of his cast, he began rehearsals at the Whitehall by "setting" the moves for each act, right or wrong, and sticking to them. On the first day there was a reading. On each of the next three days they went right through one act. On the fifth day they ran through the whole play. By this method he gave his actors a more or less rigid pattern to follow as well as giving himself a chance to see the play as a whole. Much of this pattern was clumsy and obviously wrong, but he didn't worry about that. Having got the play set, and given the actors an opportunity to "find" their characters (unworried by interjections and changes on his part), he then had something to change *from* or to build upon, when, at later rehearsals, he came to overhaul moves, business, and the reading of the lines.

It seemed to him a sensible approach (and as a producer he has, in fact, never departed from this method since), but Maurice Browne, who came to the fifth rehearsal, appeared to him unreasonably critical. Olivier particularly resented this for he was sure no play had ever been in better shape at so early a rehearsal. As it seemed impossible to reach a happy compromise, he decided that not only would he play in *Golden Arrow* and produce it; if he could, he would present it as well. He approached the backers, and they agreed to let him take over from Browne and assume responsibility. For the first time in his life he was in management.

Perhaps Maurice Browne had seen more shortcomings in *Golden Arrow* than he had disclosed. Perhaps, as so often happens in the theatre, the man nearest a play was least able to see its faults, and Olivier, caught up in all the enthusiasm of producing, had allowed his judgment to be swayed. The play lasted only a fortnight. Some critics found it very amusing; there was a certain scandal value because Olivier, moustached and in a black homburg, looked very like Anthony Eden; and Greer Garson, her hair in a short bob and her accent so good that people took bets as to whether she were really

American, was away to a flying start to her career. For the first time, and certainly not the last time in management, Olivier had his fingers badly burned. It was a relief, financially, to know that he had signed a contract with Korda a month before, and to hear that Korda wanted him to start work almost immediately in a film called *Moscow Nights*. Exactly eleven days after *Golden Arrow* closed, he was at Wharton Hall working under Anthony Asquith. Here was a pattern of fairground economics which was to become familiar. What he lost on the stage he made up in the film studios.

IV

In the autumn of 1935 no theatrical announcement caused more speculation than the news that John Gielgud was proposing to produce *Romeo and Juliet* at the New Theatre, and, as an experiment, was to alternate the parts of Romeo and Mercutio with Laurence Olivier. It was one of those bold, fortuitous ideas which quite suddenly cease to be a matter of interesting casting, and enter into the realms of inspired showmanship. Gielgud, the most popular actor in London and regarded by many as one of the greatest Shakespearean actors of all time, was at a particular point in his career when he knew that this would be the last time he could play Romeo. He had taken the part twice before and loved the play, but after thirty he would probably have passed the point of no return. To play both Romeo and Mercutio in his own production would be fascinating, the perfect way to say farewell to the poem of his own and Shakespeare's youth.

The public, violently partisan, were determined to see the production as an attempt by Olivier to challenge Gielgud's supremacy in the London theatre. If, in a sense, rivalry and comparison were inevitable, that was hardly Olivier's doing, since he was invited by Gielgud to play the parts; Gielgud had certainly envisaged no such battle, and when he had first considered the idea he hadn't even thought of Olivier. He had started by asking Robert Donat—only to hear that he was also planning a production of *Romeo and Juliet*. Donat had said he would shelve his own production, but had turned down the offer of appearing in Gielgud's. Olivier, who had been his second choice, had surprised Gielgud by saying that he, too, had a production of the play in mind.

Gielgud's offer was enough to make him shelve his own theoretical production, but he was not prepared to change his own very definite ideas about the way to play Romeo. There were only three weeks for rehearsal, and from the start Gielgud was worried about Olivier's interpretation, because in a determination to be realistic he seemed to be sacrificing the poetry. As a romantic actor, brought up in a more traditional school than Olivier, Gielgud regarded the play first and foremost as a poem, something which must retain great beauty for the ear. Olivier was not as concerned with the poetry as with the characterization. He saw Romeo as a boy of sixteen, an adolescent Italian, dashing and good-looking. He refused to make him a pale and pining lover out of some romantic book of medieval chivalry. "I think of him as a boy practically with conkers in his pocket," was how he would try to explain his ideas to Gielgud, who was very critical at rehearsals about his delivery of the verse.

Olivier hated what he called the sing-song school of Shakespearean acting in which the balcony scene became a sort of operatic duet. He was determined to make his Romeo *real*. Gielgud admitted that he was rather frightened of realism. He knew that Olivier's virtues as an actor were largely the result of a down-to-earth, factual approach, but with his far greater experience of Shakespeare he felt he had more justification for his convictions. He was firmly of the opinion that to impose an interpretation, however brilliant and original, at the expense of the poetry, would be disastrous.

It was probably a good thing that rehearsals only lasted three weeks. In that time the conflict between producer and actor, and the complete disparity of their ideas, had no time to develop into anything more ominous than arguments. As soon as he saw that Olivier would not compromise in the way he played Romeo, Gielgud tried not to over-burden him too much with his own very different ideas. As the producer he considered it his duty to tell him what, from experience, he was convinced the part required, but if his advice was ignored there was nothing he could do about it. At only one point did he become seriously annoyed with Olivier's performance—the love scene, which Olivier played with abandoned ardour. Gielgud felt bound to ask him to tone this down, despite Olivier's protest that it was a passionate love story and should be acted that way. Otherwise he largely gave Olivier his head. The tousled wig; the make-up calculated to give the impression of an olive-skinned youth from the Lombardy plains; the way poetry was dashed to smithereens to create the idea of a tongue-tied boy fumbling for words; the substitution of clumsy impetuosity for grace—all these things he feared in Olivier's conception. They were interesting, but, he was sure, fatal.

The reception was exactly what Gielgud had expected. Most of the critics and a large number of the public were bewildered by this unconventional Romeo, and disliked the interpretation. Strung together, the adverse opinions of the first-night critics formed a damning halter. Temperamentally ill-at-ease . . . a ranting, roaring Romeo . . . his blank verse is the blankest I have ever heard . . . efficient rather than inspiring . . . matter-of-fact in his methods . . . one misses the height of rapture and distress . . . approaches the mighty lines gingerly . . . one wanted over and over again to stop the performance and tell the actor he couldn't, just couldn't rush this or that passage . . . lacks poetry and more important, authority . . . instead of being romantic he was prosaic . . . plays Romeo as though he were riding a motor-bike . . .

These were some of the criticisms to which Olivier awoke on the morning after his first major Shakespearean performance. In despair he went to see Byam Shaw at his home in Putney, and together they walked across the heath, the sombre autumn tints of the dripping trees matching his melancholy. On such an occasion there is little even a friend can say by way of comfort beyond the obvious and rather futile admonition "not to worry." They damned the critics to blackest hell, and Byam Shaw, who was playing Benvolio, was genuinely sympathetic because he had liked his friend's Romeo. It was inescapable, however, that as a performance it had not quite come off, and when Olivier saw Bronson Albery at the theatre that night he offered to give up the part. But Albery told him not to worry, and as the weeks went by Olivier's confidence was restored by the opinions of people whose judgment he respected.

The very next day a note came round from Margaret Webster: "Very dear Larry, Never mind the critics—what *do* they know about it? I found your Romeo full of passion, sincerity and beauty." Most of the appreciation he received during the six weeks he was playing Romeo was from other actors and members of the profession who forgave the shortcomings because of their admiration for the ideas behind them. Tyrone Guthrie, whom he did not then know at all well, wrote to say: "This is Fan Mail! Have been deeply thrilled and moved by R. & J. and especially with your Romeo. I believe the critics are right who fault you for not getting full value out of the verse. I didn't feel this at the theatre but thinking it over as I go to bed now I believe it's true. But it doesn't matter. Your performance had such terrific vitality—speed and intelligence and gusto and *muscularity*—and you got a lyric quality pictorially if not musically. It has been a very exciting evening." Fabia Drake, the actress, who as a young girl had taken him through his first dance steps at All Saints, persuaded St. John Ervine to go with her to the New Theatre during the early days of the run, and for the second time in his career Olivier had reason to be grateful to this particular writer. He was not *The Observer's* dramatic critic but he wrote a weekly article called "At the Play" about general theatre matters, and he devoted two columns to praising the performance. Praise, however, was not exclusively from theatre people, and Olivier particularly treasured a letter written by an ordinary member of the audience whom he had never met and who was quite unknown to him.

"When the interval came I was almost in tears and could not control my voice to answer anything more than a monosyllable when my companion spoke to me," he wrote. "I do not think I ever wish to see this play again lest my memory of Olivier be dimmed. Here was the true youth untouched by love with all the shy hesitancies of inexperience when he first set eyes on Juliet at the feast. He flowered into such beauty of feeling and movement that my heart ached for him knowing what was to follow."

v

Perplexed by the reception of his Romeo, Olivier faced the prospect of Mercutio with misgivings, and during rehearsals his thoughts often turned to Ralph Richardson, who at that moment also happened to be playing Mercutio. A month before Olivier had opened at the New Theatre Richardson had left for America and, from Philadelphia on tour with Katharine Cornell and Maurice Evans, he had written a letter in which he mentioned that he was working "little jokes" into the part. Very interested and curious, Olivier wrote to ask what these were, and how his friend was moulding the character. He would be grateful, he said, for any suggestions. Richardson's reply was written in Boston:

My dear boy,

I can't tell you how to play Mercutio; you should be much better than me—don't forget you could colour Bothwell which drove me right out of the stage door. But as you ask me I will tell you my experience of it. Be careful not to hurry the "Mab" speech, as I did at first from over-anxiety to be bright. It is a speech that depends on detail and if taken slowly and all the points made will seem enormously brilliant, but if slightly rushed is just dull.

The second scene plays itself. I play it with a lazy sort of humour and come on yawning and blowing pip-squeaks after the party—but don't forget the sudden delicacy of "if love be blind, love cannot hit the mark." The next scene you should do extremely well—here I am as rapid as I can be—the real "Mercutio" tremendously smart and as full of full-up light and life as I can make him.

You should try to produce a different key every time you come on—and wear your clothes in a different way. I have a tremendous circular scarlet cloak of fine red flannelette; this I can do a great many things with.

I hope that you are not very bored with all this my dear boy—but one thing more—the *greatest* difficulty is to keep sober enough in the one hour twenty-five minutes wait you have before the end to take your call without falling into the orchestra-pit. This takes years of skill and cannot be overestimated, as much of the effect of the poetic "Mab" speech may be lost by such an incident.

I am writing this in my wait in a dressing room in a hot—you know how hot—theatre with no window or ventilation whatever.

Good-night, my dear fellow,

RALPH

The idea of the squeaker especially appealed to Olivier and he keyed his performance to that note of carnival gaiety. He got a great deal of fun from taunting Juliet's nurse, and on the line, "A sail, a sail . . !" he scandalized her by lifting her billowing skirts on the point of his sword. He made his Mercutio all dash and swagger, a Mercutio well pleased with himself, a Mercutio who had perhaps walked too much in the heat of the sun and was a little mad.

Once again Gielgud watched his development of character with some concern, fearful that he might be exaggerating, and dubious about such touches as the squeaker. At the dress-rehearsal those fears were further increased. Because they were changing parts in the middle of the week without a break, the dress-rehearsal took place on the morning and afternoon before the first night, and Gielgud was obviously upset when at last the break came for lunch at 6 P.M. Over food at the Ivy he confided to Glen Byam Shaw that he had serious premonitions. Was there going to be a repetition of Olivier's reception as Romeo? And if there was, how would Larry stand up to more hard knocks from the press?

He need not have worried. There was expectancy in the air at the theatre that night, and it was fulfilled. From his first entrance Olivier took the house. It seemed to one member of the cast that the audience was, unpredictably, *for* him—just as six weeks before it had been antagonistic. The audience loved his pantomime and applauded his business with Edith Evans, as the nurse. He could do no wrong.

"A good music hall performance" was the way Olivier was to look back on his Mercutio later, and while Gielgud was dissatisfied with himself as Romeo, the change was much to the public taste. Peggy Ashcroft continued to be the most enchanting Juliet, and the production settled down to complete a triumphant run and a short tour. It played at the New for 186 performances, twenty-five more than Irving's previous record at the Lyceum in 1882, and the longest since the play was first produced in 1597.

While he was still playing Mercutio, Olivier agreed to appear as Orlando in the film of *As You Like It* which was to star Elizabeth Bergner and to be produced and directed by her husband, Paul Czinner. In theory, as he had somewhat pompously told Walter Wanger two years earlier, he disapproved of Shakespeare on the screen; but he succumbed to what Richardson called "the artistic satisfaction of £600 a week."

Based on a "treatment" by J. M. Barrie, it promised to be an interesting film, but almost as soon as shooting started he began to regret his decision. Shakespeare had never seemed more hopelessly out of his proper element, and the character would not stand up to the test of realism demanded by the films. Olivier felt extremely foolish because the stage convention which allows Orlando to mistake Rosalind for a boy became quite preposterous in front of the camera. He even made Orlando a trifle mad in the vain hope that this might lend a touch of credibility to an impossible situation. But this distortion, and the changes which the script forced on other characters, worried him, and any sense of continuity was shattered by the studio habit of shooting scenes out of order. This lack of chronology reached what seemed to him the height of absurdity on one day when he arrived at the studio soon after dawn to hear that Bergner was not due to appear until three o'clock in the afternoon. Czinner, old in the ways of the cinema, was not in the least worried. "We will film all the close-ups of your reaction to what she is saying," he told Olivier. "And I think you had better look from side to side because Miss Bergner will probably be walking all round you as she speaks."

After a day of this sort of thing it was a relief to come back in the evening to the sanity of Shakespeare on the stage. But he soon discovered that filming by day and acting in the theatre at night was a serious strain. He often arrived back in London so late that for Mercutio he had to keep on the same boots, the same make-up, and the same padding for his calves * that he had worn during the day for Orlando. At the theatre his venture into films was treated with ribald disrespect by such friends as Byam Shaw and George Devine. They would gather in his dressing-room to hear his latest anecdotes about Bergner and the strange half-world of the film studios; and one evening he had an especially interesting story to tell them, which made them smile sceptically.

It had been a fairly slack day at the studio, Olivier said, and he had gone to see Henry Ainley, who was playing the exiled Duke in the film, and who was always good for stories of theatrical personalities of the past. That day he had told Olivier of some fine performances he recalled, and especially of one by Forbes-Robertson. It was in a play where Forbes-Robertson appeared as a general who stepped on to a balcony during the march past of his troops and exclaimed: "My men, my men! My wonderful men!"

"Well," Olivier told his listeners, "you know what a magnificent voice old Ainley has. When he came to show me how Forbes-Robertson had delivered that line, he made all the make-up jars on his dressing-table *vibrate!*"

* For the first twenty years of his professional career Olivier always had to pad his legs in costume parts because of their thinness. All that time he worked hard with exercises to develop them, but not until the production of *Œdipus* (1945) did he have the courage to show his own legs on the stage for the first time.

Olivier swore that he had seen it with his own eyes, and, when he persisted, Byam Shaw and Devine goaded him into proving it. They lined up some jars on his dressing table and challenged him to demonstrate. Olivier, looking defiantly at the jars, shouted at the top of his voice: "My men, my men! My wonderful men!" The jars remained unmoved.

"Come on, we'll give you a hand," said Byam Shaw, and moved them to the very edge of the table to help him. All three then addressed themselves to the jars; all took deep breaths and held the last word until the veins stood out on their foreheads. The room rang with their combined efforts, but the jars were still unimpressed. Further attempts were interrupted by a knock at the door and the entrance of John Gielgud's dresser.

"Mr. Gielgud wants to know what all the noise is about," he told them. "He says he can hardly hear himself speak on the stage."

VI

One January afternoon in 1936, between the matinée and evening performance of *Romeo and Juliet*, John Gielgud and Glen Byam Shaw stayed in the theatre to give an audition. They were preparing a joint production of *Richard II* which they had agreed to put on at Oxford for the Oxford University Dramatic Society. All the men's parts were being played by undergraduates, but, following tradition, professional actresses were to go to Oxford for the principal women's rôles.

Gielgud had persuaded Florence Kahn, Max Beerbohm's wife, to play the old Duchess of Gloster, and now he and Byam Shaw had only to cast the part of the Queen. That afternoon they had invited along an actress of twenty-two who had had hardly any experience but had made a big personal success in her first West End play during the previous year.

"Perhaps you'd be so good as to take your speech at the beginning of Act V?" one of them said to her.

So, unknown to Olivier, who was in his dressing-room, the audition began. At that time he only just knew the young actress and was unaware how soon their paths were to cross, and with what consequences to themselves and the theatre.

Vivien Leigh started to read.

"This is the way the king will come . . ."

BOOK TWO

Vivien Leigh

CHAPTER 1

Indian Childhood
1913-1932

I

I N THE YEARS when the Union Jack spread across the world and the British flourished in India, Alipore, the residential suburb of Calcutta, became a place of the dead at the beginning of the third week in April. Only native servants were left behind to guard the white, shuttered houses as the hot season settled over the dusty and scorching city. Their sahibs had escaped to the cool of the mountains.

Like most Europeans, Ernest Hartley, a young exchange broker, and his wife regularly made the winding train journey north to one of the hill stations which served the city as holiday resorts in the lower ranges of the Himalayas. In 1913 they spent the pleasant months in Darjeeling, and had a special reason for renting a house rather than staying in a hotel. After two years of marriage, Mrs. Hartley was expecting a child in November, and they decided she should remain there, even when the cool monsoon rains made the Bengal plain once again endurable and Mr. Hartley had returned to his desk in Calcutta. The two-storied house with the wide sloping roof, which stood in its own wooded grounds on the side of a hill overlooking the town, was a quiet and perfect place in which to prepare for the child's arrival.

With all the good wishes of the employees of Piggott Chapman

and Company, of which he was a junior partner, and the cheerful
banter of his friends at the Turf Club, Mr. Hartley went back to
join his wife in Darjeeling in time for the baby's birth. From the
veranda of the house the view seemed especially beautiful on the
evening of November 5th. Far away to the north towered the great
snow-capped peaks of Everest and Kanchenjunga; and not long after
the sun had disappeared, leaving the town a spangle of twinkling
lights in the sudden darkness, the doctor came downstairs with the
news that it was a girl. It was against this properly dramatic back-
cloth that Vivian Mary Hartley was born.

The Hartleys would probably have sent their daughter back to
England had the war not intervened when she was just nine months
old. This meant that she was to spend the first six years of her life
in India, and during four of them her father was to be a dimly-
remembered figure in the khaki and shining top boots of an officer
in the Indian Cavalry. Unlike most children at that time she was
not separated for long periods from her father. Ernest Hartley,
whose main peacetime hobby had been the breeding of race-horses,
spent most of his war in the United Provinces in the unromantic but
essential job of training remounts for Mesopotamia. Mrs. Hartley
and Vivian were able to live at Mussoorie, a hill town for Meerut
where he was stationed, and when he was moved down to the military station at Bangalore early in 1917 they followed to Ootecamund.

It was at Ootecamund that little Vivian Hartley, aged three and
a half, made her first stage appearance during a children's concert
before an audience that could broadly be divided into two sections—
adoring parents and their long-suffering friends. Among the latter
was Lady Willingdon, whose husband was then Governor of
Madras. Mrs. Hartley had taught Vivian to sing "Little Bo-Peep"
and had tricked her out very prettily as a Dresden shepherdess. On
the stage, grasping a crook in a chubby hand, Miss Hartley immediately demonstrated the most appalling contempt for her audience by
announcing to them and to her accompanist: "I won't sing. I'll recite." Afterwards Mrs. Hartley sighed that she was afraid Vivian
had been very naughty. This met with reassuring noises from other
mothers, who knew their lines and expected reciprocation in the
form of praise for their own infants. But they agreed that obviously
Vivian was a child who knew her own mind.

It was also about this time that Vivian made it painfully clear that she knew how to get under the skin of a part. Her mother, who believed in bringing home the full impact of the Bible message by acting little scenes, had cast Vivian as the lion in the story of Daniel. This allowed plenty of scope for roaring and crawling about on all fours on the bed which was the lion's den, and also for what Mrs. Hartley (Daniel) found a very free interpretation of the story. The lion sank a row of small but incisive teeth into her leg.

Although there was no professional theatrical tradition in either Mr. Hartley's family or that of his wife, Mr. Hartley was an outstanding amateur actor. Almost as soon as he had arrived in India in 1905 as a boy in his late teens, he had been swept into the Calcutta dramatic society, whose reputation was high and whose traditions stretched back over a hundred years. His initiation had principally been the result of the enthusiasm of a slightly older man in the firm of Piggott Chapman who was a keen actor and producer. Arthur George MacPherson impressed on young Ernest Hartley that, as visiting companies were rare, Calcutta had to provide most of its own entertainment, and the standard must be good. The two or three plays produced each year at the little Theatre Royal, or at the big modern theatre which was built later, called for more than the casual approach suggested by the damning phrase "amateur theatricals."

It is not easy to assess the quality of the performances in those faroff productions, and Mr. Hartley covered his tracks by deliberately destroying all his press cuttings soon after Vivien Leigh became famous. But there are still many people, who, recalling the Calcutta of those days, remember his acting very well indeed, and have no doubts at all from where his daughter got her talent. They talk especially of a character performance as the foreman of the jury in *The Speckled Band* spoken in faultless Devon dialect, and of a satirical pantomime in which he played the Bad Wolf. He also appeared as Warren Hastings in the production with which the dramatic society greeted the peace of 1918, and only gave up acting when the general enthusiasm waned after 1919 and he, personally, had to face the responsibility of his last five years in India as a senior partner of his firm.

His daughter, however, had little chance of following his example for some while, and Vivian's mother took care to avoid any confirmation of her early talent in dramatic biblical reconstruction. In the large house in Alipore, she was brought up by an English nurse and governess until she left India at six years old. If she showed any special interest beyond her pony and the dolls of which she had an enormous collection, it was in books. She loved being read to, and her mother saw to it that there were no lapses in taste. When Vivian grew out of Hans Andersen and Charles Kingsley they were replaced by Greek mythology and Kipling. The *Just So Stories* seemed to have a special fascination, and Mrs. Hartley, sitting by her bedside, had to read them night after night despite the suspicion (which was quickly confirmed if she dared to skip) that Vivian knew them by heart.

In 1920 the Hartleys had their first chance since the war of going back to England, and Vivian went with them. It had been decided that the time had now come to find an English boarding school for her, and friends had given them excellent reports of the Convent of the Sacred Heart at Roehampton a few miles from London. The idea of sending her there particularly appealed to Mrs. Hartley, who was Irish by birth and a Roman Catholic and had, herself, been brought up in a convent. They reached England in March and took Vivian to see the school which, they decided, was ideal. It was arranged that she should start in the autumn term; and there, behind the high walls of the convent in Roehampton Lane, she was left, very unhappy and tearful, in the charge of the Reverend Mother in the following September.

The first few days were bound to be miserable. Never before had Vivian been separated from her mother and father and so completely without friends. In the strange new world of the convent she was surrounded by the unfamiliar faces of girls all of whom were older than herself. As her parents lived abroad she had been allowed to enter the school at an earlier age than any of the other children. To be the youngest of the very young is usually a disadvantage; but Vivian was to find that it had compensations. The lonely and unhappy little girl with dark curly hair and large blue-green eyes was soon made a fuss of by the nuns, and because she seemed so young to be away from her home and family, they allowed her certain privileges. One of these, a matter of some envy among the older girls in her dormitory, was permission to take a kitten to bed with her at night.

Pretty though she was, the sisters found as the terms went by that Vivian's behaviour did not entirely match her angelic appearance. To one of them she was, in the time-honoured phrase of nursemaids, "a real pickle," and her teachers had a certain amount of trouble in keeping her mind on her work. Her reports that went out to Calcutta told Mr. and Mrs. Hartley that she was only good at the more frivolous subjects such as drawing and dancing. Both these accomplishments were scrupulously ladylike, but her chief shortcoming was not. In one of those secretly-kept journals beloved by schoolgirls, a friend noted that her greatest fault was a quick temper which "might be misunderstood."

It was not long before an interest in acting showed itself. In the gymnasium at Roehampton plays were performed each term, and in these Vivian Hartley took a number of parts. Starting, as little girls should, with Fairy Mustardseed, she graduated to Miranda (delivering the "O I have suffered with those I saw suffer!" speech uncomfortably perched on a hassock), and so, when a little older and in the Senior School, to the Golfing Girl in a play called *Ask Beccles*, which sounds extraordinarily racy for a convent.

At the time of the *Midsummer Night's Dream* production she entered into an earnest discussion of the future with a little girl two years older than herself who had been so bad that she had been dropped from the cast.

"When I leave school I want to fly," said the other girl defensively. "I should like to be a pilot."

But Vivian Hartley said she was quite sure she wanted to be an actress. As it turned out both were to become actresses, for the other girl, all freckles and with a trace of an Irish accent, was Maureen O'Sullivan, and they were to recall the conversation fourteen years later when they both appeared in *A Yank at Oxford*.

Besides acting, Vivian was also keen on music and dancing, and because Mrs. Hartley was musical she was only too pleased to grant any request that her daughter made for extra lessons. Although she never learnt either of them very thoroughly, Vivian could play the piano and the violin, and as a 'cellist even had a place in the school orchestra. A letter was also sent out to India with a plea for ballet lessons, an interest prompted by visits to *Where the Rainbow Ends* and pantomimes during the Christmas holidays.

By the time Mrs. Hartley came back from India in March, 1922 on her first trip home since Vivian had been sent to Roehampton, she found her daughter a keen theatregoer, if somewhat restricted in her taste. Every friend and relative, and now Mrs. Hartley herself, had been wheedled and coaxed until they agreed to take her to the London Hippodrome to see *Round in Fifty*. Before the end of the run, which lasted over a year, Vivian had established what was surely a schoolgirl's record by seeing it sixteen times. As with the *Just So Stories*, familiarity only increased her enjoyment, and her mother, sitting next to her, would marvel at the laughter—seemingly spontaneous each time—with which she greeted her hero, George Robey, as he entered from the wings carrying a pair of elephant tusks and observed: "I'll teach elephants to argue!"

The following summer the Hartleys visited the Lake District, and one morning at a hotel in Keswick the little girl of ten saw her hero sitting in the dining-room. There he was, George Robey, actually eating an egg and drinking coffee like any other human being. Robey's wife, conscious of the fixed, incredulous stare of the child at the next table, nudged him, and Robey turned and gave her a broad smile. Even better, on his way out of the dining-room he stopped to speak to her, and, in response to a strangled gasp of adoration, he promptly took ten different photographs of himself out of his pocket and gave them to her. Next term at the convent the Reverend Mother once again had to exercise special leniency, this time over a girl who secretly treasured in her locker not one, but several, photographs of a red-nosed comedian whose jokes, it was whispered, were not exactly "suitable."

Mrs. Hartley, who managed to come home every year, did not permit her daughter's taste in the theatre to remain exclusively frivolous. During Vivian's early days she had made a stand against what she termed "rubbish" in her reading, and she had no intention of letting musical comedy be the limit of dramatic education. One summer there was a visit to Stratford-on-Avon and seats were booked for *Hamlet*. This, her first straight play, might have been expected to be rather heavy going for so young a girl, but Vivian was enthralled and talked for years afterwards about the ghost who materialized under a green spotlight.

Even with annual visits from her mother and seeing her father every two years, Vivian was glad when she heard that her father was retiring and her parents were leaving India for good. She was then thirteen, and it meant she would be with them both every holiday. It was to mean a good deal more than this, for after years abroad the Hartleys had no inclination to settle down in the Anglo-Indian twilight of Torquay or Cheltenham to lament the lack of native servants and the price of a pink gin. Mr. Hartley had made a good deal of money during the five years he had been senior partner of his firm in Calcutta; now still a young man, he had every intention of giving himself and his family a very good time. This was largely to be spent on the continent, with periodic visits to Connemara for skirmishes with trout that would give him battle in the swift-flowing rivers of Western Ireland. And what, he demanded, was the use of having a pretty daughter if she were going to grow up behind the walls of an English convent? Vivian must come with them.

Mrs. Hartley mildly pointed out that education even for a girl did not end at thirteen, and schools would have to be found as they travelled. But she was pleased that Vivian was to go with them all over Europe; it would give her a chance to learn languages, which she considered a very necessary accomplishment. So Vivian began the liberal education of which any girl might dream, and which, even if she were never to acquire "roots" or have a settled home life, provided her with an invaluable background for an actress.

II

Dinard, Biarritz, Paris, Cannes, San Remo, the Bavarian Alps, Salzburg, Zurich and Kitzbühel . . . it was a feminine Grand Tour lasting three years, during which, lest the pace for a girl in her teens should be too giddy, Vivian's parents arranged for steadying interludes at schools and convents.

Her French accent improved at a school in Dinard, she was moved to a convent—another belonging to the Order of the Sacred Heart—at San Remo, where she perfected her French and learnt a little Italian.

This was the bitter-sweet period of early adolescence, a time of deep religious fervour and a time which, if recalled to-day, is somehow associated, in the tangled web of her memory, with the smell of peonies. Those were the flowers which Vivian and the other girls collected in baskets on the hillside above the town and scattered beneath the feet of robed priests as they walked in solemn procession at the Feast of Corpus Christi. The overpowering scent of the crushed petals has not faded with the years.

There was severity and some prudery at the convent. In file the girls walked down to an isolated part of the beach where the sun and the ever-blue sea called out for gaiety. There they would put on bathing costumes which were taking no risks in the violation of modesty. The basic black costumes familiar to most children of the period, with high neckline and buttons at the shoulder, had special embellishments. Long sleeves and skirts made out of calico were tacked on to them. And in this unwieldy apparel the young ladies from the convent would dash into the water and promptly sink.

On at least one occasion the unruly spirit which had been noted at Roehampton was also the subject of disapproval at San Remo. Vivian's conflict with authority betrayed itself in a letter which she wrote home and which, unfortunately, was intercepted. Opened by one of the nuns, it revealed a postscript in which she told her parents: "The Reverend Mother is a . . ." and here followed not a word but a thumb-nail sketch of a cat. Providentially the Hartleys had intended to take Vivian away at the end of the year; clearly she had outgrown the slightly oppressive discipline of convent life and calico bathing suits. During the holidays they told her that she was going to a small private school in Paris.

To be sixteen and in Paris was bliss. Vivian found that the fashionable school in the residential district of Auteuil observed none of the restrictions of the convent. Here Racine was substituted for Corneille and the world of the Parisian theatre arrived in the form of an actress from the Comédie Française, who visited the school to teach Vivian and one or two others speech training and deportment. They were even encouraged to savour the delights of the theatre for themselves. It had been decided that she should specialize in what was broadly called "drama," and this was sufficient excuse to visit the boulevard theatres to see such outspoken plays as *Marius* and to revel for the first time in the performance of the light comedy actress, Gaby Morlay. There were only about twenty girls at the school and the headmistress had no Anglo-Saxon prejudices about hard pillows, strict rules and early hours being good for the formation of character. Vivian's letters to her parents became a little too ecstatic about vague parties which went on after midnight. It was really all quite innocent, but in the middle of the term Mrs.

Hartley decided to make a visit of investigation. With the excuse that it was Vivian's birthday she arrived suddenly in Paris. She was greeted by her daughter who was wearing a hat which owed nothing to Daniel Neal and everything to the Galeries Lafayette, a complexion which had more than a hint of make-up, and a most alarmingly sophisticated manner. Before the end of the term Vivian learned that, once again, fresh plans had been made for her, and that the following term she was to be sent to a finishing school to learn German.

After Christmas in Biarritz the Hartleys drove her across France through Carcassonne to Lugano, from there to Zurich, and finally to a school in the Bavarian Alps. It had been planned for her to stay near Bad Reichenhall, on the Austrian frontier, only six months, but, with visits to the music festival at Salzburg, only an hour away, and to Vienna for the opera, Vivian enjoyed it so much that she begged to be allowed to stay on. At Kitzbühel during the following Christmas holidays she also developed an enthusiasm for skiing, and the Hartleys were happy to let the six months extend to a year.

When her mother came to collect her during the Easter of 1931 Vivian was eighteen and her schooling finished. Mrs. Hartley was well pleased to find her taste for music and the theatre even more developed. In Munich, where they spent ten days sight-seeing, they visited the opera nearly every night. Vivian loved the opera, and her mother was sharply reproved when, after nearly eight storm-wrecked Wagnerian hours, she ventured a little flippancy at the expense of the soul-searching arias of Amfortas at the end of *Parsifal*. Vivian, who throughout the performances had been leaning forward in the box, her eyes fixed on the stage, turned round quickly. "*Please*, mother!" she said severely.

III

It all happened very suddenly. To the Hartleys it seemed quite unbelievable. Only a year before Vivian had been a thin, rather pale schoolgirl of seventeen in the transition stage between Angela Brazil and Warwick Deeping. And then one day in the July of 1932 she had burst into the flat in Cornwall Gardens, waving a diamond ring for their astonished inspection, and told them she was going to be married. They had known, of course, that she had grown into a very beautiful girl, and in the few months since leaving school had not lacked for young men to take her out; yet, with the reluctance of all parents to face the inevitable, they had assumed there was nothing serious in the attentions paid by the young barrister they had met down in Devonshire.

For Vivian the year between leaving school and the announcement of her engagement had been full of excitement, even if she had not been given a formal "coming out." As her parents had never really established a London home there had been no question of a "season," and she was more than content to travel with her father and mother who were always moving from one pleasant place to another. As soon as the Munich holiday had finished Ireland had been their temporary home, and they had spent a happy summer at Aasleagh, on the border of County Mayo and Connemara. Here Vivian had seen the heather turn purple and watched her father fish for hours on end before they had tramped back together through the autumn dusk to the lodge where they were staying. By the last day of October they were back in England; but the chill damp of a London winter held no appeal for the Hartleys. In search of an Indian summer, and with the restlessness of people who have always travelled, they took a house in the West Country for the winter.

For Vivian this was splendid, as her friend Hilary, the daughter of her father's former business partner, Geoffrey Martin, lived only a few miles away at Teignmouth. They spent a great deal of time together, and one day, as they stood in the little village of Holcombe, shivering in the snow to watch the Dartmoor Draghounds come in, Hilary had pointed out a friend, a young man with wavy fair hair and a ready smile on a rather large mouth. A few days later she had been formally introduced to Leigh Holman at the South Devon Hunt Ball which was held on Torquay Pier. He had danced an old-fashioned waltz with her, and before the end of the evening he had told her that he had chambers in the Middle Temple, and had asked if he might call on her when they were both back in London. He supposed she was in the telephone book? Vivian had said yes, he could, and yes, she was.

There had been talk in the New Year of 1932 of Vivian going to spend a year in India. Many of Mr. and Mrs. Hartley's friends out there had said they would be pleased to have her to stay. But this idea was discarded for something far more important. It was decided that if she wanted to be an actress the time had come for her to study acting. Neither her parents nor her friends regarded it as a foregone conclusion even then that she would make the stage her career, but Vivian herself was quite sure about it. She saw her training as a logical development of the interest she had maintained in the theatre since her earliest schooldays and a continuation of the study she had started two years before in Paris. When her father agreed to enrol her at the Royal Academy of Dramatic Art it did not come as a sudden or unexpected surprise; it was simply a matter of course.

In May she went to the new premises of the Academy which had been opened in Gower Street only the year before, and for a few weeks the shy young barrister was forgotten in the excitement. Vivian had made an immediate impression on Sir Kenneth Barnes who heard her entrance audition, and Ethel Carrington, who took her in her first Shakespearean class, noted an assurance which was distinctive, and which established her position among such contemporaries as Dorothy Hyson, Rachel Kempson and Leueen MacGrath.

Her speaking voice was not strong and was rather high-pitched, but she had a natural stage sense and instinctive technique and grace of movement which enabled her, even in her first term, to overcome the intricacies of a stage breakfast in *Isobel, Edward and Ann*, and to make a fair showing as Rosalind in a scene from *As You Like It*. Unexpected casting of the sort peculiar to dramatic schools required her on one occasion to play Starveling, the tailor (and much-ridiculed Moonshine), in the play-scene from *A Midsummer Night's Dream*. This she did with relish, covered in a great deal of crêpe hair and with a number of her front teeth blacked out to ensure the full comic effect. So many schools and so much travel might have made her blasé, but Miss Carrington, wise in the ways of young actresses who from the start consider themselves as leading ladies, found her unspoilt and not in the least affected.

Leigh Holman, who had started to take her out as soon as she had come up to London, had been delighted when the plans for India had been discarded. As a barrister of only a few years' standing, he rarely found that the number of briefs marked for him in his chambers prevented him from reaching Gower Street at the end of Vivian's last class for the day. It was also possible for him to offer to drive her down to Henley for the Regatta. Holman, who had rowed in the Jesus College boat during his time at Cambridge, longed to show off Vivian to his friends on the lawns of Leander. In a large-brimmed hat shading her face from the July sun, she was exactly the success he had expected, and spurred by the enthusiasm, and a slight suggestion of rivalry, on the part of a Cambridge friend named Hamish Hamilton, he decided to propose to her a few days later. The final stages in the courtship were conducted with the full ceremony of flowers from Solomon's and a ring with a large diamond in it; and the conclusion was just as he had hoped.

CHAPTER 2

Birth of a Name
1932-1935

I

FIVE DAYS BEFORE Christmas of 1932 and a year almost to the day after she had met the young barrister at the Devon Hunt Ball, Vivian Hartley became Mrs. Leigh Holman. She looked pale and serene and very lovely as she walked down the aisle of St. James's, Spanish Place, on the arm of her father, and there was a rustle of interest and more than the usual amount of discreet head-turning by the bridegroom's friends and those members of his family who had not seen her before. It had been rumoured that the quiet and diffident Leigh had brought an unexpectedly beautiful fiancée to the Holmans' house on Holcombe Down. It was now obvious that rumour had not lied.

The honeymoon was spent in Kitzbühel, and during the three weeks away it was pleasant to take Leigh to Munich, Leipzig and Dresden, and to share with him all the pleasures of the places she had last visited as a schoolgirl such a little time before. Everything was the same, and yet, as she confided to her diary, having Leigh with her made all the difference. They returned to London, to a round of weekend invitations from friends and a small, easily-run flat in Eyre Court in St. John's Wood. Almost at once she saw that, with an excellent maid, she was going to have a great deal of time on her hands. The unsettling years of travel had not prepared her for idleness; equally, they had not instilled any deep affection for a purely domestic life, and her thoughts returned to the Royal Academy of Dramatic Art which she had left so reluctantly when she married. Her teachers had seen her first term's promise increase during her second, and had been impressed by her performance as Lydia in the love scene from *The Rivals*. Sir Kenneth Barnes had noted that she was working hard and, unlike some of the students, was obviously serious. He had been particularly sorry when she had come to tell him she was leaving.

"Well," he had said, "I usually congratulate people who are going to be married, but I feel you could have done very well as an actress." Her Shakespeare teacher, Miss Carrington, whom she had asked to her wedding, had been even more disappointed. "What a loss!" she had exclaimed, and had marked a tiny star against her name in the book she kept for the names of her students.

Now it seemed, as she and Leigh talked it over, that there was no reason why she shouldn't go back, anyway for a part of the course—say, just for the French classes. These were taken by Madame Gachet, under whom she had studied previously and whom she had found such a good producer and coach. Exactly ten days after she returned to London from her honeymoon she went to see Sir Kenneth. He agreed to her arranging a syllabus with Madame Gachet, and for some months nothing was allowed to interfere with her weekly, and sometimes more frequent, visits to R.A.D.A. The training cured her of a number of bad stage habits and a self-consciousness that she could not throw off about her hands. They were long and unduly large, and, because she worried about them, she began to develop tricks for getting them out of sight. One of her teachers, noticing this, asked her what was the matter, and when Vivian told her, she suggested that she should read Ellen Terry's *Memoirs*. "She had the same trouble," she said. Vivian took her advice, and it was as if Ellen Terry were speaking from the pages with her voice. "I was so ashamed of my large hands during this time at the Royalty that I kept them tucked up under my arms. This subjected me to unmerciful criticism from Madame Albini at rehearsals. 'Take down your hands,' she would call out. '*Mon Dieu!* It is like an ugly young *poulet* going to roost!'" Ellen Terry wrote that she was only broken of her self-consciousness after many years by a friend who said that he supposed she had very ugly hands, because she never showed them. "That did it! Out came the hands to prove that they were not so *very* ugly, after all. Vanity often succeeds where remonstrance fails." Vivian found it reassuring to know that someone like Ellen Terry had faced the same problem in her early days, and she decided to pretend that her hands were the smallest and whitest in the world. Perhaps autosuggestion would help her overcome self-consciousness.

After she had been back at R.A.D.A. only a few months, Vivian was once again forced to tell the principal that she was afraid she would not be able to continue her training. And this time it looked as though her leave-taking might be for good as she was going to have a baby. She did not think her husband would want her to return after the baby was born, and anyway she would probably be too preoccupied. As the child was not due until the autumn she was not prevented from finishing the term, and in the end-of-term plays she was delighted to be given one of her favourite scenes from Bernard Shaw's *St. Joan*. There had always seemed to her something very moving in the scene in the Cathedral at Rheims where Joan kneels praying for guidance about the future of France, and she had no premonition of how its beauty was to be spoilt in this her farewell performance at the dramatic school.

For her excerpt from Shaw Vivian found herself in chain-mail leggings and boots which were far too large, and there seemed nothing for it but to stuff the toes with tissue paper. Wearing these boots, whose shape owed so little to the feet inside them, Vivian clanked on to the stage and knelt down in the position in which Joan is discovered when the curtain rises. All seemed well; hands clasped, her pale face ethereally lit by a small spotlight, Joan listended to her "voices"; then her prayers were interrupted by Dunois who helped her to her feet. Vivian began to speak her lines, then happened to glance down. To her horror, she saw that the pointed toes of her mail boots were now sticking straight up in the air like a jester's. It was hardly surprising that for the rest of the scene her performance lacked much of the saintly and unworldly devotion it should have had.

II

With the calculated nonchalance of an actress who knows the effect of throwing away a good line, Vivian wrote in pencil in her small blue diary for October 12th, 1933, the single sentence, "Had a baby—a girl." If there was also in this a hint of the sudden and unexpected, it was justified, for her daughter, Suzanne, arrived a month before she was due. Once they had left the nursing-home and returned to Eyre Court it became clear that a flat was no longer large enough. The next few months were devoted to a concentrated search for a house, and this she and Leigh found at last in Mayfair. It was a small, narrow Queen Anne house in Little Stanhope Street, near Shepherd Market. It had everything she wanted, Vivian decided—even theatrical tradition. To her delight she had learned that it was here that Lynn Fontanne had rooms when she first acted in London.

Leigh Holman had a considerable knowledge of antiques and together they spent many weeks searching the shops for furniture and deciding on materials and colours for the various rooms. Pastel shades, especially lime green, predominated, and she saw to it that the heating limitations of the eighteenth century were compensated by a number of electric fires. But here, too, after six months, and once the novelty had passed and the household was running smoothly with the nurse and maid, Vivian again started to think seriously about her career. She could not shake off the feeling that she was far too young to be a mother, and was far too restless to devote herself simply to her child and home.

If at first Leigh Holman did not take her ambitions seriously he was soon to have reason to see that Vivian was very much in earnest. In the August of 1934 he had arranged for them to go on a yachting holiday in the Baltic, but just about the same time Vivian heard that there might be a chance of a part in a film called *Things Are Looking Up*, which Albert de Courville was directing for Gainsborough with Cicely Courtneidge as the star. It was a school story and Herbert Mason, the associate producer, was searching for actresses who looked really young to play the pupils. Vivian went to see him and although the part of the ingénue heroine had already been given to Mary Lawson, he said he was sure she would be suitable for a small rôle. Unfortunately he could give her no date for the start of shooting as there were several weeks of location work to be done at Cheshunt and Wimbledon before she would be wanted.

To Leigh Holman it came as quite a surprise that anything so vague and, to him, so unimportant could possibly threaten to upset their holiday. But Vivian insisted that here was a chance she might not easily get again, and she agreed to go away only after she had made elaborate arrangements to be notified when her part of the film was due to start.

She and Leigh went to Götheborg where they joined the yacht, sailed to Aarhus, and so west past Elsinore to Copenhagen. At Copenhagen there was a cable waiting for Vivian to say that she might be wanted on August 12th. This called for an immediate decision. If she were going to be in the film she must return to London at once; but she knew that if she left, the holiday, not yet half over, would be spoilt and Leigh rather upset. Whatever she decided to do, he said, he was not going to interrupt the cruise which he was thoroughly enjoying, and he hinted very clearly that he thought it ridiculous to go back to England on such an off-chance.

For Vivian the whole thing suddenly became much more than a personal issue over a broken holiday, or even a question of a possible chance of breaking into films. It was a matter of principle. If she were not playing at being an actress and was sincere about making the stage and screen her career there could be no alternative. After a long discussion she returned to England from Copenhagen, and left Leigh to continue the cruise until the end of the month.

When he arrived back in England he heard that bad weather and the Wimbledon scenes had put the film behind schedule and that, to while away time, Vivian was staying down in Sussex with their friend, Clare Sheridan. The suspicion that she had, perhaps, rushed home a little rashly only doubled Vivian's resolve that she must be in the film, now, whatever happened. If only as an extra, she must justify the broken holiday; and, at first, it was for no more than crowd work at a guinea a day that, to the accompaniment of groans from a sleepy Leigh, she left Little Stanhope Street early each morning to reach the studios in Lime Grove, Shepherd's Bush, by 6:30 a.m.

This was a time when, with few exceptions, British films had not graduated into world markets, and it was for a typical run-of-the-mill comedy that Vivian and a number of other girls were given white gym tunics by the costume department and told that they were playing schoolgirls. On account of her looks, however, Vivian was almost immediately picked to play one of the half-dozen principal girls in the story. This involved an action they would never have approved of at Roehampton. She had to put out her tongue at another girl in the dormitory scene. This lifted her into the 30s.-a-day class, and she was also given one line: "If you are not made headmistress, I shan't come back next term!"—which she delivered with great feeling.

It was difficult to make all this sound important to a maddeningly ironical Leigh, but Vivian herself felt that at least she had made a start. Each day she and the other girls with small parts (among whom were Judy Kelly, Gillian Maude, and Hazel Terry) were driven in a special car to Cobham in Kent where Lord Darnley's Elizabethan house, Cobham Hall, was being used for exteriors of the girls' school. One day while on location there she was a little annoyed to be faced yet again with a look of scepticism and with a question about her sincerity—this time by a gossip-writer. No one seemed able to believe that she was any different from a number of other young ladies with Mayfair addresses who were following the prevailing fashion of making money in the studios. The journalist asked her if she were filming just for the "fun" of the thing, and she answered tartly that she was not, that she was quite serious and did not in the least regard acting as a game.

During the autumn immediately after the completion of the Cicely Courtneidge film, Vivian's entire future was suddenly altered as the result of a chance meeting at a cocktail party between a friend of hers and a young theatrical agent. John Gliddon, a former actor and journalist, was new to theatrical agency but full of ideas on the subject. In that loud, slightly accentuated voice necessary to pierce the hubbub of a party, he began to unburden some of these on an actress named Beryl Samson, who was listening with only half an ear to what he had to say when one phrase caught her attention. Gliddon, bewailing the lack in England of young talent, said that he would like to do the trick that was so familiar in Hollywood. He wanted to find unknown girls who were beautiful but had little acting experience and build them up into film stars. The trouble was to find them—or to find the right combination of beauty, brains and the indefinable *star* quality.

At this point Mrs. Samson interrupted to say that she had the very person for him. Unselfishly for an actress in the highly competitive jungle, she wasn't thinking of herself, but of Vivian. "She's just out of R.A.D.A., has done one tiny part in films, and is ravishing to look at," she told Gliddon. "Let me bring her to see you."

No time was lost. The next day Vivian met Beryl Samson and was taken to Gliddon's office in Regent Street. Wearing a big cart-wheel hat and a light summer dress, she more than repeated her success at Leander; she actually impressed an agent. Mrs. Samson left them alone to talk, and not until the two women were on their way home to St. John's Wood did she hear from Vivian how she had got on. Vivian told her that Gliddon wanted her to come under his sole management for a year, and had promised that her days of crowd work were over. "There's only one thing," she said. "He doesn't like Vivian Hartley as a name for the stage."

"What does he suggest?" asked Mrs. Samson.

"He thought April Morn would be better," said Vivian. "What do you think?"

When she had recovered her breath, Mrs. Samson told her. As the bus passed Lord's Cricket Ground April Morn went into the limbo of forgotten stage names, never to raise her dewy head again. But as if the threat of her presence hovered over the bus, Beryl Samson settled down then and there to the task of evolving another name. By the time they had reached the Finchley Road and the conductor was calling out "Queen's Grove," the first half of Vivian's maiden name and the first half of her married name had been joined insolubly. Vivian Leigh had been born.

III

In the unashamed language of Shaftesbury Avenue, Gliddon began to hawk his protégée round London. The technique for exploiting someone who is unknown generally follows a pattern. The unknown actress, looking as fetching as she can, is escorted by her agent to restaurants, clubs and theatres on first nights, where she will be seen, and perhaps looked at twice, by people in the profession. If the agent happens to meet anyone he knows he introduces his protégée with carefully simulated casualness. If he doesn't, he is quite satisfied if a few heads are turned and there are a few whispered queries. With the sort of beauty possessed by Vivian Leigh, one or two lunches at the Ivy and a visit to the Stage Golfing Society dinner were quite enough to start the ball rolling. After five weeks of this rather embarrassing form of self-advertisement, she was given her first real part in a film made by British and Dominions. *The Village Squire*, in which she was the leading lady, was a "quickie" made to satisfy a quota law which then required cinemas to leaven the joys of Hollywood with a proportion of misery from Elstree. Vivian soon learnt that "quickie" was a phrase not idly used, for even as the leading lady her services (at five guineas a day) were only required for a week.

The *Village Squire* was followed a month later by an equally rapid and inelegant affair called *Gentleman's Agreement*. In it Vivian Leigh played the heroine who was a typist, and the film was one which even the trade papers were unable to recommend as suitable for any but "indulgent patrons." But while both these "quickies" were very bad, they served to show Vivian how unwise it was to turn down any opportunity, and how one job could lead to another. It just happened that a few weeks after the film was completed, David Horne, who was the leading man and had also been in *The Village Squire*, was cast for the part of an elderly husband in *The Green Sash*, a play set in fifteenth-century Florence that was to be put on at the Q Theatre. When some difficulty arose in finding an actress for the part of Giusta, his young and flirtatious wife, Horne thought of Vivian and told Leon M. Lion who was then managing the Q and Matthew Forsyth, the producer, that he knew of a girl who might be able to manage it. An urgent call brought her to Kew. It was too long a rôle to perfect in the short time available for rehearsal, and some of the big emotional scenes were outside Vivian's range, but she was sufficiently good on the first night for Charles Morgan to note in *The Times* that her acting had precision and lightness which might "serve her well when her material was of more substance."

The snowball of success had started. Hardly was the week at the little theatre near Kew Bridge finished than the casting director for Associated Talking Pictures at Ealing, where she had made a test a few weeks before, was on to her agent. He wanted her for a film which, in comparison with the quickies for British and Dominions, seemed very important. She was to be the heroine of a film starring Gracie Fields called *Look Up and Laugh* which was to be directed by Basil Dean.

Basil Dean had started production at Ealing three years before, and had plastered every blank wall in the studios and even the girder across the power house with one hugely-painted word, "Co-operation." This was the magic word which, he believed, would make Ealing the most efficient studios in England. His method with young actors, however, rather belied the warmly comforting sound of the slogan. The producer whom Olivier had found so terrifying five years before in the theatre had not left his bitter sarcasm behind when he entered the film studios. He was still a martinet, and Vivian, very inexperienced and with her first part in anything approaching an important film, was shown little mercy. Only the irrepressible cheerfulness of Gracie Fields helped her through the awful weeks at Ealing. After some petrifying scene in front of the cameras when Dean had pulled Vivian to pieces, Gracie would come and reassure her. "Don't worry, love," she would say, "you've *got* something!"

When the film came to be shown it was found that she had been very badly photographed. It had been the constant complaint of the lighting cameramen during the shooting that her neck was too long; and one particular technician clung to this belief for years afterwards. When she was back at the same studios as a star, he was reminded about his comment on her neck. "Well," he said lamely, "she must have done something about it."

But it was not only her neck that was at fault. Basil Dean could not decide if she was sufficiently good for the studio to retain her for another picture. Aubrey Blackburn, the studio manager and casting director, was all for keeping her, but Dean decided against it. As it turned out, it was providential that Ealing did not take up the option on her contract. Had she been forced to continue making comedies at Ealing it might have interfered with her great chance on the stage and prevented the dramatic change in her film fortunes, both of which took place within two months. Before she had time to pick up the threads of her domestic life in Little Stanhope Street, Gliddon, her agent, was on the phone with news of something which, he said, was very important. Tactfully he refrained from repeating what he had been told—that a beautiful girl was needed who did not have to be a particularly brilliant actress. He simply said that Sydney Carroll was casting a new play which was going on at the Ambassadors in May and an appointment had been arranged for her the next day.

CHAPTER 3

Success Overnight
1935

I

Although she could not have imagined anything so improbable, on the April day that she and Gliddon climbed the stairs to Sydney Carroll's office in the Charing Cross Road, Vivian Leigh was the answer to a producer's prayer. Casting for a new play had reached a standstill. There were only four main characters in *The Mask of Virtue*, the comedy which Ashley Dukes had adapted from the German, and two of them had been given to Lady Tree and Jeanne de Casalis. When George Grossmith, who was to have played the Marquis, had been taken ill, this one important male part had gone to Balliol Holloway. That left only the urgent and critical problem of finding an actress suitable for the part of Henriette Duquesnoy, the street girl whom the plot required should be passed off on a midde-aged French *roué* as a lady of unblemished purity.

One by one Sydney Carroll's producer, Maxwell Wray, had gone through the possible stars. Peggy Ashcroft, Jane Baxter, Diana Churchill and Anna Neagle had all been rung up. None was available. Then Carroll had got in touch with Aubrey Blackburn at Ealing on the off-chance that he could suggest someone, and Blackburn had mentioned Vivian Leigh. So the interview was arranged that was to have so great an influence on Vivian Leigh's career. Exactly what happened that day has now become a little clouded by time, but in the memories of three of the four people who were there the main outline is quite definite.

When they reached the offices on the first floor, Gliddon left Vivian Leigh in the outer room for a few moments while he went in to Sydney Carroll's inner office. He told Carroll, and Maxwell Wray who was with him, that he was sure Vivian would fit the part. Carroll, accustomed to the enthusiasm of agents, asked for a few details of her work. Gliddon knew that it was useless to bluff and admitted that she'd done very little. "But if you say that what you want above all else is beauty, this girl's got it," he said. While they were talking Maxwell Wray slipped out of the room and Gliddon went on to tell Sydney Carroll that Vivian had done some crowd work in films and a difficult period part at the "Q" only a few weeks earlier. "Charles Morgan saw her," said Gliddon, playing his trump card. "I expect you saw his notice in *The Times*."

When Maxwell Wray came back into the room he asked Gliddon if Vivian Leigh was the girl dressed in black who was sitting at the end of the table in the outer room. Gliddon said she was. "Then as far as I'm concerned," said Wray recklessly, "the part's cast." He saw that this intrigued Carroll, who asked for Vivian to be shown in, and was instantly conquered. With extraordinarily few preliminaries, she was given a copy of the play and engaged at the salary of £10 a week, subject to a successful audition at the Ambassadors the following day.*

If Sydney Carroll was taking a long chance he was, perhaps, influenced by the knowledge that the three principals in the cast of *The Mask of Virtue* were highly experienced. He could hardly have failed to visualize the added publicity interest that is always stimulated by the "discovery" of a new actress; two years before he had succeeded in much the same way with Victoria Hopper in *Martine*.

* In fairness to Mr. Carroll, it must be said that this description does not coincide with his recollection of Miss Leigh's engagement. As Mr. Carroll now recalls, he did not see Mr. Gliddon or *The Times* notice until after he had cast her for the part, and was guided solely by his own judgment.

II

Vivian Leigh's beauty, from which few were immune and which could make even experienced theatre men take rash chances, had a quality of youth and innocence about it which was very deceptive. It deceived Sydney Carroll and Maxwell Wray to such an extent that over lunch on the afternoon before the audition they sat at a table in the Ivy discussing not whether she could play the part, but whether she understood it. Knowing nothing about her, or even how old she was, they wondered if she had fully realized that Henriette was not at all the sort of girl she appeared to be for two thirds of the play. And how, they asked, should this delicate matter be broached? Across the restaurant they saw Lilian Braithwaite, and Sydney Carroll invited her over for coffee and explained the problem. Lilian Braithwaite was delighted by their embarrassment, and offered to go back to the theatre afterwards and have a tactful word with the protégée.

Full of excitement and unaware of the anxiety she was causing, Vivian Leigh arrived for the audition. The excitement was mixed with a certain amount of natural apprehension, and this increased from the moment she stepped out of the taxi in West Street, gave her name to an uninterested stage-door keeper, and made her way down the narrow winding stairs to the stage. In the dimly-lit theatre Sydney Carroll introduced her to Lilian Braithwaite, and, to her surprise, as he and Maxwell Wray went to the back of theatre, Lilian Braithwaite followed her on to the stage and began talking to her about the part. At the back of the stalls the two men sat waiting and wondering how the introduction to the facts of life was progressing. It was not long before Lilian Braithwaite came down from the stage and joined them. "Oh, my dears, you needn't worry," she said in her thin, quavering voice. "I have had a talk to her, and she's a very nice little girl; but when I asked her if she understood the part—what sort of gel she was playing—well, Sydney, you can put you mind at rest! Miss Leigh is married and has a child."

On the stage under a single working light, Vivian started to read, and her voice seemed either too soft or else, when she tried to raise it, went into a register which she knew to be too high. When it was all over, there was a moment's silence, broken by a whispered conference. Then Sydney Carroll asked her to come down and join them. Quickly her apprehension was dispelled. He turned to her and said simply: "The first rehearsal is next Tuesday at the Phoenix."

At first the rehearsals went far from smoothly. Quite apart from her own difficulties and the shortcomings of which she was very conscious, there was a basic difference of opinion between Carroll and Wray about how the play should be produced. *The Mask of Virtue* was the result of one of Ashley Dukes' raids on the German theatre. It was his version of a play by Carl Sternheim, who had himself lifted the idea from the eighteenth-century French author, Diderot. This comedy of intrigue seemed to Maxwell Wray to call for the light, mannered treatment that had made Ashley Dukes' pre-vious play, *The Man with a Load of Mischief*, such a success. If it was played realistically and full-bloodedly he was sure it would ap-pear as just "a dirty story." Wray's position was difficult. After some years in provincial repertory he was comparatively new in the West End, and could not easily take a firm stand with Carroll. Fortunately Ashley Dukes sided with him, and so too, as far as he could gather from the flow of German, did Carl Sternheim, who, with Dukes, attended rehearsals. But this did not prevent the first rehearsal from being an uncomfortable muddle of indecision, and from this Balliol Holloway quickly decided to retire. He probably knew that he was not rightly cast as the Marquis, and he may well have been a little less confident than Sydney Carroll about the cast-ing of so very inexperienced an actress for the heroine.

When Vivian Leigh came for rehearsal on the day after Easter she found she had a new Marquis, Frank Cellier, who quickly be-came a devoted friend and helper. With his assistance, and that of Jeanne de Casalis and Lady Tree, she began to mould her part. She often felt hopelessly bad, but they were patient, and hid their fears about her performance and her voice, which, they thought, might be inaudible even in a theatre as small as the Ambassadors. At the original audition Lilian Braithwaite had warned her that she must work to improve her range, and had given her a book on breathing exercises. She had also given her a piece of advice which Vivian was ever afterwards to find valuable. It was, simply, to take three deep breaths in the wings just before going on to the stage. They would help her to relax.

Maxwell Wray, who sometimes took her through her part alone

after rehearsals, quickly saw that she had two great qualities—repose, and the ability to move and sit gracefully—and he arranged for her to be carefully lit and shown throughout the play as effectively as possible. Her inflections were occasionally wrong, but there was always intelligence and sincerity in the delivery of her lines. As the month of rehearsal came to an end, he was quite confident that she would be able to manage the part perfectly. Her only difficulty would be with the tense and important scene at the end of the third act when Henriette asks the Marquis to shoot her; and this, he considered, was a scene which would have defeated any but an actress of great experience.

As the night of Wednesday, May 15th, came nearer, preparations reached a climax. It was especially exciting to come to the theatre one morning and see her name on the bills outside for the first time. And how curiously conspicuous one slight change in the spelling looked—Vivien Leigh! After living with herself as Vivian for so long it was a shock to see the alteration which Sydney Carroll had prevailed on her to make. Vivien, he had said, was more indisputably feminine than Vivian. That now, she realized, was likely to remain her name for life; not Vivian Hartley or Vivian Holman, but Vivien Leigh.

There were two dress-rehearsals and then, almost before she knew it, it was The Night. Last-minute good wishes arrived from friends and there was a special call on the telephone from Mother and Father to wish her good luck before she left for the theatre. Leigh Holman pointed out to her that this was also his first first night— the first he had ever attended. At the theatre she found masses of flowers, and her dresser helped her to arrange two rows of telegrams all round her mirror. They were telegrams from all sorts of unexpected people, some of them half forgotten, like the hall porter who remembered her from the time when she and Leigh were at Eyre Court. Presents were exchanged among the cast and Lady Tree, who was so kind and reassuring, gave her a whole set of *The Yellow Book*. Every few moments there was a knock on the door and someone else looked in to wish her luck and give her a kiss. At the "fifteen minutes" call Maxwell Wray came in with a word or two of last-minute advice—advice to *forget* all advice and to let the performance come naturally from herself. Now she was on her own; he was going round front and wouldn't see her until after the show. There was an excellent house and he knew she was going to be terrific. For a few moments she was completely alone with her thoughts; and then, with the awful finality of a dentist's receptionist, the call-boy came to the door and said: "Miss Leigh, please!"

III

An unknown actress given a leading part in the West End is delicately poised between sympathy and prejudice. With half their minds the audience want her to succeed, and with the other half they resent the presumption. Above all else she stimulates exaggerated expectation, and this is where she must not disappoint. To be tolerably good is not enough. She must shine; and that is exactly what Vivien Leigh succeeded in doing. She made the first night of *The Mask of Virtue* an event in the theatre which no one who was there is likely to forget.

Her producers, who had astutely calculated each effect, knew that some part of her triumph was contrived, but even they were astonished. Beyond all contrivance, Vivien Leigh gave a remarkable performance which had magic in it. Her grace and loveliness possessed a radiance which shone across the footlights and blinded the audience to technical shortcomings. Her voice lacked range but it had a peculiar soft beauty; when she spoke there was little contrast in emphasis, but an even and modulated charm; if some of her movements lacked the timing and precision of an accomplished actress, this was hardly noticed because of her general grace. By the time she came to her difficult scene she had won the house, and any imperfection was lost in the blaze of glory. At the final curtain it was Vivien Leigh who made clapping rise to a crescendo and shouts of "bravo" shower from the gallery. She took no single curtain call and there were no speeches, but as the curtain went up and down on that small cast the applause was largely for her. As the audience streamed out to the Ivy opposite or to the coffee stall round the corner in Earlham Street, the name of Vivien Leigh was heard on all sides. No actress of such promise had been seen, some people said, since Meggie Albanesi in the early 'twenties.

But Vivien Leigh was not so sanguine. Praise and congratulations seeped through her dressing-room like warm honey, but she kept her head. As her husband, parents and friends whirled her away to the Savoy and on to dance at the Florida afterwards, she recalled warnings she had heard about the hysterical enthusiasm of first-night audiences. "Was I *really* all right?" she asked Mrs. Hartley in the taxi; but it was too much to hope for a true assessment in the midst of so much excitement. She knew she must wait for the verdict of the professional playgoers. Would Charles Morgan—Morgan who had been so kind at the "Q"—like her? In the theatrical phrase familiar for a whole generation, "What would Agate say on Sunday?"

There could be no thought of bed until she had seen the morning papers. As the band at the Florida packed their instruments she and Leigh Holman got into a taxi and went down to Fleet Street to buy the early editions. It was 4 a.m., and in evening dress on that chill May morning, before the dawn came up behind St. Paul's, they opened the papers. There was the answer. NEW STAR TO WIN ALL LONDON . . . YOUNG ACTRESS' TRIUMPH . . . VIVIEN LEIGH SHINES IN NEW PLAY . . . ACTRESS IS A DISCOVERY. It was almost monotonous, but what ecstatic monotony!

It seemed that she had hardly got home and to sleep before Jeanne de Casalis rang her up, the first to congratulate her. It was a gesture which Vivien thought particularly kind, for she knew that while she had been able to shine in a short, showy part, it had been Jeanne de Casalis in a long and responsible one who had carried the main burden of the play. Soon afterwards there was a knock on the front door in Stanhope Street and the maid came upstairs to say that reporters from the evening papers wanted to see her. She got up to be interviewed, and to be photographed in every sort of pose. There was Vivien Leigh curled up on the sofa. There was Vivien Leigh sitting in white shorts playing a banjo. And of course there was Vivien Leigh, the young mother, with her baby daughter. After the flashlights had gone off, the reporters went to work.

There was something very bewildering about their questions—the sudden necessity to translate into plausible assertions ideas which at the best were half-formulated. A casual question was thrown at her about whether she was thinking of putting her daughter on the stage. Suzanne was then just nineteen months old. In the papers that night she found that she had answered: "I believe that Suzanne is going to be an actress too. I hope she will go on the stage when she gets older, and I am going to see that she is taught languages."

"How did you feel last night, Miss Leigh?"

"I was petrified when I walked on the stage at the opening of the play, but in the second act I regained my confidence and the audience was very kind."

Leigh Holman bought his paper on the way home and read with several degrees of nausea: " 'My husband does not object to me being on the stage. In fact his belief in my ability has always been an inspiration . . .' "

It was all true; it had all been said. But, somehow, in black and white under headlines like ACTRESS-MOTHER'S FAME AT 19 and VIVIEN LEIGH ON "HOW I DID IT" many of the comments seemed wretchedly banal. Also there was the first temporizing with absolute truth which so mysteriously seemed to be a requirement of theatrical publicity. She was, in fact, twenty-one, but someone had decided that for the purpose of exploitation nineteen was a better age. In the general mêlée she became a Gold Medallist at R.A.D.A., her father a senior cavalry officer, and she had not simply been taught by an actress from the Comédie Française; she had actually appeared there.

The papers showed great preoccupation with what they called "combining marriage with a career." To one reporter Vivien Leigh said that she considered it was quite possible to run a home and be an actress (with a good maid, a cook, and a nurse it was, of course), and this was seized on by a leader writer who used it as a peg on which to hang some dark observations about female emancipation.

Right from the start of her stage career, Vivien Leigh found herself plunged into the all-perplexing drama of theatrical life. Hardly had the excitement reached its peak and Sydney Carroll taken columns of advertising space to trumpet the press opinions, than Jeanne de Casalis suddenly developed laryngitis. Everyone was called at short notice to the theatre, and then the producer heard to his horror that the understudy, who was supposed to have been learning her part for three weeks, didn't know a line. Maxwell Wray, who only that morning had seen long queues outside the theatre and the public almost fighting to get to the box-office, sadly said that they would have to cancel the performance. But Sydney Carroll wouldn't hear of it. "We'll ask a well-known actress to read the part," he said. "We'll get the curtain up somehow." He rang a number of actresses, and at last found one, Oriel Ross, brave enough to take on what was a terrible ordeal. At four o'clock, four and a half hours before the show, she arrived at the theatre to read and walk through the part. A copy of the play had been bound in vellum, and with this she went on for the performance. Vivien Leigh, who had relied so much on the experience and ability of Jeanne de Casalis, now found herself in the position of having to help someone else through a part.

Once the initial excitement of her success had subsided, Jeanne de Casalis had recovered, and the artificial glamour of the first night had faded a little, Vivien Leigh, starting her first press-cutting book, had time to reconsider all that had been written about her. She had never been deceived by the highly-coloured flattery into thinking that she had not a great deal to learn, and in the careful verdicts of the serious critics she found her fears confirmed. None of them denied that she had given an extremely effective performance and that she had great beauty. To one critic it seemed that "her grace was like a magic cloak, and her whole performance so took the senses and lit up the stage as to make criticism unchivalrous." But this chivalry was not unanimous, and the cautious word "promise" was widely used. At least two spoke of her "limited range," while one said outright that it would be necessary to see her in several parts before estimating the extent of her talent. All her charm, intelligence and assurance had not blinded the majority to one great shortcoming—her voice. They said she must learn to speak more distinctly, get rid of a trick of dropping into inaudibility, and acquire a "stronger voice so that her intonation may express every phase of her feeling." "Miss Leigh has incisiveness, *retenue*, and obvious intelligence," wrote Agate. "She gives to this part all that it asks except in the matter of speech. If this young lady wants to become an actress, as distinct from a film star, she should at once seek means to improve her overtone, displeasing to the fastidious ear." This advice from one accounted a shrewd judge of acting was promptly taken. If it was to be some years before the fastidious ear was completely pleased, this was not from want of hard work. She immediately went to a singing teacher for voice production and in the years to follow was to study under Elsie Fogerty.

Only the rashest critics were prepared to rush into print and hail Vivien Leigh as a great actress on the strength of her one perform- ance, but Sydney Carroll, who combined the rôle of theatrical man-

Laurence Olivier's father and mother at Tower House, Dorking, 1904

Laurence
aged
two-and-a-half

Laurence in fancy dress
aged eleven

Laurence aged fourteen
as Katharina in "The
Taming of the Shrew"

At the Birmingham "Rep"
Laurence Olivier, aged nineteen, and, *below*, in the roles of the
Hon. Guy Sydney and Harold

In "Beau Geste"
at His Majesty's

In "Private Lives" with Adrianne Allen, Noël Coward and Gertrude Lawrence

Jill Esmond, Douglas Fairbanks, Jr., Joan Crawford and Laurence Olivier—a Hollywood photograph in 1932

As Tony Cavendish in "Theatre Royal"

"Romeo and Juliet"—the New Theatre production in 1935

Vivian, aged two, with her mother

On Bangalore racecourse, about 1918

Vivien Leigh
now appearing in
"THE MASK OF VIRTUE"
THE "FAME IN A NIGHT GIRL"

Vivien Leigh in "The Mask of Virtue." *Left:* One of the publicity postcards distributed all over London. *Below:* In a scene from the play with Frank Cellier at the Ambassadors Theatre

With Suzanne outside the Holmans' house in Little Stanhope Street

A rehearsal of "The Happy Hypocrite." *L. to r.:* Richard Addinsell, composer; Clemence Dane, adapter; Maurice Colbourne, producer; Ivor Novello, Vivien Leigh and Max Beerbohm

"Fire over England"—a scene with Flora Robson as Queen Elizabeth

p: "Hamlet" at the Old Vic. Francis
Sullivan as Claudius, Michael Red-
ve as Laertes, Laurence Olivier as
mlet and Robert Newton as Horatio

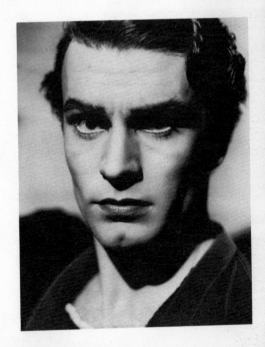

Hamlet. Old Vic—1937

Vivien Leigh joined the Old Vic Company at Elsinore to play Ophelia

Signing her contract for "Gone With the Wind," Vivien Leigh with David O. Selznick, Olivia de Havilland and Leslie Howard

Shooting a scene from the motion picture in which the population of Atlanta flees the city before the arrival of Sherman's army

Lieut. Olivier, R.N.V.R.,
training Air Scouts, 1942

Laurence Olivier on the set
of "Pride and Prejudice" plans
his production of "Romeo and
Juliet"

ager with that of journalist, was so enthusiastic that he wrote an article in which he suggested that she was an example of the material from which he hoped would emerge the Bernhardts and Duses of the future. In his Thursday article in *The Daily Telegraph* he enumerated the qualities for an "ambitious beginner," clearly hinting that these were just what he had found in Vivien Leigh. She must have, he wrote, "plenty of nerve, power of attack, power of retention, control of body and mind, imagination, sensibility, judgment, clear diction, a sense of timing, a regard for variety and a love of repose. Throw in as well beauty of figure and face, glory of voice, breadth of movement and subtlety of brain and what critic can withstand the appeal? Only the jaundiced or the would-be poseur."

It was not difficult to read into this a reply to the cautious refusal of James Agate to accept Vivien Leigh immediately as an outstanding actress. By dragging in Bernhardt he neatly baited the trap. Agate (who wrote under the pseudonym of Richard Prentis in *John O' London's Weekly*) then suggested that "greatness" was a term that needed testing and that at the age of forty, or after ten years' apprenticeship, that quality might be easier to detect. This sort of controversy gave Sydney Carroll just the chance he wanted; it not only filled his column, but focussed interest on the box-office of his theatre; he could bask in the reflected glory of the girl whom he had discovered. He came back with the argument that Mrs. Siddons had been hailed as "great" when she played Portia at seventeen; Mrs. Kendall had been sixteen at the time of her triumph as Ophelia; and Ellen Terry had made a success as Prince Arthur in *King John* when she was only eleven.

But whatever their varied opinions, one aspect of Vivien Leigh's future was emphasized by nearly every journalist. Knowing that she had come from the film studios, they clearly indicated that the unspeakable fate of becoming a film star was almost certain to overtake her. When, three days after the first night of *The Mask of Virtue*, the papers burst out with fresh headlines, their suspicions seemed justified. £50,000 FILM CONTRACT FOR LAST WEEK'S UNKNOWN ACTRESS did not, however, tell the whole story.

CHAPTER 4

Korda Shapes the Future
1935-1936

I

AMONG THOSE who had been at the first night of *The Mask of Virtue* was Alexander Korda. He had been rung up by Sydney Carroll, who had told him that he had discovered an exquisitely beautiful young actress whom he would do well to watch for the films. Carroll had said he had reason to think she was going to make a big personal success and would be snapped up by Hollywood or some British producer. Korda, whose company, London Films, was rapidly developing into one of the major film producing companies in the country, was interested. By the end of the play he was more than interested, and wasted no time in hurrying out of the theatre and round to the stage door.

Outside Vivien Leigh's dressing room door John Gliddon, weeding the influential from the merely enthusiastic, noted his arrival with especial satisfaction. It was particularly pleasant to have Korda coming to see Vivien Leigh; Gliddon still had recollections of how a few months before, when she was quite unknown, she had been in the position of having to go to him. At Korda's office in Mayfair she and Gliddon, who had arranged the interview, had been kept waiting for an hour and a half. Then, when she was on the point of going, a secretary had said that Mr. Korda would see them now. It had been a short, unsatisfactory interview, ending with a rather

vague promise of a test "sometime." Now Korda was impressed and
did not beat about the bush. When he came out of the dressing-
room he said briefly to Gliddon: "Come and see me to-morrow."

The next day, after he had helped fight back the press in Stanhope
Street, Gliddon had arrived at his office to find a number of cables
and telegrams on his desk and to be told by his secretary that the
telephone had been ringing almost continuously. Not only English
studios, but Hollywood producers too, were interested in Vivien
Leigh. With this very comforting news he went down to Isleworth
to keep his appointment with Korda. This time there were no waits
in outer offices, and Korda came quickly to the point.

"I'll take this girl under contract," he said with the certainty of a
man who had the whole matter settled.

Gliddon said he was sure Vivien Leigh would be very pleased to
hear it, but what terms had he in mind? Korda named £750 as a
first year's salary, and when he saw Gliddon about to protest he cut
him short. "I don't bargain," he said.

But for once an agent had the comfortable knowledge that he
need be neither overawed nor stampeded. He knew that at least
three American studios were prepared to make offers, and an
M.G.M. executive had been hot on Korda's heels back-stage the previous night. From Paris a Hollywood talent scout had said he would
fly to London immediately Gliddon gave the word. Gliddon sat
back easily in Korda's office knowing that he was in a position to
bargain. He said that Vivien Leigh was very anxious to continue
with stage work and had insisted that any film work must leave her
six months each year free for the theatre. Korda said that this would
suit him admirably; then the question of salary was raised again and
Korda was forced to bargain. When Gliddon could get to a phone
and ring Vivien Leigh, he was able to tell her that London Films
were prepared to give her a five-year contract, starting at £1,300
for the first year and rising, with the usual options, to £18,000 in
the fifth year. She would be expected to make only two films a year
and would have the time for the stage on which she insisted.

To Leigh Holman, bringing a professional eye to the clauses of
the contract his wife was being asked to sign, the whole business
seemed mad and quite incredible. Secretly, he had never expected
her career, or indeed her interest in acting, to reach the point where
it threatened to dominate their lives. He could find no legal faults

with the contract, but he may well have wondered what effect it would have on their ultimate personal happiness. Vivien, however, had no such misgivings. She was thrilled by the contract, and by the thought that she would be sacrificing only half the year to films; for the other six months she could concentrate on improving her acting in the theatre.

II

The Mask of Virtue was not the success that might have been expected after so much first-night enthusiasm. Although Sydney Carroll maintained a large publicity campaign, and scattered thousands of picture postcards all over London of his "Fame in a Night Girl," the play wilted after being transplanted within a fortnight of the opening. It went to the St. James's, a theatre twice the size of the Ambassadors, but the hope of correspondingly larger audiences proved over-optimistic. Altogether it survived only twelve weeks in London before going out on a short tour round the suburbs, and by the end of September Vivien Leigh was out of work and looking confidently in the direction of the film studios. She hoped that she would now be given the starring part which her contract with Korda had led her to expect.

She was very soon to be disillusioned. Korda, struggling with all the complexities of launching a major company, building a studio, raising money in the City, and dealing with a number of highly-paid and temperamental artists, had his hands full. At last, however, she was told she was to play Roxanne with Charles Laughton in *Cyrano de Bergerac*. It was exciting news, for Laughton, newly back from Hollywood and his success in *Mutiny on the Bounty*, was Korda's greatest hope and a star of international fame. But *Cyrano* was an idea which never came to anything, despite months of preparation, planning and rehearsals. Everything from the script to the false noses which, tried on and discarded, littered Laughton's flat, failed to satisfy him; and Vivien Leigh also came in for his disapproval. As Korda was against Laughton's ambitious plan to make the film simultaneously in French and English, he was not sorry when the film was shelved, but the decision left Vivien Leigh wondering if any other part was to be found for her. In December, after several months of silence from the studio, which was causing her some concern, Ivor Novello offered her the part of Jenny Mere in a produc-

tion of *The Happy Hypocrite* which Clemence Dane had adapted
for the stage from Max Beerbohm's story.

She told Novello that she would love to play the part, but that it
was difficult for her to accept because the production of the play
would come inside the six months which, under her contract, she
was supposed to reserve for films. Her agent warned her that film
companies were jealous masters, and even if Korda were keeping
her idle it would be unwise to accept the play without his permission. If she did not want to forfeit the salary due to her for a film
she hadn't made she must be very careful not to break the terms of
her contract. He also reminded her that even if Korda gave permission, she had signed a stage contract with Sydney Carroll which
gave him an option on her for her next play. It seemed ludicrous
and infuriating that she might have to remain idle when there was
a chance of a stage part she really wanted, but she was learning that
the internal politics of being a star were far more complicated than
ever appears to the public.

Gliddon advised her to be patient and to make no move that could
compromise her financial position with Korda; but on New Year's
Day she made it her first resolution for 1936 that she must play
Jenny, and she wrote to her agent from the Lygon Arms where she
was staying in Broadway in the Cotswolds: "I can't help feeling that
this play is of tremendous importance, firstly because it's essential
that I should *work* again and quickly, and that it will be a wonderful experience which is just what I want."

The possibility of filming by day and acting in the theatre by
night had been considered, but, thinking it would be too much of
a strain, she and Leigh had discarded the idea. Now, however, if
necessary she was prepared to attempt both. "After all, most people
seem to do the two now," she said in her letter to Gliddon, "and
working with Ivor can't fail to be a *big* and very good thing. Do,
do try and arrange this. If you'd read *The Happy Hypocrite* you'd
understand more how anxious I am to do it."

Her enthusiasm could not be suppressed. It meant buying Sydney
Carroll's option and a very cautious approach to London Films about
her salary, but eventually it was arranged. As there were still two
months before rehearsals began for *The Happy Hypocrite* she was
able to accept another, pleasant offer to act with the Oxford University Dramatic Society.

After the successful audition which took place at the New Theatre, during the *Romeo and Juliet* season, John Gielgud had invited
her to go up to Oxford to play in *Richard II.* Vivien Leigh soon
found Oxford very much to her liking. During the weeks of rehearsal she assumed something of the position of one of her favourite
characters in fiction, Zuleika Dobson, and short of mass suicide in
the Isis, Oxford responded by treating her much as if she were Max
Beerbohm's heroine. Undergraduates in the last drizzling weeks of
the Lent term were only too delighted to forsake their books and
lectures to see that she had a good time. There were endless parties
in her honour, and if February was too miserable for punting on
the Cherwell, there was no lack of invitations to take her riding out
Headington way.

The more serious responsibilities of the week did not prove too
exacting or strenuous. In the production of *Richard II*, Vivien Leigh
had not disgraced the professional theatre in her small part of the
Queen. She and Florence Kahn, who was Max Beerbohm's wife,
were the only professionals in what was otherwise an undergraduate
production,* and the casting of Max's wife for the old Duchess of
Gloster had been skillfully arranged by John Gielgud, part producer
with Byam Shaw, for a double reason. He had thought it would
be pleasant to attract Max to Oxford, and that the perfect climax to
the week would be achieved if he could be prevailed upon to make
a speech at the O.U.D.S. supper.

The supper was held after the final performance on the Saturday
night, and, as had been hoped, Max spoke. His speech in response
to the toast of "The Guests" was informal and characteristically witty
—"as refreshing," someone remarked afterwards, "as a bucket of
water after a surfeit of champagne." It was 3 a.m. before the party
broke up and the majority, with Vivien Leigh among them, went
back to the Randolph. John Gielgud and Byam Shaw left for bed,
but there were fourteen of the company determined to forswear
sleep, and as dawn was breaking they piled into cars and headed for
Burford and the Cotswolds for breakfast.

Vivien Leigh had her little two-seater outside, and Val Gielgud,
John's brother, and two others found a seat in front with her, while

---

* At this period women's parts in O.U.D.S. productions were invariably
played by professional actresses. Since the war it has been more usual to cast,
when possible, from women undergraduates.

Felix Felton, dressed, like everyone else, in full evening dress, climbed into the rumble seat. As it was pouring with rain the top was closed down over him. Not until she started to drive did Vivien realize how tired she was. A week of performances and late nights suddenly began to show their effect, and despite a heroic recitation by Gielgud of "The Lays of Ancient Rome," before she could stop herself she dozed over the wheel. They were doing forty m.p.h. along the Burford Road at the time. The car hit the grass verge and began to climb a bank, Gielgud leaned over and, seizing the wheel, just saved the car from turning over. Very shaken, they all got out to calm their nerves and suddenly remembered the wretched Felton in the back. The drama of the situation seemed, however, a little lost on him, for when they opened the rumble seat to tell him what had happened he emerged rather like the dormouse in *Alice in Wonderland*, murmured sleepily: "What a to-do!" and then disappeared again.

To Vivien Leigh it had come as a happy coincidence that, just when she was being treated like Zuleika and learning the part of Jenny, she should have the chance of meeting the creator of both these heroines. In London, during the long and often difficult rehearsals of *The Happy Hypocrite* at His Majesty's, she would see the slight, dapper figure in the stalls of the theatre which his brother, Beerbohm Tree, had made famous. Quietly, affably, and quite unperturbed by the flurry that eddied round him, he sat and watched the transformation of the story he had written forty years before. His own opinion of the result remained a secret, but some of his admirers thought that his fantasy of the Regency rake, Lord George Hell (who was so depraved that he "boasted he had not seen a buttercup for twenty years"), had lost a little of its light adjectival charm. It was, perhaps, too slight to be given more importance than the one-act play into which Max himself had adapted it in 1900. If Max thought this he has never said so. But across the years and from his villa in Rapallo he has recalled one thing which is of importance here. "Miss Vivien Leigh's performance," he has written, "was of exquisite sensibility—a foreshadowing of how much to come in later years!"

The Happy Hypocrite opened just before Easter and was a *succès d'estime*, but the public supported it for only a few weeks. Much to Vivien Leigh's sorrow it came off very quickly, and she exchanged the wide-eyed innocence of Jenny Mere and the eighteenth-century costume which she loved for the Tudor lawn sleeves and harder charms of Anne Boleyn. She had been asked by Sydney Carroll to appear in *Henry VIII*, one of the Shakespearean productions he was putting on that summer in Regent's Park. After a stiff financial battle, in which he had raised £3,000 by public subscription, he was continuing a theatrical venture for which he had a particular affection and which he had started three years before.

On a fine summer's night just as the sun was setting and the lights came on in the trees that formed a natural background to the stage, the Open Air Theatre possessed a magic for which audiences seemed willing to forgive many limitations. The *idea* of Shakespeare in the open air was delightful, and before she started rehearsals Vivien Leigh could hardly know that the most experienced actor was lost on that wide yawning stage; that the finest voice had to be amplified by hidden microphones; and that the most commanding presence was dwarfed by the large auditorium. She brought charm and intelligence to a stage referred to on the programme as the greensward, but her study of Anne Boleyn was said to lack "that inner hardness which might bring a cardinal down." A criticism that she was "on the slight side for park acting" also suggested that she had some difficulty in projecting herself over what, in the same idiom, would presumably be called the foot-shrubs.

The memories she carried away from this alfresco interlude were of frequent escapes from the malignant June weather, and of the heavy square-toed squelch of Lyn Harding's shoes when, as Henry VIII, he beat a retreat through the muddy undergrowth to dressing-room or emergency marquee. When the weather was fine she enjoyed acting in the Park, but even if Sydney Carroll had other parts to offer her, further devotion to damp pageantry was impossible. More than a year after she had signed her famous contract, Korda was at last ready for her at the studios.

III

As the months had slipped by and there had been no call from London Films Vivien Leigh had been seriously worried that the hopes which she had pinned on her contract with Korda were going to come to nothing. It seemed impossible that after keeping her idle for a year—idleness which had cost the studio over £1,000—Korda would take up the option and renew the contract for a second year. But at that time she did not know the strange ways of film-makers, or the lavish, slightly improvident methods by which Alexander Korda was building himself up into the most important figure in the British film industry. The Hungarian from Hollywood, whose success with *The Private Life of Henry VIII* three years before had been a turning point in British films and had helped him obtain financial backing in the City, had been engaging far more stars, writers, directors and technicians than he could use immediately. Vivien Leigh was only one of a number of unknown actresses whom he had on his books. Merle Oberon, Wendy Barrie, Diana Napier, Binnie Barnes and Penelope Dudley Ward had all been signed up in much the same way, and each had been forced to wait her chance.

With the opening of his own big studios at Denham Korda was ready to start production on a far larger scale. Historical private lives seemed to have a particular appeal for him, and Catharine the Great (Bergner), Don Juan (Fairbanks) and Rembrandt (Laughton) were among his first film subjects; then, in the August of 1936 he decided that a story about Queen Elizabeth would make a fitting successor to Henry VIII's. For this he took as his basis A. E. W. Mason's novel, *Fire Over England*, and cast Flora Robson for the Queen. He chose Vivien Leigh for the part of Cynthia, the Queen's lady-in-waiting, and for the hero, a fictitious character called Michael Ingoldsby, who falls in love with her, he cast Laurence Olivier.

By this time Vivien Leigh and Olivier had been friendly in a casual way for rather over a year. The informal masonry of the theatre makes it difficult for any well-known personalities not to be acquainted, and they had met within a few months of her sudden success. Before this, of course, they had both seen each other act. Vivien Leigh had first admired Olivier as the dashing Tony Cavendish in *Theatre Royal*, and he had come under her spell at the St. James's in *The Mask of Virtue*. It was during the run of her play that, on a date which they have both completely forgotten, they first met one night after supper at the Savoy.

Olivier was with his wife at a near-by table when Vivien, who was with John Buckmaster, Gladys Cooper's son, suddenly noticed him. While her first reaction fell far short of the romantic palpitations of a Ouida heroine, she found herself unaccountably annoyed and rising to his defence at her companion's next remark. Following the line of her gaze John Buckmaster commented casually: "What an odd little thing Larry looks without his moustache!" She replied shortly that she didn't think he looked at all odd, and there the matter might have rested had not all four of them met for a few moments in the lobby of the Grill Room. While taxis were called they were introduced. It was a casual, informal, and not particularly romantic meeting, and one which only in the months to come was to assume a special importance.

As vague as the date of that brief meeting has become the memory of their feelings at the time, but it is perhaps an indication of more than usual interest on Olivier's part that within a few weeks Vivien and her husband were invited down to the Dower House, which he and Jill Esmond had leased at Burchett's Green, near Maidenhead. If work and circumstances prevented them quickly becoming very friendly, they had at least been able to meet for luncheon on one occasion subsequently, and after the short run of *The Happy Hypocrite* Vivien had attended a matinée of an almost equally short run of *Bees on the Boatdeck* in which Olivier appeared.

Bees on the Boatdeck was a play by J. B. Priestley which he, Olivier and Ralph Richardson put on in joint management in the May of 1936. On the afternoon when Vivien Leigh, who came with Ivor Novello, sat watching the play from a box, the brilliant weather was emptying the theatres and the Lyric in particular. It was a deserted matinée, and Olivier had to hiss: "Stop groaning, Ralph!" as they struggled through the first act; and Richardson, perhaps sensing that there was someone in front whom his friend wished to impress, had only waited for the first interval to raise a bored and infuriating eyebrow and ask: "Shall we stop now?"

With the filming of *Fire Over England* both Olivier and Vivien Leigh knew that they would be thrown into daily encounter with each other, and they met for the first time down at Denham in the corridor outside the self-help restaurant where they had been lunching. Vivien Leigh said politely how nice it was that they were acting together.

"We shall probably end up by fighting," Olivier told her. "People always get sick of each other when making a film."

IV

Olivier found it less easy than Vivien Leigh to be enthusiastic about the film. While she did not consider the decorative part of the Queen's lady-in-waiting any great achievement, she was pleased to find that she had not been entirely lost in the general colour and spectacle. She had been able to instil Cynthia with a sense of humour, and had not left her just a prettily-dressed cardboard heroine. Most important of all, she had broken the spell of a year's inactivity. To Olivier it was, perhaps, a little more worth while than most of the films in which he had appeared before, but not much. Korda's practice of employing brilliant men and then not interfering with their ideas had not entirely worked out. His theory that a peculiarly "national" subject was best seen through the eyes of an alien artist had also led to an uneasy blend of cosmopolitan talent. Erich Pommer, one of the great figures of the German cinema, was in charge of production; William K. Howard, an American, directed; the art director was French, the costume designer Swiss, and the cameraman Chinese. As if all this were not sufficiently confusing, the job of transforming A. E. W. Mason's novel into screen form was partly entrusted to a Russian. Whether Sergei Nolbandov or Clemence Dane or the multiplicity of foreign fingers were to blame it is difficult to assess, but Olivier disliked the way the exciting original story had been mutilated—a sentiment fully shared by the author. A. E. W. Mason was so disappointed that he stipulated to Korda that if another film was ever made from one of his stories he must have a considerable say in the treatment.

The prophecy about fighting had not been fulfilled. Film acting consumes an unconscionable amount of an actor's time, and in the long waits and delays between shots Olivier found himself making his way more and more often to Vivien Leigh's dressing-room to joke and laugh and talk exaggerated nonsense. As time went by they both discovered that a day when the other was not "on call" and so not at the studio was curiously dull and empty. Friends like Leslie Banks, watching them act together or seeing them walking in the grounds of the studio during a lunch break, noted after a while an indefinable sympathy for which there was only one interpretation. It was a film which took a long time to shoot, and at the end of fourteen weeks when Olivier's last scene was finished and he was free to leave the studio for a holiday, Vivien Leigh was very much in his thoughts, and he had become the centre of her universe.

BOOK THREE

The Partnership Begins

CHAPTER 1

A Freudian Hamlet
1936-1937

I

ONE WEEKEND in August when *Fire Over England* had been about three weeks on the floor at Denham, Olivier was jerked out of the apathy which always overcame him when filming by some discussions he had with Tyrone Guthrie. As they sat on the lawn of Eva Moore's house at Hurley the talk turned to the coming season at the Old Vic. Guthrie, who had been producer there during the famous Laughton season of 1933 and 1934, had been invited to go back in the coming autumn. Now he was starting to make plans, and, while both he and Lilian Baylis liked to think of the Vic as a theatre without stars, he knew that it was important to have a big central personality. Olivier, whom he had admired in *Romeo and Juliet*, seemed to him the ideal choice, and he was anxious that weekend to interest him so much in his plans that Olivier would not be able to resist the offer.

He said that he was proposing to tackle *Hamlet* along unconventional lines, and, if possible, in a full-length version. For a few minutes their talk eddied round this idea. Was it not revolting, Guthrie demanded, that the convention of two and a half hours' entertainment should persist in the theatre, that the audience should pay for so much *time* in their seats as if they were in a taxi? A cut *Hamlet* was, anyway, not to be contemplated. "It leaves the skeleton without the enrichment, and above all," he exclaimed, "it is not as Shakespeare wrote it!" The thought of this awful sacrilege produced a brooding silence, and at the end of it Guthrie asked casually whether Olivier would care to consider a full-length *Hamlet*. It was an exciting but alarming thought. For a moment Olivier allowed his personal memories of Barrymore, Russell Thorndike and Gielgud to blend into a picture of himself as young Hamlet. But it was a picture that was quickly obscured by private doubts. Was he ready for Hamlet? Was he yet a big enough star or an actor of enough weight to carry the responsibility of a season at the Old Vic? These were problems, he told Guthrie, which he must think about, but before the weekend was over he had agreed to allow him to discuss the possibility—in the vaguest way, of course—with Lilian Baylis. Guthrie returned to London and the Waterloo Road confident that he had found his central personality.

For Olivier there followed a period of real worry. He was faced with a challenge. At twenty-nine he was at a point in his career when he could be a leading man in the West End, a film star, or a theatrical manager. Quite possibly he could even combine all three. But Shakespeare—Shakespeare was a different matter. Suppose his Hamlet crashed in the same way as his Romeo . . . the Old Vic was no longer a hole-in-the-corner theatre where such a failure would escape notice. It would be a catastrophe. On the other hand, what were the alternatives? Fooling about in films which he disliked, or playing some comedy in the West End. If he *was* to have a stab at Shakespeare, now was the time—now, before easy commercial success made him soft and unambitious. Yet, almost for the first time in his career as an actor, he had to admit that he was a little afraid.

Jill, who at that time was much preoccupied with their newly-born son, Tarquin, and all his closest friends were canvassed for their opinions. He went to see Harcourt Williams who had produced and acted at the Vic for so many years, and Williams, like most of the people he asked, advised him to accept. After a few weeks his mind was almost made up, but there was still one person in whom he wanted to confide, and he was in New York. He put a call through to him, and Ralph Richardson's answer to his query was the one he had expected. "I think it's a very good idea, dear boy," came Richardson's reply across the Atlantic. That was all that was needed to tip the scales. Lilian Baylis and Guthrie were informed, and the decision was made to start immediately after Christmas with *Hamlet* in its entirety. The word "star" was never heard at the Old Vic, but that was what the invitation implied. After *Hamlet* he would have, in consultation with Guthrie, virtually the choice of plays. His salary would not be large—about £20 a week. After £500 a week for films this drop was a luxury which he could easily afford.

It was not until he had been rehearsing at the Vic for four weeks that he actually met Lilian Baylis for the first time. He was invited to call on her in her office at the back of the theatre, and he went with a sense of expectancy and considerable curiosity. Like everyone else in the theatre world, Olivier had heard many tales of the homely, God-fearing Miss Baylis, who with her enthusiasm, integrity and passionate love of the theatre had done so much for the stage. He had always been deeply interested in the story of how she had carried on the work of her aunt, Emma Cons, in turning a former gin palace and the home of rowdy melodrama into an institution sanctified by the name of The Royal Victoria Coffee House and Musical Hall Foundation, and thence into a theatre of national significance.

From the time she had joined her aunt, Emma Cons, during the 'nineties in the then unthinkable venture of making the theatre available to poorer people she had stuck steadily to her resolve. She was not interested in a theatre which was just an excuse for either gowns and jewels or long hair and sandals. She was determined that it should answer what she once described as "a crying need of working men and women who want to see beyond the four walls of their offices, workshops and homes into a world of awe and wonder." Fantastic difficulties had been overcome, the books somehow made to balance, and, most important of all, Shakespeare had been made acceptable to the people living in the sprawling, overcrowded district south of the river. They had been lifted, in the words of one of Shaw's characters, "aht of the sawdid reeyellities of the Worterloo Rowd."

As he went to Lilian Baylis' office on that winter's day in 1936, Olivier knew that he was following in famous footsteps. This way had passed Ernest Milton, John Gielgud, Charles Laughton, Athene Seyler, Edith Evans and others too numerous to recall. Was he, he wondered as he walked down the long passage, regarded as the

answer to a prayer which Lilian Baylis often made—sincerely and on
her knees—"O God, send me a good actor—and cheap!" He must
prepare himself lest she ask him, as she had another actor: "Are you
pure, dear boy? Mind you, I am not narrow-minded, but I won't
have anything going on in the wings."

It was a meeting he was never to forget. He entered a room
where faded photographs, silk programmes and illuminated addresses
stared from the walls. On the desk was a tangled mess of archaic
telephones. A little dog, baring a mass of white teeth, snarled at his
ankles. Lilian Baylis, a grey-haired woman of over sixty, with pince-
nez on her rather prominent nose, met him with a volley of words
which seemed to indicate he was welcome. Exactly what was said
he was never quite sure, but their talk ended with an abrupt dismissal
which sounded to him like: "Of-course-you-really-oughtn't-to-
come-here-at-all-when-you-can-get-so-much-money-elsewhere-but-
still-it's-your-business-good-bye." From that moment he adored
her.

II

Both Olivier and Guthrie had made an intensive study of *Hamlet*
in the months before rehearsals started. When Olivier went for a
three weeks' holiday in Capri during October he carried with him
a suitcase full of books of criticism and commentaries. Every line
was mulled over, every subtlety considered. Olivier had not reached
the stage when he could agree with Cedric Hardwicke, who had
said he considered that theories were only the backwash of success;
and he had not sufficient faith in his voice to adopt Henry Ainley's
attitude—Ainley who cared less for the meaning than for the sound
of the words.

Guthrie had been hard at work on the unconventional interpretation about which he had first spoken at Hurley. In his researches
he had come across an idea which, because of his dilettante interest
in psychology and anthropology, he found particularly stimulating.
It was in a book called *Essays in Applied Psycho-Analysis* by Dr.
Ernest Jones, President of the International Psycho-Analytical Association, which had been published in Vienna in 1923.* Dr. Jones
was concerned with the old, much-debated question of Hamlet's

* Republished, 1949, in an extended and revised version, as *Hamlet and
Œdipus* (W. W. Norton & Co.).

hesitancy in avenging his father's murder, and he had an explanation of this central mystery which seemed to Guthrie far better than anything put forward by such pre-Freudian critics as Coleridge, Bradley and Goethe. Briefly, as Guthrie enthusiastically explained to Olivier, Dr. Jones' theory was that Hamlet did not take revenge more quickly because, as strong as his dislike of his uncle, Claudius, was his subconscious sense of guilt that he was "in love" with his mother. He started to doubt the integrity of his motives for killing Claudius. Was he, perhaps, being prompted less by desire to avenge his father's murder than by the feeling that he was a thwarted and jealous rival for his mother's love? Or—another parallel theory— Hamlet subconsciously desired the incestuous relationship that Claudius was enjoying with his mother, and therefore could not bring himself to kill Claudius with whom in his guilty longings he identified himself. Only after his own death became inevitable through the wound from the poisoned sword was his conscience free to take his uncle's life.

Olivier agreed that these possibilities suggested a far better justification for Hamlet's delay than the more usual explanation that he had doubts about his uncle's guilt or wanted more proof. If he had been asked by sneering anti-Freudians whether he thought Shakespeare was aware of these psychological ideas, Olivier would have answered that Shakespeare would have known them not by learning but by instinct. Acute philosopher and psychologist that he was, he would have observed the trends that are timeless but which have had to await the modern psychiatrist for their full interpretation. For an actor, facing the most varied part in the whole range of drama for the first time, this theory had an added attraction. It provided him with a consistent approach.

Guthrie's production, though ostensibly simple with a single fixed set, was, in fact, so complex for the switchboard that erratic lighting caused the dress-rehearsal to go on almost until dawn. When Olivier found himself having to repeat the line, "My thoughts be bloody, or be nothing worth" several times before the right effect was achieved, he gave way to the observation that things could hardly be bloodier. From a box he heard a chuckle; it was Lilian Baylis, still in the theatre, watching through the small hours and waiting to bring coffee down to the cast when the rehearsal was over. On such tireless enthusiasm was based the success of the Old Vic.

The first night was a nerve-racking experience for Olivier. Not only was he facing the most difficult part of his career, but he had never been through the whole play without a stop. At the dress-rehearsal there had been innumerable delays, and as a result he had no idea of even such elementary problems as where to let up for a rest, where to spare his voice, and where, in long speeches, to conserve his breath. There was the added worry that this was a great theatrical "occasion." From that night in January, 1937, onwards, he was always to have the pleasure of playing a new part mitigated by a sense of responsibility. He could not just enjoy his job as an actor; every first night was an ordeal because he was now a star tied to a considerable reputation. For *Hamlet* he had an additional worry. Guthrie had not been able to conceal from him that his coming to the Vic had been unpopular with some of the theatre's older supporters. They regarded Laurence Olivier as a matinée idol who would use the Vic as a medium for his own glory, not for the fundamental good of the theatre. Lorgnettes out, white hair piled high, they took their seats with the confirmed opinion that this was not going to be the sort of production they enjoyed in dear Ben Greet's day. Younger theatregoers were prepared to be equally critical for a different reason. They saw this as a challenge to the Hamlet of John Gielgud which had a special place in the affections of their generation.

It seemed to Guthrie, now prowling around the back of the dress circle as the house lights dimmed, that there was an intangible but definite sense of antipathy in the house. Fearing for his production and for Olivier in particular, he stood in an agony of apprehension throughout the scene on the battlements. It was as if Olivier, too, sensed the tense atmosphere, and drew on some special reserves of courage and sheer theatrical cunning. Instead of rushing into the part and trying desperately to project himself across the footlights into the dark semi-circle of unknown prejudice, he made the audience come to him. He pitched his voice almost to a whisper, took his time, and delivered his first soliloquy with what seemed to Guthrie an electrifying quality of quiet defiance. From that moment he took the house by storm; there was nothing he could not achieve during the next four hours. There were complaints, of course. Over cocoa and sandwiches during the long interval some people, looking for faults, said that he was not an "intellectual Hamlet" and that, as with Romeo, he did not do justice to the verse. But these criticisms were lost in the long and sincere applause for a great personal triumph. He had aimed high and had succeeded.

Fortunately for the peace of mind of the old ladies who were prepared to be so disapproving, Dr. Jones' particular brand of Freudian significance did not come clearly through. It might have been quite evident to Dr. Jones himself, but the majority of the audience did not notice it. Olivier had never really expected that it would; he was sure that no theory could ever outweigh the power of the rest of the play. Each member of the audience was bound to "get back" just the character of Hamlet he or she read into the part.

Nevertheless he deliberately hinted at the varied "abnormal" manifestations of the Œdipus complex in his tempestuously passionate playing of the closet scene, the gesture of wiping his mother's kiss from his face as something unclean on the line, "O that this too, too *sullied* flesh would melt," and—like most Hamlets, but for a particular reason—in his constant revulsion at the petting between the King and Gertrude. Even Hamlet's apparently straightforward question to Ophelia of "Where's your father?" was meant to convey a preoccupation in his mind about the relationship of parents and their children. In these and a dozen other ways he tried to illuminate a theory which seemed to him profoundly interesting.

The psychological subtleties were there for the initiated to see, but for the general public were obscured by a far more dominating quality in his performance. Every actor, he knew, must cut the part according to his own cloth of physique and appearance. For this reason he had been determined to bring to Hamlet a quality which he knew he possessed and which he had admired in John Barrymore. He wanted his Hamlet to be not mad, pensive and palely epicene, but a dashing young man of his period, who glorified in his ability as a swordsman and was full of all the Elizabethan zest for life. The traditionally gloomy Dane was transformed into an athlete who took terrific leaps across the stage and verged, according to one startled critic, on the acrobatic. Agate, whose wit invariably had a deadly truth in it, said that Olivier's Hamlet was the best performance of Hotspur that the present generation had seen. In *The Observer*, Ivor Brown also commented on his muscularity—a Hamlet which gave the impression of being "up to snuff." He wrote:

He is properly quick in all up-take, a master of riposte with tongue as with sword. His prose banter is admirably taken, springing quick from a quick mind. There is more of thistle and sword-grass than of sensitive plant in his composition. This means, of course, that the kind of pathos so richly established by Mr. Gielgud is not there. That is inevitable: no one Hamlet can be all the Hamlets, and Mr. Olivier succeeds in the prose of Hamlet of which Mr. Gielgud (playing a cut version) was somewhat shy. Of course there are glimpses, and acute ones, of the tender spirit; there are soliloquies in verse which are spoken with fine cadences, but the dominating impression is of

"the flash and outbreak of a fiery mind"

and of a steely body too. The weakness here is that you begin to suspect that such a Hamlet would have put through his murderous work without so much self-security and hesitation.

Mr. Brown may have missed Olivier's Freudian reason for delay (and he was in good company), but his review caught the magnetism and physical excitement of the performance. It is possible now to see a far wider significance in this, as in many subsequent performances by Olivier. He was bringing back to Shakespeare a virility which had been out of fashion for a generation.

III

It was not until rehearsals for *Hamlet* were coming to an end that Guthrie and Olivier started to consider what play they should do next. In a pub in the Waterloo Road next to the stage door of the Vic, Olivier suggested *Twelfth Night* with himself as Sir Toby Belch. As he quite frankly admitted, his idea was to give himself a chance to show his versatility and his skill with his make-up box. It would also be a little bit of a rest; on matinée days during *Hamlet* he knew that he faced nine hours on the stage with only an hour's break between performances. Then and there they began to sketch out the cast. Alec Guinness, who was making such a success of Osric, would be an ideal Sir Andrew Aguecheek; Marius Goring, a stately Fortinbras, should be given a chance with the lighter stuff of Feste. Olivier suggested Jill Esmond for Viola. Guthrie, always so full of unusual ideas, decided it would give him a chance of a production experiment he'd always wanted to try—letting the actress who played Viola also play Sebastian, a complicated manœuvre which was not to help simplicity. Thus, quickly over a pint of beer, they settled *Twelfth Night*. In those more casual days, the Old Vic did not plan its season far ahead. With productions costing about one-tenth of what they do to-day, and with fewer casting problems, it was possible to do things hot on the idea.

So rushed and improvised were rehearsals that Olivier made his gusty, tippling Sir Toby wear a pouch in which, for several performances, he carried a text so that he could take a last-minute glance at a scene as he stood in the wings waiting to go on. In front of the make-up mirror there went on the first in a royal succession of putty noses; pouches were stuck under the eyes; bits of sponge were hidden in his mouth to create bulging cheeks. A straggling moustache dominated his face, and to members of his family this gave him an unmistakable resemblance to his Uncle Herbert. His whole characterization was rich and round enough to please the groundlings, but Guthrie was disturbed by some rather grotesque overplaying. In a few weeks the play had developed into the wildest farce, with Olivier in a nightly battle with Alec Guinness for the most laughs.

This was only a breather before more heroic things. London was about to decorate its streets for the coronation, and clearly something was needed which would be in tune with the times. *Henry V* seemed most suitable, even though neither Guthrie nor Olivier cared for the play. Both of them were pacifists, and loathed the character of Henry, his glorification of heroic warfare, and what Olivier called his "scoutmaster humour." At one time they even discussed darkly a debunking production which would hold up flag-waving to ridicule. The idea never got beyond a joke, however, for both realized that the moment could hardly be more inopportune. After the abdication in the previous December the coronation of the new King and Queen was to be an occasion for the country to show its loyalty. Even a hint of irony about royalty would ill-become a theatre with the national position of the Old Vic.

Olivier had no alternative but to forget his prejudices and make something of a character of whom he disapproved. For some weeks after the play opened he could feel only a stranger to the part, and was intensely shy of exhorting his men to charge with the cry of:

"God for Harry, England and Saint George!" He could always find a humour and understanding in the delicate bi-lingual love scene with Queen Katharine, and here he really did share a fellow-feeling with Henry because of his own modesty about speaking French. But "St. Crispin" and the rest of the heroics stuck in his throat, and it was only gradually that, as he afterwards expressed it, "the words worked their own medicine." He found that as soon as he could make the poetry shine brilliantly without losing sight of the sense, as soon as he could give full rein to the rhythm but still prevent the verse becoming too near to song, and provided he constantly *felt* the character, his worries disappeared. These things accomplished, it was a comparatively short step to a more sympathetic understanding of the part, and two people helped him to change his attitude from distaste to affection. One of them was Richardson, who pointed out that, however much Olivier might dislike Henry as a "cold bath" king, Shakespeare had invested an ordinary person with superhuman splendour and beauty by making him speak with the voice of a poet, and that was the all-important thing to get over to the audience. The other was Charles Laughton whose comment was rhetorical and even shorter. Laughton came round to see him after a performance and, quite obviously moved, exclaimed, "You're *England!*" Richardson provided him with a practical solution to the problem of overcoming his dislike of the part; Laughton in two words fired his imagination. As well as its value at the time, Olivier in later years always found Laughton's remark a convenient explanation to give people who asked what he felt when playing Henry.

IV

During the Old Vic season Vivien Leigh was a loyal supporter of the higher drama even if she wasn't practising it. She saw *Hamlet* fourteen times, and was involved, with varying degrees of personal success, in two films and two stage comedies. The first film was a spy melodrama with Conrad Veidt, directed by Victor Saville at Denham. It had a highly complicated plot, and, because of the trick which prevails of shooting films in everything but the chronological order, left Vivien Leigh a little bewildered about her part. So rapid were the changes of bluff and counter-bluff, so tangled her romance with a sinister German, and so inconsistently shot were the scenes, that as a French girl, posing as a Swiss, operating in Sweden and pretending to pro-German sympathies, she found it almost impossible to keep a grasp on the story and decide whose side she was on. This bewilderment was apparently shared by some of the audience, because before *Dark Journey* was booked for Canada an extra reel was added for the enlightenment of a Dominion whose greater proximity to Hollywood was taken as no guarantee of sharper wits. Vivien Leigh made a quiet personal success, and in her next film, *Storm in a Teacup*, from James Bridie's play, had a part with character in it, and was able to bring so much charm and humour to match the urbanity of Rex Harrison that people began to talk about them as an ideal light comedy team.

Between these two films she went on a short skiing holiday in St. Moritz, the immediate consequence of which was that she had to rehearse a new play with her leg in plaster of paris. The play was *Because We Must*, which was produced at Wyndhams by Norman Marshall. Vivien Leigh could do little except try to be natural in a long, shallow part, and she was left reflecting that this was a poor play in which to return to the West End after nearly two years. On the first night she gave all the cast copies of a new American novel, *Gone With the Wind*, which she had just finished reading, and for whose heroine she felt a strong indefinable sympathy. At once, but without any thought of it being even a vague possibility, she had a wild hope that one day, perhaps, she might play the part of Scarlett O'Hara in a film.

It was not to be expected that *Because We Must*, which opened to tepid notices, would last long, and within a month she was pleased to accept an offer from the manager who took such great pride in having discovered her. Sydney Carroll had only a very ordinary part in a very conventional farce called *Bats in the Belfry* to offer her. In it she played a girl who dropped a tray, an action calling for no wide range of ability. It was hardly the part in which she might have hoped to find herself acting again at the little Ambassadors, so full of memories of the overwhelming success at the start of her career. However, she told herself that it was all experience, and that at that stage in her career she needed as many parts as possible. This was a time in which to learn her profession, and prepare for the opportunities which might lie ahead. This was a period, so darkly formative, when few people would have predicted her future success, and even Olivier, despite his growing affection for her, could not persuade himself that as yet she was much of an actress. He had been swept off his feet, like so many, by her beauty in *The Mask of Virtue*, but in these modern comedies he was discomforted by the uneasy suspicion that she had no very great talent. If she worked hard, he believed, she could improve as an actress, but he could see little promise of her future ability. Most worrying of all, although her voice seemed at times to have a wood-wind sweetness, it was light and very restricted in range. But these doubts were swept aside. He *wanted* her to be good, and from that it was a short way to a determination that she should be good—very good.

Naturally these were not opinions which he expressed to Vivien. She herself might be frank about her own shortcomings, but it is one thing to disarm criticism by open admission of one's limitations, and quite another to be confronted with them by somebody else. And by now Vivien Leigh was seriously concerned with becoming a considerable actress. Towards that end Olivier, continually bubbling over with enthusiasm, was to give her more and more advice, although as he was to insist many years later, most of what she achieved was through her own ability and hard work. He concentrated on her voice until she had a vocal range of two octaves and gave her the sort of advice that any actress might expect from a producer; but, as he always wants to tell people who jump at the idea that he has been a mixture of Pygmalion and Svengali, the strength she has developed has been entirely due to herself.

In the next film which they made under their contracts with London Films they were together again. This was Galsworthy's *The First and the Last*, for which a script had been prepared by Graham Greene. As Olivier was to be by her side, Vivien Leigh felt no qualms at the news that the director was Basil Dean, and when shooting started she found that he called the man who had held such terrors for her at Ealing by the nickname of "Sugar." Dean, who would probably have preferred a more dignified nickname, found himself in the position of a schoolmaster whose class suddenly becomes filled, not with quailing pupils, but with tough and ribald old boys. Leslie Banks was another who had outgrown schoolboy fears, and on one occasion he and Olivier were so unruly that they were asked to leave the class. Olivier became convulsed in one of the fits of giggling which had pursued him since his early days. Leslie Banks caught the infection and the shooting of one scene simply came to a stop. Dean glared through his glasses, but eventually called for a break so that they could recover. "What we need," Olivier said to his friend, "is a drink to pull us together." They had several, but no sooner were they back on the set than they found that the laughter, far from being drowned, was again swimming happily to the surface. They managed to get through rehearsals with quivering underlips, but the moment the cameras were ready and the whole studio brought to silence for the actual shot they burst again into laughter. After a long evening of this Basil Dean stopped work and walked angrily off the set.

Next day when he arrived at the studio Olivier was told that Mr. Dean wanted to see him immediately. This was clearly the summons to the headmaster's study. He went prepared for, and received, a dressing-down, but even as Basil Dean was lecturing him severely the thought that he was just a few days off his thirtieth birthday and that all this belonged to a juvenile past got the better of him. He seized on a pause to say: "Yes, of course, I agree with you entirely. But why don't you say all this to Leslie? After all, he's the senior!"

It was, perhaps, a good thing that shooting on *The First and the Last* * was interrupted after three weeks for a visit which Vivien Leigh and Olivier made to Denmark. During the closing weeks of *Henry V* the Old Vic had been invited by the Danish Tourist Association to stage *Hamlet* in the courtyard of Kronborg Castle at Elsinore. It seemed an appropriate and delightful idea, although it was difficult to keep the company together after the end of the season. Guthrie had to sacrifice part of a holiday, and Olivier had to obtain Korda's permission to take a week off in the middle of filming. Because Michael Redgrave could not go Anthony Quayle took over Laertes, and some one had to replace Cherry Cottrell, who was not available for Ophelia. Exactly how Vivien Leigh came to be chosen is not quite clear. The obvious assumption is that Olivier

---

* When the film was finished at the end of the summer it was considered so bad that it would probably never have been shown but for the subsequent success of the two stars. With the changed title of *Twenty-one Days* it was released during the war, and it was then that Olivier and Vivien Leigh first saw it. Or rather, they saw part of it. In an obscure little New York cinema they watched for about a third of its length, and then they got up and walked out. To this day, they have never seen the film right through.

suggested she should be. She suspected he had a hand in it, but Olivier, who certainly did not wish her to think that casting depended on help, strongly denied it, and it is a denial in which he has persisted whenever the question has come up since. There was certainly no hint of his influence in the letter she received from Lilian Baylis at the beginning of May. "The Danish authorities would very much like it if you could play Ophelia and we, too, would be delighted," Miss Baylis wrote. With a blameless air of spontaneity the letter arrived on a day when Olivier was abroad on a flying reconnaissance to Denmark.

So it came about that for three weeks she went through a confused nightmare of filming and preparations for *Hamlet*, with Olivier sometimes taking her through their scenes together in the car between Denham and London, and with Guthrie, recently out of a sick-bed, being very scathing at rehearsals. "Much too pretty! Much too dainty!" he would comment acidly. "Do stop all this tripping about!" She suspected that Guthrie regarded her as a jumped-up little film star who had no right to be attempting Ophelia; in actual fact, he liked her obvious determination to learn and the way she took advice, but was worried because he feared her voice would be too small for the open air and because she seemed to him to have no imaginative grip on the mad scene. He was administering a stiff dose of medicine right at the start; and, because she appreciated that with few rehearsals he could not spend much time on polite formalities, she did not allow herself to be upset. Within a few days Guthrie's criticism softened, and by the time the company left for Elsinore they were the best of friends.

CHAPTER 2

Tragedy at the Old Vic
1937-1938

I

WITH MORE TIME, less worry, and infinitely better weather the visit which the Old Vic made to Elsinore in June, 1937 might have been thoroughly enjoyable. It was a fascinating experience for the actors to play *Hamlet* in the courtyard of the ancient castle. Shakespeare might never have visited Kronborg, but he must have heard about it from travellers and imagined its pinnacled towers and walls washed by the grey rolling sea as he wrote his play about Prince Hamlet. There was an undeniable excitement about being the first English company to act there since 1585, when Will Kempe, the Elizabethan clown, had performed with the Earl of Leicester's Men. Unfortunately there was little time for either historical reflection or modern sightseeing. Even if they had wanted to, neither Olivier nor Vivien Leigh were given the leisure to make so much as a brisk pilgrimage to any of the three "authentic" graves of Hamlet which Denmark shows its tourists. Under Tyrone Guthrie's direction they were far too busy rehearsing. It was difficult to plan their performances so that they would not be lost in the great courtyard and so that they would have a chance of being audible to an audience of 2,500.

Wind and rain lashed the stage and sunshine only occasionally broke through the rolling black clouds. For two days and nights

157

they rehearsed almost continuously, with John Abbott as Claudius, under an umbrella, giving full value to the line, "Is there not rain enough in the sweet heavens?" while the rest of the cast dripped and shivered, their overcoats buttoned to their chins. Olivier, looking rather like a rowing man, carried a towel round his neck with which to wipe his hair. Guthrie, a wet mackintosh flapping against his flannels, shouted desperately at the forty Danish officer cadets who had volunteered as supers. Only through an interpreter could he at last persuade them to march in step as they carried Ophelia to her grave. The whole company battled to make their lines heard against the wind that swept across the Kattegat, and at one rehearsal had the added difficulty of contending with the noise of hammers from the neighbouring shipyards. As if warned by some sixth sense that her beloved Old Vic was being ill-treated by the weather, Lilian Baylis arrived by air during the weekend to dispense coffee and biscuits, which she clearly believed the antidote to all the ills an actor's flesh could be heir to. Those who did not share this faith surreptitiously blended the coffee with schnapps.

On Tuesday, the day before the opening, the final and complete run-through had to be abandoned, and at six o'clock on the day of the performance the tempest was still so black that it was decided that it would be impossible to follow Shakespeare's stage direction and play on " a platform before the castle at Elsinore." There was a hurried conference, and it was decided to move to the ballroom of the Marienlyst Hotel, about half a mile from the castle.

On a stage used for cabaret, and taking in part of the dance floor as a forestage, a new production was devised. It was an anti-climax, but the company took it as a challenge to their adaptability. Instructions for moves and new "business" were still being whispered in the wings as the Crown Prince of Denmark and his wife took their seats in the front row of the audience. Exits and entrances had to be improvised almost on the spur of the moment; a spectacular production, planned on different levels, suddenly developed into home-made charades. So catching was the spirit of extemporization that when Olivier noticed one of the audience in the front row chatting to his neighbour he devised an immediate reprisal. He whispered an aside to Anthony Quayle, who was playing Laertes, and when the duel started they moved the fight nearer and nearer the offender until he began to doubt if he would escape the flashing rapiers.

Out of a disappointing compromise emerged a triumph. Ivor Brown, one of the many critics from the London papers who had come to Elsinore for the production, said afterwards that it was as good a performance of *Hamlet* as he had ever seen. Like others in the cast, Vivien Leigh found herself happier in the more intimate contact with her audience. As Olivier said to her when they discussed it later, it proved that, if necessary, Shakespeare could be performed successfully in a pit shaft.

On the following evening, however, the sky was clear, and the play could move back to the courtyard. With that sense of drama which infects normally insular newspaper men when they telephone from abroad, one correspondent found himself dictating, "All is well. This morning the weather cast its nighted colour off and the sun once more looked like a friend on Denmark."

Only slightly faltering in this poetic strain he continued, "Now as I telephone darkness has covered the town of Elsinore and flung its veil across the Sound. The Swedish coast is lost; the lights of a cargo vessel are flickering on the waters. A single sentry guards the Kronborg ramparts; swans glimmer on the moat; there is no sound except the sighing of the tide. Within the turretted courtyard of Kronborg more than 2,000 people sit rapt, not a mouse stirs. Light glows upon the high stage before the northern wall of the castle where Hamlet, his task accomplished, rests in Horatio's arms and hears the throbbing of the drums of Fortinbras."

Olivier, he said, had repeated his superb Hamlet—a performance which the Danish press had hailed as superlative—and Vivien Leigh's Ophelia had shown real promise. "We shall think of these players with gratitude. Certainly we shall ever remember the glory of the setting as night sank upon Elsinore; the cheering of the great Danish audience, the tremor that passed through the courtyard when the ghost walked once more upon the battlements of Kronborg; and Mr. Laurence Olivier's last bow to the clamorous Danes before the stage lights dimmed."

II

Elsinore was a triumph for the Old Vic, and in the story of the Oliviers it also holds a place of very personal importance. In the

week after they returned from Elsinore Vivien Leigh felt obliged
to tell her husband, and Olivier his wife, that they had fallen in love;
and after the unhappiness and immediate practical problems which
such situations bring about, they themselves had to arrange a new
design for living. Engrossed though they were in these private difficulties, there was no respite from work; in fact, their jobs helped to
provide them with a refuge from their thoughts. There was *The
First and the Last* to complete at Denham, and then, after a holiday
which took them to Venice, Olivier started on *The Divorce of Lady
X*, a bright and amusing film comedy with Merle Oberon.

At about the same time Vivien Leigh was loaned to M.G.M. for
A Yank at Oxford, the first film the company was to make in England. A great deal of fuss was made about the casting of the part she
played with Robert Taylor. It was much put about by the studio
that dozens of actresses had been tested, all of which gave her added
prestige when it was finally announced that she had been cast.
Maureen O'Sullivan, her friend of so many years before at Roehampton, came over from America to play the heroine, but to
Vivien Leigh went the delightful part of the scheming and flighty
wife of an Oxford bookseller. Wearing cheap flashy clothes and a
preposterous hair style she had, at last, a real character to play on
the screen. It was not a large part, but it was rounded off with one
line which stamped it with success. Because of her demoralizing
influence on the undergraduates she has been asked to leave Oxford,
and, in reply to a question as to where she and her husband are
going, she says with wide-eyed innocence, "We are moving to
Aldershot." This reference to England's great military center,
which never failed to get a laugh, was not in the original script, and
was only added on the morning the scene was shot. It was the inspired suggestion of a young assistant director, Sidney Gilliat, who
may have recalled how, in similar circumstances, another Oxford
siren called for a Bradshaw to look up the trains for Cambridge.

Olivier decided to return to the Old Vic that autumn and wanted
to appear as Macbeth and Richard II. This, however, looked as if it
might conflict with the plans which John Gielgud was making for
a season at the Queen's. They talked it over, and Gielgud agreed
not to play Macbeth while Olivier left him a clear field for Richard
II. Shakespeare thus neatly apportioned between them, Olivier
started rehearsals under Michel Saint-Denis for *Macbeth*. It was

a production which was to have tragic associations for the supporters of the Old Vic.

Saint-Denis, a French producer, who had made his name in England with the production of *Noah* and who in 1935 had started a dramatic school on highly original lines in north London, quickly showed Olivier that his ideas were unusually provocative. For every line Saint-Denis suggested half-a-dozen subtleties and overtones. He coaxed the Motley sisters into devising some very mannered costumes and curious, barbaric masks for the witches; from New York he brought Judith Anderson to play Lady Macbeth on the recommendation of Gielgud, with whom she had appeared as Gertrude on Broadway the previous season.

Legends feed and grow fat on their own tradition. Everyone in the theatre can contribute a story of bad luck about some production of *Macbeth* with which he has been associated. So the superstition has grown up that it is a play of ill-omen. While Olivier refuses to acknowledge the superstition, he has to admit that this particular production lent considerable weight to the legend. It saw not only bad luck, of the sort which is easily accountable, but tragedy as well.

The bad luck started with Saint-Denis being involved in a taxi accident; then a dog of which Lilian Baylis was very fond was run over and killed; and Olivier caught a bad cold. Worst of all, there were endless delays and complications during rehearsals. At 3 a.m. on Monday, the night of the dress-rehearsal, when they had only reached the end of the first act it became clear that they could never open the next night. As they broke up at dawn it was decided to postpone the opening until Friday, but as this was almost unheard of in the history of the Old Vic some explanation had to be made. To say that Saint-Denis' elaborate production simply wasn't ready was bad publicity; so, using Olivier as a scapegoat, the theatre decided to twist the *Macbeth* superstition to its own ends. Olivier's cold was exaggerated into a complete loss of voice—just another example, it was insinuated, of the traditional bad luck of *Macbeth*.

Then, as if the furies had no intention of letting actors mock their abilities or try to improve their work, news of genuine gravity followed a few hours later. Lilian Baylis was seriously ill. She had gone down with a sudden heart attack at her home in Stockwell. That was on the Tuesday evening, and she recovered sufficiently to send one of her staff round to the theatre the following morning to reassure the company. But then, on the Thursday, a rehearsal was interrupted for an announcement of the news which everyone was dreading. Lilian Baylis had died. Should there be a further postponement? What would "The Lady" have wanted? Her companion who had been at her bedside was able to supply the answer. Among her very last questions had been: "Is everything all right at the Old Vic?" and she had asked that her illness should in no way interfere with the first night.

For the first time in the memory of anyone, that familiar, thickset figure wearing a sable cape over a taffeta coat was missing from the box she always occupied on first nights. Sitting there beside an empty chair was her companion, Miss Prevost, who had accompanied her to first nights for many years. Lord Lytton, as Chairman of the Board of Governors, paid a tribute before the curtain to the woman who, after thirty years of guiding the theatre's destiny, had died at the age of sixty-five. The whole audience rose in her honour before the play began.

It was an evening of deep emotion, but for Olivier the full sense of loss was not brought home until he went back to his dressing-room, the play over and his personal tension relaxed. On the dressing-table was a letter. He opened the envelope to find a short note from Evelyn Williams, the theatre secretary, saying:

Dear Larry,
   The Lady had done this little card on Monday, and I thought you'd like to have it, though I knew you'd rather not be given it before the show to-night.

Attached by a paper clip was a plain copperplate visiting card on which was written in Lilian Baylis' own hand the message, "Welcome return to dear Laurence Olivier. May you be as happy in *Macbeth* as in *Hamlet* last season."

About the production itself opinions were sharply divided. The dim lighting and sombre tones of barbaric exaggeration in which costumes and scenery were conceived did not help. It started well, but deteriorated at the end in a battle of Dunsinane so silly that it defied adequate description. Perhaps J. G. Bergel, who was not only an erudite dramatic critic, but also had the advantage of being a Rugby correspondent, came nearest to it when he leaned over and whispered to his companion that in his professional opinion *every-one* was off-side! Masked witches and a masked ghost of Banquo suggested at once the stylized continental expressionism which has always been slightly suspect in England. There was even sympathy for more reactionary playgoers who said that the Old Vic was a place, not for highbrow experiments but for solid traditional virtues.

Olivier's *Macbeth* was conceded to be a fine performance for a young man, and one which was likely to be even better when he was twice as old, but there were criticisms of his voice—the same criticisms which pursued him so consistently through all his early performances in tragedy. Despite the resonance of his voice and tricks of variation, he could never disguise the fact that he was a baritone, and that for Macbeth, as for Othello or Lear, a tragedian requires a bass voice to get the maximum effect from the verse. He tried hard to train his voice, and always hoped that as he grew older it would deepen in pitch; but since he still has not developed the bass voice needed for the great tragic rôles he has on several occasions had to force his lower register at the risk of being occasionally let down.

It was in key with a production whose over-elaboration seemed to suggest a lack of self-confidence that his make-up should also be exaggerated. Olivier, who had just been given Macready's make-up box by Vivien, put in false gums to make his lips protrude, slanted his eyes and raised his cheekbones in yellow pallor so that he assumed the appearance of some Mongol emperor. As Vivien Leigh put it, when describing the performance to a friend: "Well, you hear Macbeth's first line, then Larry's make-up comes on, then Banquo comes on, then Larry comes on."

Whatever the shortcomings, it was a financial success at the Old Vic and seemed too interesting a production to run for only a month. Towards the end of December when it had to make way for a special Christmas presentation of *A Midsummer Night's Dream* it was transferred to the New Theatre. But for some reason audiences which had flocked to the Waterloo Road were not tempted to St. Martin's Lane; to Olivier's bitter disappointment it closed in three weeks after losing £2,000.

The production of *A Midsummer Night's Dream*, in which Guthrie invited Vivien Leigh to play Titania, was to be remembered for years because of the original idea of staging it in the Victorian

manner with Mendelssohn's music, painted gauze drops, and a flying
ballet of fairies in Victorian ballet skirts. Oliver Messel, paying out
of his own pocket for effects which the Old Vic simply could not
afford, gave way to a riot of white muslin and pink roses and fairies
with tiny wings and red sashes. Moonlight shone on silver crowns,
and everywhere there was the twinkle of sequins and tinsel. Ninette
de Valois arranged the ballets, and among the many things for which
the production was notable was the appearance of Robert Helpmann
as Oberon. It was his first speaking part on the stage. Vivien Leigh
was particularly excited to hear that he was to be in the play for, as
a keen follower of ballet and a frequent visitor to Sadler's Wells,
she had admired him as a dancer for a number of years. They had
met several times, but this was to be the start of a long and close
friendship. Like Vivien Leigh, Helpmann was to prove a little in-
expert in his handling of the verse, but he moved with such grace
and rhythm that Guthrie was well pleased with this unusual piece
of casting. Both dazzled the eye and made what he considered was
"a nice noise," a combination which for fairies was probably more
important than a reading of great variety.

It was a production to take the town, and was to live like an
enchanted dream in the memories of hundreds of children who
crowded the matinées throughout the Christmas holidays. Here
was scenery so beautiful that it made even the glitter of pantomime
look dull and a Bottom, in Ralph Richardson, who was funnier by
far than any red-nosed Dame.

Among these many children who sat in awed wonder before the
magic of the play were a little girl of eleven in a high-buttoned coat
and short white socks and her sister, aged seven, who was dressed
exactly the same. One afternoon in March they saw the production
from the Royal Box and during the interval Vivien Leigh, Richardson, and Helpmann were taken round so that the girls could meet
and shake hands with them. Their mother, the Queen, was keeping
a long-standing promise she had once made to Lilian Baylis that
Princess Elizabeth and Princess Margaret should see their first
Shakespeare at the Old Vic.

When the time came for the players to return back-stage Vivien
Leigh and Robert Helpmann curtsied and bowed in the narrow
doorway and just as they were about to straighten up suddenly
became aware that their head-dresses were entwined. They tried to

shake themselves free but the elaborate wire and gauze confections which Messel had designed for his Titania and Oberon were quite hopelessly tangled. There was nothing for it but to walk gingerly backwards with heads bowed until they reached the stairway and passed out of view of the royal party. It was hardly the happiest of exits, but they took comfort from the hope that their curious retreat was mistaken for loyal self-abasement.

III

For some years Ralph Richardson and Olivier had had an ambition to play in *Othello* together, as Othello and Iago, and it was decided that this should be the first play to open the second part of the winter season in the February of 1938. It had a fine cast which included Anthony Quayle, Stephen Murray and Andrew Cruickshank, and settings by Roger Furse. Everything seemed to be in its favour; yet few of those connected with the production look back on it as anything but the direst failure. Perhaps it was ill-fated from the moment that Guthrie wrote to Dr. Jones, the psycho-analyst, to ask if he had any theories comparable to those he had given them for *Hamlet*. Dr. Jones replied that he had never published anything on the subject, but that he would be glad to discuss it, and suggested that they should meet. Without telling Richardson, Guthrie and Olivier went to see the doctor at his house in Regent's Park, where they found him, a Welshman in his middle sixties with a noble head and manner which made Guthrie think irresistibly of Merlin. His ideas were startlingly unconventional and as such immediately appealed to both of them. Dr. Jones told them that to his mind the clue to the play was not Iago's hatred for Othello, but his deep affection for him. His jealousy was not because he envied Othello's position, not because he was in love with Desdemona, but because he himself possessed a subconscious affection for the Moor, the homosexual foundation of which he did not understand.

This was a little startling, but once they had accepted the premise it was remarkable how easily all the lines and situations could be made to fit the theory. Here at last was a plausible explanation of the problem of why Othello was so irrationally influenced by Iago. The great climax in Act III, when Iago and Othello kneel together planning the death of Cassio, became virtually a love scene with Othello's "Now art thou my lieutenant," and Iago's reply, "I am your own for ever" taking on a new significance. Even Iago's often-repeated "I hate the Moor" was easily explained away by the psychologist; it was simply the stubborn protestations of a man unaware of his true subconscious emotions.

As they left Dr. Jones' house Olivier asked Guthrie what he thought of the theory. "I think it is inescapable," said Guthrie firmly, "on an unconscious plane, of course." "Oh, of course," echoed Olivier, and added: "I don't think we dare tell Ralphy." He felt rather guilty about such treachery, but was sure Richardson would disapprove of any hint of perversion, however unconscious. So rehearsal went on with Richardson quite unaware of Olivier's ideas about the Iago-Othello relationship. "Never mind your psychology!" he would exclaim whenever the subconscious was mentioned. "The beauty of the play to me is the magnificence of its rhetoric. Leave me my 'monumental alabaster.'"

It would probably have been difficult to get across so revolutionary an interpretation to an audience even with the full co-operation of both leading actors. With one of them left completely in the dark it was quite impossible. It was, anyway, an idea which could only be suggested very subtly if it were not to give grave offence. The audience were therefore not unreasonably bewildered by an Iago who was not the sinister schemer to which they were accustomed, but a smiling, flippant, strangely affectionate fellow. As with his Hamlet, the critics missed what Olivier was getting at, and it might never have been made public had not James Bridie, a doctor as well as a playwright, written a letter to the *New Statesman* to point out that this Iago was a vital and intelligent man with a diseased and perverted sexual "make-up."

IV

At that time Bridie had a particular interest in the work at the Old Vic because the next play there was to be his subtle mystifying comedy, *The King of Nowhere*. The idea of inserting a modern play in the Old Vic repertory was a radical departure from policy. For forty years the theatre had been dedicated to Shakespeare, and only occasionally had established Restoration or eighteenth-century plays been included in the repertory. Chekov, Ibsen and Shaw were reluctantly admitted as modern classics and R. C. Sherriff had once got under Lilian Baylis' guard with a costume play about Napoleon.

Now they were breaking every precedent by presenting a new play
with a contemporary setting by a living playwright. The reason for
the innovation was largely theatre politics on Guthrie's part. He
wanted to establish the Old Vic in the widest and fullest sense as a
"national theatre" so that if the long-planned National Theatre was
ever built it would look to the Old Vic for a nucleus. But Bridie
came under heavy fire, and within a month the theatre returned to
Shakespeare and tradition. *Coriolanus* went up on the posters with
Sybil Thorndike as Volumnia and her husband, Lewis Casson, as
producer, to restore the methods of the classical school.

It was strange for Olivier to be working again under the producer
who had given him almost his first chance as an assistant stage manager only thirteen years before, and to be playing the lead with an
old friend of the family who remembered him as a schoolboy in
Pimlico. Casson's influence may well have decided him to conceive
the part in a more heroic manner than he would have done otherwise. At rehearsals Casson would frequently pull him up for little
informal tricks which were so much a part of modern, realistic acting. He severely censured any throwing away of lines. He knew
that Olivier was critical of anything in the classical tradition which
he considered pompous or insincere, but during the lively arguments
that arose during rehearsal Casson would reiterate over and over
again his belief that too much realism would take away from the
overall magnificence of Shakespeare's conception. Olivier was himself slowly and grudgingly coming round to this point of view, and
for the immensely exacting part of Coriolanus he allowed his performance to be slightly more in the traditional Shakespearean manner. He would not entirely discard an occasional flash of comedy,
and again his make-up was so heavy—"buried beneath loam and
plaster," muttered Agate—that he robbed his face of much of its
character and seriously reduced his range of expression.

But generally faults were noted to be in abeyance, and he reaped
the reward for following Casson's advice. For the first time his performance was hailed as great. Privately he was a little amused to
see how easily praise was won if he toed the accepted line. Like so
many artists he was inclined to be contemptuous of the work which
was most acclaimed, and annoyed to be appreciated more for the
easily-achieved success than for the failure which cost so much
thought and effort. Olivier regarded his Coriolanus as a great show-

off performance, lacking variety; the one thing he rather liked about it was his death scene when, with his penchant for the acrobatic, he threw himself down the staircase in a complete somersault, rolled over three times on his side and crashed to his death just short of the footlights. He noted cynically that this sort of thing brought up the applause and assured the accolade; this made the critics acclaim his Coriolanus as his best performance to date. One of them even pronounced: "There is now no doubt in my mind that the only sign of a great actor in the making in England to-day is Mr. Olivier."

He might pretend to be careless of such praise, but he could not entirely ignore it. And he could not fail to be thrilled by his experience on the last night of *Coriolanus* and the last night of the Old Vic season. For the first time when he came out of the stage door there was a huge throng of fans waiting to cheer him and besiege him for autographs. This was the sort of popular success which an actor can only enjoy to the utmost when he is young. Olivier was just thirty-one.

CHAPTER 3

The Reluctant Heathcliff
1938-1939

I

EVERYONE HAS his perfect holiday, the one holiday in a lifetime which is always recalled with deep affection because of the certainty that there can never be another quite like it. It belongs to the period between youth and middle-age and before life has acquired too much responsibility; and for many the recollection is more poignant for being part of the tranquillity which existed before the war.

As they lay on the beach at Agay or swam lazily in the sheltered little bay between St. Raphael and Cannes during the long, idle days of that last summer of peace in 1938, Vivien Leigh and Olivier were enjoying just such a holiday. They could not know it, but both were mid-way in their careers; they were both on the brink of the sort of fame which recognizes no privacy and from which there was to be no escape. They had driven down through France in a battered old Ford V8 belonging to Vivien, and after a few days at the fortified town of St. Paul in the Alps above Nice had found a quiet spot on the coast. The little hotel called the Calanque d'Or where they were staying possessed nothing but a tiny restaurant, two rooms and—a final enchantment for Vivien—eighteen Siamese cats owned by the proprietor and his wife. Both felt that they deserved a holiday; Olivier had put another season at the Vic behind him, and

Vivien Leigh had just finished filming with Laughton in *St. Martin's Lane*. Now they lay in the sun and let their talk wander aimlessly over the uncertain future. Olivier wondered if he should follow Bridie's advice and tour in the provinces, to build up a country-wide following as all actors had been forced to do in the days before the cinema. Should they act together, and how much would they be separated if they allowed their careers to develop separately? What would happen if Hitler went too far and there was war? This was a question which they came back to frequently—the only tiny cloud to pass over the face of the sun. Sometimes the idle pattern of their day-to-day existence would be changed for a few pleasant hours, when John Gielgud and Hugh Beaumont, who were staying at Vence, came to visit them, or when they went to stay for a couple of days at the house Gielgud had taken there. Many of their friends were on the Riviera that summer, and Peggy Ashcroft, Glen Byam Shaw and his wife Angela Baddeley were among those who dropped in from the various places where they were staying along the coast for a meal and a bathe and a few hours' talk.

Only faintly did the problems of the immediate future ripple the serene surface of the perfect holiday. Agents sweating it out in London through July were liable to send querulous cables and be rather pained if they got no answers. In a sprawling, spider-like hand the clerk at the local post office would diligently copy out the only partially comprehensible messages and deliver them to the Calanque d'Or. Over Dubonnet before lunch they would adjust their sun-soaked minds to the contents of these cables. ARE YOU INTERESTED GOLDWYN IDEA FOR SEPTEMBER FIRST FOR VIVIEN YOURSELF AND OBERON IN WUTHERING HEIGHTS STOP ANSWER AS SOON POSSIBLE STOP. This sounded all right, but Olivier sent back an evasive reply. He was determined not to go through what he termed "the fire" of Hollywood again unless the whole set-up was absolutely ideal. He had allowed himself to be stampeded by cables before, and had learnt his lesson. There was also the suspicion that Sam Goldwyn and Emily Brontë might prove strange bedfellows. In an attempt to influence them a bulky parcel arrived a week or so later at the hotel. It was the script of *Wuthering Heights* as wrought on behalf of Mr. Goldwyn by Ben Hecht and Charles MacArthur. It appeared a good script, in so far as long Victorian novels can ever be condensed without seeming melodramatic, but from Vivien Leigh's point of view there was one definite shortcoming. Merle Oberon was to play Cathy, and she did not find the part of Isabella sufficiently important or interesting. It was not just a question of personal vanity; she had now starred in half-a-dozen British films, and Olivier insisted that it would be bad policy for her to go to Hollywood as a supporting player. As he had no wish to go to Hollywood unless she came too, he wrote to his agent turning down the offer, but added a "feeler" that it would have been nice if only Vivien Leigh could have played Cathy.

There the matter seemed to end; they had almost forgotten about it by the middle of July, when the time had come to turn the nose of the Ford north and say good-bye to Agay and the Calanque d'Or.* They spent a week or more on the pleasant tour through France and at Roanne on the Loire, where they stopped on their journey to Boulogne, a letter was waiting from Cecil Tennant. He was an executive in London of Myron Selznick, Olivier's agent, and wrote to say that he hoped Olivier would change his mind about *Wuthering Heights* because of the importance of the film, and added that the director, William Wyler, was at Juan les Pins and anxious to get in touch with him.

Ever since the conference about casting which he had had with Sam Goldwyn earlier that year, Wyler had fixed on Olivier as the ideal actor for Heathcliff. He had seen him on the stage, and his only reservation was whether he would be too polished and handsome for the early scenes as a gipsy stable boy. He had naturally been upset when Olivier had turned down the idea without any particular explanation, and having missed him in France, decided to look him up on his way back through London.

Olivier had never met Wyler. As far as he could recall Wyler could only have seen him act twice. The first time was in *The Green Bay Tree* in New York, and second at the dress-rehearsal of *The Ringmaster* at the Shaftesbury, when he had heard that Wyler and his wife, Margaret Sullavan, had been in front. He hadn't even a very clear idea of the films Wyler had made, and before the director came to see them he and Vivien took the precaution of going to

*In 1949 they went on a sentimental pilgrimage to Agay and found that the hotel had been destroyed. Vivien Leigh, making inquiries in the little village, asked after the proprietor and was told that both he and his wife had been found guilty of collaboration and were executed by the Resistance.

see his latest film. It was *Jezebel*, with Bette Davis, and certainly seemed to justify Wyler's growing reputation.

Wyler visited Olivier twice at his new home, Durham Cottage, a small seventeenth-century house which stood in a little walled garden not far from Chelsea Hospital. Talk at their first meeting was neatly steered by Olivier away from *Wuthering Heights* to the wines of Wyler's native Alsace and to abstract discussions on the art of the films. Wyler, who loved the cinema and knew every aspect of the industry, did what he could to awaken Olivier's interest, but it was clear that Olivier had a dislike of Hollywood and a love of the stage which could not be altered for all the dollars that Goldwyn could offer, and Wyler left frustrated. He tested Robert Newton for the part, but the tests did not please Goldwyn; so Wyler paid another visit to Durham Cottage.

This time he tried a different tack. He knew he didn't stand a chance of persuading Olivier that he could do as worth-while an acting job in a film as in a play; now, he believed, the answer lay in converting Vivien Leigh. If she could be persuaded to play Isabella he thought Olivier might change his mind. Wyler had been sufficiently impressed by a preview he had seen of *St. Martin's Lane* to think she would be good in the part. "Look," he said to her, "you want to go to America . . . you're not known there . . . you'll get better parts after a while . . . but for *a first part* in Hollywood you'll get nothing better than this!" They were both to have reason to smile at this prophecy within a year.

Persuasion failed, but the conversations had served to make one thing clear to Vivien Leigh. Olivier liked the part, and, whatever he said to the contrary, rather wanted to do it; he was turning it down simply because he didn't want to leave her behind in London. She saw very clearly that this sort of self-sacrifice might seriously upset their future. They had a long discussion, and after much heart-searching, finally decided that the only logical thing to do was to adapt their lives to fit the mould of their careers. Anyway, she said as cheerfully as she could, he would only be away for three months, and during that time she, too, would be busy. Norman Marshall had asked her to play in *Serena Blandish* at the little Gate Theatre in Villiers Street, and at Christmas she was going back to the Old Vic for a revival of the Victorian *Midsummer Night's Dream*. Half-convinced, Olivier agreed, and one day down at Denham, where they were filming together in *Q Planes*, he talked the matter over with Ralph Richardson. "Bit of fame! Good!" was Richardson's terse comment, and on the strength of it Olivier cabled to Goldwyn. He sailed for America in the *Normandie* on November 5th, Vivien Leigh's birthday.

II

Whatever it looked like from a seat in the cinema, *Wuthering Heights* was a battleground for an actor's soul. Olivier went back to Hollywood against his better judgment, found himself in immediate opposition to his director, and was miserable during most of the time the film was being made. Yet *Wuthering Heights* changed his whole attitude to the cinema, and William Wyler was the man who brought about his conversion. The two of them disagreed—often bitterly—in the studio, and away from it sat up into the small hours discussing their violently conflicting theories. The antagonism ended, like the traditional school fight behind the gym, in friendship. By then the influence on Olivier as a stage and screen actor had been incalculable.

From the moment of his arrival in Hollywood, things started badly. When he had been in New York the idea of Vivien Leigh playing Cathy had suddenly and quite unexpectedly been reopened. After schooling himself to the idea that there was no question of her accompanying him to Hollywood, all his hopes had suddenly been revived by a long distance call from Goldwyn himself saying that it might be necessary to make a last-minute change, and, if it were, would Vivien Leigh be available? Then, on his arrival at the studios, all his hopes were dashed again; whatever the trouble was, it had been patched up. Merle Oberon was definitely cast as Cathy.

Unusually for Hollywood, the whole film was rehearsed before shooting started, and Olivier soon became aware that he and Wyler were completely out of sympathy. The director from Alsace who had been so agreeable in London now seemed brusque and sometimes even rude, "That's lousy!" he would exclaim after a difficult and emotional scene. Olivier had the suspicion that perhaps he was attacking the part of Heathcliff too melodramatically, but it was hard to judge the shades of emphasis for himself, and he could never get Wyler to put into words precisely what he wanted. It seemed to him that Wyler was too much of a technician and not sufficiently concerned, as a director should be, with the problems of his actors. Olivier couldn't help admiring the way he would spend hours on a scene until he got it exactly right. His standards were high, and perfection had to be obtained even if it meant shooting a scene over and over again. But how much easier on the nerves it would have been, Olivier thought, if he could only have explained what he wanted first! He was also slightly resentful that such care as Wyler gave to actual acting he concentrated on Merle Oberon. She was co-star of the film and this was partly to be expected; but to an actor struggling with a part in which he was not happy, it was no help at all.

All these thoughts were, of course, unspoken, and Wyler was un-conscious of growing resentment. He was quite happy about Olivier's interpretation; indeed, it showed far more strength and imagination than he had expected. If he was over-acting in some scenes, so much the better; Wyler infinitely preferred an actor to over-act because he found it simpler to subdue a performance than to add to it if there was little there to start with. The constant cor-rection which Olivier began to regard almost as persecution was Wyler's watchful insistence that there should not be a false note in a period piece which was already melodramatic enough.

To make matters worse Olivier found that, not only was he losing patience with his director, but he was not getting on at all well with his leading lady. This was difficult to understand because there had been no disagreements during the making of *The Divorce of Lady X* at Denham only the year before. Perhaps he was annoyed that her performance, unlike his, seemed perfectly acceptable to Wyler. A feeling which for some while was nothing more than friction even-tually developed into an open clash. It came during a love scene. Its setting was the romantic meeting-place on Peniston Crag. Dur-ing the first run-through Olivier spluttered slightly on one of his lines. "Please don't spit at me!" Merle Oberon requested, and it seemed to him that her tone was unnecessarily frigid. Once more they played the scene and the same thing happened. Involuntarily he spluttered. "You spat again!" said Merle Oberon, and at this Oliv-ier suddenly lost his temper and said a number of things which he afterwards regretted. His rudeness magnified a trivial incident into ridiculous proportions, and they both marched off the set really angry. Wyler remained apparently unconcerned, and after a suitable pause asked them to come back. In the best tradition of the ruthless commanding officer who orders his pilots into the air immediately after a crash to prevent them losing their nerve, Wyler informed Olivier and Merle Oberon that he wanted them to play the scene again—the same scene. Still inwardly raging, the lovers returned to the conversation which had to suggest great depths of mutual passion. The camera searched their faces in vain for expressions of anything but love. "Cut!" called Wyler triumphantly when they had finished. "That's it! Perfect!"

Few actors would retain their reputations if the public saw the worst shots of every scene in which they appear. Fortunately most of the shots are never printed, and generally only the very best get beyond the cutting room. Goldwyn, however, made a point of seeing nearly all of them, good and bad, at the daily show of "rushes" and he was far more critical than Wyler of Olivier's performance. Wyler had been afraid he would not get enough of the dirty stable boy; Goldwyn thought he was getting far too much. He had gone to endless trouble to coax this difficult and expensive young man from England. He'd been assured Olivier was the best leading man available, and he was nagged by the suspicion that he wasn't getting value for money. As he complained explosively on one occasion, "His face isn't even clean." One day, shortly after he had watched the rushes of a scene in Cathy's bedroom in an early part of the film, he came on to the set, sought out Olivier and Wyler and placed one hand on each of their shoulders. Olivier half-expected a friendly benediction, but instead Goldwyn came out with an alarmingly direct remark. Turning to Wyler he said: "If this actor goes on as he is, I'll close the picture!"

This was a point in his career when Olivier was not accustomed to being treated like a schoolboy, even by someone as disarmingly frank as Goldwyn. He would have flared up, but he knew that Goldwyn was right. His interpretation in some scenes had been slap-dash; he hadn't evolved—hadn't bothered to evolve—a film technique. In his discussions with Wyler he might sneer, "Your poor anæmic medium can't take a full-scale performance," but he knew it was the actor who must conform to the medium.

Realism, as opposed to convention, was a quality he had always regarded as all-important on the stage; now, he saw, realism must be carried a stage further in the film studio because the camera, prying nearer than any audience, demanded the most delicate shades of subtlety. The camera could sometimes disguise an actor's inadequacy, but it was ruthless in exposing any hint of insincerity. As the weeks went by Olivier found that a considerable change was taking place in his acting. With an increased sympathy for Wyler's theories came an instinctive understanding of what was wanted. Sincerity became the key-note and his acting automatically more disciplined. In place of a "performance" of Heathcliff, theatrical and slightly larger than life, he substituted a real person in whom he himself could at all times believe.

III

A great deal of play was made by the studios about the authenticity of *Wuthering Heights* and the integrity with which Emily Brontë had been brought to the screen. The whole cast was British. A cameraman was sent to Yorkshire to take photographs of the moors so that they could be matched—stone walls, crags and heather —on a bleak stretch of country forty miles from Hollywood. Hecht and MacArthur had courageously used much of Miss Brontë's original dialogue. Merle Oberon's well-manicured hands were chapped and roughened by the make-up department. Museums were ransacked for sampler frames, and a doctor's stethoscope was banished when it was discovered that stethoscopes were not used before 1850. Somewhat less emphasis was placed on the fact that Goldwyn had switched the period forty years on from 1801 to 1841 because he did not like Merle Oberon in Regency dresses; that a bathtub scene had been introduced, and that the heath, a variety of heather several feet tall and cultivated in hot houses, was rather more luxurious than is usual in the West Riding. Only after the film was finished did Goldwyn decide to have the transparent ghosts of Cathy and Heathcliff reunited on Peniston Crag, and in the absence of Merle Oberon and Olivier had the scene shot with their stand-ins. Mr. Goldwyn's apologists were quick to point out that the cinema is a different medium to the novel and that therefore liberties were justified.

A few people may perhaps have wondered at the virtue of making a fuss about some details, if others were so flagrantly disregarded. Were these discrepancies the reasons why the film, rather like the translation of a foreign book, left them feeling, in a way which they could not explain, that the subtleties of the original had probably been lost? The general reception was enthusiastic, and the fine performances as well as Wyler's fastidious direction were highly regarded. And despite the enormous changes and inevitable condensing needed to bring the novel within the scope of a film, it was praised by a great many people from whom criticism might have been expected. Alexander Woollcott (under whose hospitable Vermont roof the script had been prepared) cooed: "Sam has done right by our Emily" and even stern members of the Brontë Society confessed themselves completely satisfied.

To the box-office, of course, obscure literary quibbles were a matter of absolute indifference. Nothing could prevent the success of a film billed as "The Strangest Love Story Ever Told"; however critical Olivier might be of his own performance, this one film was to build him into a star of international popularity. Within a few months a pleasant reputation among British theatregoers was inflated out of recognition. Under huge red lettering—THE MARK OF HELL WAS IN HIS EYES—Olivier's face, tight-lipped, suffering, and with a touch of green about the jowl, stared with hypnotic fascination from billboards all over the United States. His fan mail began to create a technical problem for the post office.

Popularity meant power, not just in terms of money, but in prestige. If he wanted to return to the studios in the future he would be able to choose his own films and to a large extent determine the way they were made. The danger of losing that independence by signing a long-term contract was neatly avoided. He was determined that nothing should divert him from the steady course of his career as an actor, and even while the film was being made he was arranging to return to the stage. A play in New York with Katharine Cornell was to be the corrective to an excess of movie fans.

The most important thing about *Wuthering Heights* for Olivier had nothing to do with fans who fought for his autograph, the reverent respect of the man on the studio gates, or the size of his name in lights over the entrance to cinemas. What was to matter in terms of his future was that for the first time he had found an interest in the cinema for other reasons than making easy money. Having previously rejected anything but the theatre as unimportant, he was now convinced that here was a medium in which he might one day do something really interesting. And it was William Wyler who had brought this about. The man whom he had described in a letter home soon after his arrival as "quite inarticulate and almost impossible to understand" he now regarded as something of a genius. He had come round to Wyler's theory that the cinema was potentially as interesting as the stage because there was equal fascination in trying to achieve perfection in either medium. As an actor he was to continue to find the stage infinitely more satisfying, but the technical side of films—the work of the director—was beginning to interest him more and more.

CHAPTER 4

"Gone With the Wind"
1938-1939

I

IN LONDON during the late autumn of 1938, while she was waiting impatiently for Guthrie to start rehearsals for the revival of *A Midsummer Night's Dream*, Vivien Leigh soon began to regret the decision she and Olivier had made. The high-minded insistence on a separation to suit their careers was not working out at all as they had planned. The sensible, business-like idea of spending three months apart, each artistically preoccupied, hardly survived three weeks. Letters, heavy with melancholy and air-mail stamps, were posted almost daily in the little hexagonal Victorian letter-box on the corner of St. Leonard's Terrace in Chelsea. In return, envelopes containing pages of distant woe from California dropped with a dull thud on to the mat at Durham Cottage.

Vivien Leigh read that Larry was exhausted (this heavily underlined) but putting on weight; that Wyler was difficult, and that he was not getting on well with Merle Oberon. Another letter announced that he was in pain and on crutches suffering from "athlete's foot." Yet another gave a highly-coloured description of his trouble with Goldwyn. To Vivien it seemed that all Hollywood was conspiring against Larry, and one day, when his moans reached a particularly mournful crescendo, she went straight out and bought a ticket to New York on the *Queen Mary*, booked an air reservation

179

from there to Hollywood, and sent a cable to say she was leaving immediately. She could be in Hollywood only five days because of rehearsals, and her friends said it was sheer madness and reckless expenditure. Vivien, hurriedly packing a small suitcase, agreed and hummed a little tune.

This holiday, which promised to establish a record for distance over duration, was to have unexpected and completely unpredictable consequences. As sudden as the change from the grey skies of an English December to the sunshine of Hollywood, was to come the chance to play Scarlett O'Hara in the film of *Gone With the Wind*. Little more than a week after she left London there was to be a revival of an idea which she had nursed as a fanciful dream ever since she had read the book in the September of 1936 soon after its English publication.

Over the years she had read snippets of news about the film in the papers. The screen rights of Margaret Mitchell's book had been bought by David O. Selznick for $50,000, a sum much publicized as the largest ever paid for a first novel, and Vivien Leigh had followed every report of the deal.

In May, just before the book was published in the United States, one of Selznick's New York staff, whose job it was to find stories, had airmailed a synopsis and a copy of the book, saying, "I beg, urge, coax and plead with you to read this at once. I know that once you read the book you will drop everything and buy it."

But Selznick did not drop everything; he just had a look at the synopsis. Any enthusiasm he might have felt for Civil War stories was tempered by his knowledge that Paramount had been saddled with a failure in *So Red the Rose;* also the price seemed very high. Nevertheless, he took a chance, and bought it. When the book became a best-seller throughout the United States he was confronted with a problem. It was going to be impossible to treat it with the usual disrespect and slash it, as he would have done an ordinary novel, to conform to the average film length. Too many people were going to be angry if the story were tampered with. So, reconciled to the idea of a long film, he handed the book over to Sidney Howard, the American dramatist, and asked him to prepare a script.

It was at this point that *Gone With the Wind* disappeared temporarily from the news, and Vivien Leigh only heard occasional gossip from Hollywood friends about what was happening. It seemed that a film shot from Sidney Howard's original script would have taken five and a half hours to show. He rewrote it twice, and then, in the time-honoured Hollywood tradition, everyone was dragged in to have a go at the adaptation. Such well-known authors as John van Druten, Scott Fitzgerald, Ben Hecht and Charles Mac-Arthur, among others, beat out their brains in the task of making a novel of over a thousand pages conform to cinema requirements. They all fell away frustrated, and, in fact, no final shooting script was ever completed.

Difficulties about the script were as nothing compared with the casting; but at least casting problems had publicity value. As Selznick knew, he could create interest even by the most tentative announcements. Only one character was so completely identified with a particular actor that he found himself powerless. The public seemed to have decided unanimously that Clark Gable was the one man for Rhett Butler, and this meant striking a bargain with M.G.M. to whom he was under contract. M.G.M.'s terms were high and made no allowance for the fact that Selznick was Louis B. Mayer's son-in-law. In return for Gable and an investment of $1,250,000 in the production, they were to have exclusive distribution rights and a half-share in the profits. Over the casting of Scarlett Selznick had more difficulty. To start with, both he and his director, George Cukor, thought it would be easier to recreate the book if the actress who played Scarlett had not been seen on the screen before. "Scarlett O'Hara Contests" were held all over the United States; magazines and newspapers canvassed their readers for suggestions; and the studios put it out that 1,400 girls had been interviewed and ninety tested.

All this sounded like the most outrageous stunt, and Selznick, who has a genius for whipping up publicity, was not unconscious of its value. But, in fact, he genuinely hoped to find a completely unknown girl for the part. Not until test after test had been made and the results thrown aside did he realize that the part was too exacting to be entrusted to any but a trained actress of considerable experience. So then began the testing of established stars among whom were Jean Arthur, Joan Bennett and Tallulah Bankhead. Rumours, whispered in Hollywood and spreading all over the world, gave the part at various times to Bette Davis, Paulette Goddard, Katharine Hepburn and several others.

It is now part of a legend, from which it is almost impossible to sift fact from fiction, that on one occasion Selznick's stunts rebounded on himself. Awakened one morning by his butler, he was asked to go down to the living-room and there found a huge copy of *Gone With the Wind*. The cover of the book was pushed back like a door and a girl dressed as Scarlett stepped out and asked him for the part. If this nightmare scene ever took place it may well have been closely paralleled by Selznick's actual bad dreams. As the date on which shooting was to start came nearer, the elusive Scarlett had still not been found.

This was the situation early in December when Vivien Leigh landed in Hollywood with no other idea than to see Olivier and to enjoy to the full her five days in the Californian sunshine. If she gave the matter a thought, or, after so much conflicting rumour, even knew that the part was still not cast, the idea of playing it seemed beyond her possible dreams. It had not, however, been beyond Olivier's. When he had heard that Vivien was coming to Hollywood he had asked his agent, Myron Selznick, who was David Selznick's brother, if it wasn't worth trying to get her the part. Perhaps it was a long chance; but it was just a chance. Myron Selznick, who knew his brother was in the fantastic position of starting the film without a Scarlett, said he'd think about it. Would Olivier like to bring her along to see the big exterior scene that was being shot in a few days' time? He'd give him a ring and fix a time to pick them up in his car. It was going to be the big fire in Atlanta, and promised to be very spectacular.

So it was that, a few days after she arrived in Hollywood, Vivien Leigh, with Olivier beside her and Myron Selznick at the wheel, drove along the road from Los Angeles. As they neared Culver City they saw the blaze, reflected against the night sky. On a forty-acre lot at the back of the old Pathé studios dozens of disused sets had been piled together to represent the city that Sherman so ruthlessly destroyed before starting his march to the sea. In a single night $26,000 worth of timber buildings soaked in kerosene was going up in smoke and flames.

For the production unit it was a long, hard night's work complicated by the fact that a number of differently-proportioned stand-ins had to be photographed in silhouette and long-shot to represent the still undecided Scarlett, in the scene where Rhett Butler drives a four-wheel cart through the blazing streets while the terrified Scarlett sits on the box beside him. It was 1 a.m. when the party from Hollywood walked up behind the seven Technicolor cameras which were shooting from different angles, and to the platform from which George Cukor, the director, and David Selznick were shouting through microphones. As they stood watching, Olivier glanced at Vivien Leigh. Her hair was streaming in the breeze; her eyes were alive in the reflection from the flames.

"Just look at Vivien to-night!" he said, taking Myron Selznick by the arm. "If David doesn't fall for that I'll be very surprised."

During a few minutes' break Cukor and Selznick turned their backs on the flames and, wiping the smoke from their eyes, came over to the party of visitors. David Selznick gave Olivier a friendly smile and turned with outstretched hand to the dark girl beside him.

"David," said Myron Selznick, "I'd like you to meet Scarlett O'Hara!"

It was said half-jokingly; but it might have been an embarrassing introduction. As it was, Selznick just nodded, and muttered something about having to get back for the final shots, and said he hoped to see them a little later. There was nothing to suggest to Vivien Leigh that this was a meeting which was to acquire almost Stanley-Livingstone fame in cinema history.

But an hour later, as they all sat chatting in his office, Selznick asked her if she was really serious about playing Scarlett. Vivien said she was—very. "All right," said Selznick, "you'd better have a word with George, here."

She and Cukor went off to an adjoining office to talk it over. At that stage in the game it was a matter of routine for Cukor to run actresses through the test, and he had stacks of scripts in his office. He selected one or two scenes, indicated them to Vivien Leigh, and, late as it was, asked her to read them. Simply, naturally, and in her English accent, she did so. Apart from her abilities, which impressed him considerably, Cukor was struck by her personality. There was a directness, candour, and general lack of affectation about her approach which he liked. She seemed a very probable candidate, and he reported so to Selznick later, adding that she had said that, given a fortnight, she was sure she could master the required Southern accent.

Vivien, too, had taken an immediate liking to George Cukor, and

it was with mounting excitement that she heard him say that, as
there was some urgency, he would like her to make a photographic
test as soon as possible. She told him that she was quite free.
"Good," he said. "Then shall we say to-morrow morning at the
studio—ten o'clock?"

A test. As they drove back to the Beverly Hills Hotel in the early
hours of the morning, Vivien did not allow herself to think of it
as any more than that. Just a test. She was merely going to follow
the ludicrous, over-publicized path of other girls who had been
tested for Scarlett. She was to have the honour of joining the galaxy
of distinguished rejects.

Cukor was true to his word. The next day she was putting on
the costume of Scarlett. "I strongly suspect," she told Olivier that
evening, "there was hardly time for the previous actress to get out
of it." She made no attempt for the first test to use an authentic
accent, and it was with her ordinary voice that she played the two
highly-contrasted scenes she was given. The first, which came
early in the film, was where she was laced into her dress by the
coloured Mammy before the barbecue; the other—considerably more
dramatic—was the one in which Scarlett tells the unwilling Ashley
that she loves him and that he *must* love her. All the other actresses
who had been tested had made it sentimental and tearful; she carried
it off with a high hysterical laugh which Leslie Howard (who had
been cast for the part of Ashley) thought very effective. It also
impressed George Cukor, who until then had thought her sufficiently
beautiful but had feared she might not be temperamental enough for
a woman so passionate, so full of fire, and so strange a mixture of
gaiety and petulance as Scarlett.

Selznick said he would be getting in touch with her as soon as a
decision was made, but several days went by without a message.
Her five-days' holiday was up, and on the day rehearsals were due
to start for *The Dream*, instead of being on the stage of the Old Vic
she was still in Hollywood. She sent a cable to Guthrie and followed it up with a tactful letter. To her relief Guthrie wrote back
to say that he would not stand in her way if she had a big chance
in Hollywood and that Dorothy Hyson was taking over the part
of Titania. Vivien Leigh made more tests to prove that her assurance about acquiring a Southern drawl had not been over-optimistic,
but still there was no decision, and she began to reconcile herself to

the belief that she had been consigned to the limbo of discarded Scarletts. She could not know that Selznick was delaying his announcement until he had sounded public reaction to his choice. He knew that to cast an English actress in the rôle of a girl who had virtually become an American national heroine was dangerous, but he thought the controversy it would arouse would be good publicity. He had the additional worry of whether Vivien's personal background could be made to fit the sugar-coated formula which publicity required for "unknown discoveries." Finally, however, he decided that publicity about the film was going to be so big that he need have few misgivings. On Christmas morning Vivien Leigh heard the news.

She and Olivier were invited by George Cukor to a party at his home in Beverly Hills, and when they got there Cukor took her to one side. As they sipped their drinks in the garden he told her casually that the final casting for *Gone With the Wind* had been made. Vivien Leigh, who had heard that Cukor secretly wanted Katharine Hepburn, prepared herself for the worst as she asked with equal casualness who they'd finally settled on for Scarlett.

"Well, I guess we're stuck with you!" he said cheerfully.

Nineteen days later, on Friday, January 13th, 1939, the contract was signed. At the same time Olivia de Havilland and Leslie Howard were announced for Melanie and Ashley. It was an announcement that went round the world, and film correspondents who had made so many fruitless attempts at exclusive prophecy sighed with relief.

Strangely enough it was not the American press which greeted the casting of Vivien Leigh as Margaret Mitchell's heroine with protests. Even in the South, which might reasonably have been expected to be prejudiced, comments were kind, a fact which puzzled her until she remembered how strong were the traditional associations of states like Virginia with Great Britain. It was the English papers which demanded to know how such a "Dresden figure" (the descriptive cliché that Vivien Leigh dislikes more than any other) could hope to play a fiery Southern belle. And how about her accent? Rather tartly she replied that it was part of an actress' equipment to be able to assume, and perfect, any accent within a short time. Eagerly she set out to acquire the Southern drawl, and this was achieved by much repeating of phrases like "Fo-o-ur door

Fo-o-ord" under the tuition of Will Price, then Maureen O'Hara's husband, who came from the South. She had a good ear and after a while Sue Myrick, the technical adviser from Georgia, would only occasionally have to pull her up with the tactful caution, "That's a bit *too* Southern, dear!"

From Vivien Leigh's point of view, the contract was not the one she would have chosen. It tied her to Selznick for seven years, but those were the only terms on which he would let her play Scarlett. He argued that if he was going to buy her contract from Korda, and build a little-known English actress into an international star in a fabulously expensive film, he wanted her for other films afterwards. She had no wish to be forced to spend so much of her time in Hollywood, and she knew that it would inevitably mean that she and Olivier would be separated for long periods. But once again, as before *Wuthering Heights*, this was the sacrifice that ambition demanded, and it was one which had to be faced. As Olivier wrote to Vivien Leigh's mother a month or so later: "It is difficult to make a decision to work apart, but I believe we were wise to make it, and that it will bid more for our ultimate happiness together to choose to work (even if we don't like it very much) at the expense of our temporary personal happiness."

Contrary to conventional ideas about Hollywood contracts Vivien Leigh's salary was not a large one. *Gone With the Wind* cost $7,000,000 (and was to take more than $45,000,000 at the box-office), but for playing Scarlett, the most coveted part in Hollywood, she was to be paid about $30,000.

II

During the early part of the five months it took to film *Gone With the Wind* Vivien Leigh was very happy. Each morning at six-thirty she would leave her home in Beverly Hills for the Selznick Studios, breakfast while being made up and having her hair done, and be on the set for the first scene at eight-forty-five.

From the very first day when she played the scene which opens the film—as the girl of fifteen in a white dress sitting on the porch at Tara flirting with the Tarleton twins—she was given great help with her performance by George Cukor. He always seemed cheerful and bubbling over with good humour, and she quickly discovered why so many actresses liked to be directed by him. He had a natural sensitivity, a quick sympathy when she was worried, and a pleasant way of gently overcoming any lack of self-confidence. Cukor found her all that he had hoped. As well as being hard working and adaptable, she had even rarer qualities of intelligence and of being unconventional in her approach to the part. Clark Gable, too, she thought, was kind. As he was a well-established star and she very much the newcomer—the unknown English "discovery"—he might easily have been less helpful on the set and less friendly off it. As it was, he let her teach him backgammon, which they played together while waiting, and he was soon confiding to her that he disliked the part of Rhett Butler. When she protested that surely he was ideally cast she discovered that his dislike could be reduced to the fact that he was never very happy in period costume. Leslie Howard also surprised her by saying that he did not like the part of Ashley. This was equally incomprehensible, for she found it difficult to imagine anyone who corresponded more with her idea of the character. As the days went by she found Gable a highly accomplished technician, nearly always easy to act with, while Howard, though charming and sensitive, was rather less predictable. The quiet vagueness, the almost spiritual quality which gave him so much of his charm on the screen, was also true of his own personality. It was comforting to find a player in the film who was more likely than she to forget or fluff a line.

It was just ten days after shooting started, when Vivien considered that everything was going perfectly, that she heard a rumour which sent both her and Olivia de Havilland flying to see David Selznick. Was it true, they asked, that George Cukor was to be replaced? Selznick said it was. They pleaded with him to retain the director whom they both so much liked, but he appeared determined on the change. The only reason he gave was that perhaps Cukor "lacked the big feel, the scope, the breadth of the production." It was more widely rumoured that Clark Gable, whose contract gave him the right of choice, wanted a director who would allow a rather more forceful and dramatic interpretation. Cukor, the specialist in delicate, intimate scenes, concentrated his attention more especially on the women's rôles. Whatever the true reason, he left, and at once Vivien found herself lonely and more than a little worried. She wrote home that she was badly upset by the change because she had loved working with Cukor and because the "poor wretch" of a new director, as she called him, was very tired, hadn't stopped working for ages, and had not even had time to read the book. Just how upset she was could be gauged from the last sentence in her letter. "I will never get used to this," she wrote. "How I *hate* film acting!"

The "poor wretch" was Victor Fleming, who had been chosen by Clark Gable from four directors whom Selznick had suggested to him. A tall, grey-haired man, whose experience dated from the early Hollywood days when he had worked with D. W. Griffith, Fleming seemed an excellent choice. But so disorganized was the production, and so internecine the studio politics, that within a month he was talking about quitting. He did not hit it off particularly well with Clark Gable, and Vivien Leigh was at first discouraged by his seemingly gloomy disposition. She was soon to discover, however, that he possessed a somewhat unusual sense of humour.

One day when they were filming the scene in which Rhett carries Scarlett up a long flight of stairs, a number of technical things went wrong and the scene had to be reshot six times. At the end of the sixth time Fleming had a whispered conference with the cameraman and sound engineer and then said: "Sorry, Clark! Just *once* more!" Clark Gable made a face and again picked Vivien Leigh up in his arms, only to be stopped by a laugh and a shout of "Cut!" from Fleming. "I don't really need another shot," he said, "I just had a bet you couldn't make it!"

Days at the studio were long, and Vivien Leigh was often on the set until nine at night. Meeting her for a few hours at the weekends, her friends were sometimes worried to see how exhausted she was, and one Sunday afternoon at George Cukor's she fell asleep on a couch beside the swimming pool in her wet costume. The sun was going down and Cukor was frightened that she might catch cold but had not the heart to disturb her. She looked completely tired out. He covered her with a thick blanket, and she continued to sleep there for hours. Working at high pressure was also bound to lead to tension and short tempers on the set, and on one occasion when an important scene she was playing with Leslie Howard kept going wrong Vivien was shocked to find herself behaving ungraciously. "For goodness' sake," she exclaimed to Fleming, "let's go and see the test scene that I did with Leslie . . . when George was directing!"

Afterwards she was sorry for the remark, especially when she saw the determined attempts which Fleming made to keep everyone in a good humour. "Take it easy," he would say to the cast, "we've only got three more days' work to do to-night!" Then, after time infuriatingly wasted in setting up the cameras for a difficult shot, he would come over to where she was waiting, give an elaborate bow and, using the nickname he had given her, say, "Now, Fiddle-de-dee . . ." Hardly had she got used to his methods, however, than he left after a serious disagreement with Selznick. In *Gone With the Wind* directors were expendable.* Sam Wood, who had just finished *Good-bye, Mr. Chips*, was the next to take over.

On one occasion Vivien worked from early in the morning until eleven o'clock at night at the studios, and then went out to the country for the scene (which had to be taken against the sunrise) where Scarlett falls to her knees in the fields of Tara with the vow that she will never be hungry again. They took the shot, and when she got back to her hotel at 4:30 a.m. it was almost twenty-four hours since she had left it. Long hours were less of a strain to her than the difficulty of maintaining consistency in Scarlett's psychological development—the development of a character who has so many varied emotional experiences between the ages of fifteen and twenty-eight. The episodic method of film-making always presents a problem for an actor or actress who has to convey subtle gradations of age, and in *Gone With the Wind* this was made even harder because the script was constantly being changed, scenes switched round, and dialogue rewritten.

Foreseeing this, Vivien Leigh asked for an opportunity to rehearse as many scenes as possible in their chronological order, but any hope of this soon went overboard. Often the cast only received late at night the lines they had to memorize for the next morning. She was faced with the problem of skipping from one unrelated scene to another with very little preparation. A single day's shooting schedule might include:

* Fleming and Cukor were only two of a number of people who started on the film but, because of fierce dissension within the studio, did not finish it. Among others were Lee Garmes, the cameraman, Sidney Howard, the author, and Hobe Erwin, the set director. Victor Fleming was credited as director on the final film, but considered that he had been so badly treated that he would not attend the Academy Award Dinner at which he would have been awarded the Oscar he had won for his work.

(1) Interior. Aunt Pitty's parlour, Spring, 1866.

(2) Exterior. Approach to Tara, Spring, 1861.

(3) Exterior. Rhett's house, Spring, 1872.

These scenes would not only require her to alter her age three times over this span of eleven years, but also to vary her mood to cover in Scene (1), Scarlett's good-bye to Rhett after his proposal, Scene (2), her anger when Gerald tells her that Ashley is going to marry Melanie, and Scene (3), her reaction when her daughter Bonnie falls from a pony and is killed.

If she was not to lose the thread of continuity, Vivien Leigh found she had to keep the novel constantly by her. This was a source of some surprise to the producer, who had rather lost sight of Margaret Mitchell in the rapidly changing drafts of the eleven different script-writers. Vivien saw some of her favourite dialogue thrown away—dialogue which she considered vital to an understanding of the character—and her occasional protests were met with the request from David Selznick that she "put away that dam book" and please just concentrate on the picture.

In twenty-two weeks Vivien Leigh took only five days off, a self-imposed strain which was quite unnecessary and was really the result of a longing to get the film finished. Much of the despondency she felt during the making of the film could be traced to the fact that Olivier had been forced to leave for New York a few weeks after she had started work. He rang her up frequently, regardless of the coast-to-coast charges, but however reassuring he was, she missed his advice and the day-to-day chance of quietly talking over any worries she had about the way the film was going. In his absence she grew to rely a great deal on the good counsel of George Cukor. Even though he had ceased to direct *Gone With the Wind* his influence on the film continued. Hardly a Sunday went by when he and Vivien did not meet so that she could confide in him, talk over her lines, and discuss any problems she had about the part. It was the basis of a friendship which has existed ever since.

III

No Time for Comedy had opened in Indianapolis at the end of March and after a month on tour settled down to a long run in New York. Olivier had accepted the part of Gaylord Easterbrook, the tempestuous young playwright of S. N. Behrman's comedy, because he wanted to act with Katharine Cornell and get back on the stage, and also, as he wrote home at the time, because he thought it "very important to get established in New York again if I can." It was a part which he quite liked, but he took it principally because of the value which he knew it would be to his career. He was casting his net widely. If he could build up a reputation on Broadway as well as in Shaftesbury Avenue, he need have no fears for the future. Behrman's play was just the success he expected, and, in a light comedy part which he could act on his head, he won exactly the sort of praise for which he had hoped.

Just before the New York opening at the Ethel Barrymore Theatre, he was given permission to fly to Hollywood for a day to see Vivien Leigh, and after they had talked over all her problems at the studios she asked him how he was enjoying his return to the stage. He thought for a moment and then said it was a strange experience. Although Behrman's play was a modern comedy, and acted in what was regarded as strictly "naturalistic" style, after the three months with Wyler it seemed to him that stage acting was highly artificial.

"It is difficult to explain exactly," he told her, "but Willy seems to have doused my old temptation to take off on exploratory flights —you know, the search for an unknown dimension! I'm quite shocked to find how exaggerated stage acting is after the films, I simply didn't notice it before; but now it seems to me that in the theatre audiences swallow dialogue and acting conventions which on the screen would draw howls of derisive laughter."

Vivien Leigh, looking for an explanation of her present dislike of film acting, found her feelings summed up much more by something he said a little later. It seemed to her that he hit on the perfect simile when he described film acting as just about as satisfying as looking at a Michelangelo fresco through a microscope.

"You may spot a few details that you might otherwise miss," he said, "but you lose the whole. It is impossible to get a full, free characterization. Frankly, I don't see how any actor can ever have the freedom to shape a character as he chooses on the screen. For instance, however much thought you put into Scarlett, and regardless of how well you play each individual scene, the sum total of your performance is going to depend entirely on the way the director and the blokes in the cutting room put the mosaic together."

If he admitted this, how on earth, she demanded, could he regard film acting as of any value?

"It gives you a chance to study your own technique," he said, "and it also teaches you the difficult trick of working up enough emotional voltage to act for the camera—the stimulus you get on the stage from the audience."

Leaving Vivien with this cold comfort to sustain her through the months which followed, he returned to New York and was soon to face a problem which had nothing to do with acting theories.

Wuthering Heights had its New York première during the early weeks of the run of *No Time for Comedy*, and suddenly the acclaim which had seemed pleasant enough outside the stage door of the Old Vic a year before became magnified into a regular nightmare at the Ethel Barrymore. After every performance he was besieged by admirers who mobbed him outside the stage door, thrust autograph books at him, and carried the battle for attention into the foyer of his hotel. One even insinuated himself into his suite by giving a false name on the house phone. Fans climbed on to the running-board of his car, and one night a particularly enthusiastic woman jumped inside. He asked her to get out, and when she refused said he was sorry, but he must insist. She then turned on him and called him a "lousy stinking so-and-so." The incident left him with the unpleasant sensation that the real feelings of fans hover on a thin dividing line between love and utter loathing.

Not all his fans were so hysterical and assertive, and he had a particularly soft spot for three girls of about sixteen named Nancy,* Beth, and Franny who attended the matinée performance regularly each week and whom he could see across the footlights sitting together in the front row of the orchestra stalls. As unfailing as their appearance was the carnation which they sent him. He would wear it as he left the theatre, and it was, paradoxically, this carnation which led to Olivier having a serious row with his more unruly admirers. After one matinée as he came out of the stage door the fans pressed forward as usual, seized his handkerchief, and dragged at his tie and coat. One grasping hand caught at his buttonhole, and the crushed petals fell on to the sidewalk. The destruction of the

---

* Nancy Perkins. Her enthusiasm was to have its reward seven years later. She became Olivier's New York secretary during the visit of the Old Vic, and again during the *Cleopatra* season on Broadway in 1952.

present from the three girls thoroughly irritated him. For too long, he decided angrily, he had accepted this sort of treatment as an occupational hazard; now they had gone too far. He announced that in future he would sign no autographs in the street.

Somehow the newspapers got to hear of his decision and interpreted it as unbounded conceit. Reporters were sent to ask him his reasons and he was unwise enough to tell them that he considered the request for autographs meaningless. "As for the autograph-hunters themselves," he said, "they want to see you, they want to touch you, but they are not nice about it. In fact they're dreadfully rude." He was being quite frank, but for a British actor on Broadway it was undiplomatic. When he opened his papers the following day he found the reports were highly sarcastic. The venom and mischief of a hostile press seemed to be unlimited and he was horrified to see himself quoted as saying, among other things, that he found playing opposite Katharine Cornell very boring. Under the headline LIFE AND LAURENCE OLIVIER ARE VERY DULL—BUT DEFINITELY there was an interview in the *World-Telegram* which, it seemed to him, was angled to make him look as pompous and conceited as possible. At this point his entire sense of humour deserted him and he resolved not to give any more interviews to a number of papers.

His resolution was strengthened when he found among the fans at the stage door, now considerably fewer in number, some who, to his mortification, actually showed signs that they had been crying. A deep-voiced boy in his early teens stepped forward and waved one of the papers under his nose. "Did you really say all this about us, Mr. Olivier?" he demanded sternly. Olivier replied that he mustn't believe all he read, but this did not seem to comfort him, and he disappeared shaking his head and muttering ominously, "I don't think this is very good publicity!"

Olivier was quite sure it wasn't, and from then on declined to talk to reporters. As, anyway, interviews always embarrassed him this seemed to him a wise move. He was not free to discuss his private life even had he wanted to, and he felt little more comfortable in answering intelligent questions about the stage. As he told one reporter, he still regarded himself as a student of acting, not a professor.

If his attitude about autographs had seemed like conceit his refusal to see reporters was regarded as only just this side of anarchy, and

for a while the papers gave him a very rough time. The stir die
down, but it left Olivier with a very definite prejudice which was to
last for the next ten years, and which has never quite disappeared
Because he would give only a few interviews over a period of years
and believed that an actor's performance should be its own and com
plete publicity, what little was known about him became embel
lished, and half-truths were twisted out of all recognition. And the
more nonsense he read about himself, the less sympathetic to the
press did he become and the more determined in his attitude. He
was left in a curiously unresolved position as he and Vivien Leigh
became more and more famous. To be part of a profession which
thrives on artificial publicity and not be tainted with it; to be "ap-
proachable" without being constantly accessible; to decide exactly
where public life ends and privacy begins; these are problems which
influenced by his experience in New York in 1939, he has never
completely solved.

IV

Towards the end of June *Gone With the Wind* was finished at
last, and Vivien Leigh found herself a little sad as she said good-bye
to the other members of the cast, the studio technicians—and to
Scarlett. She was longing for a holiday, but, although she was looking forward to joining Olivier in New York, and afterwards returning to England to see her parents and friends, the part in which she
had been immersed for so long had claimed more of her affection
than she had realized. When it came to the point, Scarlett was a
difficult person to discard.

In New York she went to see one of the last performances Olivier
gave in *No Time for Comedy* before he handed over the part to
Francis Lederer. By careful planning they had made their dates
coincide nicely. They could both sail to England on the *Ile de
France* and then, after a month's holiday, would go back to Hollywood together. Vivien had to be there in August for any retakes
which Selznick might find necessary, and Olivier would be starting
work, also at the Selznick Studios, in *Rebecca*. While he was reading Daphne du Maurier's book Selznick had apparently visualized
Olivier as Max de Winter. When he had come to the description
"His face was arresting, sensitive and medieval in some strange, inexplicable way . . ." he was said to have pencilled Olivier's name in

the margin. Olivier suspected that Selznick would have preferred Ronald Colman, but was well content to lend his face, medieval or otherwise, to so interesting a part.

They arrived in Plymouth at the end of July, and spent a short time in Malvern and London. For Olivier the pleasure of homecoming was lessened by a private sorrow. In the previous March, while he had been touring with Katharine Cornell, he had received word that his father had died after a stroke. The Reverend Gerard Kerr Olivier, who had become so proud of the son he had put on the stage, had been just a year away from his seventieth birthday when he died. He had been buried in the churchyard at Addington, the pretty Buckinghamshire village which had been his last parish.

It was also a holiday heavily overshadowed by fears of something always fastidiously referred to as "a state of emergency." But however much the dreaded word "war" might be avoided, there was an unmistakable significance in the air-raid shelters which were being dug in the parks, the filling of sandbags and the fitting of gas-masks at town halls. Hitler was threatening Danzig, and Europe had mobilized. Yet serious as the situation looked, it did not seem to Vivien to be as bad as after Munich the year before when she and Ursula Jeans had hurried to Chelsea Town Hall together to volunteer for civil defence work. The excitement of the 1938 crisis had given way to a mood of sombre resignation. Certainly in those early August days of 1939 there was nothing which seemed, either to her or to Olivier, to justify breaking the contracts which required their return to Hollywood.

Vivien thought that her mother badly needed a holiday, and impulsively swept her into a rush of packing and getting visas so that she could go to America with her. As Mrs. Hartley, her daughter, and Olivier stood on the deck of the *Ile de France* that carried them down Southampton Water and out to sea, they looked back at the fading coast-line of an England which, had they known it, was to be at war within three weeks.

CHAPTER 5

Failure on Broadway
1939-1940

I

THE ISLAND of Santa Catalina lies some twenty miles off the Californian coast and is just sufficiently far from Los Angeles to deter the great masses of holiday-makers. It provides a pleasant sanctuary for more leisurely visitors, and on the first week-end in September, 1939, Douglas Fairbanks, Jr., and his wife chartered a yacht and invited a few friends to sail over there. They would leave on the Saturday morning and there would be no need to return until the Tuesday, for Monday was Labor Day, when all the studios would be shut. Vivien Leigh told him she would be glad to join the party; it would make a pleasant break during the wearisome business of retakes for *Gone With the Wind* and something to keep her mind off the bad news from Europe. Fairbanks asked if her mother, who was staying with her, would also come along. Olivier, too, was able to take a few days away from the studios before he started work on *Rebecca*.

When they got down to the docks they found that Nigel Bruce, David Niven, Bob Coote, and a doctor who was a friend of the Fairbanks', were to be their companions. It promised to be a good weekend, for a number of other friends, including the Colmans, were taking their own boats over to the island. It was difficult, however, to avoid discussing the threat of war. "I see that Nevile Hen-

196

derson's flying back from Germany to-morrow with a personal message from Hitler," somebody said; and after that, although worry was uppermost in their minds, the sense of personal helplessness made them drop the subject. But try as they would to think of other things, it was impossible not to listen to every radio bulletin, and on the Sunday morning of September 3rd, as the yacht rocked at anchor in Emerald Bay, the whole party was up early. At about 8 a.m., Californian time, they switched on the portable radio and crowded round to hear the news. Suddenly all talk was stilled by the announcement that Britain was at war, and this was followed a little later by the solemn voice of the Prime Minister which was being re-broadcast from London. Like millions all over the world they heard how Germany had been given until 11 a.m. to promise withdrawal from Poland; they listened in almost unbearable suspense until the final phase, which was so simple, but which was to mean so much for everybody: "I have to tell you now that no such undertaking has been received and that consequently this country is at war with Germany."

Vivien Leigh was suddenly conscious that tears were running down her cheeks, and after the radio was switched off nobody spoke for a long time. Each was busy with private thoughts. Nearly everyone in that party was British; all had friends or relatives in a London which even then, they knew, might be having its first air-raid. Vivien's thoughts were centred on Suzanne her daughter, and the hope that she was somewhere safe in the country. When drama is so vast adequate response is not possible; with a few perfunctory remarks everyone broke away to different corners of the ship to keep his own counsel.

Douglas Fairbanks and his wife went to their cabin, and Vivien Leigh and Olivier also felt the need for privacy to talk things over. It was difficult to make plans; impossible to know—when you were abroad and your country was at war—what to do for the best. Ought they to go straight back to England? And if they did, would Olivier be able to join up at once? Surely there was to be no repetition of 1914, with volunteers flocking gallantly to recruiting centres to take the shilling and join the Colours? Wasn't there something about "age-groups"? And, most important of all, what about their children? Would they be able to bring Suzanne and Tarquin to Amer-

ica out of danger of air-raids, and would that be the fit and patriotic
thing to do?

With little decided, they rejoined the others who were slowly
drifting back on deck. They found Douglas Fairbanks setting out
glasses. "I know it's early," he said, "but I think we should drink
a toast to victory." The toast drunk, David Niven announced cheerfully that he was going water-skiing. That broke the tension and
everyone began to smile. As he watched him fitting on the skis and
the motor-boat was started, Olivier could not help admiring Niven's
coolness. As a former Regular Army officer Niven was on the Reserve, and would leave for home and active service almost immediately. At the same time Olivier rather envied him; all problems
of his immediate future were solved. In wartime it is rather pleasant
not to have to make your own decisions, and to allow fate and the
High Command to take over your destiny.

II

As soon as they got back to the mainland Olivier, like the rest of
the British Colony in Hollywood, got in touch with the Consul in
Los Angeles for advice. The Consul said the directive was for actors
"to stay put" and "not to panic." Olivier was not panicking in the
very least, but he was fretting; at thirty-two he had no wish to
remain in Hollywood making films while England was at war. He
had little patience with the policy of the British Embassy in Wash-
ington, which had now decided that it would be good propaganda
in America for "the best type of Englishmen" to be seen on the
screen. He thought it much more likely that Americans would
wonder why, if they were the best type, they weren't at home in
uniform. However, it was apparently no good returning until his
call-up was due and so he and Vivien Leigh tried to forget their
frustration in work at the studio.

Their own decision not to act together had quickly worn thin,
but no sooner did they plan to be in the same film than they were
promptly confounded by the studios. Vivien had rather hoped for
the part of the gauche and timid second wife of Max de Winter in
Rebecca, but Selznick had apparently decided that Scarlett had now
firmly placed her in the tempestuous class. The idea that the film
public could accept an actress as tempestuous and timid in successive
films was beyond reason, and the part went to Joan Fontaine. But

when *Rebecca* and the retakes of *Gone With the Wind* were finally finished there seemed a real chance of playing together—in fact, two chances.

The raiding of Victorian classics was providing hostages for the latest Hollywood "cycle," and M.G.M. had decided to film *Pride and Prejudice*. This would normally have been a matter for alarm, and not only among the Janeites; but it seemed (until the public saw the result) that Jane Austen's integrity was guaranteed by the fact that Aldous Huxley was preparing the script. Edmund Gwenn was the obvious choice for Mr. Bennet and George Cukor who was then going to direct it, thought Olivier would be ideal for Darcy and Vivien Leigh for Elizabeth Bennet. Almost concurrently S. N. Behrman was preparing the script of *Waterloo Bridge* with Vivien Leigh in mind for the ballet dancer and with a definite idea of Olivier for the hero. Vivien longed to play Elizabeth Bennet, but the studio announced her for *Waterloo Bridge*. So she asked George Cukor to do some lobbying on her behalf. If he could persuade Louis B. Mayer to replace her by Joan Crawford, she and Olivier could both be in *Pride and Prejudice;* if that failed, they could still be together in *Waterloo Bridge*. For days the alternatives hung in the balance, but the arrival of Greer Garson in Hollywood unexpectedly tipped the scales. M.G.M. decided she was the ideal Elizabeth Bennet, and at the same time cast Robert Taylor for *Waterloo Bridge*. It was an almost classic example of falling between two stools.

III

In the middle of October Vivien Leigh, writing to her mother who by then had returned to London, told her that *Gone With the Wind* had been shown privately. This was the first intimation of an event for which the drums were to beat louder and louder until December, when the film had a première in Atlanta on a scale which deprived even the publicity men of sufficient superlatives.

Selznick invited all the stars who were in the film to fly down, and, for good measure, a number who were not. With Olivia de Havilland, Vivien Leigh, Claudette Colbert and Olivier, he flew from Hollywood in a specially chartered plane. Clark Gable and his wife Carole Lombard followed in another, which trailed a streamer proclaiming in large letters: M.G.M.'S GONE WITH THE WIND.

But Selznick's understandable displeasure at M.G.M.'s arbitrary claim was quickly swallowed up in the general excitement. The Governor of Georgia had declared a state holiday in honour of the event and Atlanta itself was dedicated to a five-day fiesta.

As the planes came to a halt on the tarmac crowds surged forward and huge bouquets of roses were thrust into the arms of Vivien Leigh and Olivia de Havilland. The cars in which they travelled from the airport to Atlanta moved at the pace of a coronation procession through three miles of cheering people. It was a crowd, according to one reporter's caustic estimate, larger than the combined armies which had fought for Atlanta in 1864. Confetti was thrown at a smiling and waving Vivien; Confederate flags were waved, as well as being flown (in amity with the Stars and Stripes) from every flag-pole.

The Grand Theatre, at which the première was held, had its entire façade altered by the fixing of white columns to the front to make it look like Tara, the home of the O'Haras. Seats for the première were being sold at the box-office for $12 each, and, unofficially, one block of eight seats went for $1,250. At a costume ball, Atlanta's and Selznick's most elaborate publicity stunt, costumes from the films were worn and the guests appeared in crinolines, cut-aways and top-hats. It had been feared that the arrival of Olivier with Vivien Leigh in Atlanta might give rise to gossip, and at the ball where the famous from Hollywood were introduced over the microphone the mayor was warned of this pitfall. With the worldly air of a man who knows how to dispel any hint of indiscretion from the atmosphere he indicated Olivier. "And now," he said, "I am going to introduce a gentleman who is here in Atlanta strictly on his own business!"

After Atlanta the circus moved on to New York where there was another première on an only slightly less exuberant scale. The film opened simultaneously at the Astor and the Capitol, and the papers, noting Vivien Leigh's absence, decided she was scared of the reception. While all the ermine, chinchilla and mink in Manhattan appeared to be converging on the two cinema houses, she and Olivier had slipped away quietly for dinner at the Chambord. After all, it was a very long film; and they *had* seen it before. More important to Vivien than craning necks and whirring news-reel cameras was the estimation of the few critics and fellow-artists whose opinions

she trusted. She had risked disappointing the public simply by accepting the part of the most famous heroine in modern fiction. She
herself did not consider she was as good as she should have been,
but nevertheless one critic's verdict was particularly welcome.

"Any other actress in the part," wrote Frank S. Nugent in the
New York Times, "would be inconceivable." This was a vindication
of Selznick's choice and justification for her belief, sustained over
two years, that she could play Scarlett. It was an instinct which she
was to feel again some years later when she read the parts of Sabina
in *Skin of Our Teeth*, Antigone in the modern version by Jean
Anouilh, and Blanche Du Bois in *A Streetcar Named Desire*. Scarlett was the first of four blows aimed at the "Dresden figure," the
popular image of herself which she so much disliked.

Gone With the Wind established her, as *Wuthering Heights* had
Olivier, as a screen personality of world-wide popularity, and won
her an "Oscar" for the best performance of the year. To people in
Hollywood who had seen so many actresses develop into stars,
Vivien's reaction to her fame was surprising. Although this one success made her a far more important star in the motion picture world
than Olivier, her sense of values remained unchanged. As one of
their closest Hollywood friends, a famous director, was to write
some years later. "As a result of *Gone With the Wind* Vivien was
the 'hottest' thing in pictures; she was a really big movie star. In all
this her professional attitude to Larry never changed in the slightest;
she deferred to his professional judgment; in her eyes their relative
positions had not altered in any way; he was the great, talented
actor, and she the promising, young, not too important actress who
had not yet accomplished a great deal. Her success as a picture
actress never seemed to matter to her. She wanted to accomplish
things on Larry's terms. She always felt that his was the great and
important destiny, and she never let anything interfere with this. I
think her incentive for her development as an actress was to be on a
par with him."

The film itself was to create every sort of record. According to
those statistics which bring art down to terms in which it is immediately comprehensible from Sheffield to Seattle, it was seen by 100,-
000,000 people before October, 1947, and by that date had already
taken $35,000,000 at the box-office. In Britain 12,000,000 people
have seen it, which is not entirely surprising when it is remembered

that at one cinema alone, the Ritz in Leicester Square, it ran for four
and a half years, or two hundred and thirty-two consecutive weeks.
Even in provincial cities it established comparable records with
nearly six months in Manchester, four and a half in Glasgow, and
four in Birmingham. To Vivien Leigh it is a flattering if somewhat
unnerving thought that there is one member of her adoring public
who has seen it thirty-three times.

IV

During the early part of 1940 it was noticed in the M.G.M.
studios, where they were filming *Pride and Prejudice*, that Darcy
was unusually preoccupied. A stills cameraman taking an informal
picture of Olivier between scenes produced a photograph which
showed him, a neglected film script slipping down between his
knees, writing in a portfolio with fierce concentration. In another
part of the studios where *Waterloo Bridge* was being filmed, Vivien
Leigh was devoting her lunch period in her dressing-room to mysterious conferences, and regularly at mid-day Dame May Whitty
would call on her. At night in the large drawing-room of the house
which Olivier had leased next to Danny Kaye's on San Ysidro
Drive, voices were to be heard declaiming Shakespeare. For as long
as it is possible to keep anything quiet in Hollywood they managed
to conceal what was afoot. But in a letter to her mother Vivien
wrote: "We have a beautiful plan to do *Romeo and Juliet* in New
York, and I do pray we can. Larry would direct it himself; we can
hardly think of anything else all day. I am having voice lessons
four times a week and Larry has suddenly started to *compose* music
and nothing will stir him from the piano. He is extremely proud of
his achievements and writes them out and *signs* them! When I say
'them' I mean 'it'—so far, but still *it's* very good! It's his own
entrance music for Romeo. Now he's going to compose mine for
Juliet—unless I can do it for myself."

The idea, which had been in Olivier's mind ever since he had
planned his own unrealised production four years before, had been
revived in a determination to have one last fling in the theatre before
going back to Europe and war. "Why don't you do *Romeo and
Juliet* for a few weeks?" George Cukor had suggested when they
discussed the idea, and he had written to Ralph Richardson, who by
now was quite accustomed to being consulted like a Delphic oracle

before nearly every big step in Olivier's career. The oracle, now in the Fleet Air Arm and on active service, had written back to say that he thought *Romeo and Juliet* sounded "a bit too luxurious for wartime," but for once Olivier ignored his advice. Elizabeth Montgomery and Peggy Harris, who (with Miss Harris' sister Sophia) made up the firm of Motley, were invited from England, and arrived with rough sketches for the production which were irresistible. Search began for a suitable cast, and Olivier persuaded Dame May Whitty, rather against her will, to take on the nurse, Alexander Knox, an old Vic companion, to play Friar Laurence, and Edmund O'Brien Mercutio.

Once started, there was no going back, and Olivier and Vivien Leigh poured their entire savings of about $60,000 into the venture. A backer among the film magnates was easily found to put up the same amount. With $120,000 they could have a sumptuous production, and satisfy Olivier's long-standing wish for a décor which really suggested Italy of the Renaissance. At the old Vitagraph studio a large and intricate set was built on a revolving stage, to allow the rapid change of the twenty-one scenes and yet still retain the time unity. In the past Olivier had often felt that slow or clumsy changes obscured the sequence and the swiftness of the tragedy. Everything must be concentrated on conveying the idea of the meeting of the young lovers on Sunday, the marriage on Monday, the separation on Tuesday and their death on the morning of Thursday. "I wanted to stress," he wrote later, "the human tragedy of the play, the tight, driving tragedy that catches the characters like straws in a whirlwind and drives them on to their inevitable destinies."

It was a tall order, but working on Olivier's basic idea of a permanent set the Motleys devised one which ingeniously gave the audience a view of the three most important scenes in rapid succession. Its design was logical and functional. In the first scene, which showed the inside of the Capulets' house, was a staircase which led to Juliet's bedroom. It was a genuine staircase and really *did* lead to the bedroom as the audience saw when the stage revolved and the bedroom was revealed. Similarly, in the bedroom was a glimpse of a balcony beyond long windows; with another turn of the stage the balcony was seen from the front and from the outside of the house, with the garden below, showing the wall over which Romeo was to climb. The Motleys enjoyed devising the costumes and scenery for the play, but were appalled by the American production costs. They would insist, half seriously, that they had built the whole London production of *Macbeth* for the cost of the wigs in *Romeo and Juliet.*

Ever since he could remember, Olivier had visualized Juliet as a slight, dark-haired girl, little more than a child. To emphasize her extreme youth in the scene when she waits in Capulet's orchard for the nurse with a message from Romeo, he made Vivien play with a ball, which she bounced against the wall, altering the rhythm with childish impatience to suit the varying moods of the soliloquy which starts: "The clock struck nine when I did send the nurse . . ." On the line when she sees the nurse—"O God, she comes!"—the ball was flung away with sudden abandon.

Vivien Leigh, on tiptoe with excitement at playing Juliet, realized at once how difficult a part it was and what immense reserves an actress had to have at her disposal. She was cheered by the knowledge that Fanny Kemble had played Juliet at seventeen, but she quickly learnt the truth of the old theatrical saying that no actress can play Juliet until she is too old for the part. She found that her main difficulty was not the potion scene, which is usually regarded as the greatest challenge for a young actress, but the lyrical passages such as those in the balcony scene. At the great climax the emotional sweep of the tragedy carried her along; it was in the delicate love scenes that she was conscious of her lack of technique. Then, she knew, she lacked variety in her reading and had not the maturity and knowledge that would have helped her project the subtleties she wished to convey.

Olivier's performance was not radically different from the one which had caused so much controversy at the New Theatre. He now gave the verse more music and had tidied Romeo's hair, but he still pictured Romeo as the immature, awkward boy who in a few days comes to manhood as a result of his love. He saw Juliet as the more dominating character of the two, and with infinitely more humour. Romeo, he decided, had no sense of humour, but, for once, this did not make him like the character any the less. "I shall never love a part as much as Romeo again!" he wrote enthusiastically to his sister during rehearsals.

Carried along on the tide of their own enthusiasm, encouraged by

magnificent advance publicity, and with the good wishes of all
their Hollywood friends, they opened the play in San Francisco.
Alexander Woollcott added his always ready voice to the preliminary fanfares. Turned actor for a season, he was playing in *The
Man Who Came to Dinner* at the Curran Theatre in San Francisco,
which was next door to the Geary where *Romeo and Juliet* was to
open. He was there a week ahead of them, and this meant that for
the second week of his run Shakespeare would be running in direct
competition. This did not prevent him devoting his nightly curtain
speech to them. He told his audience that he had seen Olivier's
Romeo in London, and there had never been a Romeo like it. His
enthusiasm, always expansive, extended to treating Olivier and
Vivien Leigh to oyster breakfasts on the balcony of his hotel, and
during one of them, they agreed to give an extra matinée so that he
would have a chance to see the production.

Between the completion of filming at M.G.M. and the opening in
San Francisco there had been a short, precipitous and utterly exhausting rush. The combination of acting, producing and supervis-
ing music imposed a great strain on Olivier, who worried continually
over every detail of the elaborate production. It had been a greater
strain than he realized, and only on the first night, and at a most
unfortunate moment, did he discover how physically fatigued he
really was. When the moment came for him to vault over the wall
out of Capulet's garden, he caught the top of the wall, but found
he had not sufficient strength to jump over it as he had always done
successfully at rehearsals. To his extreme mortification he was left
hanging, weakly kicking his legs, until obscured by the merciful
black-out.

There were a few caustic comments from the critics, but, on the
whole, the press gave the production an enthusiastic send-off, and
after playing to record business, they moved to Chicago. A welcome had been guaranteed in the Middle West by advance trailers
in cinemas which announced the arrival of "the Great Lovers in
Person," and thousands of fans swarmed to the Union Station in
Chicago to greet them with cheers and banners. They played in
the Chicago Auditorium, a vast theatre almost twice the size of
Drury Lane, which had been built for opera. From its four thousand seats fans shouted themselves hoarse every night. The cheers
at the final curtain seemed a more substantial argument in the pro-

duction's favour than slick newspaper wisecracks. Finding fault
with Olivier's bouncing performance, one writer retitled the play
"Jumpeo and Juliet," while another compared him with "a bump-
tious football half-back." Such criticisms could not be taken seriously, and it did not occur to them that cheap levity might be a
cloak for deeper, more genuine misgivings about the production.
Into it Olivier had put his whole heart and years of experience, and
had filled it with charming details and subtleties; all would be well,
he felt sure, when they got to New York and faced the really dis-
cerning critics and serious theatregoers. There was no complacency
in this belief. He took no chances; much of the play was re-re-
hearsed in Chicago, fresh scenery built, and hours devoted to lighting rehearsals with special equipment which was rushed from New
York. More money was recklessly poured into the production, and
any protests by the business manager were silenced by Olivier's insistence that everything must be ready for the great opening at the
Fifty-First Street Theatre on the second Thursday in May.

One thing neither Olivier nor Vivien Leigh reckoned on, simply
because they knew nothing about it. This was an undercurrent of
public resentment which, encouraged here and there in the press,
was being built up in New York long before they arrived. Many
people took it as significant that the theatre into which the production was going was owned by a film company and had only recently
had its name changed from the Hollywood Theatre. Here were
two English film stars, one of whom had never appeared on Broadway before, covered in cinema glory and backed from the bottom-
less coffers of a Hollywood magnate. The publicity that shrieked
ahead from Chicago was of unabashed vulgarity ("See real lovers
make love in public"). None of this was Olivier's own fault except
that, as he agreed on reflection later, he should have had the foresight
to see that an all-Hollywood set-up might create the wrong impression. If only they could have come modestly and unheralded into
a small New York theatre and allowed the critics and public to discover for themselves the quality of their production, all might have
been very different. As it was, it would have required a superlative
production to overcome prejudice.

There was absolutely nothing to warn them about all this. They
were too deeply involved to be able to step outside the play and
gauge something as intangible as public opinion. Cheerful figures

told of advance bookings in New York which amounted to hundreds of thousands of dollars, and, with everything apparently set for a triumphant opening, they made lavish preparations for a long run. Olivier sent to California for his car, booked an expensive apartment, accepted Katharine Cornell's offer of her house at Sneden's Landing on the west shore of the Hudson for weekends, and ordered in crates of wine for the parties they would throw to celebrate their success.

On the first night the play went smoothly until the scene in which Juliet takes the vial of poison and then, during the long tragic soliloquy which is Juliet's invocation of death, Vivien Leigh suddenly became aware of a banging of doors, fierce whispering, and some sort of commotion in the orchestra stalls. When she came off-stage she was told that a crowd of fans who had been swarming outside the theatre throughout the performance had succeeded in breaking in from the street. They had come through a side exit door, had stampeded into the gangways, and had had to be forced out by the theatre attendants.

This disturbance did not upset the play unduly, however, and at the end a packed house applauded with apparent enthusiasm. The first hint they had that all was not well came only after the curtain had fallen for the last time. Hardly any of the friends they knew had been in front came round to see them. Instead of the usual congratulations of the dressing-room and the sycophantic assurances that they had been wonderful there was only an exclamation of appreciation from Sam Goldwyn and some polite, but far from overwhelming compliments from their friend, John C. Wilson, the Broadway impresario. But it was not until the following morning when their secretary, her eyes red and swollen from crying, brought in the papers that their worst fears were confirmed.

"The worst Romeo ever," said one paper. "Laurence Olivier talked as if he were brushing his teeth," said another. In a third the critic commented that, should it be argued in favour of the production that the audience had taken it quietly, the most likely explanation was that they were fast asleep. Quickly they turned to the *New York Times* for the more temperate judgment that could always be expected from Brooks Atkinson. But here, once again, they stared at a description of disaster which was all the more chilling for being obviously sincere and considered. He wrote that the production had swallowed up the play and that "excepting a stray scene or so little of it can be heard. None of it recaptures the heat and passion of the tragedy."

Although Miss Leigh and Mr. Olivier are handsome young people [he went on] they hardly act the parts at all, and Mr. Olivier in particular keeps throwing his part away. His only passion is one for detail. In twenty-one pedantically staged scenes he has gone through the text with an eye for spectacle. Everything is solid; the doors close with a proper bang; the hardware makes an honest rattle. The costuming is full of splendour and Robert Edmond Jones' lighting follows the clock round accurately and handsomely. Bells ring off-stage. The orchestra is busy all the evening with music and "traditional" airs. Palestrina chants point up the religious episodes. But you cannot have this sort of spectacle and a play at the same time. To mount it Mr. Olivier has had to set it deep in the stage where the mechanical equipment moves easily. Even from the orchestra seats the performance seems remote from theatre-going and too far away to be heard. Mr. Olivier's industry is more admirable than his judgment.

Miss Leigh's slender, girlish beauty is perfect for Juliet. Fourteen years are not too few for the willowy innocence of her personality. Let it also be said in her favour that she makes an earnest attempt to act the part as it is written. But she is not yet accomplished enough as an actress to go deep into the heart of an imaginative character wrought out of sensuous poetry.

Mr. Olivier is more gifted personally than most actors who play the part of Romeo, and he is also a widely-experienced actor. The superficiality of his acting is difficult to understand. He is mannered and affected, avoiding directness in even simple episodes. In costumes that flare extravagantly at the shoulders, he looks like a belligerent sparrow when he scurries across the stage. Most of the time he speaks for Juliet's private ear, dropping his voice at the end of the lines as though they did not matter. As his own director Mr. Olivier has never heard himself in the performance. That is just as well; he would be astonished if he did. . . .

After such a broadside the other quickly scanned comments on their production and performances—"plodding and uninspired," "explosive and incomprehensible," "singularly hollow"—were light wounds from grapeshot, but still painful. In everything they read there seemed to be animosity. No paper went so far as to say that the disturbance during Juliet's death scene was actually a publicity stunt, but the implication was that such hysterical behaviour was all that could be expected if film stars were allowed to appear on the stage.

"This can't be us—it can't!" muttered Olivier after they had opened all the papers, and then, as if to shake off the nightmare and get a grip on reality, he phoned the theatre. He asked the box-office manager if there was any reaction. "Yes, they are queueing up right round the theatre," came back the reply. "Queueing?" A moment's renewed hope. "Yes, they are asking for their money back. What shall I do, Mr. Olivier?"

"Give it to them," he said. "If that's how they feel, give it to them!" It was a decision that was to cost him $1,250 a day for the next fortnight.

Quite suddenly and coldly he knew that they were going to lose every penny of the savings they had put into the production. He acted as if constant failures had conditioned him to deal with such emergencies. Lifting up the house phone, he told the manager of the hotel that he would be checking out. He told his secretary that he would live permanently at the house at Sneden's Landing; he called the floor waiter and asked him to arrange for the immediate return of the wine. In the midst of all these tactical withdrawals, their secretary came in with the announcement that John had arrived. "John? Who the devil's John?" Olivier asked, turning to Vivien Leigh, and then suddenly he started laughing. This was taking the absurd too far. It was their chauffeur who had been driving their Packard night and day from Hollywood so that they would have the car in New York for the triumphant day after their opening.

That night there was a "War Relief" Ball, organized by Noël Coward, which was being held at Radio City. They had agreed to attend some time before, and, as it was in aid of Britain, they decided that they must fulfil their promise. Noël Coward was there to meet them with a slightly strained smile. His greeting, about which they were all to laugh in the years to follow, confirmed their worst suspicions. "My darlings," he murmured, "how brave of you to come!"

BOOK FOUR

Marriage

CHAPTER 1

Secret Wedding
1940-1941

I

DURING THE WEEK the star-crossed production of *Romeo and Juliet* opened in New York, events in Europe tended to make theatrical misfortune seem comparatively trivial. The Low Countries fell, and the same newspapers which were damning the play were carrying screaming headlines on the front page to say that England faced the threat of immediate German invasion. The safety of their children now became the chief concern of Olivier and Vivien Leigh. As the play limped towards the close of its four weeks' run they determined that whatever happened both Tarquin and Suzanne must be brought across the Atlantic. Olivier's son was not yet four; Vivien Leigh's daughter six. Already, they read, children were being sent over by the shipload, and so Olivier wrote to Jill Esmond, and Vivien Leigh to her mother to ask if the children could possibly be brought to America. The trouble was to know how to support them once they arrived.

Each night Shakespeare's lines came—as lines in plays so often will —to taunt them. "It is too rash, too unadvised, too sudden," Juliet would say from the balcony, and Romeo, calculating his financial losses below, thought the words hideously true. It did not help that during this speech he had to stand in a way which gave him a stiff neck while he listened to them. "Not only is it a most uncomfortable position," he would comment, "but it is costing me $1,250 a night."

After a fortnight he countermanded the order that anyone who wanted could have his money back on advance bookings. Pride was becoming too expensive. Even so, it was obvious that they were going to lose every penny of their $60,000. Quite apart from the problems of the children and finance, what was their duty now that the phoney war was over and England directly threatened? While the British Embassy was still deprecating the return of British citizens from America, to go back home penniless and with no qualifications for service seemed senseless. But Olivier sent a cable to Mr. Duff Cooper, an old friend and the Minister of Information, asking if he should come home. At the same time he wrote to Richardson about his chances for the Fleet Air Arm. From Duff Cooper he received a somewhat mystifying reply. "Don't hurry home," said the cable. "You may be more use where you are." Richardson was equally discouraging. He said there was no chance in the Fleet Air Arm for anyone without experience over the age of twenty-eight. Pilots were accepted, however, up to the age of forty-five according to experience, and Richardson wondered if he couldn't get some flying practice. A few years before Richardson had taken Olivier to the London Aero Club at St. Albans and later to Hatfield at the weekends. Olivier had taken lessons, had borrowed Richardson's plane, and had actually flown a couple of hours solo. He didn't care much for flying, but at least this was a chance to do something while still in America. There was a little seaplane base at Sneden's Landing on the Hudson, opposite the house he had been lent by Katharine Cornell, and he started to learn all over again. Gallantly and with an assumed confidence she was very far from feeling, Vivien Leigh would sometimes go up with him, furiously knitting Balaclava helmets to avoid looking out at the lurching landscape below.

At the back of Duff Cooper's mind when he sent the cable had been the arrival of Alexander Korda in America. Korda stopped in New York long enough to see *Romeo and Juliet* before flying out to Hollywood, where, he told them, he was planning to make a propaganda film. His film *The Lion Has Wings* had been an outstanding success in America, and now his idea was to make another patriotic British film. He had come to the States because, apart from practical advantages of filming in a country at peace, he wanted American distribution. This would help to get the film shown in the neutral countries where support for Britain was most needed. Korda told them he was still searching for a suitable subject—a film about Chatham, perhaps, or the younger Pitt—and if possible he would like them to play in it. With this prospect, vague as it was, he left them a little more optimistic about their future.

Although they did not hear about it until much later, in the plane which carried him across the United States to Hollywood Korda became engrossed in a book by Admiral Alfred Mahan, the American naval historian, and from it he suddenly got the idea for a film. It would be the story of a war which had an extraordinary parallel with the one which England was fighting, and two main parts which would suit Olivier and Vivien Leigh perfectly.

They first learnt about it when the telephone rang one evening a few weeks later in the house at Sneden's Landing and the operator said that California was on the line. A few moments later Olivier heard the excited voice of Korda, who, with hardly any preliminaries, demanded abruptly, "You know Nelson and Lady Hamilton, eh?" Quite unprepared for such a suggestion, Olivier said he didn't think he did. "Yes, Larry, you *know* them!" Korda insisted. The film he had in mind was a story of Nelson; R. C. Sherriff was already working on the script; Korda's brother Vincent was to be art director; and he himself was going both to produce and direct. It was, he thought, the ideal subject for a propaganda film. "Propaganda, Larry, can be bitter medicine," he said. "It needs sugar coating— and Lady Hamilton is a very thick coating of sugar indeed." He knew they wished to return home, but he would be ready to start in September and to keep down costs it would be made fast—in probably not more than six weeks.

It seemed a heaven-sent chance. Out of their salaries from the film they would be able to pay for the children to stay in America for the duration, and save just enough to live on in England until Olivier was wanted in uniform. As it was then only the middle of July they had time to visit a few friends in the East before going to California. They went to see Woollcott on his island home on Lake Bomoseen and Katharine Cornell at Martha's Vineyard.

During the exhilarating week they spent on Woollcott's island they soon learned why someone had called it the Isle of Unrest; the

strenuous schedule of activity demanded by their host left them no
time for reflections about their recent catastrophe. With George
Kaufman and Alice Duer Miller, who were fellow-guests, they were
briskly dragooned into bathing or into a special brand of rough
croquet which, as Woollcott admitted, was "no game for the soft
of sinew and the gentle of spirit." It was croquet which recognized
few rules and no limits and which was played far beyond the edges
of a lawn, through trees and over hillocks. Competition became
hardly less fierce with nightfall, for then there were elaborate quiz
games and endless cribbage. Respite was only granted when, enthusiasm radiating from his bulky figure, Woollcott pulled a volume
from a shelf and regaled the company with his favourite excerpts
from Dickens.

Their holiday over and once again in Hollywood, Olivier started
to concentrate seriously on flying. He went daily to the Clover
Field and later to the Metropolitan Airfield where he was trained by
an instructor who was a caricature of the hard-bitten martinet of
the movies. Completely indifferent to Olivier's reputation, he treated
him like a young rookie. Exacting discipline would seem to have
been needed, for Olivier succeeded in breaking up three planes during his training, and it was only with the greatest difficulty that
Korda persuaded a company to insure him once the filming of *Lady
Hamilton* had started. Vivien Leigh, who received dramatic phone
calls about these crashes, could only hold her breath every time he
went up and pray that he would get through the necessary two hundred flying hours all in one piece. Due largely to his tough and
caustic instructor, he did, and as they walked across the tarmac from
the training plane after his last lesson the instructor ran true to
movie form. Beneath the gruff exterior must beat a heart of gold.
This was the moment to relent and allow a hint of wintry approval
to shine through. "You fly a good airplane, bud!" he conceded.

II

In the weeks before the start of *Lady Hamilton*, and while both
were engrossed in books about Nelson and Emma, news arrived
from England of very great personal importance. After three years,
during which they had come to know they could never be happy
apart, they were free to marry. For both of them divorce had been
a serious matter because they had a deep affection and respect for

the people to whom they were married, and because each had a child. A natural unwillingness to repudiate vows solemnly taken had delayed the final decision of all four. But now Jill Esmond, Olivier's wife, and Leigh Holman, Vivien Leigh's husband, had decided that divorce was the only solution. It had been decided sensibly and with little rancour, and, while they lost legal custody of their children, it was arranged in a friendly way that they should see them whenever it was practicable. It was on August 28th that they received news of their decrees, and Olivier immediately got in touch with Ronald Colman, whose own marriage to Benita Hume had been managed with so little fuss two years before. Colman told him that Californian law required a full three days' notification and registration before marriage. If this was done in Los Angeles it would be in all the papers in a few hours and he and Vivien could say good-bye to any chance of a quiet wedding.

"The best thing you can do," he said, "is to go a hundred miles away to Santa Barbara, register with the county clerk who will have no interest in informing the press, and then go back there in four days' time and be married by a judge. Why not have the ceremony at my cottage on the ranch?"

Benita Colman then came on the line to have a word with Vivien and warn her about buying the ring. Neither she nor Larry could very well go into a Hollywood jeweller's for such a thing without exciting speculation. It was arranged that Benita should go to her own jeweller and say that she wished to add a gold ring to her present one. As Vivien's fingers were bigger, she would have to pretend that she wanted it a little larger. This last piece of cunning nearly upset the plan, for the jeweller took the change in size as a personal affront to his previous judgment. It was a bore to have to go to such lengths to safeguard their privacy, but they made the best of it by treating the whole thing as a sort of spy drama in which they were pitting their wits against the American press. By the time the wedding day arrived they and the Colmans confessed that they were in a fever of suspense. Code words, dark looks and whispered conferences became so commonplace that Benita Colman said she would not have been in the least surprised to see any of them in a false moustache.

Ronald Colman and his wife decided not to attend the actual

marriage, which was fixed for Friday, August 30th, but arranged to meet them both after the ceremony at San Pedro, where his schooner *Dragoon* would be waiting in the harbour to take them on a few days' honeymoon.

Vivien Leigh said she wanted to have a pre-wedding party for all their friends. Then, even if they couldn't be told what was afoot for fear of a leakage, at least they wouldn't feel slighted. At the end of the party Olivier and Vivien Leigh mystified their guests by wishing them the best of luck when they came to say good-bye. With Garson Kanin and Katharine Hepburn, who were close friends they started on the three-hour drive to Santa Barbara. When they arrived it was discovered that the three days' notice did not expire until midnight, but the local judge agreed to perform the ceremony at one minute past twelve. It was a brilliant moonlit night, and when at last the time came the two walked out into the moonlight and with a deliberate gesture stood facing east, facing towards England.

The judge, perhaps unused to being robbed of the benefit of daylight, said he was going to keep things short—very short indeed. He was as good as his word. After only one quickly murmured "Yes" from Vivien Leigh, he said, "I now pronounce you man and wife." Then, the ceremony at an end, with a charming disregard of rubric he gave a sudden and unexpected cry of "Bingo!"

Meanwhile the other partners in the carefully prepared plot, the Colmans, were at work on the *Dragoon*, transforming the one small stateroom for guests into a bridal suite, complete with gardenias, lace-edged pillows, and champagne. On deck, where they sat trying to keep awake until the arrival of the Oliviers, was a little white wedding cake and a large bottle of champagne. It was not until sometime between 3 A.M. and 4 A.M. that a car appeared out of the darkness and the Colmans watched their chauffeur take elaborate security precautions before allowing the Oliviers to climb from the back of the car on to the quay.

Secrecy had triumphed. They embraced and toasts were drunk. Ronald Colman told the captain to weigh anchor, and for half an hour or more they all stayed on deck laughing and talking until the San Pedro light at the entrance to the harbour was passed and the *Dragoon* headed for the open sea and Catalina Island. Just as the first glow of dawn showed itself, the Colmans went below, leaving the two of them standing at the prow of the ship looking out to sea.

They awoke to a glorious morning and found the schooner anchored in a small, quiet bay. After a swim they lay on deck drying in the sun and once again raised their glasses to the success of their plan. It was just about then that, quite unmistakably, reaction set in. The plan had been almost too successful; a hoax is not much fun unless one can see the discomfiture of the hoaxed. Ronald Colman recalls the sense of anti-climax:

We had just finished lunch when Larry asked if we had a radio on board. I said that we had and that we might just catch the two o'clock news. "That would be interesting," said Vivien. "Wouldn't it," said Benita. I turned on the news. Fifteen minutes—and no mention of any wedding. "Wonderful," said Larry, "Ronnie, you really managed it superbly." "Oh, it's nothing," I said modestly, "but the four o'clock news has the more important events." "Indeed," said Larry, stretching himself out in a deck chair. It was, of course, only by coincidence that at four o'clock Larry pulled himself out of a siesta. Benita said: "Would you two mind if Ronnie and I listen to the news?" "Not at all, but keep it down, won't you?" said Larry, rolling over a little closer. "It's a pity to spoil the quiet of this idyllic spot," said Vivien, coming over and sitting by me. I turned on the radio—still no news of the Oliviers. "Of course," I said quickly, "you can't expect to escape Winchell at six o'clock—he gets *everything*." "Oh yes, *he'll* have it," said Benita, helpfully. "Have what?" said Vivien, opening those large and wonderful eyes at us. "Oh, darlings, you *can't* think for one minute that we are the least bit interested in . . ." Larry interrupted this with a laugh that started the rest of us off, but by nine o'clock we might have been described as definitely fidgety. After all there's not much point in having a secret the other fellow doesn't want to know. "We certainly pulled it off, didn't we?" I said. "We certainly did," said Larry gloomily, downing some apple pie. At ten o'clock, thank goodness, the story broke, and thinly disguised relief was plain on every face. "Too bad," said Larry heartily. "Too good to last," sighed Vivien with an incandescent smile. "Well, that's the way it goes," contributed Benita wittily. After that we had a very happy evening.

There was an infectious enthusiasm and a sense of common endeavour about the making of *Lady Hamilton*. It was filmed on a
low budget in a small studio. To save expense all the scenes in Sir
William Hamilton's house in Naples were shot against one composite
set and the naval battles were all fought with models. It was make-
shift and shot largely "off the cuff," with Sherriff, Walter Reisch,
Korda and Olivier improvising dialogue on the set at the last minute.
But despite all these seeming disadvantages, and although all their
work was rushed through in six weeks, the Oliviers found it the most
enjoyable film they had ever made.

It was a film which set out to be patriotic propaganda and which
gauged very nicely the sentiment of the time. Probably never before or since could Olivier have shouted with more conviction the
melodramatic cry, "Look out, Bonaparte; by gad we shall lick you
now!" Every line seemed to have its modern parallel, and tight-
lipped sentiments such as, "You can't make peace with dictators.
You have to destroy them—wipe them out!" could be delivered with
sincerity. (Afterwards in New York this line was to produce a
round of applause nearly every time the film was shown.)

Vivien Leigh appeared to have a certain amount of trouble with
her accent; probably one result of under-rehearsal. In the early
scenes her Emma wavered uncertainly between Irish and Cockney
and then seemed to find gentility with startling suddenness, but it
was a performance of great charm, especially in the comedy sequences, which were played with an exquisite lightness of touch.
Olivier had become passionately interested in the character of
Nelson, but reluctantly decided that for the purposes of this film it
would have been a mistake to venture beyond the popular conception of a great naval hero. This was neither the film nor the time
to present Nelson as the man he really believed him to have been, or
to build up a character in which hysteria and egotism were mixed
with genius. Both he and Vivien Leigh were quite happy to play
their parts for their immediate surface values.

For America the title of the film was changed to *That Hamilton
Woman*, a seemingly dime-catching device, but in fact historically
justifiable. It was the description of Emma given by Nelson's son in
a letter written to his mother from Naples. America also required

one other change. Because sin must never appear to pay even such returns as were enjoyed by Nelson and Emma, a special prologue had to be shot. The Hays Office insisted on a scene showing Lady Hamilton in later life, down-and-out in Calais, being flung from a café into the gutter. The whole story was then told in flashback. When the film was first shown in Britain this prologue was kept in, but Korda subsequently cut it as a piece of moral humbug and artistically unsatisfactory.

At the box-office the film succeeded in breaking records all over the world. In Russia especially, where Vivien Leigh was adopted as the Red Army's Pin-up Girl, it was highly praised, ran for month after month in Moscow, and was to remain popular long after the end of the war. It had, too, the unsuspected result of inspiring a Prime Minister beset by war worries. Winston Churchill, who saw it several times, described it as one of his favourite films, and arranged for it to be shown on board the *Prince of Wales* in August, 1941, on the way to the Atlantic Conference with President Roosevelt.* Sir Alexander Cadogan wrote in his diary:

> Film *Lady Hamilton* after dinner, excellent, P.M. seeing it for the fifth time and still deeply moved. At the close he addressed the company: "Gentlemen, I thought this film would interest you, showing great events similar to those in which you have just been taking part."

Married, the film finished, and flying hours completed, the Oliviers were able to draw a neat line at the end of a phase of their lives. At last they could pack for home and prepare to face England at war. Most important of all, they had the satisfaction of knowing that their children were now safe. By a coincidence, Mrs. Hartley with Suzanne and Jill Esmond with Tarquin had found themselves on the

---

* Mr. Churchill's interest dated back to the time when it was first announced that the film was to be made. Within twenty-four hours he had cabled Korda in Hollywood with a suggestion for a title and this had been followed up by other cables with other suggestions. Korda, alive to the importance of security, kept very quiet about these cables, but when he returned to England in January, 1942, Mr. Churchill invited him to Chequers for the weekend, and the first thing he asked was whether Korda had received them. Korda thanked him and said he had, and added that of course he had kept them absolutely secret for fear of vulgar publicity. Churchill looked at him quizzically. "I *meant* them to be used," he said. "I sent them to put your stock up!"

same boat sailing for Canada. Vivien Leigh and Olivier had flown up to Toronto to meet them, combining the visit with personal appearances in cinemas to raise money for Britain. Jill Esmond and Tarquin had gone to New York before travelling to Hollywood where they were to spend the rest of the war; Mrs. Hartley had taken Suzanne to Vancouver, as it had been arranged for them to live with friends until a boarding school could be found for Suzanne.

Towards the end of November Vivien Leigh flew to Vancouver to see Suzanne for the last time before she and Olivier left for England, and for what would almost certainly be the last time until the war was over. To avoid publicity she travelled under her former married name, and this was to have unexpected consequences.

With Suzanne happily settled in a convent school, Mrs. Hartley was thinking of returning to England; but the events of a few hours were to change all her plans. Somehow the papers heard that Vivien Leigh, travelling as Mrs. Holman, had arrived at Vancouver Airport, and they succeeded in tracing her to the address in Belmont Street where her mother and daughter were staying. Reporters and photographers, mystified by the secrecy, swooped on the house. Vivien Leigh wondered how to get rid of them, and at the same time dissuade them from writing anything about Suzanne. As her daughter was only seven, she did not want her to be the subject of a lot of publicity. Her friends' son said he had an idea. He was sure it would work, especially if he appealed personally to one of the reporters, who had been a friend of his at college. He went to the front door and explained that Vivien Leigh had come to Vancouver for a rest and to see her daughter and mother. If he had left it at that all might have been well, but unfortunately he took his friend confidentially aside and appealed to him not to run the story because, he whispered, Vivien Leigh was afraid her daughter might be kidnapped. That was why she had come to Vancouver as Mrs. Leigh Holman and why Suzanne's identity had not been revealed at the school she was attending.

Here was a better story than the reporters could have hoped for. Vivien Leigh in Vancouver would have made front-page news by itself, but here was almost an embarrassment of angles. Arrival under assumed name . . . daughter's identity at school secret . . . fear of kidnapping . . . *kidnapping!* It was too stern a test for even a college friendship, and the story hit the front page only slightly less prominently than "Greeks Hurl Italians Back from Coast Base."

The consequences were swift and unexpected. So strong was the fear of kidnapping, so vivid the memories of the Lindbergh tragedy in the minds of many mothers, that parents whose daughters were fair-haired and blue-eyed like Suzanne immediately removed them from the convent. The Mother Superior told Mrs. Hartley that she was sorry, but she was afraid Suzanne must leave. This was upsetting enough, but, even worse, no other boarding school in Vancouver would take her. Eventually a day-school agreed, but only on condition that she was accompanied to and from school every day. Mrs. Hartley had to write to her husband to say that she looked like being stuck in Canada for the duration.

IV

Three days before Christmas, 1940, the Oliviers closed up the little house which they had taken just after they were married, said good-bye to Hollywood, and left for New York. A passage had been secured for them on a ship leaving for Europe on December 27th. After three months of waiting they were now going at short notice. Behind them were all the preparations for Christmas, and as they looked round the rooms of their house in Cedarbrook Drive the little Christmas tree surmounted by a Star of Bethlehem seemed a symbol of the peace they were forsaking. A sad and shaggy sheepdog which appeared to be let with the house and which Olivier had adopted was left behind; so, too, was a large stray called Old Tom which fell rather short of Vivien Leigh's ideal cat, but which had adopted her. There was only just time to ask a few people in for a farewell drink, and then they were heading east. Whatever lay ahead, it was a departure made with a sense of relief. It had been bad enough to be abroad during the quiet months in the autumn and winter of 1939; but with the fall of France and the mass air-raids which had started on England they had felt, more and more, that they must get home. To read day after day in the American papers the guarded and censored accounts of the bombing had become unbearable; they should be sharing the dangers about which their friends wrote from London with such cheerful understatement.

The *Excambion*, an American ship which had arrived in New York with four hundred passengers from Europe, was returning to

Lisbon with twenty-three. In the voyage across an Atlantic which
was infested with U-boats it was not entirely comforting to find
that the captain, chief engineer, and chief steward were all German.
The ship's doctor confided that he suspected some of them of being
pro-Nazi members of the American Bund, a suspicion which Vivien
Leigh, who speaks German, also began to share. The ship was
technically neutral, but if she were challenged by a U-boat the
Oliviers could see themselves being taken off as prisoners. With this
unpleasant feeling they scanned the grey horizon praying that the
coast of Portugal would appear before the periscope of a surfacing
submarine. When they had made Lisbon without incident they
began to laugh at their fears; but their suspicions had not been entirely unfounded, for later they were to hear that several of the
crew had been arrested on espionage charges.

Lisbon was full of people trying to get to England, but with a
little help from the British Embassy seats were obtained on a plane
after three days. *Rebecca* had just opened at a Lisbon cinema, and
the name of Laurence Olivier possessed the sort of prestige which
leads so smoothly to priorities. Their pleasure at this piece of luck
was somewhat mitigated by the flight. The black-out cabin windows provoked acute claustrophobia and when they were still over
the sea and an hour or more from Bristol airport the door of the
pilot's cabin swung open to reveal flames all round the cockpit. One
of the crew had made the classic mistake of firing off the recognition
signals without opening the window.

At Bristol they heard for the first time the melancholy wail of
the air-raid sirens. After the lights of New York, Bristol seemed
a place of the dead. At the reception desk of the only hotel where
they could get a room they were told, almost as a matter of course,
that the glass had been blown out of all the windows. That would
be jolly fine, said Olivier, hoping he sounded sincere.

This was their introduction to England at war. But after the lotus
interlude of Hollywood and Broadway they found it exhilarating
as well as frightening. Whatever the conditions, they were home.
It was a bitter January night, and they went to bed fully clothed.
Vivien Leigh even wore gloves. Hardly had they settled down to
sleep against the noise of falling bombs and ack-ack than there was
a violent knocking at the door. Expecting yet another wartime

alarm, Olivier hurriedly got up to answer it, and Vivien Leigh heard a prolonged conversation. "What was it, darling?" she asked as he came back to bed.

"The Press," he said. "They wanted to know if we'd had a pleasant journey!"

CHAPTER 2

The Acting Sub-Lieutenant
1941-1943

I

ANYONE WHO HAD chanced to be on the Portsmouth Road on a particular day in the middle of April, 1941, might have witnessed an unusual sight. At the wheel of an ancient and open Invicta, whose radiator boiled and bubbled on every hill, sat a young man wearing a Naval uniform which was almost embarrassingly new and had a single wavy gold band round the sleeve. Attached by a tow-rope to the back of the Invicta was a little open four-seater with a broken clutch and a formidable amount of luggage in the back. As the young officer, who had yet to see a day's Naval service, glanced periodically into the driving mirror, he grinned at what he saw. Sitting rather anxiously at the wheel of the car behind was his wife, and on the seat beside her, bolt upright and displaying enormous dignity, was their black-and-white cat, Tissy. Thus did Temporary Acting Sub-Lieutenant (A) Olivier, R.N.V.R., and his wife set out for the wars determined on the confusion of the King's enemies.

It was three months since the cold January night when they had landed at Bristol, and they were on their way to Lee-on-Solent where Olivier was to undergo a three weeks' "conversion course" to adapt his American flying experience to British planes. They had not been idle during those intervening months. Almost as soon as they had arrived home and surveyed the damage which blast had

226

done to Durham Cottage, Olivier had been to the Admiralty to
apply for admission to the Fleet Air Arm. Here he had met with an
initial set-back. He was rejected as unfit. At a medical examination
the M.O. told him something which he knew very well. One of his
ears was faulty—the legacy of a flight through a blinding storm in
America the year before. The nerve of the inner ear had been
permanently affected, but it had never occurred to him that it would
be regarded as a disqualification. After his medical he immediately
consulted a number of specialists, and one of them wrote a strong
letter to the Admiralty saying that the complaint was not serious
and would get no worse. As a result the decision was reconsidered
and he was accepted for non-operational flying.

During the month between his rejection and acceptance Olivier,
who had put all ideas of acting out of his head the moment he
landed in England, found himself again in a film studio. This was
for the film *49th Parallel*, in which he gave a remarkable character
study as a French-Canadian trapper. He had also been on the stage.
With Constance Cummings, Ben Levy, John Clements and Jack
Melford, he and Vivien Leigh had visited aerodromes and launched
the R.A.F. Benevolent Fund with their all-star concert party. Together they had played the wooing scene from *Henry V* and Olivier
had regularly reduced the rest of the company to helpless laughter
by his performance in Farjeon's sketch "How to Get There." And
there had been no escaping the microphone. In the early hours of
one February morning they had broadcast with C. B. Cochran to
New York, and afterwards had breakfast in the Mansion House
before taking a drive through the ruins of the City.

Most important of all had been a visit to Burnley, which had become the wartime headquarters of the Old Vic and Sadler's Wells.
They had wanted to see Tyrone Guthrie, who had been keeping
the companies going ever since they had moved out of London at
the beginning of the war. It was partly a friendly visit, and partly
so that Vivien Leigh could find out if there would be any possibility
of joining the company once Olivier was in uniform. She and Olivier had talked over the problems which now confronted her; she
was conscious that her fame as a film star far exceeded her experience on the stage, and, if it could be managed, she was keen to subject herself to the discipline of acting again with the Old Vic. This
set Guthrie rather a problem. Personally he would have very much

liked her in the company, and knew that she would have been of
tremendous value to the box-office. But he, too, was worried about
her fame. Vivien Leigh might be prepared to play small parts, but
he believed that already she had reached a point in her career when
this was no longer possible. If her name were on the bills the audience would naturally expect to find that she was the star; even if
they would accept her in supporting rôles, Guthrie was afraid that
she would throw productions out of balance. He remembered her
as a hard-working, conscientious actress, but was still doubtful if she
would fit easily into the company. At the time it was slightly difficult to put all this into words, and Vivien left Burnley with nothing
settled. A few days later Guthrie wrote to her explaining as well as
he could all the doubts he felt, and Vivien was still undecided about
what to do next when Olivier was ordered to his training station.

When at last the steaming Invicta and its mixed cargo reached
Lee-on-Solent the Oliviers sought out Ralph Richardson who had
a cottage near by where they were to stay for a week or so. In the
morning Olivier reported to his Commanding Officer and Vivien
went round to the local house-agents in search of somewhere for
them to live. After several days she announced that she had found
a late Victorian house with a pleasant garden and orchard overlooking the Solent. It was at Warsash only a few miles away, and apart
from a forbidding collection of beaten brass-ware the only disadvantage as far as she could see was the name of the house. "And
what is the name?" asked Olivier curiously. "*Forakers,*" she said
and spelt it out.

They had brought just one or two personal treasures from London to modify the discomfort of living with other people's furniture.
Some Indian rugs and a little Aubusson carpet were put down on
the floor, a small round black frame containing a four-leafed sham-
rock that Elsie Fogerty had sent Olivier on the day he joined the
Navy went up on the flowered wallpaper; a painting by Sickert and
a small Boudin replaced two of the landlord's water-colours. Soon
the house was as fair an approximation of home as anyone in uniform
had the right to expect, and from there each morning Vivien saw
Olivier off to the seaplane base with entreaties to be careful. And
then, with the aid of a cook they had brought from London, she set
about being a housewife, content for the moment to forget she had
ever been an actress.

For Olivier, plunged into the perplexing new world of the Fleet Air Arm, it was not quite so easy to shake off the past. He was genuinely anxious to make a success of his new part, to respect the customs and taboos of Ward Room life, and to understand the mentality of the people with whom he was now thrown in contact. He had Richardson to show him the ropes, but, like everyone else new to the services and rather as he had expected, he quickly found there were small obstacles designed to prevent civilians, who did not conform to a pattern, from being readily at ease. All the self-confidence gained as an actor was useless in warding off the feeling that he was a new boy back at school, automatically unpopular, and with all the new boy's terrors of saying the wrong things and opening the wrong doors.

All his life, from the time he had first gone on the stage, he had been aware of the unspoken criticism of people outside the world of the theatre that actors and the like were superficial and unreal. Now here at last was his chance to meet *real* people, even perhaps become a real person himself. Only slowly, and hardly permitting himself to recognize the fact, did he reach the conclusion that the real people about whom he had heard so much were, in fact, no more real than his fellow-actors. Worse still—the final plunge into the pit of disillusion—apart from being no more real he found that they weren't even quite so nice! Although these sentiments were kept hidden behind a well-disciplined façade, the antipathy he felt sometime later for an officer who was senior to himself was so strong that it made him understand with new clarity Iago's hatred of Othello. It was something far removed from Dr. Jones' Freudian conception and could be explained simply by a dislike of being subordinate to a man for whom one has little respect.

The three weeks at Lee were quickly over and when he had passed his test he was transferred to Worthy Down, near Winchester, an airfield condemned as unsuitable by the R.A.F. in 1920, but which had taken on a new lease of life with the war. Arriving there, full of good intentions and determined to impress the Commanding Officer that he was a serious-minded pilot and not an irresponsible actor, he met with initial disaster.

It was a disaster which could not easily be concealed or the news of it kept from his friends. One of them, Robert Douglas, who was also in the Fleet Air Arm, and had been away on duty at another station, strolled into the Ward Room on the very first evening after Olivier's arrival and out of friendly interest asked the Commanding Officer how Lieutenant Olivier had been getting on. Perhaps there may have been a sudden stiffening in the C.O.'s manner which gave him a faint premonition of the answer; perhaps he may have suspected that the impetuous Olivier (whose part he had taken over when Olivier broke his ankle in *Theatre Royal*) was likely to be an erratic pilot. But even so, he was not prepared for the shock when the C.O. grimly and silently pointed out of the Ward Room window at a crippled plane which Olivier had been flying that morning and another wrecked plane into which he had taxied. "Good heavens, sir!" exclaimed Douglas in horror, "Not *two!*"

II

As the months went by Olivier found himself being given more and more of the dull routine duties which were the inevitable lot of a second-line pilot. There was no chance of operational flying against the enemy unless the aerodrome were attacked, and the ennui he began to feel was relieved only by talk of the theatre with Vivien in the evenings. Frequently they discussed the question of whether Vivien should continue to rusticate away from the stage. The Theatre Guild had written to ask if she would come to New York to play in *Cæsar and Cleopatra* with Cedric Hardwicke, and she had written back to say that while she would be very interested to do the play sometime, she could not come at present. But even if she could not think of going to New York during the war and while Larry was in uniform, it would be quite a different matter to do a play in London. She could still come down to Warsash each night after the performance. Once again they were anxious to find a part completely within her range, and the idea of one Shaw play led to another. After much discussion over several weeks, Olivier suggested Jennifer Dubedat in *The Doctor's Dilemma*. At first Vivien Leigh did not care much for the part, and recalled that Shaw had once warned Lillah McCarthy that she would have her work cut out to make Jennifer fascinating. But after reading the play several times Vivien saw that it had a number of advantages. Jennifer was the only woman in the play, and the play itself seemed to her a good one. She recalled the Katharine Cornell production in New York and realized that there would also be the chance to wear lovely

Edwardian clothes. Here was a rôle totally different from Scarlett and, in the absence of a better alternative, it seemed as good a play as any in which to make her return to the stage.

The idea was suggested to Hugh Beaumont, the managing director of H.M. Tennent Ltd., who eagerly undertook to put on the play. With settings by Michael Relph and costumes designed by Sophia Harris, the production at the Haymarket should have the maximum of style and elegance. It should lift people out of the drab wartime London of uniforms and blackouts, and transport them for a few hours into the golden Edwardian age.

Before the dawn of the golden age, however, the play toured the provinces for six months. After opening in Manchester in September, 1941, it did not arrive in London until the March of the following year.

At the Haymarket, despite air-raids, the play ran for thirteen months—a record for a Shaw play—and any monotony which might have been caused by acting the same part night after night was relieved for Vivien by having four different leading men. Within a fortnight of the opening, and on St. Patrick's Day, to be precise, Cyril Cusack, the Irish actor who was playing Dubedat, was suddenly taken ill in the middle of a performance, and the play had to be completed with an understudy carrying the book. The understudy played for a week and then Peter Glenville took over. But after a few months he went down with jaundice on a Thursday night. Once more the understudy was called on, but during the weekend John Gielgud told Hugh Beaumont, with whom he was then sharing a flat in Park Lane, that he would like to play the part until Glenville was well again. It happened that Dubedat was one of the only two Shaw parts he had ever wanted to do—the other was Marchbanks—and here was the opportunity. It meant a quick study at very short notice. On the Saturday and well into the early hours of Sunday morning he learnt the lines, rehearsed through Sunday afternoon and evening and all Monday. On Tuesday the curtain went up to a surprised and delighted audience many of whom had only learnt of the change when they were already in the theatre. Gielgud was nearly word perfect, but the tartan rug on the knees of the dying Dubedat that night did double duty. It concealed a prompt copy of the play.

During his later years Bernard Shaw made it an invariable rule never to attend his own plays. Although he still had his flat in Whitehall Court and was sometimes in town, he did not go to *The Doctor's Dilemma* even though he was rather interested to see Vivien Leigh. Gabriel Pascal, with whom he was working on the preliminary plans for the film of *Cæsar and Cleopatra,* had told him that he was anxious for her to play Cleopatra, and that she, too, was very keen on the idea. Was she old, tall and fat? he asked, and seemed greatly surprised when he was told that she was in her twenties and both small and slim. "It is a curious fact," he is said to have commented, "that ladies who set their hearts on that particular rôle are invariably giantesses or over fifty. Miss Leigh must be exceptional."

He was soon to have a chance of judging for himself. During 1942, when the casting was still not finally settled, Hugh Beaumont took her round to meet him for the first time at Whitehall Court. It was a meeting charged with more than usual significance, for, while both she and Pascal were agreed that she should play Cleopatra, Shaw's consent was essential. But that afternoon at his flat Vivien with shrewd diplomacy behaved as if the idea had never been mooted.

Beaumont, who knew her secret hopes, marvelled at the way she steered the conversation away from the subject which must have been uppermost in her mind. Perhaps Shaw enjoyed the game as much as she, for it was not until a few moments before she left that, with a twinkle in his eye, he said suddenly, "You know, what you ought to do is to play Cleopatra!" Vivien Leigh protested, but Shaw insisted that she had reminded him of a Persian kitten from the moment she had arrived and would be the perfect Cleopatra. But, she argued, would she be good enough? Shaw had a prompt answer for pride disguised as humility. "You'd *look* wonderful," he said shortly. "You don't need to be an actress. The part's fool-proof!"

When he came to say good-bye a few minutes later, Shaw said something which puzzled Vivien Leigh for years afterwards. "You are the Mrs. Pat Campbell of the age," he told her admiringly as they shook hands at the door. A possible explanation of this remark came only with the recent publication of the correspondence between Mrs. Campbell and Shaw. Many of Mrs. Campbell's early letters are concerned with subtle stratagems and long battles of wits with Shaw for getting her own way as an actress.

III

While *The Doctor's Dilemma* was on tour both Vivien Leigh and Olivier had made long weekend journeys to see one another. He went up to Aberdeen and Leeds, and she came down from Edinburgh, Derby and Glasgow. By this time they had moved from Warsash to a bungalow at Worthy Down, and they continued to live there when the play opened in London. Olivier had to be up at 6:30 every morning to drive on his motor-cycle to the aerodrome, and Vivien did not get back until late at night after the performance. The journey from London and the tedium of travelling in the smoke-laden, blacked-out trains was relieved for her by Dickens, for whom she had developed a great passion. At the time of their marriage, Alexander Woollcott had sent her Dickens' letters for a wedding present and they had filled her with enthusiasm. Now, each night, under the dimmed lights, she was reading her way steadily through all the novels.

It was during one of these journeys that, as she sat huddled in the corner of the carriage, she overheard two men from Worthy Down discussing Olivier's abilities as a pilot and the way he flew in formation. "He's a duck out of water," one of them said, quite unaware of her presence. The airman was echoing an opinion which she had held privately for a long time and which, if it was a libel on him as a pilot, was probably true of his feelings. His complaint was that he was a duck out of rough water. While he had been fretting in America to get home, he had mentally been casting himself for, if not an heroic rôle, at least an active one. His duties as a second-line pilot were falling very far short of expectation. Apart from the training flights, which were monotonously uneventful, he found himself involved in running a camp on the aerodrome for the young members of the Air Training Corps. This was all very well, but it was difficult to become reconciled to such routine while many of his friends such as Tony Bushell, Cecil Tennant, Glen Byam Shaw and George Devine, were facing danger. News of fellow-actors being killed on active service did not make it any easier. Frustration and depression reached a point where he simply could not throw them off. He tried to get his feelings down on paper during this period and wrote:

I think the thing that hits one so when hearing of a war is not the thought so much of the horrors of it, but the terrible irremediable *mess* that everyone's lives are to be turned into until the thing is over. It is a state of affairs in which surely *nobody* on earth can ever feel happy again until the end of it. It means the whole earth is under a sort of pall of sickness, distress, and anxiety and self-disgust in some way or another. So many millions of people trying to feel something they don't feel or trying not to feel something they do.

In an England which was being transformed into an island under arms there was a great deal of emphasis on what Whitehall called "keeping up morale." Entertainment had a priority, and Olivier was called on more and more frequently to combine his duties on the aerodrome with all sorts of semi-theatrical activities. His Commanding Officer was for ever receiving chits from the Admiralty asking for his release for twenty-four hours so that he could make a patriotic broadcast or deliver some ringing orations at the Albert Hall in a "Battle for Freedom" or a "Salute to Russia" Pageant. "Look here, this is getting a bit thick," the C.O. would sometimes complain, but would generally add in sympathetic man-to-man tones. "Mind you, I know that it must be a bit embarrassing for you, Olivier, all this stage business." Then he would call on Olivier's Squadron Commander to do a little juggling with the duty roster. After that when the question of entertainment for the station came up Olivier could hardly decline to help, and he soon found he was organizing a concert party. He himself appeared singing a sea shanty (an episode called "Shantasia" on the mimeographed programmes) and in a specially devised excerpt from *Henry V* with officers, Naval airmen and Wrens in smaller rôles.

The concert party acquired sufficient prestige for the C.O. to give his proud permission for the whole show to go to Aldershot, and there on one fatal evening in February, 1942, a special performance took place at the Garrison Theatre. For Olivier it was a performance ever to be engraved on his memory as the worst experience of his career. There could hardly have been a more unfortunate week-end for members of the Fleet Air Arm to arrive in a military town; certainly it was no moment for them to be appearing on a stage. Newspaper headlines were informing a bitterly-disappointed country that the German battleships, *Scharnhorst* and *Gneisenau* and the

cruiser *Prince Eugen* had slipped out of Brest under the nose of
the Navy. Despite attacks by Swordfish, the planes of the Fleet Air
Arm, all three had successfully run the gauntlet up the Channel and
reached the safety of Heligoland. On such a day a cheerful opening chorus of "Wings over the Navy" was unlikely to be popular
with an audience in khaki.

A few turns on the programme were allowed a fairly quiet hearing, but when the curtains went back on the *Henry V* episode it
seemed to Olivier, standing in the wings, as if all Bedlam had been
let loose. A soldier was discovered marching on sentry-go up and
down the stage, and between whistles and jeers he was offered a
great variety of free advice from all parts of the house. Olivier's
own entrance, carefully prepared and built up, was a cue for even
more barracking. As he stepped on to the stage in the best suit of
armour he had been able to hire from Simmons he was greeted with
howls of derision. The words of his opening speech: "And what
have kings that privates have not too, save ceremony—save general
ceremony?"—were completely drowned. His every move produced
shouts; but for laughter, laughter with an ominous howl of rage at
its core, there was nothing to equal the moment at the start of the
Crispin speech when he drew his sword and flourished it above his
head. The house rocked.

Completely inaudible in a theatre for the first time in his life,
Olivier hoarsely addressed himself to the first few rows and tried
to inform them that gentlemen in England now a-bed would think
themselves accurs't that they were not here upon Saint Crispin's day.
But it was no good; Shakespeare's finest rhetoric was lost in cat-calls
and for a moment Olivier contemplated just walking off the stage.
Then something prompted him to one last endeavour, a final dramatic gesture which would either command silence or have the audience throwing the chairs. He strode forward right down to the
footlights, turned his eyes upward, and sank on his knees. This
action surprised the audience into a moment's pause in their shouting, and in that pause he managed to get out the start of Henry's
prayer before the battle, an impassioned cry of:

"*O God of battles! steel my soldiers' hearts
Possess them not with fear . . .*"

It worked. They heard him to the end, and when the curtains swung together there was a burst of applause.

After that, the most hazardous mission that the Fleet Air Arm could offer a pilot would seem positively dull, but during the months that followed Olivier decided that he must get a posting to duties that would involve him in operational flying. Surely there was something he could take on at the not exactly advanced age of thirty-five? He made inquiries and was told that his only chance was to become a pilot of a Walrus. He immediately applied.

Knowing how upset she would be, Olivier put off telling Vivien Leigh of his decision as long as he could. But when at last he was informed by his C.O. that he had been granted his transfer he had to break it to her. And what exactly, she demanded, were Walruses? Trying to make it sound very commonplace and unexciting, he said they were small, "general-purpose" amphibians that were catapulted from battleships. But she was not deceived and, as he had feared, was very worried by the news. He tried to comfort her by saying that it would probably be three months before he took up his new appointment, and, as it turned out, those three months were to see a change in all his plans.

Faced with the uninspiring routine of Worthy Down until he transferred, he heeded the siren voices which were trying to lure him back to the film studios. A suggestion was made to him about a film which he was assured would have a valuable propaganda value and which had the backing of the Ministry of Information. It was to be called *Demi-Paradise*, a whimsical affair about an earnest young Russian engineer who comes to England and is apparently won over to the British Way of Life by such national idiosyncrasies as the B.B.C.'s recording of nightingales. Filippo Del Giudice, the Italian producer, swept aside Olivier's initial objections by saying that, through the M.O.I., he could arrange for his temporary release from the Fleet Air Arm while he was waiting for his transfer. On the understanding that the release would not prejudice his new appointment, Olivier allowed him to go ahead, and by the January of 1943 had started filming at Denham.

In some obscure way *Demi-Paradise* was supposed to serve as pro-Russian propaganda, and, if nothing else, it helped the British public (spinning from the rapid changes expected of their affections) to accept the Red Menace as nothing more sinister than Larry Olivier with a severe hair-cut. Amiably satirical, it turned out to be splendid pro-British propaganda and only made the Russians look a little foolish. Olivier took infinite care with his accent, in which he was coached by a Russian, but was so little interested in the film that he never bothered to see the finished result.

It was while the film was being completed that news came through which meant the final frustration of all Olivier's plans for taking up operational duties. To Vivien Leigh's infinite relief, Walruses were taken out of commission. Faced once again with the bleak prospect of Worthy Down, he felt no moral compunction in allowing an application to be made for the extension of his release from the Fleet Air Arm. Another film was being planned which seemed to justify a suggestion to the Admiralty that one of the Navy's lieutenants would be better employed in acting than in training air gunners. It was a film of Shakespeare's *Henry V*.

IV

The idea of a film of *Henry V* had been in the air for some while. Although it was made at the time of the campaign in Europe and seemed to have a parallel with the events of D-Day, the topicality was little more than a coincidence. It's origins could be traced to a television script, written and discarded as long before as 1938, and its actual realization as a film was an example of how a good idea can hang in the air for a long time until, at a given moment and as if by some miraculous coincidence of thought, all the right people seize on it and bring it down to practical reality. Three people were principally concerned, and although Olivier naturally received most praise as the film's producer, director, and star, he has never failed to give credit to Del Giudice, who backed the enterprise, and Dallas Bower, who had the germ of the idea, brought Del Giudice and Olivier together and nursed the whole project through its formative days.

For Olivier the complicated and intricate train of events started when he agreed to take part in a fifteen-minute radio programme, produced by Dallas Bower, called *Into Battle* in May, 1942. He came up from Worthy Down to deliver the "Crispin" speech and the Harfleur speech from *Henry V*. It was a broadcast which Bower deprecated as "unashamed flag-waving," but out of it discussion arose in very general terms about the possibilities of *Henry V* as a film, and Bower told Olivier that he had actually worked out a film treatment. When he had been a television producer before the war he had scripted it for television, but it had been shelved as too elaborate for Alexandra Palace. He'd forgotten all about it for nearly a year, and then, after he had joined the Army, he had taken it out in the barrack room at Whitby and, simply as an exercise, turned it into a rough film scenario.

Bower, who had been in films for many years before he went into television, was seconded from the Army to the Ministry of Information and there, as Supervisor of Film Production, he had once or twice suggested that a film should be made from his script. His superiors, more concerned with one-reelers about A.T.S. recruiting and saving pig food, had not been enthusiastic. So the film was still just an unrealised dream when Bower had left the M.O.I. in 1942 to work at the B.B.C.

Olivier told Bower that he was naturally interested in the idea of the film, but there the matter rested until, shortly afterwards, the B.B.C. asked him to take part in a full-length radio version of the play. It was to be produced by Howard Rose in Manchester, and by the time this broadcast was made Dallas Bower had at last succeeded in getting a company to accept his film script. An Italian, who had spent the first four months of the war interned on the Isle of Man, had seen in it the potentialities to which English producers had been blind, and had bought an option on it.

Filippo Del Giudice was accustomed to overcoming difficulties, and his company, Two Cities, had already made Noël Coward's *In Which We Serve* in the face of considerable initial opposition from the M.O.I. *Henry V* was obviously an even more fantastic undertaking for wartime, but Del Giudice enjoyed doing things which he was firmly told were impossible. Everyone said he was crazy even to consider it, and in Wardour Street the very idea of Shakespeare on the screen was received with horror. Despite all this (and at that time with no idea of Olivier for the part) he bought the script, and Dallas Bower joined Two Cities. Preliminary plans for the film were just starting in the autumn of 1942 when Olivier made his broadcast from Manchester. Del Giudice, who was listening-in, decided then and there that he was the ideal actor for the film, and the next day told Bower that Olivier must somehow be persuaded to take it on. Bower said he would arrange a meeting, and next time

Olivier was in London he took him along to meet Del Giudice at his offices in Hanover Square.

Interested as he was by the idea in general terms, Olivier was not going to be rushed into a decision. He did not want to be associated with any film version of Shakespeare over which he did not have complete control. Experience of film-making had taught him how dangerously easy it is for work to be delegated to the wrong people. If he were going to make *Henry V* he wanted to have the final say in the way it was produced and cast. The script, music, costumes, and art direction must be done by people whose integrity he trusted. There must be no compromising, no accepting of half measures, and no fighting against the sort of minds which set standards simply by the box-office.

He thought Del Giudice seemed a man who would see eye to eye with him about this, but even so, he was aware that to ask for such powers might easily look like egotism. He therefore put it to Del Giudice as tactfully as possible that he would not feel justified in asking for release from the Fleet Air Arm unless he accepted the dual responsibility of producing and starring. By this time Olivier had decided to use a completely new script, but, because Dallas Bower had nursed the whole idea, he was determined that Bower should be the associate producer; the rest of his team he also wanted to select personally. Del Giudice was delighted. This was exactly how he liked to work. To inspire someone whose abilities he admired and then give him complete control was his idea of the function of a film impresario.

Having asked for complete control, and having been given it, Olivier then began to have misgivings. He had never done anything on the technical side of filming, and he had grave doubts about his ability to direct. He recalled the director with whom, in the heat of a discussion in Hollywood, he had once argued that Shakespeare could never be done on the screen. By chance William Wyler, then a major in the American Army Air Force, was at that moment in London and enduring the rigours of the campaign at Claridge's. Olivier went to see him, but Wyler, who was making documentary war films, and was shortly to go on active service, told him he was not interested in directing a commercial film at the moment, and that he would, anyway, be quite the wrong person for Shakespeare. He held to his assertion that Shakespeare *could* be done on the screen, but would not even consider himself for the job. Carol Reed and Terence Young were both approached but could not accept, and at last Olivier decided to take the plunge himself. To prompt him on any technical points about which he might be in doubt, he chose Reginald Beck, who was the editor of *Demi-Paradise*.

While he was making *Demi-Paradise* during the early months of 1943, he and Vivien Leigh moved from Worthy Down to the little Buckinghamshire village of Fulmer. So that they could be near Denham, where most of the film was to be shot, they leased a house called Hawksgrove, which Noël Coward had occupied shortly before. Here, after a day's work, Olivier assembled his team and planned *Henry V*. On Dallas Bower fell a large share of the preliminary organization, and the responsibility for getting actors and technicians out of the services. All this had to be done through the Ministry of Information where, fortunately, he had good friends. Even so, the services were extremely unwilling to release men for a film only a few months before D-Day. Leo Genn, whom Olivier wanted for the Constable of France, was an officer in the Army; Robert Newton, who was to be Ancient Pistol, in the Navy. Their Earl of Salisbury was a private in the Pioneer Corps under the name of Griffith Jones. And only with difficulty could the Admiralty be persuaded that Roger Furse was more essential to the film than to the staff of the Naval Officers' training station at Lancing.

Service chiefs, however, proved more amenable than at least one Hollywood film executive. Olivier had taken it almost for granted that Vivien Leigh would play Katharine, but David Selznick, to whom she was under contract, cabled that he would not hear of it. He had been dismayed when the actress whom he considered he had made world-famous as Scarlett had turned her back on Hollywood and her seven-year contract, and returned to England. He had kept up a creeping barrage of cables suggesting various parts from Jane Eyre to the heroine of a highly dramatic film about Yugoslavia, but Vivien Leigh had declined to leave England. So, when she asked for permission to play in *Henry V* Selznick refused on the ground that it was too insignificant a part for the star of *Gone With the Wind*. Olivier had to search for another Katharine, and found her at the tiny Mercury Theatre at Notting Hill Gate where, curiously enough, she was playing Vivien Leigh's original part in *The Mask of Virtue*. She was Renée Asherson, whom he had first met eight years before when she walked on in his season with Gielgud at the New.

From the start it had been decided that the Battle of Agincourt would be the pictorial and dramatic high-spot of the film and must have a highly spectacular treatment. But this was virtually impossible to manage in England. To suggest on the screen Henry's army of thirty thousand and the French army, which was twice the size, it was calculated that they would need at least 650 men and over 150 horses. It was out of the question to recruit them in England. Also it was difficult to find any spot in England during the spring and early summer of 1943 which was not alive with the hum of aeroplanes or covered with modern military defences which would seem strange in fifteenth-century France. "Where," demanded Olivier, "can we find a really poetic countryside?" Dallas Bower had the answer; Ireland, he believed, would provide the right setting, and he went over to reconnoitre. He returned to say that he had found just the place near Dublin. It was an estate at Enniskerry belonging to Lord Powerscourt, whose family had a great military tradition, and who was quite agreeable to their filming there. He was Irish Commissioner of the Boy Scouts, and as the park was used as a permanent Scout camp it had many facilities which would be most useful. The Irish Local Defense Force would provide men under semi-military discipline, and he had been assured that horsemen could easily be obtained.

Preliminary calculations showed that it would be a costly business, even if the weather were good, but Del Giudice waved aside the question of money. "That is my worry, gentlemen," he would say, and little knowing how insecure the financial backing was, Olivier set out with the unit for Ireland at the end of May.

CHAPTER 3

An Oscar for Henry
1943

I

L IKE MERCENARIES coming to join some medieval army, young men
from all over Ireland converged on the standard raised by
Olivier at Powerscourt. Farmers from as far as the shores of
Lough Neagh; plough boys who turned the dark earth of Kilkenny;
stable boys who could play truant, and even a Dublin cab-driver
who took his nag from between the shafts; anyone who could strad-
dle a horse rode into the camp of khaki tents and long marquees to
take part in the battle of Agincourt. Most knew that it was in aid
of some film or other, but there were a few who had never been inside a cinema and who came simply because they were offered £ 3
10s. a week and another £2 if they brought their horses as well.
Nearly all had a stiff stubble on their chins, for the advance agents
who had recruited round the villages put men on the payroll from
the moment they started to grow beards. In the camp these mounted
irregulars joined the more disciplined ranks of the Irish L.D.V. who
paraded to the call of the bugle. Stables, sleeping quarters, cook-
houses, and a bar were built to accommodate them and the film unit
which arrived from London. Olivier, in the best tradition of modern
generals, had a trailer, and from this he conducted his film-making
operations.

It was his first experience of being in control of a large number of men, and he approached it with some diffidence. The thing to do, he decided, was to get them all together so that he could explain what he was doing, and the co-operation he needed if the battle scenes were to be a success. Rather carried away, he ended his speech by saying: "I may be asking you to do some dangerous things in the weeks to come, but I promise you I won't expect you to do anything I won't first undertake myself."

This splendid promise in the very best Sandhurst tradition was taken extremely literally, and on several occasions, after explaining some complicated, rather unpleasant fall, there would be a smiling, faintly ironic chorus from the men, "Sure and we see what you mean, Mr. Olivier, and now perhaps you'd be so good as to be showing us yourself what it is you have in mind." He was let in for all manner of athletic prodigies, and, to show them how he wanted the English soldiers to fall on the French horsemen, he once had to fling himself from the lower branches of a tree. For several days he had both arms in a sling, and had to walk with a crutch as the result of spraining his ankle. This was not his only injury. One day a horse charged into the heavy Technicolor camera just as he was looking through the view-finder. He was aware of a violent blow on the mouth, but was more concerned with the fate of the camera as it was the only Technicolor camera then available in the British Isles. Only when he put his hand up to his face did he find that his upper lip had been cut through to the gum.

The first week was devoted to costuming and rehearsals. Horses were turned from rough hacks, some with the marks of the plough harness on their backs, into gaily caparisoned mounts for armoured knights. Roger Furse and his wife Margaret concentrated on the banners which were to be carried by the knights and which would, it was hoped, give the impression of even greater numbers than really existed. Numbers were large, but unlike some film spectacles, they did not exceed the historical proportions.

Not all the men could be dressed in real armour. Olivier's helmet and gorget were of bronze and his armour of metal; and so were those of some of the other leading players, but Agincourt had proved a battle to exhaust the combined stocks of all the theatrical costumiers. Wartime shortage of material called for more than usual resource by the costume and property departments, whose most ingenious idea was for the manufacture of chain mail. It was knitted and crocheted in heavy twine which was then sprayed with aluminum paint.

Preparations involved teaching the members of the L.D.V. to fire the long bow for the dramatic moment in the film where the mounted French army is brought up suddenly by the hail of English arrows. Also Olivier had to put in several hours of riding practice under an ex-sergeant of the Scots Greys. Riding in full armour was difficult enough, but to ride in a medieval knight's saddle, which was ten inches higher than the horse's back, provided an added hazard. At times he felt as if he were on a camel.

After ten days the men were trained and costumed, the horses more used to their unaccustomed rôles, and Olivier out of sling and bandage. They were ready to shoot.

In a journal-letter, Olivier wrote to Vivien Leigh:

June 7.

Your second letter has just arrived. Your first was undated, but I gather took two weeks to reach me. . . . Things, I suppose, have gone fairly well but sometimes it seems that they are not going at all, and I get panicky and nervous.

I have just this minute moved into my caravan [trailer], it is about ten-thirty, and Dallas and Reg., having conducted me to my new home for the first time, have just left me. I have been promising myself to write to you the first moment I was here alone, and now I am—by candlelight. I will describe the caravan to you to-morrow in detail—it is very nice and comfortable. The horses are about 100 yards or so below me, and I suppose the dear beasties will make themselves heard by snorting and stamping at their lines all night. I am on top of a little hill—very solitary—where I can see the whole lay-out of the camp and the location. I have a "master view" as Ralph would say and it's a very beautiful one. I shall dress, make-up and sleep here, but feed during the day in the camp.

My back is much better tho' I still feel it a bit especially when tired at the end of the day, but it *is* improving all the time. My arm, however, is another matter which is quite maddening because I don't remember doing it at the time. Carl Cook * says I must have clutched at an overhanging branch during the fateful pursuit of

* Olivier's osteopath.

Duffy * and wrenched my elbow. Anyway that was getting all right when I strained it again yesterday. It's quite painful to-day, and as I'm beginning to feel it straining a bit I think I'll stop writing now and go on with this to-morrow. Three (two?) weeks gone— oh I wish I knew how much more!

Tuesday 8th. It has been a difficult day and a very long one. I enjoyed my night in here, only disturbed occasionally by sheep and odd animals scratching their backs against the side of the caravan. I rode "Blaunche Kyng" as I call him (one of Henry's horses) at 8.0., rehearsing the charges nearly all day, and when I wasn't doing that (because the *dear* horses can't work too long at a time, until they're in better training) I was hareing about vast stretches of land with little flags and quantities of red tape laying out one shot after another.

After a little while at this the camera crew sent word that "really it wasn't the sort of work they were supposed to do." So I sent word back that if they would rather do nothing and watch me working that was all right with me, as they weren't much help anyway. So Reggie and I fell to it for the rest of the afternoon while some of the workmen made a show of helping.

At 5.30 it was time to take the horsemen again through another shot of the charge which I did till 6.30. Had a cup of tea, bath, dinner, changed, came back and sent for —— who, alone of all the outfit, has been temperamental, sulky and awkward. Had a lengthy row with him, after which he apologized and we shook hands (!) I hope things will be all right, but if not I shall get rid of him, or anybody who doesn't pull his weight. The Irish are being so marvellous that it's just not good enough to take any nonsense from our own people.

Wed. 9th, 11.45. Well, we got our first shot to-day and on the day we said we would! It wasn't exactly the shot we intended to start with as we weren't quite ready for that, and it wasn't exactly perfect, but it was *something.* The sun played lovely games with us all afternoon. Clouds changed their course deliberately from all directions and just got in front of the sun, leaving the sky perfectly blue everywhere else! When a very large patch of no-cloud that we had all been looking forward to came along it opened itself out

* Their cat, which he had chased up a tree at Fulmer.

to disclose that the only high cirrus in the sky had just got in front of the sun way above it. By the time *that* had moved, (very slow, of course, being so high) the lower clouds by putting on an extra spurt were just able to cover it up again.

All this time the horsemen were getting frightfully hot in their armour, and the horses had stood themselves into a stupor and were too sleepy to charge properly. But we got it eventually, as I say, at 6.0. Of course the morning was perfect, but it *takes* all morning to dress the men and horses—at least so far—it'll get quicker I think (hope). This particular shot, luckily, was a very simple one with four platoons of horses, increasing in size, advancing over a hill in V-shaped formation. It sounds simple enough but none of the men are cavalry-trained to keep in line, so I'm afraid it wasn't too good. Still it wasn't too bad, and the flags and the colours generally looked all right. Roger and Paul [Sheriff] far from satisfied, but if I waited till everyone said they were ready we really wouldn't get it done— not in this climate anyway. They have all worked wonderfully— Roger and Maggie most particularly have done a fantastic job with 160 men and horses who really do look more like a thousand.

I felt a bit nervous at first, but v. excited, dashing about all the time on Blaunche between the horses and the other side of the hill and the camera, yelling instructions through a megaphone tied round my neck. Blaunche who doesn't like the megaphone *won't* behave well in front of the other horses—wants to be with them all the time. As soon as the shot was through I felt quite emotional with relief that we had really started.

To crown it, on the way back Paul met me with the news that the tracking car was at last all right. Oh yes—*great* trouble with the tracking car there's been—the most magnificent track you've ever seen which stretches for half a mile. Steel tubular rails on sleepers raised off the road when it dips—the tracking car also runs very gaily on it but *too* gaily as it shakes like a jelly! And so does everyone on it including the camera. But now we've got different tyres on it and a different car and I think it'll be all right.

After Dinner. I had to go over with Reggie to have a conference with Roger and others about the calls for to-morrow to see really what they can manage. I am lying in bed as I write. *How* I wonder what you are experiencing every minute. It has started to rain— gentle little patters on the roof.

Thurs. 10th. Have just had lunch and I am giving this to Margaret to get off now or you will never get it. Cloudy to-day, but it gives a chance to repair the damage from yesterday a bit. Five hundred men came in last night so we are now full complement . . .

II

With all the men and horses assembled, they were ready to shoot a sequence destined to make film history and so exciting that time and again it was to win a round of applause in the cinema. It was the scene where the French cavalry break into a trot, which develops into a full gallop as they charge down on the ranks of the English, who stand resolutely waiting and so helplessly outnumbered that annihilation seems certain. It was for this charge that the little single track rail, stretching for half a mile, had been built, and the camera mounted on a car so that the whole charge could be kept in the camera's eye. It was a scene that had to be endlessly rehearsed so that every detail was right; and its full shooting was seriously delayed by bad weather.

Altogether the unit was shooting for thirty-nine days, but fourteen of these were spent in miserable contemplation of rain pouring from dark clouds. There were many other days when the sun shone so fitfully that only a few minutes of work was possible. These delays sent the costs soaring above the original budget, and in London Del Giudice faced serious financial difficulties. No hint of this, however, was allowed to reach the unit. Every night he rang up full of encouragement, telling Olivier that the "rushes" were superb, and always ending with the assurance: "Larry, you're making a masterpiece!"

Olivier would have had good reason for depression if he had had the least idea of what had really been happening in London, and how, for several days, the whole project of *Henry V* trembled in the balance and was very nearly abandoned.

Although he was the producer of the film he had at that time only a superficial idea of its financial backing. Film finance is so complex and baffling that anyone except an expert financier may be forgiven for failing to comprehend all its intricacies. Del Giudice was one of the industry's acknowledged geniuses at raising money, and so neither Olivier nor Dallas Bower had gone carefully into the question of whether the money was absolutely guaranteed. Unfortunately, in the middle of the filming in Ireland the chief "backer" withdrew, and Del Giudice was faced with the task of persuading someone else to finance Shakespeare on the screen to the tune of £300,000, the largest sum ever spent on a British film up to that time.

He found support from J. Arthur Rank; but it was support given only after some considerable initial reluctance, for among the things weighing in the balance against it were the earnest supplications of one of Rank's most influential advisers, who was horrified to find Shakespeare's play full of bad language. He implored Mr. Rank to have nothing to do with the film, but Mr. Rank overcame his scruples and said he would back the film on the understanding that Two Cities Films came partially under the control of the Rank Organization. This was a blow for Del Giudice, who greatly valued his independence and was artistically in violent opposition to the "big business" conception of film-making and distribution. But it was something which he had to accept. When Olivier got back from Ireland Del Giudice told him how he had made a personal visit to Rank's home near Reigate one night at the height of the crisis to discuss the whole matter.

"I must say," Del Giudice said, "when I was able to speak to Mr. Rank alone my task was easier. Somehow I could make him feel my point of view, and my poor English at times helped a good sense of humour. That night he agreed on an amount to be spent for such a film—not over and above £300,000. I knew very well that with that money it was practically impossible to do *Henry V*, but it was the start and I hoped to convince him along the way of spending more."

As Del Giudice recalled it, Gabriel Pascal also arrived at the house later that evening and helped him to persuade Rank to put up the money. It never seemed to occur to Del Giudice that a backer might pardonably be annoyed if, after agreeing to put up a certain amount of money, he was later called on for more. *Henry V* ran away with £175,000 more than was agreed on that night, and the total cost was exactly £475,000, but Del Giudice, the artist, always considered that Mr. Rank, the business man, should never have weighed the extra cost against the privilege of being associated with so worthwhile a film.

So, with Rank as chairman of Two Cities and the financial risk under-written, *Henry V* was saved, and Del Giudice continued to send soothing, reassuring messages to Ireland. It was often much-needed assurance. Every second day the black-and-white prints were flown over and shown to the production team at a little cinema on the coast. Technical defects meant that nearly five days' work had to be thrown away and the scenes refilmed. Olivier, unaccustomed to seeing the rough shots (which lose a great deal of quality in the black-and-white prints of a Technicolor film), was often very worried and grew increasingly depressed as the weather got worse. Some of his worries were expressed in a letter which he wrote to Vivien Leigh, and which she read under the kindlier skies of North Africa where she was entertaining the troops.

Powerscourt, June 26, Saturday.

It is days since I have written to you, but things for the last three weeks have been getting so troublesome that what with not being able to hear anything from you (for three whole weeks now) I have really been so down in the mouth that I could write nothing but how anxious and perplexed I was . . . Anything I might have written would have been one long moan. But the day before yesterday Lady Powerscourt sent me over an old copy of *The Times* which reported of your exciting doings on the 19th * and my heart was so uplifted to know that at least you were all right up to that time that already everything was much better and happier for me.

It's been a very hard fight the last three weeks and I wouldn't like to go through them again. But yesterday after lunch the weather suddenly started to improve and we got eight set-ups in the day, and to-day we really had our first wonderful day—absolutely perfect, and it was such a joy and made everybody feel so much better, restoring the humour of the camp which was getting very depressed and presenting quite a formidable problem to me. To-day we did six lovely set-ups—including two master shots, employing the whole complement of 664 men—the French camp and the Agincourt procession—for both of which two days each were scheduled! The Procession was really lovely and gave me a great lump in my throat

* This refers to Vivien Leigh's presentation to the King after a performance at Tunis. See page 262.

at each of the two takes we made. Bunnie * rode Lyard (another of Henry's horses) for me as it was very distant and looked splendid. As Lyard turned down the hill round the last bend towards Agincourt, he gave his tail a beautiful swish, which you could see quite clearly right in the distance. It was a terribly gallant and touching little effect; it sounds silly I know, but it's tiny things like that that make all the difference between all right and really good in a shot.

Sunday 27th. I've had a lovely restful day and am feeling much better. I lazed in bed and had breakfast sent in to me here in my caravan at about 9.30. I got up very lazily and slowly and at about eleven I joined a party riding down to the waterfall and back—about eight miles. I rode ahead on Lyard with Bunnie Hare who has been an absolute angel on the location. Fred the wardrobe master came, and Peter, one of the camera boys, Dottie,** one of my many secretaries, and also Reggie who rode far behind getting his legs very sore through his thin trousers. Darling, I do hope you're not too uncomfortable, I expect your conditions are not of the smoothest. I've had to light my candles. It's been a beautiful day with a fine calm sunset this evening, promising well.

I am so wretched without you . . . In fact, I'm like the king that never smiled again at present. People avoid me like the plague. Everyone is having a whale of a time except me; they keep saying how they dread going home and couldn't we stay on? I don't think anybody imagines the real reason why I'm driving through it like a maniac and worrying so at any delay. They just think I'm a madly conscientious director!

To-morrow there's one of the most difficult shots of all—"the morass." Reg. and Dallas have betted me it will take a week and I have betted them I shall rehearse it in the morning and shoot in the afternoon. It's a longish tracking shot starting on an argument between a large party of retreating Frenchmen and a reinforcing party of horses who are trying to get past them. Then it tracks back to a troop of crossbowmen who come rushing in and are checked by the wodge of argument in front of them and a mass of dying and dead horses and men in a swamp. More reinforcements come up and one by one are pushed into the morass by weight of the numbers behind.

---

* Ernest Hare, who was Olivier's stand-in for the acting sequences when Olivier was behind the camera.

** Dorothy Welford, now Olivier's personal secretary.

After we have tracked over about forty yards of this we pan round to a cow at a gate watching it all unconcernedly—and this having given us a "detached" view, we can now cut to the aerial shot again.

Monday, June 28th. Overjoyed to get your two cables to-day. At LAST, after more than three weeks with nothing. And so you're in Cairo. How peculiar. Be careful of the donkeys! I hear they're *very* forward. *What* joy. . . ! I sent you off a cable at once. . . . I am so thrilled it's been a lovely day. First hearing from you and second we got the shot I was telling you about, so I won my bets. *First Take!!* What a director!

We rehearsed it all the morning and it was very tough trying to get the horses to lie down in the water and pretend they were dead. I had all the footmen in bathing shorts in the morning and made them push me in the mire first. I'd always heard, you see, that you could lead an Irishman through hellfire, etc., but you couldn't drive them and bless the dear boys they took to it literally like ducks to w. When we arrived at the end of the track I couldn't believe my eyes when we panned round and saw the cow's head at exactly the right angle with quite an amused look on its face—it was marvellous! I pray God the film won't have a scratch on it or be spoiled in the labs as I've dismissed 150 of the footmen to-night which is what's known as burning one's boats I believe.

We had two other shots and three retakes after the tracking shot. We're having such perfect weather now that if it keeps up I think we might almost be ahead of schedule. It all looked so hopeless a week ago.

I'm playing two parts to-morrow, my own and the French messenger. So when I'm through my own I have to make up to look like Jonathan Field. . . .

By the end of the third week in July the last of the young men had jogged away on their horses to the remote villages from which they had come, their pockets full of money, and with stories to tell about the mad ways of the film people. The part of the film in which they had played cost £80,000 to make, and represented only just over fifteen minutes in a film which was to run two and a half hours. It was a good deal of money, but these scenes of Agincourt were the most important in the dramatic structure of the film. To make them might well have intimidated a director of far longer experience than Olivier, for whom they represented a personal triumph, and when printed in colour they assumed a new beauty.

Although the scenes were achieved with little actual violence, the fighting looked realistic; and apart from Olivier himself, almost the only casualty was an old horse which lost an eye, and whose story did not end when its owner, a Dublin cab-driver, returned to the city to ply the streets. Within a few weeks he was involved in a petty traffic charge. When the magistrate asked if he had anything to say, the old cabby whined: "Sure, yer honour, an' you wouldn't be taking it out of an old war horse that lost an eye fighting for the Oirish at the Battle of Agincourt." Olivier has always assumed that the magistrate must have been the only person in Ireland who knew nothing about the filming of *Henry V*, for he promptly penalised the cabby for contempt of court.

III

The period when he is planning a film, creating a new part, or has a play in the early stages of rehearsal, is all-important to Olivier. It is the time he really enjoys, and his whole mind is fixed on the problems ahead of him. He becomes completely abstracted, and his friends and fellow-actors know the signs well; they have long-since ceased to be offended if they get no answers to their questions; they have learnt not to be surprised if they see details of "business" rehearsed at the most inappropriate moments; they are quite prepared for Olivier suddenly to become lost in fierce contemplation. The world outside his thoughts is forgotten and inspiration can, and frequently does, come suddenly and unexpectedly—anywhere.

The solution to the main problem of *Henry V*, which had been worrying him for weeks, arrived in a taxi in Gower Street. He was coming away from the Ministry of Information with Anthony Asquith, partly listening to what Asquith was saying but far more engrossed in something which was fretting at the edge of his mind. What would be the best and most effective way to adapt the Shakespearean Chorus to the cinema?

As he had seen it up to that time, it would be spoken by a disembodied voice which would be heard at various stages in the film, and then at the end . . . at the end the camera would come to rest on the figure of Chorus himself. What would Chorus look like? Of course —but of course—*an Elizabethan actor!* . . . an actor actually taking part in a performance of *Henry V* in seventeenth-century London at the Globe! The only trouble was that to cinemagoers not versed in theatrical history that might be a little mystifying. At that moment in his train of thought, suddenly and lucidly the whole idea crystallized. The film should not only end in the Globe Theatre; it should *start* there as well. With this framework he would not have to lose the fine speeches or the famous excuse (which the resources of the cinema made ridiculous) that the "vasty fields of France" could not be crammed into a "wooden O."

The moment he had thought of this idea Olivier found that other things clicked into place. For instance, it solved the wider, even more worrying problem of how to blend the artificiality of Shakespearean verse with the modulated sincerity to which audiences are accustomed in the cinema.

If in this Bankside prologue the performance had all the broad bombast of Elizabethan acting, then, by contrast, the verse and prose dialogue of the film proper, which would be spoken quietly and sincerely, would seem natural. The audience would experience considerable relief when, on Henry's line, "Now sits the wind fair . . . ," the scenes at the Globe blended into those of the film and they realized that the whole film was not to be in the highly artificial manner in which it had started.

Even with this device, Olivier knew that if the rest of the film were acted against strictly realistic backgrounds, these backgrounds would be at odds with the verse, and so he began to search for inspiration for the settings. The original idea of filming at some such place as Kenilworth Castle had immediately struck him as wrong. "If it's a *real* castle why are they talking so strangely?" would be the logical sub-conscious reaction of the ordinary filmgoer. What was wanted was a castle and backgrounds as poetic as the words. Paul Sheriff, the art director, brought him roughs of various ideas, and while Olivier liked them, none of them seemed quite right, although he couldn't explain exactly why. He had a vague, half-formulated idea that the buildings in the scene of Harfleur were too big, and that was all.

"Somehow I feel that we don't want tiny men against a big superstructure," he said to Sheriff and his assistant, Carmen Dillon. "Couldn't we have big men . . . little town . . . oh, I don't know!" Even while they were talking Carmen Dillon made a rough sketch of a little ship with about a dozen huge soldiers in it—something conjured, perhaps, from her recollection of the Bayeux Tapestry, and at once Olivier seized on it. That was the idea he was after. Now, couldn't that be developed in some way even a stage further? He had some reproductions of illustrations from a medieval calendar of the months called *Les Tres Riches Heures de Duc de Berri* which he thought caught the spirit he was after. He showed them to Sheriff, and Sheriff's next sketches with their formalized backgrounds and lack of perspective were completely right. The calendar directly inspired the background for the scene of the quarrel between Fluellen and Pistol over the leek and also the distant view of Katharine's castle.*

The cinema has evolved its own technical conventions, and one, so usual that it is hardly noticed by the audience, is the way the camera is brought slowly forward as an actor begins anything verging on a long speech, so that he is in close-up by the time the speech is under way. Olivier had noticed that when M.G.M. had made *Romeo and Juliet* the same method had been used, and in the potion scene Norma Shearer's face had been brought into enormous close-up, so that she had been forced to whisper just when the verse demanded a more dramatic rendering. After talking it over with Reginald Beck and other technicians, he decided that with the great speeches in *Henry V* he must break away from this tradition; in fact, completely reverse it. He began with close-ups and then the camera receded to a long-shot to permit a full declamatory reading. How well this worked was especially noticeable in the great "Once more unto the breach, dear friends" speech in the scene before Harfleur. Technically the script read:

Crane Shot. Close-up Henry.

Henry: *In peace there's nothing so becomes a man*
As modest stillness and humility:
But when the blast of war blows in our ears,

(On "But when the blast of war" the camera starts to move back

* By a coincidence the Duke of Berri (1340–1416), a famous collector of art treasures and illuminated manuscripts, is actually mentioned in *Henry V* (Act II, Scene IV). In recognition Olivier decided to have him in the film and took the historical liberty of making him the French Ambassador. The part was played by Ernest Thesiger.

very slowly, discovering, as it does so, more and more of the army,
standing perfectly still as they listen to Henry's speech.)

> *Then imitate the action of the tiger . . .*
> (and so the lines to) . . . *The game's afoot:*
> *Follow your spirit, and upon this charge*

(Camera stops tracking on this line. Camera as low as possible.)

> *Cry "God for Harry, England, and St. George!"*

(On the word "George" cut to a medium close shot of Henry
with the camera kept low to give dramatic emphasis to the way the
horse rears up into the camera at the climax.)

Now that *Henry V* has been accepted as an imaginative piece of
film-making these various departures from convention do not seem
so revolutionary, but at the time they were new and carried the
stamp of original minds. As such they were met with foreboding.
Even a number of people inside the unit told Del Giudice that they
considered the Globe Theatre prologue would ruin the film, and
wanted him to persuade Olivier to abandon the idea. But Del
Giudice ignored these criticisms; it was an essential part of his
method that he did not interfere once he had placed power in the
hands of someone in whom he had faith. For once the multiple
voices, petty and destructive, which generally bring all films down
to the lowest imaginative level, chattered unheeded. Olivier had
asked for complete power with good reason.

The film took eighteen months from conception to completion,
not because of technical shortcomings, but largely because of the
difficulties of filming under wartime conditions. It had cost more
than Rank had stipulated and yet it had not been wasteful expenditure. In Hollywood they reckon to throw away almost twice as
much superfluous film as they eventually show in the cinema; at one
time British studios reckoned to throw away fifty per cent. Olivier
on his first film as producer and director kept the wastage down to
a quarter of the whole. But even so, experimenting in a new medium,
he was often confused and overwhelmed with doubts. Only a director with a lifetime's experience could hope to judge as he went
along, from a mass of unrelated shots all of which had to be woven
into a comprehensive pattern, whether the film as a whole would
be good. Reginald Beck, his cutter, on whose abilities he now had to

rely, was quietly confident, but not until the day when the rough-cut was synchronized with the score which William Walton had composed, was Olivier certain that, even if it was a financial failure, people could not say it was bad.

Doubts about the financial chances were fully shared by the Rank Organization, and when the film opened at the Carlton in London it seemed at first that not even a brilliant press or the name of Laurence Olivier could turn film fans into patrons of Shakespeare. Del Giudice himself began to be seriously worried. He had so bravely defended his enterprise against the dismal prophecies of the men in Wardour Street, but for a few fateful days it looked as though they were going to be proved right. Then the word-of-mouth advertising, which means more to entertainment than the largest posters, came into its own. By the fourth week the queues outside the theatre were so long that the Carlton, leased for only a month, had to be booked for a further three months. At the end of that time the film was doing such huge business that it was immediately transferred to the Marble Arch Pavilion, where it completed a London run which was to amount to eleven months altogether.

To prove his theory that the film had created its own audience, Del Giudice arranged for people in the queues to be interviewed, and discovered that six out of every ten were not regular filmgoers; they had come to see the film because other people who had seen it had told them it was so good that they ought to go. This prompted his suggestion to Rank that the best way to show *Henry V* was not to "release" it like other films, but to put it on for an indefinite run—the length to be decided by its popularity—at special cinemas in the provincial cities. From a business point of view this sort of selective screening would have meant slower financial returns, and for this reason it was turned down. The film did unexpectedly well, but there was a certain amount of sales resistance, and it was booed off the screen at some cinemas in the north by audiences who, Olivier remarked, were probably not prepared for the shock of it coming between Grable and Raft.

Del Giudice, whose hatred of the business side of film distribution is unlimited, loves to tell of how he attended a special showing of *Henry V* for some of the chief executives of the American company who were considering distribution in the United States. The film was received in ominous silence, and afterwards the whole party

As Jennifer Dubedat in "The Doctor's Dilemma." Laurence Olivier's
favorite photograph of Vivien Leigh

Entertaining the troops, 1943

"Spring Party" at Gibraltar

Mediterranean bathe during the North African tour. Kaye Young, Vivien
Leigh, Beatrice Lillie and Hugh Beaumont

Vivien Leigh with Bernard Shaw and Gabriel Pascal at Ayot St. Lawrence

"Henry V" on location in Ireland. *Above:* the English camp, and (*below*) the railway track built to film the charge of the French cavalry at Agincourt

Laurence Olivier receiving an honorary degree at Tufts College

Backstage after the first night of "Venus Observed." Olivier, in his make-up as the Duke of Altair, with his son Tarquin

Sergius—1944

Astrov—1945

Hotspur—1945

Oedipus—1945

Mr. Puff—1945

Lear—1946

Antony—1951

Caesar—1951

Vivien Leigh as Sabina
in "The Skin of Our Teeth"

As Blanche Du Bois in
"A Streetcar Named Desire"

Anna Karenina

"Hamlet" filmed at Denham, 1947.
Below: Olivier directs Jean Simmons in the Play Scene

On board the *Corinthic* going to Australia

The Oliviers besieged as they arrive at the Embassy Theatre, Sydney,
for the première of "Hamlet"

Vivien Leigh as Antigone

The Oliviers with Danny Kaye sing a number at the Sid Field Memorial Benefit

Two scenes from the motion picture of "Streetcar," and (*below*) in the studio with Elia Kazan and Tennessee Williams

Vivien Leigh as Cleopatra in "Antony and Cleopatra"

moved off to the hotel where a special lunch had been arranged. "We formed a kind of cortège," he recalls, "which moved from the theatre, and slowly like a funeral march we moved towards the restaurant. Nobody dared say a word. I myself felt like an undertaker, if not the corpse," In the restaurant, as they sat down to a large meal, the silence continued until the English representative of the distributing company asked one of the Americans what he thought about the film. "There's a lot of work in it," he replied shortly, and another of the Americans observed that it would never be understood in the United States. The man who would be responsible for the film's publicity said that Henry's proposal to the French princess, which took two thousand words, might seem a little long to the steel workers of Pittsburgh. "They are accustomed to make their own proposals," he said, "in two words or none at all." Then, as Del Giudice remembers it, they turned to him for his opinion. His comment would seem to have been heroically phrased in view of the importance of the Americans on the future of the film. "I was frightened you would like it," he said. "Now I feel better. Now I know that this will be the greatest success in film history."

As a booking in a chain of cinemas in the United States did not promise well, Rank decided to follow Del Giudice's idea of "roadshowing" the film, and *Henry V* opened in Boston where it played for eight months, and in New York it ran for eleven months, the longest run a British film had ever had. There was one unforeseen hazard. The Hays Office lived up to its reputation by banning it until Shakespeare had been trimmed of words like "damn" and "bastard," and references to God deleted. In Boston a specially scissored version was shown on Sundays. Once, however, it was free from anything likely to ruffle the sensibilities of the most fervent women's clubs, it did even better business than in England. Within a year it had been shown in twenty different cities, and, whatever the reaction in libelled Pittsburgh, it had made a profit of £275,000.

For Olivier, who was given his first "Oscar," the award of the Academy of Motion Picture Arts and Sciences, it was an artistic triumph, and for Del Giudice, who had fought so many battles on behalf of his ideal, its success was particularly sweet. Conscious of all the Italian producer had done to make the film possible, Olivier went to visit him at Sheepcote, his home on Wooburn Common, one day in 1947 just after he had received the Oscar from Holly-wood. When he arrived, Del Giudice noticed he was carrying a parcel, but had no idea what it contained or why Olivier took it into the study on the first floor; not until he joined Olivier a little later did he find out the answer. Standing on his desk was the golden statuette. "I wish you'd have it, Del," Olivier said to him. "*Henry V* would never have been made without you, dear fellow." It was a gesture which, coming at a time when Oscars were not so profuse as they are now in the Olivier household, Del Giudice has never forgotten.

Olivier had his own memento from *Henry V*. It was the grey gelding he had first ridden in Ireland and which had been brought back with the unit for studio shots at Denham. Over the months Olivier grew very fond of Blaunche Kyng, and when the film was finished and the horse's future in doubt, he took him back to Old Prestwick, the country house which they had taken at Fulmer, only a few miles from their previous house, Hawksgrove. Once de-mobilized, Blaunche was inclined to get lazy and put on weight, and on several occasions his wartime dignity suffered seriously. In those days of strict petrol rationing, he was harnessed and put be-tween the shafts of a cart in which Olivier would drive down to the station to pick up friends who were arriving for the weekend.

Blaunche showed some resentment at this treatment, and would dawdle slowly on the way back to the house completely unimpressed at the privilege of drawing Noël Coward or Lady Colefax. But Olivier had a pretty trick up his sleeve which never failed to amuse his guests. "Watch this!" he would say, and, standing up in the cart, would begin to recite: " 'Once more unto the breach, dear friends, once more . . .' "

At this Blaunche would find his lost soul. With ears back he would break into a lumbering gallop so that the last stage of the journey to Old Prestwick was as brave a charge as was ever seen at the battle of Harfleur.

CHAPTER 4

The Desert and Cleopatra
1943-1945

I

IN THE WESTERN DESERT through which they had so successfully
chased Rommel, the Eighth Army had often to be satisfied for
entertainment with "Ave Maria" played on an accordion, cook-
corporals with a talent for humorous recitations or rather travel-
stained concert parties from Cairo. Then, while training in Tunisia
for the invasion of Sicily, the troops heard that a really brilliant
company had arrived by air from London.

The principal stars of *Spring Party* were Beatrice Lillie, Dorothy
Dickson and Leslie Henson, and the name of Vivien Leigh was a
welcome but rather surprising addition to a cast of artists who were
otherwise all well-known in musical comedy or revue. Under the
terms of the wartime agreement which the Ministry of Labour had
with the theatrical profession an artist had to devote six weeks in
every year to entertaining factory workers with C.E.M.A. or the
troops with E.N.S.A.* As Vivien Leigh had been playing in *The
Doctor's Dilemma* at the Haymarket for over a year, she said she
would be delighted when Hugh Beaumont asked her to join the

* C.E.M.A., the Council for the Encouragement of Music and the Arts, was
founded in 1940 and financed by the British Treasury. E.N.S.A., the Entertain-
ments National Service Association, was concerned with providing service
entertainment throughout the war.

company which he was helping to organize for North Africa in
April of 1943. She was due to appear in *Cæsar and Cleopatra*, but as
it looked as though Pascal's plans would be more than usually protracted she could easily manage to be out of the country for about
two months.

She had warned Beaumont that she thought she would be pretty
hopeless in concert party, but if there was any way she could help
she was naturally keen. Her only problem was to decide what she
could do. She had felt the disadvantage of any straight actress who
is asked to go on and hold a stage by herself. She was assured that
the troops would be quite happy just to *look* at her, and while this
was flattering, it didn't seem quite enough to stand about looking
decorative while Beatrice Lillie sang about a little fish that swam
right over the dam and Leslie Henson wrecked Rachmaninoff.

At a conference at Drury Lane, the E.N.S.A. headquarters, she
put forward a hesitant suggestion that perhaps she might try the
potion scene from *Romeo and Juliet*. There was rather a horrified
silence when John Gielgud, who was helping to produce the show,
said blithely, "Oh no, Vivien! Only a great actress can do that sort
of thing!" Less embarrassed than anyone, Vivien Leigh asked for
ideas, and, after a good deal of discussion, it was decided that as well
as appearing in sketches, for her own individual "spots" she should
recite Clemence Dane's heroic poem "Plymouth Hoe," and, in contrast to the patriotic, a piece of nonsense verse, Lewis Carroll's "You
are old, Father William." The ingenious versifier known as "Sagit-
tarius" was also asked to supply her with some material, and, recalling the part in which Vivien Leigh was most famous, provided her
with a satirical lyric as a not so scarlet Scarlett O'Hara.

At one time it was thought that the company would leave before
the *Henry V* unit went to Ireland, but the final defeat of the German army in Tunisia ran a little behind schedule. It was not until
the middle of May, and when Olivier was at Powerscourt, that at
last the order came and *Spring Party* flew to Gibraltar, via Lisbon,
on the first stage of the journey.

For the next three months the company sweltered under the
North African sun from Gibraltar to Cairo, giving one, two and
sometimes three performances a day. They presented their brilliant
little revue on the decks of aircraft carriers and in hospital wards,
in the Miramare opera house in Tripoli, against a woodland set in

the theatre at Constantine, and at Suez on a stage rigged up in the middle of the sand surrounded by an audience of six thousand. It was exhausting work in a heat to which they were not accustomed, but, as she wrote home to her mother and father, it was "one of the most exciting and often most moving experiences I have ever had."

Every wartime concert party tells stories of extraordinary places in which it has had to play, and for the company in *Spring Party* no setting was more unexpected and at the same time more appropriate than the one in which they performed at Leptis Magna, a few miles east of Tripoli. The great Roman theatre, probably dating back to the seventh century, which had been excavated only shortly before the war, was being put to modern and proper use by the 7th Armoured Division which was stationed around Homs. There the E.N.S.A. company entertained eight thousand troops who sat tier upon stone tier in the great semi-circular auditorium, and their last performance, which was at night, had a special magic about it. For at least one "Desert Rat" there was a memorable moment when Vivien Leigh stood all alone on the vast stage, picked out in the darkness by a spotlight, and hardened soldiers who had fought through a gruelling campaign sat spellbound as she recited Lewis Carroll's poem.

Among the sun-scorched men in khaki or white drill she would sometimes find old friends such as Alec Guinness and Peter Bull, longing for news of home, and it seemed to Vivien Leigh that the touching gratitude of all the troops to whom they played owed something to the fact that the company from England had come so recently from the place which filled their thoughts. To the men they were the next best thing to their own wives and families. Sometimes at the end of the show when they all joined in "God Save the King" she found it almost unbearably moving.

So famous a company was bound to find its tour somewhat gilt-edged. In Algiers they were the guests of General Eisenhower and Sir Arthur Tedder; in Tripoli they met General Montgomery; in Constantine they stayed with General Spaatz and General Doolittle; and in Tunis the girls were lent Von Arnim's villa and Vivien Leigh slept in the room which had been occupied by the German general up to the last days before the surrender a few weeks earlier. In Tunis, too, they gave a very special performance one evening on the terrace of Air Marshal Cunningham's villa overlooking the sea.

It was a performance which was attended by His Majesty King George VI, a report of which Olivier had read in Ireland. They played in the open air on a white marble terrace with three great arches behind them, through the centre one of which they made entrances and exits from the villa. The King, fresh from a bathe in the Mediterranean, sat with the audience of about eighty people on a lower terrace. It was a perfect night with a huge moon which shimmered in the sea, and lent a special beauty to the whole performance. Afterwards the company were formally presented, and later, during a party at the villa which he did not leave until 1:30 in the morning, the King told Vivien Leigh how much he had liked her "Plymouth Hoe." As they talked she mentioned how difficult it was for a straight actress to find material suitable for a concert party. After a moment's reflection the King suggested that she should try a favourite poem of his, Alice Duer Miller's "The White Cliffs of Dover."

After Tripoli the company flew to Cairo, which, now that the war had moved so many hundreds of miles away, had resumed its atmosphere of torpid luxury, and there they played to the half-forgotten troops in the Delta. At Tripoli where, on General Montgomery's special invitation, they stopped on their return journey, came the exciting news of the Sicilian invasion, and after farewell performances at Bougie, Bone and Phillipville they said good-bye to North Africa. Vivien Leigh had lost weight, and like the rest of the company she had suffered bouts of illness. Yet despite this and the appalling heat, when the time came to fly back to Gibraltar the whole company were sad to leave. Apart from interest in the work, for the women especially, North Africa had seemed a place of enchantment; there they could buy material, clothes, trinkets, and such essential trivialities as safety-pins, which had long since disappeared from the London shops. The costume skips began to bulge with exotic acquisitions. For Vivien the bazaars exerted an almost magical influence, and she was for ever dashing off and returning triumphantly with bargains. At Tripoli the stage door of the Miramare Theatre was only a hundred yards from the entrance to the Old City and the Kasbah, and nothing could restrain her from visiting it between performances. On one occasion she arrived back at the theatre with a length of vivid scarlet material which failed to impress the others in the company to whom she proudly showed it.

Not in the least disconcerted by their lack of enthusiasm she bundled it up. "Oh well," she said cheerfully, "I can always sell it to Pascal for *Cleopatra!*"

At Gibraltar Vivien was faced with a conflicting pull on her loyalties. Telegrams from Larry, some of which had set the cabling clerks a problem by being in verse, were full of ecstatic excitement about her immediate return to England, but there was also a request from E.N.S.A. headquarters to the whole company asking them to extend their tour for a further three weeks so that they could entertain smaller units and hospitals. She felt very homesick as she read Larry's letters full of trivialities about home (the scorched garden, and cats having kittens), but she felt bound to send a cable to say that she thought she must stay a week or so longer, even if she did not complete the last few days of the tour with the rest of the company. He wrote back that he was disappointed, but that he supposed he could just manage to wait a little longer until he saw her. Before she finally flew home she received another letter from him in which he mentioned that Gabriel Pascal had gone to Hollywood to find a leading man for the film of *Cæsar and Cleopatra.*

II

Cæsar and Cleopatra, which Gabriel Pascal first had the idea of filming in 1938 and which started at Denham six days after the Normandy invasion of 1944, was not a happy film. It was planned with high hopes and a great deal of initial enthusiasm, but, rather as if some curse hung over it, the film fulfilled hardly any of its expectations.

Arthur Rank, faced with a large financial gamble, hoped that it would increase the growing reputation of his company and establish British films in the world market. To Bernard Shaw, in the twilight of his life at Ayot St. Lawrence, it seemed to offer an even wider extension of his fame. Gabriel Pascal looked forward to a repetition of the success he had enjoyed with *Pygmalion*. Vivien Leigh saw it as her greatest chance since Scarlett.

Each of these personal hopes collapsed in ruins. *Cæsar and Cleopatra* did not in the least help Mr. Rank or British film prestige; Shaw was reported to have said privately that the film reminded him of the coloured illustrations in a cheap Bible and that he thought it very bad; Pascal's expenditure—a budget of £470,000 soared to something like £1,300,000—was hardly justified by the finished film. For Vivien Leigh it was a film tinged with tragedy, for six weeks after filming started she was taken ill and lost the child for which both she and Larry had so much hoped.*

If she had any reason to remember the film kindly it was because it gave her the chance to meet Shaw again on two occasions. She went with Pascal to Ayot St. Lawrence, and spent a little time with him talking in the sunshine as they sat on the steps of the revolving summerhouse which was his workroom in the garden of Shaw's Corner. As they strolled back to the house she asked him if he would autograph her copy of the play. In writing even more squiggly than usual he inscribed it: "Cleopatra's copy. B.S." He apologized for the brevity, saying, "I can't write to-day; there are some days I simply can't write."

The next time they met was when he visited Denham and after looking round commented prophetically: "I pity poor Rank. The film will cost him a million." After this he took a great interest in the film, and while he abruptly dismissed Rank's suggestion that he should add a little love interest, he was prepared to write a completely new scene (which unfortunately was never filmed), and a stream of postcards of advice and instruction poured from Ayot St. Lawrence. Alterations to the script were permitted only if he suggested them, and after he had met Claude Rains who was to play Cæsar Vivien Leigh received one of the inevitable postcards:

> Your Claudius Cæsar is not rather thin and stringy (I have just seen him); so will you say instead: "You are hundreds of years old; but you have a nice voice, &c."
>
> I think this is the only personal remark that needs altering; but if there is anything let me know.
>
> G.B.S.

Vivien Leigh was amused by the reference to "Claudius" Cæsar, but was disappointed by the change as she much preferred the original line, and at once wrote off from the studio asking to be allowed to retain the description as it was in the play. A little vaguely she suggested that she was sure that she could make Claude Rains *look*

---

* When the film was first shown she could not even bring herself to see it, and six years were to pass before she agreed to go to a special private screening which was arranged during the rehearsals of the production of the play at the St. James's Theatre in 1951.

thin and stringy—simply by the way she spoke the lines. This produced an immediate rebuke from Shaw:

> No. Rains is not stringy, and would strongly resent any deliberate attempt to make him appear so.
>
> Besides "you are hundreds of years old" is a much better line, as it belongs to the childishness of Cleopatra in the first half of the play.
>
> I never change a line except for the better.
>
> Don't be an idiot.
>
> G.B.S.
>
> Why don't you put your address in your letters?

These astringent exchanges with Shaw were the few stimulating features about a production which very soon lost all its enchantment. It was impossible to retain interest, much less vital enthusiasm, in the protracted delays and conflict of emotions and personalities at Denham. Pascal apparently decided after a fortnight's shooting that everything was going far too smoothly and that if the film were to have any life he must make a few enemies. He protested that he found this repugnant because he was really a simple, kindly man. But as he seemed to succeed, nevertheless, it was hardly surprising that shooting was soon behind the timetable and costs were soaring.

The tedium of constant retakes, the strikes of technicians, and the general sense of mismanagement were not calculated to inspire a leading lady who was, anyway, despondent because of her own private misfortunes. Blue with cold and shivering miserably in Cleopatra's thin and wispy gowns, Vivien Leigh tried hard to suggest the stifling heat of an Egyptian summer in scenes which were being filmed in a field at Denham in November. Hollywood, however, had taught her equanimity and technical efficiency, and people watching her on the set noted how effortlessly she fitted herself to the part. One minute she would be sitting in her dressing-gown with *The Times* cross-word, and the next in front of the camera, catching with quiet certainty all the subtleties of a scene. She could repeat it again and again with just the same precision of timing and inflexion if a scene had to be reshot for the benefit of another actor.

With the relief with which one wakes from a long and unpleasant dream, Vivien Leigh completed her part in the film. The final stages in the elaborate and reckless production were accomplished without her. She did not have to accompany the model of the Sphinx, weighing eighty tons, which was shipped from England all the way to Egypt for location scenes. She was spared the ordeal of trying to act in an artificial sandstorm created by two R.A.F. aero-engines. Her only regret was that she was not present at one of the most remarkable banquets that can ever have been witnessed. For the desert battle scenes 1,200 Egyptian troops were employed, but their effectiveness was marred by their discovery that the papier-mâché shields, imported from England, contained a fish glue which made them both edible and appetizing.

With such unlikely excursions it was hardly surprising that well over a million pounds was spent on *Cæsar and Cleopatra* in the eighteen months it took to make and before it was eventually shown to the public in December, 1945. If it had been a brilliant film such prodigal expenditure might have been forgiven; as it was, it proved very far from brilliant, and Vivien Leigh, a sparkling and enchanting Cleopatra, was about the only person who came out of it all with much credit. In the three and a half years between this and her previous appearance before the cameras she seemed to have acquired a much greater accomplishment as an actress. Especially in the banqueting scene in which Cleopatra orders the murder of Pothinus, her performance revealed a depth and authority which had hitherto been only hinted at in her films.

III

Early in 1944 the Oliviers had received from New York the script of a play which at first reading was a little confusing and difficult to understand, but which excited them so much that they bought the British rights. Olivier had read it first, and then, purposely refraining from expressing his own enthusiasm, had passed it over to Vivien for her reaction. She had been entranced by the heroine, and thought the play more than justified the praise she had heard from a friend who had seen it in New York. The night after she had read it she could not sleep for thinking about it, and as soon as she was free of Cleopatra, all her enthusiasm was concentrated on returning to the stage as Sabina in Thornton Wilder's *The Skin of Our Teeth*.

She was not, however, able to shake off the hold of the film studios at all easily. Over her wartime career hung the obligations of the seven-year contract which she had signed with David Selznick in 1939. This had prevented her appearing in *Henry V;* Rank had been forced to pay Selznick heavily for the right to use her in *Cæsar and Cleopatra;* and there was no denying that a certain amount of ill-feeling existed in Hollywood because of her failure to go back and make films there. Over the years a great number of letters and immoderately long cables had been sent by the Selznick Organiza- tion to Vivien Leigh on the subject, and their friendly tone had assumed a certain edge when, with diplomacy and charm but in- flexible firmness, she had consistently declined to desert England in the middle of the war and return to Hollywood.

Eventually Selznick's lawyer had dropped all façade and brought the thing down to brass tacks. "We are aware you do not care whether you ever make another film," said one cable acidly, "but obviously this cannot be our viewpoint and equally obviously we could not believe and still cannot believe you would expect us con- tinue give you consents do plays and have our own interests suffer." Whether they believed it or not, Vivien Leigh continued to stall gracefully. Nothing on earth would make her leave England and Larry, or to let the terms of a five-year-old contract interfere with her plans. Legal advice was taken, and she went ahead with *The Skin of Our Teeth,* which Olivier was to produce and which was to be put on by H. M. Tennent's. A cast of thirty was assembled and rehearsals had started at the Globe when the blow fell. Selznick applied for a legal injunction to prevent her appearing.

The case, which was heard in the Chancery Division, was fought over points of legal nicety which so delight opposing barristers and give a judge an opportunity to deliver a verdict which may create a precedent. There is much learned reference, and fees mount agree- ably while paradoxes are pointed and parried across the court.

It was the contention of Sir Walter Monckton, K.C. (for David Selznick) that Vivien Leigh was "an exotic plant" whom his client did not wish to be subjected to "unwise exposure." "A screen per- sonality is something so expensive and so valuable," he told Mr. Justice Romer, "that a person investing in it a large sum of money will naturally say, 'I want to prevent you entering into adventures otherwise than with my consent.' "

Pulling the exotic plant briskly out of the hothouse, Sir Valentine Holmes, K.C. (for Vivien Leigh) stated that Mrs. Laurence Olivier was a married woman of thirty-one and subject to National Service regulations. At the end of *Cæsar and Cleopatra* she had applied to the Ministry of Labour for a further period of exemption from being directed. This had been granted so that she could appear in the play, and if she did not she would be idle. Surely, he argued, it was against public policy to prevent anyone working in wartime?

When he heard the verdict David Selznick must have felt that Gilbertian love of paradox was almost too ingenious in the English courts. Mr. Justice Romer had said he must consider what was in Mr. Selznick's best interests and that he could not see that it was against Mr. Selznick's interests for Vivien Leigh to appear in *The Skin of Our Teeth*, whereas if she was forced by an injunction to be idle she might be directed by the Ministry of Labour. This, though he did not say so, clearly conjured up the picture of the exotic plant unwisely exposed and wilting in a munitions factory. The injunction was therefore refused, and Mr. Selznick had only the cold-comfort reflection that, according to the interpretation of the learned judge, it had really been to his advantage to lose the case he had brought at such cost.

While the verbal battle had been going on in the court, rehearsals had continued with defiant optimism at the Globe, and when the evening papers arrived with the verdict a cheer went up from the company. Olivier took it in his stride. "Well," he observed, "we seem to have won—by the . . ." Leaving the sentence incomplete he carried on with the rehearsal.

IV

In April Wilder's "history of mankind in comic strip" opened to a bewildered Edinburgh. Not only Edinburgh found difficulty in grasping the full meaning of this unconventional, allegorical play in which Vivien Leigh appeared as the eternal woman—in the guise of beauty queen, housemaid, and *vivandière*. As someone said, it was a wise, silly and diverting play, and each of these seemingly incompatible descriptions was accurate. An eccentric "morality" play, it was a highly theatrical novelty which spilled ideas all over the stage. To tell the basically simple story of the strength of the family in the face of all sorts of danger, and the survival of the wife in the face of the eternal enchantress, Wilder used every technical trick. He allowed the actors to move inconsequentially in and out of the framework of the play, complain to the stage manager that a scene was not worth playing, soliloquize, and speak as individual characters or symbolic figures. It was symptomatic that, during one performance at the Piccadilly, a distraught member of the audience, who climbed on to the stage from the stalls, was bustled into the wings without the rest of the audience realizing that she was not part of the play.

People who battled too conscientiously to understand it were apt to get angry because, however hard they tried, the symbolism would not resolve itself tidily. During the try-out tour and later in London Vivien Leigh began to collect the outraged comments. She liked the military voice which was overheard to say: "I do think they ought to get better *organized*, yer know!" and this assumption of confusion was echoed in the remark of a landlady in Liverpool. Because the characters appealed to the audience, she thought they did not know their lines, and reported to a friend: "Ooh, it's a proper shambles up at the Royal Court!" Best of all was the conversation of the two elderly ladies at a matinée at the Phoenix, one of whom said in the first interval, "My dear, I *am* sorry to have brought you. I'm afraid I didn't read the critiques—I had no idea it was *that sort* of play. Please let me get you a cup of tea." To which came the severe reply: "No, dear—don't let's give them another penny!"

Ten days after London had cheered itself hoarse with excitement at the end of the war in Europe the play opened at the Phoenix to the sort of first-night audience that might have decorated just such an occasion in the 'thirties. Many were Vivien Leigh's personal friends whose genuine good wishes for her success were testified by flowers in her dressing-room; but there were also, she knew, a few who would be whispering damp prophecies about her ability to manage the rôle of Sabina. There would be a ready audience for the well-travelled V.I.P. who could say casually in the bar ". . . of course, in New York Tallulah . . ."

It was therefore a night which offered more than a usual challenge, and she met it with a brilliance which routed all petty denigrators. From the applause at the end she knew that she had made a great personal success, and the press was to confirm that Sabina was the most outstanding performance she had so far given. All the critics seemed to vie to give her the most praise, and two of them even used exactly the same phrase—"entrancing mischief"—to describe the quality which she brought to the part. Everyone talked in terms of "a dazzling triumph" and many asserted, like A. V. Cookman, that it was "a long way ahead of anything else she has done." "As volatile as quicksilver," wrote W. A. Darlington in the *Daily Telegraph*, "and she carried the piece on her shoulders." For the first time she had a part which gave her scope for comedy, a character in which she could lose the conventional Vivien Leigh and change the attitude of those who associated her with a series of beautiful but rather ordinary screen heroines. Now there were comparisons with Beatrice Lillie, and perhaps she owed just a little to the lessons which she had learnt as, performance after performance during the tour of *Spring Party* in North Africa, she had stood in the wings studying Beatrice Lillie's brilliant technique. Certainly she could ask for no greater compliment. Praise also came from one unexpected quarter. It was with more than usual apprehension that Vivien Leigh and Olivier opened *The Sunday Times* to read James Agate's notice, and with good reason. On the first night Olivier had hit him.

Conflict between the artist and those who criticize him rarely reaches violence. Hannen Swaffer on one notable occasion had his face slapped by an actress who considered he had insulted her, and in Paris it would seem that even to-day dramatists sometimes demand satisfaction from editors in the cold light of dawn in the Bois; but for the producer of a play actually to hit a critic—albeit not very hard—in the stalls on a first night is probably unique. Although they were on nodding acquaintance, and Vivien Leigh was actually quite friendly with him, there had never been much love lost between Olivier and James Agate. Over the years he had sometimes been praised, and praised highly, in Agate's columns, but like so many other actors and actresses he had often been taunted by Agate's caustic pen. In his action, taken ten minutes after the curtain had gone up on the third act of Wilder's play at the Phoenix on the night of May 18th, 1945, Olivier has always considered that he struck a blow for his profession.

The circumstances, which reflect no credit on Olivier's patience or Agate's punctuality, were briefly as follows. It was a first night which proved something of a producer's nightmare because in the second act the lighting cues were all late, never a happy thing and particularly fatal in an experimental play with a complicated lighting

plot. Characters were often left speaking in the dark while unoc-
cupied parts of the stage were fiercely illuminated. The audience,
already in some confusion, probably took this as just another hazard
which they were being asked to negotiate, but Olivier in a gangway
seat in the middle of the stalls was in agony. Although he had tried
to calm his nerves with a stiff drink he was in a far from placid
frame of mind when he slipped back into his seat after the second
interval. It was then, as the lights dimmed, that he noticed that
Agate, whose familiar squat figure and bald head he had previously
seen in a seat across the gangway, was absent.

It would be pleasant, but a distinct falsification of the theatrical
scene, to suggest that it is without precedent for critics to be a little
late back after the interval, but the thing which infuriated Olivier
on this particular occasion was that Agate was missing for ten minutes, and they were ten minutes which Olivier knew to be essential
for a full understanding of the play. So when Agate finally appeared
he could not restrain himself from getting up and crossing the gangway to his seat. With the hissed accusation of "You're late, blast
you!" he hit him a glancing blow across the shoulder. For the most
part the incident went unseen; there was no confusion; no blowing
of police whistles. Understandably startled, Agate simply peered up
and muttered: "Who's that?" To which Olivier replied, darkly and
savagely, "You know who I am all right," and then returned to his
seat.

After this assault Agate's review in *The Sunday Times* was almost disappointing; it suggested no lasting bruise, no umbrage beneath a bandage. In fact he said that Vivien Leigh's performance
was the best of its kind since Yvonne Printemps, and Olivier's production ingenious and inventive. This caused Olivier to regard the
incident with satisfaction. "I've always thought the only way to
treat critics was to hit them!" he confided to his friends, and there
was a speculative note in his voice which might, perhaps, have
alarmed some of Agate's colleagues had they heard it.

In Sabina Vivien Leigh had an exciting and stimulating part, but
after two months she found she was becoming strangely overtired
and quite alarmingly thin. When the play had been in Liverpool
she had developed a cough and a doctor there had advised her that
it would be wise to see a specialist when she was in London. She
had put this off, but, now seriously worried, she decided to have a

thorough examination. X-rays were taken and the doctor who saw her looked very grave. He asked where her husband was, and when she told him that he was on tour with the Old Vic playing to the troops in Germany, he said that he should be sent for. She had a tubercular patch on her lung and must stop acting immediately; it might be necessary for her to go to Switzerland or a sanatorium in Scotland. This was very frightening, but before making a decision which would mean the end of *The Skin of Our Teeth* and serious complications in the Old Vic tour, she took a second opinion from another specialist. His verdict was less dramatic. He simply advised her to stop work as soon as possible.

By this time Olivier was in Hamburg and until she saw the second doctor Vivien Leigh did not say anything in her letters for fear of worrying him. Unfortunately, while he was playing there he had a vague and very disturbing hint that something was wrong from their friend, Anthony Bartley, a young pilot who, flying frequently between Germany and England, had seen Vivien more recently than he had. Olivier immediately wrote imploring news, but Vivien's letter of explanation never arrived, and the next he received was even more upsetting as it contained the phrase, "now that you know the worst," but did not amplify it. Still without news he arrived in Paris and there immediately got in touch with Alfred Lunt and Lynn Fontanne who were just over from London to play *Love in Idleness* for the American troops. The Oliviers' friendship with the Lunts went back to the early days of the war when they were in New York, and even before. Since the Lunts' arrival in London during the winter of 1943 they had all seen a great deal of each other, and there could have been no more sympathetic people to break the bad news and gently try to reassure him that, dreadful as the idea of T.B. sounded, there was no reason for serious alarm. Nothing, they pointed out, would be known definitely until the end of the month when Vivien was going into University College Hospital for observation, and by then he would be back in England and with her. Over lunch which the three had together the Lunts tried to keep the conversation away from Vivien's illness, and afterwards, for fear that he would brood if left alone, Alfred Lunt said he would be very grateful if Olivier would come round to the theatre where they were due to open in the Rattigan play and help him with the

lighting. He shrewdly guessed that work in the theatre would be
the one thing which would occupy Larry's mind.

Fears, based on the first alarming diagnosis, proved out of all proportion to actual seriousness. When *The Skin of Our Teeth* closed
at the end of July Vivien Leigh went into hospital, and after six
weeks was told that neither Switzerland nor Scotland would be necessary; provided she spent several months quietly in the country and
in bed the patch on her lung could be cured. And so it came about
that, towards the end of September, Notley Abbey became not only
her home but a temporary sanatorium.

Notley was the house at Thame in Buckinghamshire which the
Oliviers had bought soon after *Henry V*, and which had been the
end of a two years' search for a home. Ever since they had returned
from America they had moved from one furnished house to another
while Durham Cottage, a bomb casualty, waited on extensive repairs.
Then, while they were living at Fulmer, they heard of Notley, and
one bitterly cold winter's day they had driven over to see it. Originally founded in the reign of Henry II for the Augustinian Canons,
the Abbey, a thirteenth-century house of grey stone and mullioned
windows, had passed into private hands at the time of the Dissolution
of the monasteries. When he heard its history, Olivier was blind to
burst water pipes, the tangled rose garden and the great cold and
draughty rooms which depressed Vivien Leigh. And when he learnt
that Notley had been endowed by Henry V it seemed like destiny
that he should buy it. As they left, they looked back from the car
and both delivered an opinion simultaneously.

"Well," said Olivier happily, "that's it!"

"That," said Vivien Leigh, equally positively, "is *not* it!"

They spoke at precisely the same moment and each had to ask
what the other had said. When they discovered how completely
opposed they were they sought the opinions of their friends, and
Robert Helpmann and Lady Colefax were only two who were taken
to look over the house. As clearly as Vivien they saw all the work
needed to make Notley "livable" and sided with her against the idea.
But Olivier would not be deflected. Already, in his mind's eye, the
rough fields leading up to the house from the little river were transformed into a lawn. Vines and creepers which they would plant
already lent colour to the mellow walls; already the now-unkempt
Italian cypress stood clipped and serene. As for the restoration and

the cost . . . well, they would slowly get licences . . . make the rooms comfortable one by one . . . do just a little each year. Here was the place of refuge to which they would come, tired from London and their work, to be refreshed and to entertain their friends. In the grounds of Notley they would watch the changing of the seasons. It was perfect. In the face of such enthusiasm Vivien Leigh had known it was useless to argue, and within a few months of the end of the war Notley became theirs.

It was a little sad that for her first stay of any length she had to be in bed, but the doctors were quite definite in their instructions. For four rather depressing months she lay in bed reading her way through books as diverse as the maxims of Confucius, Montaigne's essays, and the few novels of Dickens she had not devoured on those dark wartime journeys from London to Winchester. As spring began to bring out the white conical flowers on the chestnut trees in the grounds, she was allowed up for a few hours each day, and when the weather became warmer she started gardening. In the quiet of the country she slowly won back her health, and for the first time, she felt, Notley became her real home and not simply a weekend refuge from London. She was to be there, away from the theatre and the studios, for nine months.

CHAPTER 5

The Great Parts
1944-1946

I

ONE DAY during the last few weeks of filming *Henry V* Olivier had two visitors at Denham. Ralph Richardson, still an officer in the Fleet Air Arm, and John Burrell, who for the previous four years had been a drama producer at the B.B.C., came to see him on a combined mission. Walking round the studios they told him that the Governors of the Old Vic considered that, as London now seemed finally free from air-raids, the time had come for the company to return from provincial banishment. The Old Vic was seriously in debt, but there would be capital from the bountiful wartime patron, the Council for the Encouragement of Music and the Arts, to help through the first season or so. Richardson said that Guthrie had asked if he would help to build up the new company which would open in London in the autumn. His reply had been that he would be delighted provided he could be released from the Navy and could have the help of John Burrell; then, when he and Burrell had discussed it, they had wondered if they could possibly persuade Olivier to join them. Would he lend a hand in the formidable but very worthwhile job of restarting the company?

As they talked they came to the large model of Elizabethan London which had been used for the early sequences of *Henry V*. They looked down on the city as it had been in Shakespeare's day. There

275

was old St. Paul's on the further side of the river, London Bridge covered with houses, and, in the foreground just to the right of them, the Globe Theatre. Most of the foreground consisted of the open meadows of Paris Gardens and the marshy fields of Southwark, and suddenly all three of them realized that they were standing on the exact spot where, in the real London of two hundred years later, the Old Vic had been built in 1818. It was an irresistible piece of symbolism, and then and there Olivier agreed to join them. But thinking of the old theatre reminded him that the building in the Waterloo Road was a bombed shell. Where, he asked, were they going to open? Richardson told him that Bronson Albery, who was joint administrator of the Old Vic with Guthrie, had promised the New Theatre.

So it was arranged, and the Governors were asked to apply formally to the Admiralty for Olivier's and Richardson's release. Surprisingly for Whitehall which, in the early summer of 1944, had other things on its mind, the reply came back almost by return of post. "We were released," said Olivier ruefully, "with an alacrity on the part of my Lords of the Admiralty that was almost hurtful." Three years and one month after he had been commissioned he could finally put away a uniform which during his long period in the studios had been acquiring a pronounced smell of camphor. After being absent from the London stage for six years—except for a special matinée he had done nothing since *Coriolanus* in 1938—he was coming back with a company which was the nearest thing to a national theatre that England possessed.

It was a company for which he retained a considerable sentimental attachment, and he remembered that he had once said it was rare for players to appear only once at the Old Vic and not return. Now he was making his own prophecy come true. Two Old Vic veterans, who had returned several times, also rejoined the colours. Sybil Thorndike, a member of Lilian Baylis' first company in 1914, was one of them, and Harcourt Williams, who had produced nearly fifty plays in the Waterloo Road, was the other. With the addition of Nicholas Hannen and George Relph, the company had a firm backbone. Joyce Redman, Michael Warre, and Margaret Leighton were the younger players still with reputations to win.

While the company was being selected the three directors were simultaneously choosing the plays. Plays were harder to choose than actors, but Olivier found that, as always, Richardson had deep-laid plans, and a cut-and-dried idea of the play in which he wanted to take the lead. It was Ibsen's *Peer Gynt*. As neither he nor Olivier had done any stage work since the outbreak of war, they decided they needed at least a week's out-of-town canter in a comedy before opening in London with anything as exacting as Ibsen. There was talk of Pinero's *Dandy Dick* but they eventually decided on *Arms and the Man*. This left one play still to be settled. Unlike Richardson, Olivier had no plans or ideas for the third play of the season— the play in which he would be the star. The parts of Hamlet, Macbeth, Henry V and Coriolanus were all behind him, and he had no wish to revive any of them yet. Burrell suggested *Richard III*, but Donald Wolfit had recently scored a success with it and Olivier did not wish to appear to be vying with him. Eventually, however, he agreed to play Richard because he could think of no suitable alternative.

To start with the fates did not seem to bless their enterprise. Rehearsals began in the critical weeks just after the Normandy invasion when England was being rocked by flying bombs. The V-1's sailing over London made things far from comfortable for actors rehearsing in the echoing and empty rooms of the National Gallery. It was almost impossible not to hesitate in a speech as the hideously unpredictable planes droned over; and only by stern self-discipline did they manage to carry on and not waste time waiting for the dreaded cut-out. Harcourt Williams arrived at rehearsals one day with the triumphant news that he had read in tea-leaves that the "doodle-bug" menace would be over before they opened; but the question was, would they open at all, and where? Already players were leaving the town, rather like their Elizabethan predecessors during an outbreak of plague, until only six theatres remained open.

With a certain amount of relief, they themselves departed for the comparative peace of Manchester in the middle of August for the try-out of *Arms and the Man*. They left London with the opening fixed for August 30th, and hoped that before that date the tea-leaf prophecy would have come true and that there would still be a New Theatre left for them to return to.

Manchester gave Richardson good notices for his Bluntschli, and as the phlegmatic "chocolate-cream soldier" he had a part which suited him perfectly. Although he disliked the priggish Sergius,

Olivier was nervous of caricaturing him and playing him, as he was written, just for comedy. His pride as an actor would not allow him to take the obvious interpretation, and because he disliked the character he was all the more determined to play him "honestly." The result was a performance which missed the comedy and also failed, on the serious plane, to make Sergius sympathetic. In the Manchester papers he was faced with phrases which began, "Laurence Olivier on the other hand . . ." Perhaps because they were the first notices for a very long time he was quite inordinately upset by this reception. As he walked from his hotel to the theatre the following day he was full of self-pity, which he confided to Guthrie. "It looks," he said, "as if I've come out of the Navy just to be a flop."

As a producer Guthrie was used to the despairing cries of actors, and, like a doctor, searched his mind for the correct diagnosis of why Olivier was not succeeding in the part. After a moment or two he asked Olivier if he loved Sergius.

"*Love* him?" Olivier exclaimed. "Love that . . . that . . ." He broke off, unable to think of an apt description.

"Oh well," Guthrie told him, "if that's how you feel you'll never be good in the part."

He never expected Olivier to take the remark seriously, but he did not know that he had touched a chord in his memory. Olivier suddenly recalled how, seven years earlier, he had started by despising Henry V, and then, as in human relationships, understanding was born out of familiarity and affection out of amusement. Once again he had been given a timely reminder of something which for ever afterwards he was to remember as a basic necessity of a good performance. Sympathy—as much as realistic character drawing—was the essential key to acting.

He was often to ponder that advice, and slowly developed what may be termed an Actor's Philosophy for the Playing of Villains. According to Olivier, however much an actor may loathe a character he must try to comprehend the cause of his evil nature, and then (being careful not to play for sympathy) make the cause known to the audience. In studying the part of a bad man, an actor must use all the versatility of mind and imagination of a priest in the confessional. It is no good being so horrified that he rejects the man out of hand. He must have a real knowledge of the human heart, and must promote its understanding.

Exactly two nights after the last of the flying bombs was brought down, and as Harcourt Williams had so mystically prophesied, the Old Vic was able to return to London for a triumphal opening at the New Theatre on the date planned. With a nicely-gauged sense of showmanship Olivier chose the part of the Button Moulder in *Peer Gynt*, a character who has only one short, effective entrance towards the end of the play. This caused everyone to compliment him on making a self-sacrificing gesture—"the true spirit of repertory" was the theme—and, as he had intended, helped to stimulate interest in his performances to come. As far as he was concerned, *Arms and the Man* was simply a romp, and all his interest became focussed on the third play of the season, *Richard III*.

He had forebodings about Richard, and these were made all the worse because of the interest that had been aroused. He was haunted by quite unaccountable fears that the play was going to be the "ugly sister" of the three, and that he was going to fail in his first important part after so many years. After planning his make-up, as he always does, by sketching on a full-face and profile photograph, he spent hours in front of the mirror, perfecting the thin reptilian nose, adding a wart to the cheek, and stressing the thin, hard line of the mouth. A wig of lank black hair streaked with red completed an appearance which was so satanic that, as one of the cast recalls, members of the company were to give him a wide berth even in the wings. During rehearsals he put himself to some pain with a finger and one leg pulled back to give him the feeling of deformity.

All this helped to mould the character of the savage and twisted man whom no creature loved, but Olivier seemed to have set up such a neurotic state of worry within himself about his performance that he suffered lapses of memory. Normally he learned lines easily, but in *Richard III* even at the dress-rehearsal he didn't know his words and had to call on the prompter. For him this was almost unprecedented, and he put it down partly to the fact that as he grew older, it was getting harder for him to learn a long part. On the night before the opening he was up until 4 a.m. in a room at Claridge's going over and over his part while Vivien Leigh and an old friend, Garson Kanin, the American producer, gave him the cues.

He went to the theatre the following evening full of doubts, but his doubts were really the earnests of success. The curtain had not been up two minutes before everyone at the New Theatre from the stalls to the gallery was holding his breath in anticipation. In the first great soliloquy which starts:

> *"Now is the winter of our discontent*
> *Made glorious summer by this sun of York . . ."*

he emerged, his back half-turned on the audience, from the shadows; there was a sardonic humour beneath the savage whip of his tongue which excited speculation, while the variety of pace, the cut-and-thrust of his delivery completely held the attention. In the same way as he had captured his audience with the first performance he had ever given at the Old Vic, eight years before, he started by playing down . . . and so made the audience come to him. He was able to take more time than most actors in creating his effect because he had expanded the speech to twice its usual length. He incorporated part of Gloster's long soliloquy from Act III, Scene II in *Henry VI*, a device which he considered justified, as the play is in the same historical cycle, and the speech helped to explain Gloster's character. He was careful to avoid the conventional trick of making Gloster too hideous and villainous from the start; he won a reluctant admiration because of his swift asides and the vicious and cunning smile which flashed on and off with the speed of a viper's tongue; he minimized the deformity to a limp and slight stoop (no vast padded hump); and very subtly he suggested the accumulation of evil until, at the climax of his villainy, he accepted the crown. The death scene was given the full Olivier treatment. After a terrific duel which he fought with Richardson as Richmond, he went down on the ground but died slowly, with a convulsive and frenzied contraction of his limbs. His writhing shook off Richmond's triumphant foot, and it seemed that his black soul might never leave his body until, in his death agony, his eyes caught sight of the cross-shaped hilt of his sword. Then, all grace spent, he finally collapsed.

He was given an overwhelming reception on that first night at the New, and, while nearly all his forebodings were swept away by the cheers that greeted the final curtain, he still waited a little anxiously for the morning papers. He was sure, as far as any actor can be, that he had given a good performance, but he recalled that he had sometimes felt the same before, and was on guard against over-optimism. He must steel himself against possible disappointment. But never before or since in his career had apprehension less foundation; for when the papers were brought up to the bedroom at Claridge's the following morning, and he and Vivien, separately and secretly holding their breaths, opened them, it was to read of "an outstanding occasion in the history of the English theatre," and to see his characterization described as "a masterpiece." "Mr. Olivier I have always considered a good actor," wrote one wise and elderly critic. "His Richard entitles him, I think, to be enrolled in the company of the great."

Every daily and evening paper showered its praise, and the following Sunday J. C. Trewin was to describe his performance in *The Observer* in these terms:

> Too often an actor of Shakespeare's *Richard III* has offered us the mask without the mind. When the brains are out a part should die, and there an end. Not so here. . . . It is the marriage of intellect and dramatic force, of bravura and cold reason, which so distinguishes Mr. Laurence Olivier's study at the New Theatre. Here indeed we have the true double Gloucester, thinker and doer, mind and mask.
>
> Blessedly the actor never counterfeits the deep tragedian, the top-heavy villain weighted by his ponderous and marble jaws. His Richard gives to every speech a fire-new glint. His diction, flexible and swift—often mill-race swift—is bred of a racing brain. If, outwardly, he is a limping panther, there is not lameness in his mind. Other players have achieved the Red King and developed the part with a relishing theatrical imagination; none in recent memory has made us so conscious of the usurper's intellect, made so plausible every move on the board from the great opening challenge to the last despair and death.
>
> Mr. Olivier's speed and variety, the deceptive early lightness which cloaks decision and steeled hatred, the refusal to yield sword to spiked mace—these qualities are not incompatible with Shakespeare's Richard. There is no attempt to force excitement. From the first the actor, dark-haired, evilly debonair, pale of cheek, has Richard's measure, whether as sea-green corrupter or as scarlet sin. He preserves the man's pride—this Plantagenet is from the aery in the cedar's top—he has a glittering irony, in rage he can terrify ("Out on you, owls! nothing but songs of death!"), and his silences, mocking or malign, are infinitely charged.

When, at the matinée following the first night, he walked on to the stage, Olivier felt, for the first time in his life, that his audience was immediately with him—that they wanted to hear every word and did not have to be won over. Beneath the twisted form of Richard he almost swaggered; he knew that he had—to use his own words—"come off." How, he wondered, after years away from the stage, and with only the preparation of two light-weight performances, had he managed to achieve his greatest success at that particular moment? He could find no better answer to the question than the simple explanation that it must be because he was older.

Richard III, far from being the ugly sister, became the outstanding play of a season which was itself outstanding, and before long it was being asked if Olivier should not now be considered the greatest living actor. After fifteen years during which Gielgud had held the unchallenged title, there were those who were determined to raise the arm of a new champion. Papers began to invite readers' opinions and solicit the views of the critics on this delicate matter, and it fell to James Agate to pass the judgment of Solomon in a letter to the editor of a theatrical magazine who had asked him which of the two he considered the better.

> Dear Sir (he wrote from Grape Street), Many years ago I asked my ancient caddie at St. Andrews which was the better golfer, young Tom Morris or Bobby Jones. He looked at me distastefully and said: "Baith o' them played pairfect gowf!"

Olivier, who hated such empty comparisons, was naturally perturbed about his friend's feelings. He need not have worried; Gielgud's reaction was characteristically generous. He had in his possession a sword with a great theatrical history. Edmund Kean had worn it as Richard III, and it had passed, by way of a gift from William Chippendale, the actor, to Henry Irving on the first night of his appearance as Richard on January 29th, 1877. Gielgud decided to give it to Olivier and asked Alan Dent to call on him at the Haymarket so that he might be the bearer of the gift. Dent had temporarily forsaken his position as a dramatic critic, and it was in the uniform of a Naval Sickberth Attendant that he carried the sword to the New with much preoccupation and grandeur. On the way at least one Naval officer who should have been saluted found himself completely ignored.

On the blade of the sword was inscribed its history up to the time
it was presented to Irving. And, turning it over, Olivier read with
considerable emotion the new, clearly engraved words:

This sword given him by his mother Kate Terry Gielgud, 1938,
is given to Laurence Olivier by his friend John Gielgud in appreciation of his performance of Richard III at the New Theatre, 1944.

II

There had never been much doubt that, with the names of Laurence Olivier and Ralph Richardson on the bills, the Old Vic's
return to London would be a success. It would have been less easy
to prophesy that the success would mount steadily for two years
until the huge wartime debts were reduced, thanks largely to a new
generation of theatregoers, many of whom paid their first visit to
the New Theatre in uniforms and returned as civilians.

That first season paralleled events on the continent. When *Peer
Gynt* opened the allied armies were advancing across France to
Paris; on the first night of *Richard III* they were across the frontier
and fighting inside Germany; the set-back in the Ardennes during
the bitter January of 1945 coincided with the opening of *Uncle
Vanya*, the one disappointment in the Old Vic's first season. And in
May, when the bells were ringing for victory, the company put
on uniform and took all the plays except the Chekov across the
Channel so that they could be seen by the troops who had been
too preoccupied to come to them. The short tour, which included
Antwerp, Ghent and Hamburg, ended in Paris. There, after a week
at the Marigny, the Old Vic company were given a great honour.
They were asked to appear for a fortnight at the Comédie Française
—the first foreign company ever invited to play in the national
theatre of France. On the last night Olivier decided to make a curtain speech in French which, as his French was shaky, he learnt by
heart. For the end he was given an idea by a story he had been told
about Molière. To obtain silence and order before a rehearsal Molière would walk briskly into the theatre and deliver one terse reminder: '*Et maintenant . . . place au théâtre!*' At the end of the
Old Vic's last performance Olivier stepped to the footlights and
repeated the two hundred-year-old phrase with a slight variation.
'*Et maintenant . . . place au théâtre—Française!*' he said, and so

with a kiss of the hand restored the theatre to its rightful owners.

Even while they were touring in Europe the three directors were starting to plan the next season. Once again Olivier and Richardson decided to divide the weight of acting responsibility. Richardson wanted to play Falstaff, and they planned to present Parts I and II of *Henry IV* in succession, so that the whole sweep of the historical story could be chronologically developed.

On the face of it this did not seem to give Olivier much to do, but he said he was quite happy with the much smaller parts of Hotspur and Mr. Justice Shallow. It was a clever choice, and in both he made a great success. Especially with the Hotspur, a part rarely taken by a star actor, he even managed to divert some of the limelight from Richardson's brilliant Falstaff. Taking his cue from Lady Percy's remark, in the Second Part, that her dead husband had had a way of "speaking thick, which nature made his blemish," he made Hotspur stammer. Other actors have done this, but Olivier was a little different in choosing the letter "w" as the one on which he faltered. His reason was to provide a climax of unusual pathos when the stammer seemed to prevent Hotspur from completing his own courageous and dying epitaph: "No, Percy, thou art dust and food for w-w . . ." and he died on the struggle to get out the word and left it for Prince Hal to finish it with ". . . For worms, brave Percy." The death scene had the same dramatic effect he had achieved with Richard. After the mortal thrust from Hal's sword, Olivier stood for some moments quite upright, while blood oozed through his fingers as he tried to staunch the wound on the side of his neck. Then he suddenly plunged forward down two stairs on to his face.

If theatrical showmanship was suggested by following Hotspur with the quavering sharp-nosed Shallow in the second part of *Henry IV*, suspicions that he was playing to the gallery were aroused even more by the double bill that followed. It was altogether too dazzling a display of pyrotechnics to fire off the giant rocket Œdipus on the same night as the squib of Mr. Puff. *Œdipus* (in a translation by W. B. Yeats) lasted only an hour and a half, and was obviously an incomplete and rather heavy evening's entertainment by itself, and certainly Sheridan's *The Critic* sent everyone out into St. Martin's Lane delighted. Fifteen minutes after he left the stage as the tragic Œdipus, his eyes streaming with blood, Olivier was back as the foppish, foolish Mr. Puff. The wisdom of so daring a contrast was questioned by some of his friends who were afraid that he would be accused of showing off.

It was difficult to find fault with either performance individually. Olivier's Œdipus, played in what might be described as a restrained classical manner, was at times almost unbearably moving; and his Mr. Puff was all lightness and froth, a brilliant display of technical virtuosity and acrobatics. The general public, less captious than those few, perhaps over-fastidious, critics who were upset by the one following hot on the other, were delighted by the contrast. Their applause and cheers were a measure of success with which he was quite satisfied; they showed him that he had succeeded in one thing he set out to achieve. Here was the key to nearly every decision he was to make in the future about the parts he was to act and the plays in which he was to appear. He wanted to bring back a sense of theatrical *excitement* to the stage.

The last night at the end of the second season of the Old Vic saw a scene outside the New which was unique in the history of the theatre. For an hour St. Martin's Lane was closed while a crowd numbering about 2,500 blocked the road and the narrow alleyway which runs from the front of the theatre to the stage door. Delirious fans, among whom were hundreds of young girls, called out for Richardson and Olivier, and sent up a wild chant of "We want Larry! We want Larry!" Nothing would move them, and escape by way of front-of-house was impossible because the entrance was as tightly jammed with people as the courtyard outside the stage door. They waited in their dressing-rooms for a full hour after the curtain; when the shouting showed no sign of abating, Olivier asked three of the toughest stage hands to form a bodyguard and told Richardson that he supposed they would have to face it.

As they came out the noise rose to a crescendo, and despite the bodyguard the journey was a desperate struggle. It was scarcely more than thirty yards, but it took them nearly ten minutes to get to their taxi, and during that time hundreds of clutching hands tore at Olivier's coat and ripped off the buttons. Only when he and Richardson had been forced on the roof of the taxi did the shouting die away to allow them to make a short and slightly incoherent speech of farewell.

They drove off to supper reflecting that if hysteria were any indication of success, then the Old Vic had succeeded. It was difficult to assess what possible relation such a demonstration bore to appreciation of Shakespeare, Chekov and Sophocles, but it was apparently spontaneous and sincere. As such it was a fitting climax to one venture, and its echo carried them forward to another.

The following day thirty-one members of the company climbed aboard a specially chartered plane at Hurn airport to fly to New York, where they were due to open at the Century Theatre a week later. It was the first time in history that an entire theatrical company had been flown across the Atlantic. Scenery and publicity had travelled ahead, the scenery on the *Queen Mary* and the advance bally-hoo in the newspapers on a scale unknown for any British or foreign company since the original D'Oyly Carte. Even before they arrived advance bookings for a six weeks' season were said to be over $300,000.

Vivien Leigh, who had now recovered completely from her illness, was able to accompany Olivier, and at La Guardia Field told reporters she had just come along "for the ride." How did she like being back in the United States, she was asked. "It's like going from home to home," she said with infinite tact. At the St. Regis the Oliviers found their room looking rather like a tent at the Chelsea Flower Show. It was a mass of red roses, hydrangeas, daffodils and narcissi, and Vivien, walking round and examining the labels, half expected to find their Latin names. They carried the welcome and good wishes of the Lunts, Helen Hayes, George Cukor, Katharine Cornell and other American friends. There were even presents from fans of whom they had never heard. It was all a little unnerving, and remembering the last time they had swept into New York on a tide of advance enthusiasm, they wondered if excitement was not being pitched too high.

During the six weeks in New York the Old Vic played to 87,000 people, and had to turn away a third as many again from the box-office; but however much the public clamoured for seats, the critics showed a disinclination to be swept off their feet. As one of them said, the "build-up" would not have been unworthy of the Creation with the original cast; and this may have put them on their guard. The second part of *Henry IV* was better received than the first, and *Uncle Vanya* very coolly. *Œdipus*, however, was not only greeted by cheers from the audience, but was given unanimous praise in the papers, and John Mason Brown said that he believed Olivier's performance deserved "that precious, dangerous, final objective 'great'." In a piece of criticism which itself deserves much the same adjective he went on:

> . . . I may be right. I may be wrong. I do not know. I can remember only William Hazlitt's sustaining line. "I am not one of those," wrote he in his theatregoing days, "who, when they see the sun breaking from behind a cloud, stop to ask others if it be the moon."

This line gives me the courage to overcome that cowardice—that fear of commitment and that embarrassment in the presence of emotion—which is as much the curse of criticism as are its thoughtless, churlish misappropriations of the dictionary's fund. I can only say that in *Henry V* and *Œdipus* I have seen the sun rise. And I refuse to mistake it for the moon, or salute it as such, when for me it is the sun.

Mr. Olivier's *Œdipus* is one of those performances in which blood and electricity are somehow mixed. It pulls lightning down from the sky. It is as awesome, dwarfing and appalling as one of nature's angriest displays. Though thrilling, it never loses its majesty.

His Theban king is godlike in appearance. Although he has Henry's authority, the extrovert has disappeared. The proud figure from the tapestries, the warrior monarch, the dashing symbol of those days when all the youth of England was on fire and silken dalliance in the wardrobe lay, has become a Græco-Roman statue brought to life; sullen, wilful, august, and imperious. There is something of the young Napoleon in him too, but he is a Napoleon pursued by the Furies rather than following the Eagle.

At the outset his is the arrogance of a man who feels himself secure. He can judge others rapidly, because he believes he is himself above judgment. He speaks slowly, with a frightening casualness at first, when addressing the suppliants. His decisions are as swift as his speech is deliberate. He dares to take pauses of uncommon length. Yet the passion of his nature makes itself felt at once; the passion and the violence.

He prepares us completely for the man who, in his maturity, has been condemned by his youthful hot-headedness. Mr. Olivier's *Œdipus* is, as it should be, the victim of his character. His character is his own evil destiny. His instantaneous surrender to torrid impulses, which we have demonstrated for us in his conversations with Creon and the Old Shepherd, is what has doomed him. It is this self-same instability which has embroiled him, in an even fierier form, in that fight at the crossroads long ago during which, without meaning to, he had killed his father, King Laius.

Œdipus's gradual comprehension of his guilt, which is scored so inexorably in Sophocles's text, is given its fullest theatrical expression in Mr. Olivier's performance. The evening's suspense is draining and almost unendurable. When the fearful realization at last inundates him, and his Theban king knows beyond doubt that he has murdered his father, married his mother, and had children by her, Mr. Olivier releases two cries which no one who has heard them can hope to forget.

They are the dreadful, hoarse groans of a wounded animal. They well up out of a body that has been clubbed by fate. They are sounds which speak, as no words could, for a soul torn by horror; for a mind numbed by what it has been forced to comprehend. Yet fearful as these groans are in their brute savagery, they serve only to magnify the stature of Œdipus's kingly woe. The subsequent moments when Œdipus appears, self-blinded with the blood trickling down his face, are almost more terrible than audiences can bear. But even these final scenes are redeemed from gruesomeness by their grandeur. The question is one of spiritual scale rather than physical detail.

As if alternating Œdipus and Mr. Puff with Hotspur, Shallow and Dr. Astrov were not sufficiently hard work, Olivier also had to broadcast every Sunday for the sufficient, if unexpected, reason that it was the only way in which he could pay his hotel bill and buy Vivien a fur coat. His salary of £100 a week might sound ample, but paid in dollars and for a star in New York, it went nowhere. These various activities would not in themselves have been too great a strain, but they came at the end of a two years' period in which he had been driving himself hard and almost without a break or a holiday. Suddenly, during the hot June days of 1946 in New York, he became aware that he had been giving too much of himself for too long and was on the verge of a nervous breakdown. He developed a neurosis that he was going to be killed, and was pursued by a recurring nightmare in which he was crashing in an aeroplane or falling from the flies of the theatre while playing in *The Critic*.

This last fear was partly prompted by experience, for during the London run he had barely escaped a serious accident in the startling acrobatic climax which he had devised for the play. At the end the gesticulating Mr. Puff, straddled on a painted cloud, was hauled into the flies and out of view of the audience. The next the audience saw of him was when he reappeared clutching the curtain as it swung down only a few seconds later at the end of the play. It was an elaborate piece of "business" which, to be fully effective, required him to climb down a rope from the flies like a trapeze artist. At one matinée at the New he had stretched out for the rope and was just about to swing from the cloud and climb down the rope when it came away in his hand. He had toppled forward, grasping desperately on to the thin wire cable which carried the cloud. For several moments he had clung there, with a drop of thirty feet on to the stage below him, until he was rescued by the men in the flies.

That experience and a number of subsequent near-accidents were the root of the nightmare which crept into his waking hours so that, mentally, he began to cross off the number of performances of Mr. Puff and wonder if he could make the last one before he had a serious injury. Had he not been so tired and run down he could have laughed at this fantasy; and he did, of course, reach the last performance without an accident . . . or nearly without one. On the very last occasion on which he played Mr. Puff the whole routine went perfectly, and he felt such an overwhelming sense of relief when he was at last safely on the ground that he took two somersaults across the stage. With a thud his heels came down on the boards, and he was aware of a sudden sharp pain. He climbed to his feet to take his curtain, and managed to hobble to his dressing-room, but the pain was so acute that a doctor was summoned. After an examination he announced that the Achilles tendons were torn.

Although he could barely walk, nothing would persuade Olivier to cancel an engagement he had made for the next day. Vivien and he had arranged to fly to Boston, where he was to be given an honorary degree by Tufts College as "the real interpreter of Shakespeare of our age." The real interpreter, feeling on the whole a thoroughly bad advertisement for his profession, could only just limp on to the platform to receive his diploma and academic hood. He was conscious that the whole visit was slightly unbecoming, for, the moment his installation ceremony was over, he would have to rush back to the airport and catch the return plane to New York in order to keep an important appointment the same night.

The plane was due to leave at four-forty-five, and the ceremony, which seemed to call for a certain amount of elaborate formality,

did not start until three. When it was over, Vivien left as arranged
for the airport, but he felt bound to go to a reception to which he
was invited by Dr. Carmichael, the President of the College. But
no sooner had he got there than he began, suddenly and quite illogi-
cally, to panic. An ill-defined fear insisted that he must catch that
plane. He and Vivien had always vowed never to fly separately, and
either her plane or the next one in which he would be following
would be certain to crash! If he didn't make the airport in time he
would never see Vivien again! Polite conversation about the higher
drama with the faculty and graduates who crowded round him became intolerable. Surreptitiously he kept glancing at his watch, and
at last could bear it no longer. He made hurried excuses to a puzzled
Dr. Carmichael, snatched up his M.A. hood and its brown and pale
blue lining which was in a cardboard box in the hall, and rushed out
to the car which he had kept waiting. A woman reporter who came
up imploring a story was bundled in too. There was no time to
argue. "Logan Field!" he shouted at the driver.

At the airport Vivien Leigh had managed to hold the plane back
for a few minutes, but at last, when there was still no sign of Olivier,
the pilot said he was sorry, but he couldn't wait any longer. Just as
the engines roared and the chocks were pulled away, the car arrived
on the tarmac. But it was too late. Olivier hobbled frantically out
and was within a few yards of the machine when it moved down the
runway for the take-off. It was then that he fully realized what a
highly-strung condition he was in. He lost all control and burst into
tears. The girl reporter, who to her eternal credit never wrote the
story, suggested briskly that they go to the airport canteen for a
stiff drink. "Just a cup of tea," said Olivier, grasping in the moment
of crisis at his national beverage.

Despite all premonitions, Olivier arrived safely in New York, but
his nerves were to be given no chance of recovering. Two days later
it seemed as if his long-dreaded nightmare had at last come true.
After attending the American première of *Henry V* at the City
Center, he and Vivien had climbed into a plane for England with
visions of a good holiday ahead of them, and feeling that all worries
had been left behind. Their sense of relief was short-lived. Half an
hour after they left La Guardia Field one of the Clipper's four
engines caught fire, the flames burnt their way into the wing, and
the engine fell off. There followed seven minutes of awful suspense

for the fifty-two passengers while the pilot searched for a suitable field, and they were told that as the landing gear had been affected they would have to crash-land. Eventually they came down at Willimantic in Connecticut, and although the plane ploughed and skidded for more than half a mile, no one was hurt.

While another Clipper was being flown up from New York to take them on to England, Larry and Vivien discussed whether they should take it or go back to New York, and catch a boat. A boat seemed the obvious answer, and yet—an actor's objection—it would be an anti-climax. Also, terrifying though it had been at the time, the experience had dispelled some of Olivier's fears. Now that he had actually been in the crash which had haunted him for so long, the worst was over. Imagination had been defeated by reality. "Anyway," Olivier explained afterwards, "it was impossible for us to remain. We were practically cleaned out. We had exactly seventeen dollars and forty cents between us."

III

July in Buckinghamshire worked its balm. Long peaceful days at Notley, tennis-parties at the weekends, weeding of flower-beds, and time to stand and stare with idle vacancy at the Jersey cows newly bought for their private farm, all had the required effect. The doctors told Vivien Leigh that she could act again in the autumn, and it was decided to revive *The Skin of Our Teeth*. Olivier, now rested as completely as he would ever allow himself to be, was planning the next season at the Old Vic. He had settled on *King Lear*, and, as well as playing the part for the first time, he decided to produce it as well. He knew it was a big step, but he was so full of ideas that he could not face the awkward business of a three-way discussion through a producer every time he wanted to explain them to the cast.

It was not easy to be producing from the stalls and acting on the stage at the same time, but he overcame the difficulty as best he could by asking David Kentish, his stage manager, to walk through the part and read for him during the early rehearsals. Once the general pattern was formed he had little reason to be out front. With as good a cast as he had, there was no need to be continually correcting every move and inflexion. In fact, he particularly wanted to avoid giving them any suggestion that he was "showing them" how to play their parts. He knew only too well from experience that subconsciously an actor fights against his producer's ideas if they conflict with his own. It was far better to have long, informal discussions, plant certain ideas and then let the characterizations develop in their own natural way. Being both star and producer did not present its greatest difficulty until the dress-rehearsal, when all the technical problems of lighting and scene-changing had to be considered, and when, as well as giving a good performance, he had somehow to step outside the play and see the overall effect.

On the first night at the New Theatre in September there were some small mechanical difficulties, and while the actual production was not unanimously hailed as a great one, Olivier has always considered that it was his best, principally because his cast seemed to him to be as nearly perfect as any for which a producer could hope. Never before had he seen Goneril, Regan and Cordelia played with what he termed "such perfect rightness of colour" as they were by Pamela Brown, Margaret Leighton, and Joyce Redman. He was particularly pleased with Alex Guinness' Fool, George Relph's Gloster, the Kent of Nicholas Hannen. And a cast which, in smaller parts, included Harry Andrews, Michael Warre, Peter Copley, Cecil Winter and George Rose all contributed performances which, he thought, were simple, unaffected and in harmony with his ideas. "Action" on the stage, Olivier believes, should fulfil certain basic requirements. First, and most important, it should be the best expression of the text, should convey the maximum of intensity and meaning, and should, in a word, be the *exaltation* of the scene at the particular moment the action takes place; secondly, it should be as comfortable and natural for the actors as possible; and thirdly, it should look (without giving the least suggestion that the producer is showing off) attractive, decorative and exciting to the eye of the audience. It seemed to him in *Lear* that all the positioning, the movements, and the relation of the actors, each with the other, completely fulfilled these demands, and that in a production which had rhythm and a Gothic symmetry of design, the meaning of the play had never been made clearer.

There were disappointments, the main one of which was that visually it fell short of what his designer, Roger Furse, and he had hoped. On the day before the production the basic principle on which Furse was relying for his effects had to be abandoned. Technical problems made it impossible to project shadow slides (which were to be used to suggest interiors) on the cyclorama. As a result the complete illusion was lost, and the simple functional sets which Furse had designed to conform with Olivier's conception of the production seemed a trifle too stark and, especially for his first scene, were criticized as "drabbish" and "unimaginative."

To his surprise on the first night Olivier found himself approaching his performance as Lear with none of his usual fears. He was less frightened than ever before or since, and he put down his sense of relaxation to the fact that the odds against him were so great that they ceased to be terrifying. How could he hope to bring *everything* off? He was a little sorry that his Lear had to be judged on his first-night performance. For him first nights are nearly always his worst, and it was to take him four or five performances before he considered he was doing the part and himself full justice. By the end of the forty-eight performances (during which there was never an empty seat at the New and £1,500 profit was made), and by the time they took the play to Paris, he was, as he would say with quite professional objectivity, acting Lear very well. But to judge from the review which appeared in *The Times* the next morning, it would seem that he had little reason to fear that his first-night performance had fallen short of the highest expectations. "Mr. Laurence Olivier, lately come to the plenitude of his powers," he read, "plays the part with the magnificent ease which testifies that it is for him a completely solved problem." The notice went on:

> To this solution, this genuine re-creation of character, goes an unexpected humour, unfaltering analytical acuity, a beautifully keen emotional sensibility and such steely abundant natural vigour as to afford that extra half-ounce of energy which compels immediate assent even to what on reflection may be questionable, may, that is to say, be different from our own or somebody else's solution of the same problem. . . .
>
> As the benevolent autocrat dividing his kingdom without a thought for the consequences of abdication Mr. Olivier knows his Lear well enough to set him in a judicious comic light which exposes what is vain and tyrannical in the old man's affection for his daughters. By sudden vacant stares and the dropping of the jaw the failing powers and natural weaknesses later to be developed in a tragic contest are lightly and amusingly conveyed. Mr. Olivier is seldom

declamatory in the frets and rages lit with flashes of savage irony
that seize upon Lear in the first throes of outraged affection and
outraged self-will, but when he lets himself go, when for instance
he threatens the terrors of the earth, the roof rings with the controlled resonance of his full-toned utterance. The fear of madness is
a recurring motif which Mr. Olivier casts into grimly comic form
which is somehow terrifying, and when madness comes and the old
man sits crowned with rank fumitory indicting the universe the
actor reaches what is perhaps the height of a wonderfully fine performance, though as spiritual illumination breaks in and in the pit-
eousness of the end there is no faltering.

Perhaps more than any performance Olivier had given up to this
point in his career, his Lear deserves our consideration of the assess-
ments made at the time. James Agate, in a letter to his friend,
George Lyttleton, while more cautious in his praise than the majority of critics, wrote "I have the conviction that Olivier is a comedian
by instinct and a tragedian by art. He keeps his sense of fun under
control in his tragic parts, but I can see him controlling it. Of his
Coriolanus in 1938 I wrote: 'I think, too, that he must resolve to
discard that clowning which he probably adjudges to be mordancy.
There is not much of it in the present performance, but what there
is is wholly bad. For where it is used it turns into a naughty boy a
figure whose dignity should be pauseless.'"

This theory—much favoured by others since—that Olivier was "a
comedian by instinct and a tragedian by art" was given strength by
the way he invested Lear with a certain quizzical sense of humour.
This was probably only a device to get him over the absurdity of
the scene in which Lear divides the kingdom between his daughters,
but it was widely commented on, and "tender humour" was also
mentioned by Alan Dent in the *News Chronicle*. After summing
up Olivier as "a great Lear," he wrote in part:

> In its wide range and variety, assurance, authority, certainty, and
> all-prevailing grandeur even in ruin and madness, Olivier's King
> Lear is nothing short of a tremendous achievement.
> Here is the old king, always old and always kingly, in all his suc-
> cessive stages—doting, indignant, raging, breaking (rather frighten-
> ingly), broken, mad, and then at the end trembling on the verge
> of a returning and almost unwanted sanity. He looks like a hoary
> patriarch drawn by Blake. But—what is far more difficult to encom-

pass and imagine—he *sounds* like a Blake! Hardly once throughout the immense evening do we think of the young actor made up to look venerable. We think only of Lear himself, and identify our own ideal with what we gaze upon and heed—white hair pelted by the pitiless storm, royal moods and caprices, and even touches of tender humour, eyes that turn with a rare gradualness from full authority to dismay and oblivious madness, tones that rake the welkin and then whisper us to tears. If there is a better, a more expressive Lear in human recollection, it is certainly not in my experience.

BOOK FIVE

In Their Own Theatre

CHAPTER 1

"An Essay in Hamlet"

1947

I

YAWNING AND TIRED after a late party, Olivier was still in pyjamas when he put the call through to Switzerland. It was the morning of January 1st, 1947, and he had made his first, and certainly his most important, New Year's resolution. He had decided to film *Hamlet*. Now he must confirm it so that there could be no turning back, no more arguing. Firmly he told the girl on the Continental Exchange the number he wanted in Zurich, and when Del Giudice came on the line he gave him the news.

Ever since the success of *Henry V* the Italian producer had been worrying Olivier to make another Shakespeare film. Olivier had already delayed so long that Orson Welles had forestalled him with *Macbeth*, and *Othello* was threatened. *Hamlet* remained the obvious choice, and in the middle of the previous month Del Giudice had invited him to lunch in his apartment at Grosvenor House in a final attempt to persuade him. Olivier had an unwritten agreement with the Old Vic which gave him some months off to make a film, and now that the run of *Lear* was finished Hollywood was beckoning both Vivien and himself with an offer of *Cyrano de Bergerac*. Cecil Tennant, his agent, had been all for Hollywood, but Olivier was tempted by the thought of *Hamlet*.

Seeing that one of the things which was influencing Olivier in

favour of Hollywood was the chance of having a holiday before
filming started, Del Giudice quickly suggested an alternative. If
Olivier would make *Hamlet* he would arrange for him and Vivien
to have a holiday first on the Italian Riviera; and he could promise
that they would find it far lovelier on the Mediterranean than in
California. Nothing had been finally settled over lunch, but before
the party broke up he had given Olivier his Zurich telephone number. So confident had he been of the outcome that, flying to Switzerland the following day on the same plane as Sir Stafford Cripps,
he had confided to him that *Hamlet* was a certainty.

On the phone Olivier reminded Del Giudice of his promise about
the holiday, and the delighted producer assured him that if he
would combine pleasure with some work, everything could be arranged. Overcoming restrictions and arranging the impossible were
Del Giudice's speciality and in a remarkably short time he had
persuaded Rank to allow him to take a floor of a hotel at Santa
Marguerita Ligure for a "planning group" on *Hamlet*, and had
coaxed the Treasury into making a grant. It may be guessed that
he had carefully prepared the ground on the aeroplane journey he
had made with the President of the Board of Trade. Then, as later,
he would have been full of plausible arguments to show that a few
preliminary thousands spent in Italy were really a good investment.
Given a small holiday—no, not a holiday: more a quiet place to work
—he was sure Olivier would make *Hamlet:* and *Hamlet* would be
a great dollar-raiser like *Henry V*. It was a fool-proof argument,
and once he had the necessary currency Del Giudice splashed mag-
nificently. In the months to come hard-headed men in South Street,
faced with the bills, were to wonder if it had been entirely necessary
for the Oliviers to have a five-room suite at the Hotel Miramare,
and if it had been essential for the suite to be furnished with specially hired antique furniture. "I wanted their first evening to be a
happy one," Del Giudice explained simply.

The journey to Santa Marguerita, in slow, freezing trains by way
of Milan and Genoa, was not an encouraging start. Genoa was covered in snow, and as they left by car Vivien Leigh felt tempted
to tell Del Giudice that in California there was no snow in February.
By the time they had reached Nervi, however, she was glad she had
made no reproaches. The sun was shining, the trees were full of
oranges, and as they passed over the highest point of the climbing

road at Ruta, the Gulf of Rapallo, spread out below them, looked a place of enchantment.

After ten days of the promised holiday, Alan Dent, who was to work with Olivier on the script, arrived from London, the first of the team who were to plan the entire film in minute detail in the hotel overlooking the Mediterranean. They decided that the film should last two and a half hours, and this meant that a full two hours of the play had to be sacrificed. It meant, in fact, not Shakespeare's *Hamlet*, but a simplified essay in Hamlet, a new pattern to be made out of the larger pattern of the play. If it was to be a good *film*, it was necessary to be quite ruthless, and to simplify a highly complex and diffuse psychological study into a straightforward, logically-told story. It must be easy to follow, which meant that they would have to discard irrelevancies of plot, transpose scenes, even move phrases in certain speeches, and modernize a few of the more incomprehensible Elizabethan words.* Olivier knew, as every artist knows when he tries to reduce something complex into brief, simple and popular terms, that he'd be disliked by the purists and the scholars, and by those critics who demand absolute integrity. But he believed that was compensated by bringing part of Shakespeare to a far greater audience than had ever seen or heard him before. There would only be time to present one main facet of Hamlet's personality, and this must be kept constantly to the front; so he decided they would concentrate on "that particular fault" of Hamlet—irresolution. "We must think of Hamlet," he said to Alan Dent, "as a nearly great man —a man damned, as all but one in a hundred of us are, by a lack of resolution. Our *Hamlet* will be the story of a man who couldn't make up his mind." That phrase, later spoken in the prologue to the film, was the Argument; for those who would listen it said that this film did not pretend to be the whole of *Hamlet*.

After the daily conferences, as he walked with Vivien through the February sunshine past walls on which mimosa was just starting to bloom, he told her that he thought it was a good thing they were planning the film in a place so completely foreign to their subject. Here, in a country which was pictorially and emotionally as far from Denmark as could be imagined, he could visualize the whole

---

* For example, in Hamlet's line: "By heaven, I'll make a ghost of him who *lets* me," it was considered that "lets" in its archaic sense of "hinders" would not be understood, and it was therefore changed.

film objectively. As an actor he had always seen the problem of Hamlet as eternal and universal. That was the idea he must impress on the designers, Roger Furse and Carmen Dillon, when they arrived. This should not be *Hamlet* in Elizabethan or more modern costume, but as far as possible a timeless *Hamlet* in a setting which, stripped bare of all but essentials, would belong to no particular country or period. They must make a point of not cluttering up the sets with any furniture or props which were not demanded by the action. If they were going to sacrifice Fortinbras, Rosencrantz and Guildenstern, as Vivien suggested, and important soliloquies like "Oh what a rogue and peasant slave am I," there should be visual austerity as well. It would all help the audience to concentrate on the story.

Soon Reginald Beck and Desmond Dickinson also arrived at the Miramare for the technical planning of the shooting sequences, camerawork and lighting. The main question was whether the film should be made in colour, which has considerable box-office appeal. But, whereas colour had been an asset for *Henry V*, Olivier thought it might be too "pretty" for tragedy. He considered the possibility of having very subdued colours—greys and sepias—but even so he would be unable to avoid the "apricot-coloured faces" he so disliked. Also colour would mean using a cumbersome Technicolor camera, and to keep the action fluid he wanted a mobile little camera that could dart in and out of the scenes. Black and white also had one outstanding advantage. He could use deep-focus photography, which keeps foreground, middle-distance and distance all simultaneously in focus, so that it would be possible to have an actor with his face showing perfectly clearly although he was 150 feet away from the camera. "Tracking"—the stealthy advance of the camera for close-ups—and cutting would thus be reduced to a minimum. As had been seen in *Citizen Kane*, it gave scope for very dramatic effects, and as it is a slightly heightened form of normal vision it might be in keeping with the poetic quality of the film.

Cut off from all but essential telephone calls from London, and with the key-technicians and planners in conference together, it was possible to prepare the "master-scene script," in which every scene and action was described in minutest detail, as well as the more technical "first shooting script," in little over a month. Olivier leaned heavily on the knowledge and experience of his collaborators, and was anxious to give them credit for their work. They were equally determined to acknowledge that most of the original ideas came from him, and that his inspiration was felt in every department. Reginald Beck was to admit quite frankly that working with Olivier taught him what a lot of dust and bric-à-brac a technician collects without question in his repertory. Olivier would often simply sweep away these prejudices with the single question, "Why?"

In London Del Giudice was already coming under fire. As the bills for the "planners" rose to £7,000 for the month he was faced with all the criticisms of extravagance that had dogged him ever since *Henry V*. He argued that £7,000 was not an excessive amount of money to spend on so important a script; the accountants replied that as they believed the author of *Hamlet* was dead they might reasonably have expected to get the script for nothing. Reflecting, not for the first time, that the men who controlled film finance were devoid of all soul, Del Giudice flew out to Italy to receive the script. After so much contention it is, perhaps, not surprising that he has never forgotten the great moment when the script was actually handed to him. Olivier brought it down to his room himself, and Del Giudice describes the incident with characteristic artlessness: "I was moved to see a great man like Larry make such a gesture, and, excited by the marginal notes and corrections in Larry's own hand, I was kept awake by the script all night." Burbage receiving the manuscript of *Hamlet* from Shakespeare could hardly have shown more touching reverence.

II

During the month that the others were in Italy, Anthony Bushell, the assistant producer, had been casting in London. It was a task which, except for Gertrude and Ophelia, was not difficult, for he soon found that his was a film in which everyone was very anxious to appear. Felix Aylmer and Basil Sydney, Olivier's first suggestion for Polonius and Claudius, were both available. Norman Woolland, who had been in partial eclipse as a radio announcer, was chosen for Horatio, and of five young actors tested for Laertes, Terence Morgan proved easily the best. The women, however, were not so readily settled.

The problem of finding a suitable Gertrude was not new. Actresses, young enough to be physically interesting to the King and yet old enough to be Hamlet's mother, have always been rare, and incompatibility naturally increases with the age of the actor playing Hamlet. As he would be forty soon after filming had started Olivier considered himself at the extreme age limit for the rôle, and the only advice he could give Bushell was not to cast round him, but quite independently. "Get all the other people's ages right," he said, "and then let's hope if I can give a half decent performance the audience will accept me." The result was a mother who was thirteen years younger than her son, a defect in nature for which Eileen Herlie compensated by allowing herself to be unflatteringly made up and photographed.

For many reasons, of which the casting of Gertrude was only one, Olivier wished he were younger, but in a way he was relieved not to be directing someone else in the part. For the same reason which had decided him to act and produce *King Lear*, he wanted to be on his own. He had so many personal ideas about Hamlet's every inflexion, movement and line that to have impressed them on an actor of sufficient importance to star in the film would inevitably have been resented, and would, anyway, probably have been impossible.

Bushell was familiar with the often-repeated assertion that there is a great mass of young undiscovered female talent on the English stage, but he strongly began to doubt its truth after a long fruitless search for an Ophelia. Ninety-four girls were interviewed, and thirty tested, and in the end they came back to Jean Simmons, whom Olivier had originally said he would like for the part. They had been forced to rule her out in the first place because she was working in one film and was due to leave soon afterwards for Fiji to make *The Blue Lagoon*. But when Olivier arrived back from Italy and was shown the other tests, he said that, if it could possibly be managed, they must try to get her.

The Rank Organization were agreeable provided all her scenes could be completed within thirty days, and, with this in mind, Olivier went to Pinewood where she was filming. At first Jean Simmons, who was eighteen, was so amazed and overawed that she said she couldn't possibly do it. Olivier told her he was quite sure she could, and in the car which took them back to Denham explained the part to her. When they arrived he asked her to read Ophelia's speech, "As I was sewing in my closet . . ." She did so, a little falteringly, but he discerned what he was subsequently to confirm, that she possessed a great natural talent. There were a number of readings and discussions, and Olivier decided that she had a warmth and sensitivity which would make up for her lack of experience. And during the weeks to come he found her quite extraordinarily quick to catch any subtlety or inflexion she was given; she had, too, the ability of a natural actress to achieve instinctively effects which could otherwise be acquired only after years of experience. Olivier considered that she brought subtleties to Ophelia's demented ramblings in the second mad scene which on a conscious level she could not have known anything about.

III

Shooting began at Denham in May virtually behind locked doors. Olivier would not permit visitors on the set, a decision which mystified Wardour Street, where it is more usual to shout your wares than to be secretive. He did not want journalists, school outings, or provincial mayors disturbing him in the double job of acting and directing, and also he believed that visitors were apt to make actors nervous and a director show off. Except in unusual circumstances visitors are not allowed at rehearsals in a theatre, and he saw no reason to make any change for a film studio. To a journalist who once complained about this he summed up his feelings in a question. "How," he demanded, "would you like to have me looking over your shoulder while you are writing an article?" To publicity men who complained he gave his old reply that he considered a performance should be its own and sufficient publicity, and, as he was shrewdly aware, this insistence on privacy had the result of creating mystery and speculation which was in itself good publicity.

Preparations were infinitely more interesting than the actual filming, and to Olivier, who enjoys work and believes in having a happy company around him, it was a little disturbing to find that making *Hamlet* was not nearly so much fun as *Henry V*. There was no tangible reason for this; everything was going smoothly; there were none of the rows or personal feuds which sometimes upset a unit. It was not until he was discussing the question with Carmen Dillon one day that he discovered the probable answer. She suggested that the characters in *Hamlet* were not such pleasant people to know. The sense of gloom that broods over the tragedy was enough to create its own subtle, malignant atmosphere.

The technicians, less responsive to mood than actors, had their own problems and reasons for occasional fits of despondency. Deep-focus photography, with its need for intensely strong lighting, the unusual camera shots, and the difficulty of working in one more or less permanent set, all contributed to the complexities of production. A normal film is mostly made up of a series of short, highly selective shots with little depth, but here, to keep a flowing rhythm, the camera ranged widely and, because foreground and background were in focus, made unusual demands on art director and lighting cameraman. Desmond Dickinson, the director of photography, said that in thirty years in the film industry he had never experienced any film which presented so many problems. It called for intense concentration over the whole period of six months; it was without relief or the spontaneous fun that often enlivens humbler films. *Hamlet*, he said, sent him grey.

Quite the most stubborn problem, artistically and technically, was the ghost. The first idea was to have a transparent figure—a *negative* image which would be super-imposed on the film. As all whites come out as blacks in a negative the actor playing the ghost (Olivier himself) wore a black make-up. White pupils gleamed out of the dark sockets of the eyes, and, because shadows, such as those under the arms, also came out as white, the figure had a weird, incandescent appearance. This would have been excellent if double-exposure ghosts had not become almost a cinema cliché; as it was, it had to be discarded simply because it obtruded as a familiar camera trick. After several months of vain experiment in which everyone was baffled in the search for an alternative idea, the final solution came with the comparatively simple device of smearing a little vaseline on the lens of the camera to give the figure, photographed in the ordinary way, an indistinct outline. To produce the eerie noise which preceded the appearance of the ghost Olivier subsequently went to enormous trouble. He made as many as fourteen separate sound tracks. On one he had recorded fifty women shrieking; on another the groans of as many men; a third consisted of a dozen violinists scraping their bows across the strings on a single screeching note. These various tracks had then to be blended in different volumes and intensity until he produced a noise which seemed to him to resemble—on what authority is uncertain—"the lid of hell being opened." Supernatural horror was further increased by the pulsing heart-beat which heralded the ghost's every entrance. This sound, Olivier remembered, had been used by Jean Louis Barrault in a stage production in Paris; he made it doubly effective on the screen by bringing the camera in and out of focus to synchronize with the pulsing. Before he would use it, however, he wrote to ask Barrault's permission and insisted on paying for the idea. Because no copyright is possible Olivier is particularly scrupulous about borrowing other people's production tricks or another actor's business.*

It was one day during the filming of the ghost scene that Olivier's secretary, Dorothy Welford, came on to the set and handed him a letter. It looked rather formal, and was marked "Private and Confidential." He opened it, to find that it was from the Prime Minister's secretary, who wished to know if, should such an honour be offered, he would be prepared to accept a knighthood. This came as a quite unexpected surprise, and was all the more pleasant because it followed so closely on the knighthood which Ralph Richardson had received in the New Year's Honours List.

Richardson had told him how important it was to keep the P.M.'s request absolutely secret. A leakage in the press before the announcement in *The London Gazette* meant almost certainly that the honour would be withdrawn. He tried to continue work as if nothing had happened, but after a short while he could not resist surreptitiously showing the letter to so old and trusted a friend as Anthony Bushell, and could hardly wait until he rang up Vivien Leigh that night. She was in Paris, being fitted for clothes for *Anna Karenina*. "You won't take it, of course?" she asked with mock innocence. "Of course not!" he answered, and promptly sat down and wrote to say that he would be honoured to accept.

The notice which appeared in *The London Gazette* announcing the Knights Bachelor in the Birthday Honours gave the very brief citation: "Laurence Olivier, actor. For services to stage and films." Equally briefly Olivier noted the date of the investiture in his pocket diary. In the space for Tuesday, July 8th, he wrote: "Buckingham Palace 10.15" and underneath he drew a little sketch of a sword.

---

* When he played *Richard III* he remembered an amusing piece of business which Emlyn Williams had used in his performance at the Old Vic in 1937. Williams made Gloster assume great sanctity in view of the crowd by reading a Bible, and then showed up the artificial pretence by turning over several pages at once without reading them. After he had Williams' permission Olivier borrowed the idea for his own performance.

On the morning they went to the Palace together, he considered that Vivien, who was dressed in simplest black and wore no jewellery, looked very beautiful, but he himself felt a bit of a mountebank. His hair had been bleached for Hamlet, and he was wearing Anthony Bushell's braided morning coat and a black waistcoat belonging to Ralph Richardson. The waistcoat had seen similar duty before and was, Richardson had insisted, *de rigueur*. It was small comfort that at least his trousers were his own.

Few stage appearances had made him feel more nervous. He was guided into the Bow Room which served as an ante-room, to find himself surrounded by admirals and generals, all of whom seemed to know each other. They were preoccupied in hearty conversations and were so blandly self-confident that, until he spotted his friend Malcolm Sargent, who was also to be knighted that day, he felt lonely and ill at ease.

As he stood waiting his turn to appear in the Grand Hall where the investiture was being held, he might have reflected that knighthoods were not often or lightly given to men of the theatre. Since 1895 when Irving was summoned by Queen Victoria to Windsor to become the first actor to be knighted there had been only nineteen actors besides himself in more than half a century. And if he had ranged over the great names . . . Bancroft . . . Tree . . . Alexander . . . Forbes-Robertson . . . and curiosity had prompted him to some rather wearisome arithmetic he would have found that, at forty, he was the youngest actor ever to receive the honour.

At last his turn came, and beckoned by an almost imperceptible gesture from the Lord Chamberlain, the Earl of Clarendon, who stood beside His Majesty the King, he walked forward. His head bowed, he went down on one knee on the red plush stool at the feet of the King. He felt the light touch of the sword on each shoulder, and it was all over. He rose henceforth entitled to the style and rank of Sir Laurence Olivier, Knight Bachelor.

IV

Hamlet, which took six months to shoot and cost £500,000, was completed at Denham in November, and as a comparative newcomer to film production, who had somehow acquired a reputation for being "artistic" and extravagant, Olivier was pleased to be able to point out that the film had been completed on schedule and within his financial budget.

The dramatic scene in which Hamlet leapt from the balcony to kill Claudius at the end of the duel was not filmed until the very last day, as Olivier had privately planned something in the great heroic and acrobatic tradition which was becoming his trade mark, and in the performance of which he might very easily get hurt. Basil Sydney, who was playing the King, shared the apprehension of the rest of the unit about this leap, and was not reassured by Olivier's promise that he would hardly notice it. When he heard that his back would be to the camera in the scene Sydney firmly said he thought it would be better if he had a stand-in. A professional strong-man named George Crawford was brought down to the studios, fitted into the robes of Claudius and, as Olivier climbed the winding stairs to the balcony high above the throne, squared his shoulders for the impact. He needed to. At the last minute Olivier changed from the jump he had planned, which would have meant that he landed only half on the King. With the cry of "The venom of thy work!" he threw back his arms and performed a complete swallow dive on to the stand-in. Even strong men have their limits; this one was knocked unconscious and lost two teeth. Crawford's sacrifice also went without honour, for the publicity department, unwilling to divulge the secret of the stand-in, was forced to pretend to the world that the scene went off "without mishap."

But even when Olivier could dye his hair back to its normal brown and shooting was over, the film was not finished. There was still the enormously complicated job of editing. Reginald Beck was working against time, because Olivier was due to leave for a tour of Australia with the Old Vic in the following February, and he naturally wanted to see as nearly perfect a rough-cut as possible before he went. He had final decisions to make about several scenes, one of which was the "How all occasions do inform against me" soliloquy. He considered it to be the most illuminating in showing the development of Hamlet's character, and, though often cut on the stage, of great importance because it is the one speech in which Hamlet says categorically that he is powerless to take action but does not know why. The trouble was that it was nearly five minutes long and, coming at a moment when it was unwise to be discursive, he was not sure that the film would, as he put it, "hold" the scene. Would it mean anything to the audience as a whole? What, in the private joke he had with Desmond Dickinson, would Gertie think of it? Gertie was an imaginary young woman in the one-and-ninepennies who, Dickinson had told Olivier early during the making of the film, would not understand a particular sequence. Throughout the film Gertie was constantly at Olivier's elbow, and he was careful never to forget her. A few of the critics were subsequently to call the omission of this soliloquy unforgivable; they did not know how much heart-searching it cost Olivier to cut it, and how he put off the final decision until the last possible moment before he left for Australia.

He toyed, too, with the idea of cutting the whole of the final sequence in which the body of Hamlet is carried through the castle, each part of which is heavy with memories of scenes in the tragedy which has gone before. That survived, against his better judgment, almost out of a superstitious respect for its origin. In the very earliest days, when he was turning ideas for *Hamlet* over in his mind, he had first conceived this shot; pictorially it was beautiful and he was loath to see it go, but he had a suspicion that it would be far better to end on the line, "Good night, sweet Prince and flights of angels sing thee to thy rest!" He kept wondering if that last leisurely scene would not just have people groping for their hats.

Perhaps because he did not ignore the one-and-nines, even if he did not unduly pander to them, *Hamlet* made money at the box-office, and is still making it. After a première at the Odeon, Leicester Square, in London in May, 1948, when the film was seen by the King and Queen, the two Princesses and the Duke of Edinburgh, it started on a run of twenty-six weeks which was to be followed by a triumphant progress through the provinces, in America, and eventually all over the world. In the United States there was an initial battle with the censor, who at first wanted to cut forty minutes because Shakespeare did not conform to cinema "morality codes"; in Boston, where Roman Catholic opinion has considerable influence, a specially expurgated "Sunday" version was shown. But after a while the controversy as to whether Shakespearean indelicacies were absolved from guilt died down, and the film was even more successful financially than in England. Arthur Rank had learnt his lesson with *Henry V*, and sent *Hamlet* out to special cinemas in the main cities, and let the returns come in slowly and steadily over a period of two years. It made a great deal of money at a moment when the British film industry particularly needed it; was given almost unanimous praise from the critics; and won all those "awards" which, like school prizes, are accepted as a yard-stick of merit. The awards, made by film festivals, magazines, and more serious bodies such as the New York Film Critics' Circle, are too numerous for all of them to be taken as seriously as their sponsors would like; but the trophies presented each year by the Academy of Motion Pictures Arts and Sciences continue after more than twenty years to retain their glory. *Hamlet* established a record by winning five "Oscars." It was the Academy's "best motion picture of the year" for 1948 and Olivier's performance was also voted the best of the year; it won two awards for Roger Furse for his sets and costumes, and another for Carmen Dillon for her art direction.

These things were satisfactory, judged on a material level, and Olivier felt a certain sense of achievement after reading all the letters from people who said the film had given them pleasure. But looking back on it he decided that for him the most interesting part of *Hamlet* had been the days in Italy when it took shape in the mind's eye. And then, after the stimulating period of creation, there had followed the satisfaction of seeing some of the ideas captured for ever on celluloid. In the theatre he had always regarded working to a climax as the actor's and the producer's greatest challenge—the ability to gauge to a hair's breadth and the fraction of a second the length of time which a scene, a speech or a pause can be held to give the maximum effect. In the cinema that had proved an even more subtle and difficult thing to judge accurately. But several times, notably in the shot when the camera's eye was held on the retreating figure of Ophelia as she made her long last exit down the corridor of the castle, he believed he had succeeded. It confirmed what had, until then, been just a hope. *Henry V* hadn't been a fluke; given the right support, he could be a good film director. It also proved that the business men of Wardour Street, who for so long had said that Shakespeare on the screen would be box-office poison, were hopelessly wrong. He had often marvelled that for hundreds of years indifferent actors in bad productions had succeeded in bringing the house down with Shakespeare in remote provincial theatres on tipsy Saturday nights. That thought had made him certain that Shakespeare, and *Hamlet* in particular, possessed a romance

—some quality which was indefinable—that would not be lost simply because the play was transferred to the screen. It had strengthened his belief that a film, made with care and drawing on some of the best modern talent available, *must* succeed. Now, as it became obvious that caviare had been made palatable to the general, his theories had survived the practical test; he could feel, humbly, that he had repaid some of the enormous debt he owed to Shakespeare.

CHAPTER 2

Australian Journal
1948

I

W HEN THE OLIVIERS accepted the invitation to tour Australia
and New Zealand in 1948 they foresaw that the ten months
away from England would not be a holiday. Inevitably a
great deal of hard work would be involved in taking three major
plays and a company of more than fifty over vast distances to cities
and audiences unaccustomed to regular professional performances.
They also knew that they, personally, would be under a special sort
of strain; their fame had travelled ahead of them with the films, and
their arrival was likely to cause more than usual interest. But what
they did not envisage was the number or magnitude of the public
engagements they would be expected to attend, and that it would be
impossible for them to go out of a theatre or leave their hotel without being mobbed. They had no idea that, as they moved from city
to city, they would be involved in the most arduous of social mar-
athons.

Exactly how this came about is not quite clear. It gathered mo-
mentum as the tour went on, and probably had its genesis in the
endeavour of the British Council, which was partly sponsoring the
tour, to see that they had a good time. The Council made such
elaborate arrangements for their reception, entertainment and sight-
seeing that a theatrical occasion merged into a social one. The civic

313

fathers of each city they were to visit heard the thunder of advance publicity and decided to outdo each other. It was even whispered that some officials welcomed the tour as a dress-rehearsal in miniature for the visit planned for the King and Queen in the following year.

They were grateful for the hospitality, but began to wish that their engagement book were not quite so full. As actors they were worried because they knew their work was bound to suffer. At night they had to give performances in major rôles in huge theatres; by day they found themselves attending official receptions, visiting hospitals, universities, art galleries and museums. Always there were large, clamorous crowds, cameras, microphones, and a series of handshakes so hearty that once, at least, Vivien Leigh withdrew her hand with a cry of "How d'you—*Ow!*" There were innumerable bouquets and endless requests for a "few words."

It was an enthusiasm and kindness which they appreciated, but the pomp and circumstance sometimes threatened to get a little out of proportion, as on the occasion in Melbourne when Olivier was asked to "review" a march-past of the Royal Australian Navy. As he stood at the saluting base feeling acutely embarrassed while the contingent gave him an eyes-right, he considered that this went rather beyond the duties which might reasonably be expected of a visiting actor.

The tour was the outcome of a suggestion made by Sir Angus Gillan, head of the Dominions section of the British Council, when he visited Australia and New Zealand soon after the war. One of his concerns was to see the best in British entertainment in the Antipodes, and he put it to D. D. O'Connor, a New Zealander, who before the war had been a well-known concert impresario, that he should go to England and try to arrange the visit of some companies. He would have all the support the British Council could give him.

O'Connor went, and he returned with the triumphant announcement that he had secured the Boyd Neel Orchestra, the Ballet Rambert and, as the greatest attraction of all, an Old Vic Company headed by Laurence Olivier and Vivien Leigh. The company was first expected during the late autumn of 1947, but even two years after the end of the war shipping space was still a problem, and it was not until the February of the following year that a ship could be found that could take forty actors, and ten managerial and technical staff.

The choice of plays for such a tour presented a considerable problem. They must be varied, representative of the best in English drama, and likely to appeal to their audiences; and as well as having important star parts for Olivier and Vivien Leigh they must, in the Old Vic tradition, provide good opportunities for the rest of the company. For economy's sake it would be wise to include old productions. It had to be remembered that they were receiving no subsidy, and while success seemed certain they were, in fact, only guaranteed by the Old Vic against half the loss if the tour went badly. After a good deal of discussion Olivier decided on two classical plays and a modern one: Shakespeare's *Richard III*, Sheridan's *The School for Scandal*, and Thornton Wilder's *The Skin of Our Teeth*. This last was the most dangerous and controversial choice because it was American, and because, if London had regarded it as unconventional, it might well prove too puzzling for the taste of audiences unaccustomed to regular theatregoing. Its inclusion in the repertory seemed justified to Olivier because he thought it a brilliant play and because Sabina was by far Vivien's best rôle. The three plays gave them a nice balance of opportunity—one starring play each and the honours divided in the Sheridan.

The only completely new production was *The School* for which costumes and sets were specially designed by Cecil Beaton, who had first heard about the Australian tour exactly a year before. On their way to Santa Marguerita to prepare the script for *Hamlet*, the Oliviers had stopped for a few days with their friends the Duff Coopers at the Embassy in Paris and had talked ideas over with Beaton who also happened to be staying there. Olivier had asked him if he would care to design the production, and on their return to England Beaton had shown them sketches with which they were delighted. By using only painted backcloths and "drops" (with highlights and shadows to convey the impression of deep perspective), he gained a double advantage. Here were sets which could easily be toured and adapted to shallow stages and which at the same time captured the atmosphere and style of the eighteenth-century playhouse.

The company, on the whole, was a young one, with a backbone of experienced principals. Eileen Beldon, George Relph and his wife, Mercia Swinburne, were invited by Olivier to go on the tour, and so were Terence Morgan and Peter Cushing [the Laertes and Osric of the film of *Hamlet*], Dan Cunningham, Thomas Heathcote, and Morgan's wife, Georgina Jumel, who was Vivien Leigh's understudy. It was no coincidence that many of the company had played with him before and were old friends. If possible Olivier always casts his plays with actors and actresses with whom he has worked previously. It is a quite deliberate policy, adopted not only because he knows their capabilities and if they are sympathetic personalities, but because he believes the public likes it. Rather in the way audiences develop an affection for the players they see week after week in repertory, he hopes that they will welcome the familiar faces they associate with his productions and management. But although he allows this to prejudice his casting, he is also quite ruthless if an old friend proves unequal to the part he has been given. At that point sentiment stops abruptly.

II

Just before they left for Australia a well-wisher sent Olivier a leather-covered diary on the outside of which gilt lettering proclaimed: "My Trip Abroad." Inside there were spaces for "Name . . ." and "Address . . ." and "Accompanied By . . ." and on each page room was provided for Autographs. Although it seemed to him a volume rather more suitable for an American debutante of Edwardian days on her first trip to Europe, he resolved to keep it up day by day. He settled down to this undertaking with great initial gusto which lasted for several months but which unfortunately faded as the tour in Australia became more and more strenuous.

It began on the Saturday they left:

Feb. 14th. Johnnie and Mary [Mills] had stayed the night in the study. Some 70 intimate friends had been to drink us "Bon Voyage." Danny Kaye and Roger [Furse] making final exit. R. left overcoat but took a lot of whitewash from garden wall. Only three hours in beds. Called at 8. Staggered through dressing and packing. Said good-bye to New [Vivien's Siamese cat named after the theatre], who stayed in ruined drawing-room. Met by station master in top hat at Euston. A great many flash bulbs. High Commissioners of

Australia and N.Z. Interview with Leslie Mitchell for television camera at top end of platform. Interview with somebody else for another movie camera at lower end of platform. Flash bulbs of course. Retake with L.M. at top end. Flash bulbs. Many sweet people seeing us off. Many sweet fans and many sweet flash bulbs. Liverpool about 3. Masses of flowers on board, about 100 wires, books from Jamie [Hamilton] of course. About 4.15 tugs pushed us out and round. Cecil [Tennant] and Dorothy [Welford] waving from gantry on landing stage until we were nearly mid-channel. Beautiful boat and very comfy. Unpacked for the night, dinner alone together in cabin. Vivien not eating much. Went for a walk by myself wearing duffle-coat. Poured bath, but went to bed without it. Read Logan Pearsall Smith's "English Aphorisms" for a while before turning out light.

Feb. 16*th.* Went round with Purser location-hunting for rehearsal space. Eventually picked on dining-room and gently extricated promise of quite a few more tables being removed than originally suggested. Did some study of Sir Peter. Burning pain like white-hot needle in right toe getting v. bad. Went to see Doctor afterwards. He said it was not gout. He said rest it, so I played deck quoits.

Feb. 17*th.* A good night. Woke with no gout but stiff neck. To-morrow it'll be something else. Studied Sir Peter over breakfast. Anointed and soaked foot, studying Sir P. Went up on deck and met Hugh [Stewart] who heard me Sir P. To-night at dinner at the Captain's table Vivien turned to me suddenly with an alarmingly wild look and said: "To-night I should like to play dominoes."

Feb. 20*th.* First pretence at work to-day—just a little flutter. Prancing and singing in Forward Lounge. The boat was rolling in a mocking way which made the prancing even less graceful than usual. Level with Cape Blanco at noon. In bed now, Vivien reading me occasional passages from "All Trivia." She has stopped now. I must get on with Sir Peter against the morning.

Feb. 21*st.* Rehearsed "School," going through for words mainly. Also in hope of some impressions for future guidance. Starting at 10.30 and packed it up at a quarter-to-twelve so that the dining saloon could be put straight for lunch. Back to "School" in the dining saloon at 2.45. We had finished by tea-time, and I had a hard time trying to put my thoughts into shape, or rather trying to find some shape in my thoughts about it. The thing eludes me somehow —somewhere. I know I was tired when I was planning it, but even now I can't feel how else to plan it. I think the first scene must be every director's Waterloo. Of all authors' dialogue, it seems to me, Sheridan's indicates least movement where it seems to require most. Where it is human it comes instantly alive and presents no difficulty, where it is artificial it seems hearsed in death unable to burst its cerements, and, to prevent the audience dying as stiff as our ancestors in 1780, has to have arbitrary choreography thrust upon it. How are the two to be married? I can only think by the spirit and vitality of the playing. At any rate that is the baby I left with the company in a talk after the rehearsal. A lot of their Speech is awfully bad—talked to them about that. Cape Verde Islands. Our first sight of North Africa.

Sunday: Feb. 22nd. Tony Garvin said to-day: "The worst of it is that all our tooth glasses taste of Gin and Andrews." Noon off Sierra Leone. Played tennis and bathed. Saw many flying fish and a beautiful hammerhead shark. After lunch rehearsed the first scene at Lady Sneerwell's, all the afternoon, and quite a heartening improvement. At five, V. and I rehearsed the second quarrel—no improvement, but some beautiful porpoises and another shark cheered things up.

Feb. 25th. Read the "Wild Duck" to-day. It's wonderful, lovely for Vivien; and I should dearly enjoy working on it, but worried about casting it with this company. Nothing for the three boys.*

Feb. 26th. Screen scene all day. Not quite finished yet—going very much better.

Feb. 27th. Sun directly overhead. No shadows. Thornton [Wilder] was saying when we saw him in England that I should try and write, so I thought I'd better start with a foreword to his play for the programme. I've been working on it to-day quite a bit.

March 1st. Did Clarence scenes [*Richard III*] in the morning. Afternoon stood about with others on boat deck waiting for Table Mountain to appear, misty and bad for photographs, not that it would make much difference to ours. Docked by five o'clock, came below and changed for dreaded Press party. Flowers, fruit, messages

---

* This was a reference to a play which, looking well ahead, might possibly have been included in the Old Vic repertory on the company's return to England.

and mail in profusion came flying into the cabin. Had very little to say to the Press, I fear, and indeed, they didn't have much to say to us. After a bit Gwen [Ffrangcon-Davies] arrived, which was wonderful, and Ivor [Novello], Bobbie [Andrews], Roma Beaumont and Vanessa Lee, Ivor's new find. Everybody madly sweet to us and bulbs flashed many times. Vivien looking v. lovely in New Look black and white. Ivor's car took us to the Alhambra to see "Perchance to Dream." Wonderful having to come all the way to Capetown in order to see it. Lots of ripping applause from the publique on the way in. Found "Perchance" and Ivor's performance highly enjoyable.

After the company had spent two days sightseeing, had been constantly prevented by the notorious "tablecloth" from catching even a glimpse of the top of Table Mountain, and had attended a party given by Sir Evelyn and Lady Baring at High Commission House ("Twelve-and-a-half per cent, I suppose!"—Vivien Leigh's comment), the *Corinthic* sailed out of Table Bay. They were on the last four thousand miles of the voyage to Perth, where the tour was due to start on March 20th. An advance party of technicians had gone ahead in a previous ship to prepare the converted cinema which was to be their theatre.

Twelve days after leaving the Cape the *Corinthic* arrived at Perth at 8 a.m. on a Monday morning. The Old Vic tour had created its own publicity, and anticipation throughout Australia was so great that practically every newspaper in the Commonwealth had representatives to meet them. They arrived in the middle of a quite unpredicted heat-wave, and as the temperature went up to nearly 100 degrees, the reception on board was made almost impossible. As all Vivien Leigh's light dresses were packed she was forced to swelter in a tweed suit, and, like the rest of the company, felt absurdly overclothed. The diary continues:

Monday, March 15th. First day in Australia. Woke at seven, feeling worse than I remember since first evening of Irish whiskey with Roger and Dallas in Dublin 1943. Very unfortunate. Vivien quite all right. Press on board, interviews, flash bulbs, newsreels and a broadcast before we knew what we were doing. Came ashore eventually. Drove here, 16 Bellevue. *Terribly* hot. Wonderful view of

Perth, having been round University and King's Park. Lunched by Charles Wilmot and Philip Lee of the British Council at the Esplanade Hotel. Then the theatre. Kind efforts by Mr. Harvey the manager had been made to make the dressing-rooms respectable, but def. not enough of them. A movie was going on—English, Glynis Johns, Jeanne de C., Barry Morse etc. About 12 people in front. House holds 2,280, but does not seem as vast inside as the Century, N.Y. We are the first "live" show ever to play in it. Went out to Scarborough Beach, for wonderful drive as sun went down. A black swan flew over us afterwards. If I don't sleep to-night I never will.

March 16th. I wish I hadn't said that. I woke after an hour or two being eaten by mosquitoes. Up at nine. Theatre 10.30. David [Kentish] had not been to bed. Company arrived, called them at 1.30 for words. Worked out dressing-rooms with David. Vivien and I will dress on the stage. She has a huge cage which girls will use for quick-change room. Boys will use mine. Broadcast 1 o'clock A.B.C. with V. 4 o'clock tea with Lt.-Governor Sir James Mitchell and Lady. Both extremely charming. Talked of the land, labour, etc. 5 o'clock *large* cocktail party at Esplanade. We shook hands with Perth. Dinner with Prof. and Mrs. Currie of the University. Went on to students' show of "Œdipus." Met them after and then went and said hallo to the people queueing up for seats who were v. sweet. Quite a day. Exhausted.

By their decision not to take two of the only six dressing-rooms in the cinema, the Oliviers set the tone and example for the company throughout the tour. Vivien Leigh's dressing-room was simply a part of the stage screened off by wire netting and covered with a curtain. Olivier dressed on the O.P. side of the stage with nothing more than a chair, table and piece of carpet in the wings. During the days before the opening he worked in his shirt-sleeves with the stage hands who were adapting the narrow stage for the play, while in an improvised wardrobe room Vivien Leigh helped to iron costumes.

March 18th. Finished lighting, staff rehearsal and rehearsal with orchestra. First dress-rehearsal with orchestra in evening. —— has made my shoes so small, right foot began to hurt badly. Make-up much too old for Sir P.

March 19th. Check on lighting and stage work. Too hot to make actors dress twice so full rehearsal in afternoon with piano for stage work. Evening final dress-rehearsal with orchestra. Make-up for Sir P. now too young.

March 20th. Foot now very painful. Words in afternoon and actually home for a rest before the show. Decided to be very royal and play six bars of the "King" at opening and full company sing whole at end of each performance. Rang up a little late so that Lieut.-Gov. could get to his seat. Harold [Ingram] had difficulty with orchestra which was very untrained though very nice and enthusiastic. Trumpeter had incurable vibrato and on a consistent quarter-tone sharp. Oh dear, Sir Thomas would not have been pleased. Audience very quiet and strangely disinclined to laugh. It became obvious during the evening that they could not hear. And we were really bashing over Sheridan's gossamer trifle like Hellza-poppin' with everything we knew and had. However wonderful applause at end. I was rather embarrassingly given a wreath before any girls had anything. Darling V. was almost left out. Made quite good, fairly long speech. "Welcome to Old Vic . . . first perf. of prod. in Perth . . . added fillip being in cinema . . . like reclaiming land from sea . . ." Brought in Western Australian cricket victory —all went well and I blessed Danny Kaye for advice. "If you pre-pare every speech you are asked to make," he said, "you'll have a nervous breakdown. If you make enough lousy speeches—lovely! They'll stop asking you to make any more." Nice party after beer get-together with the quality in the foyer.

March 22nd. Run through Richard in afternoon with foot up. Still painful. Gave way to amplification installed by University peo-ple for evening perf. Difference clear—plenty of response to com-edy. Made speech mildly apologizing necessity for amplification. "If all went round with binoculars strapped to eyes . . . soon forget to see . . . etc. . . . naturally world forgetting how to listen, etc." Suggested that if all the 2,000 people in audience gave £1 at each of our ten performances, by end of stay £20,000 would have been collected—a nice start for proper theatre.

March 23rd. Lord Mayor's reception 12.0. Premier Western Aus-tralia, General Whitelaw. Very hot indeed and responded to toast in heavy sherry, champagne and good beer. Made rousing speech extolling theatre—"the readiest and most acceptable glamorizer of thought." Vivien followed with a few words. Straight from Lord Mayor to University for lecture on "The Use of Poetry in Drama." Dear Professor Currie introducing V. She makes the most damn awful fuss but I think she's beginning to like it; anyhow have tiny feeling she could not be discouraged even if that were necessary. "There are many advantages to being married," she told the delighted students, seizing the mike like Lamoret's duck, only even more bewitchingly. I started denouncing myself as a theorist . . . "learnt to fly by seat of pants". . . delved mildly into use of poetry, structural and practical, rhythmical and atmospherical. Rehearsal Richard 2.30. Peter getting first class as Clarence.

March 27th. My foot quite well now and I am dancing in play instead of my would-be comic old man act which I was rather enjoying. Matinée. Speech getting quite Sheridanesque: "Truly, ladies and gentlemen, a little laughter from the mouths of babes and sucklings is very heartening on a hot afternoon like this" (for the kids in front). Show getting better. Vivien loosening up no end, but she must bubble with delicious laughter both inner and audible. My make-up is still lousy, not that it matters much with a theatre this size. I've got a great deal to do on Sir P.

Perth, which of all cities in Australia considers itself closest in spirit and atmosphere to England, went a little mad during the fortnight of the Old Vic's visit. The company was cheered at the end of each performance and the Oliviers were mobbed the moment they appeared in the streets. At the box-office they took £15,000.

At the finale of the play on the last night the company sprang a surprise. They startled the audience by making the library of Sir Joseph Surface's house ring with the unexpected, and secretly rehearsed, choruses of "Waltzing Matilda." As a gesture this was much appreciated, but it was a little disconcerting for the English company to discover how much better they knew the words than the Australians. At the end of the song the applause and cheering threatened to go on indefinitely, and at last Olivier had to step forward and say that he was sorry, but he would have to ring down the curtain for the last time. Planes were waiting for them at the airfield to fly them through the night to Adelaide.

Only with a police escort on motor-cycles was the bus carrying the company able to force its way along William Street and out to the airport. When the Oliviers themselves appeared they had to fight their way to the taxi while the crowd sang "Auld Lang Syne," and once again the police had to provide an escort. Even at the airport at one o'clock in the morning there were several hundred people to wave and cheer until the Skymasters took off. The Oliviers had had their first taste of the receptions to come.

During the fortnight in Perth the heavier and more elaborate sets for *Richard III* and *The Skin of Our Teeth* had been sent on by sea to Adelaide in advance. This was part of an ingenious plan so that all three plays could be toured as cheaply as possible with the minimum of delay. The sets for the Sheridan by Cecil Beaton were virtually only painted backcloths and "drops" which could be set and struck very quickly and were light enough to be carried by air. While the Shakespeare and Wilder were played in Adelaide, Sheridan was leap-frogged by air to Melbourne, so that it was ready for the opening week there and bridged what would otherwise have been a gap while the heavier plays followed more slowly.

After all three plays had been performed at Sydney, Shakespeare and Wilder were again sent on in advance by sea, this time to Auckland, New Zealand. Sheridan had a fortnight in Brisbane and was then flown with the company so that all three could be played there. This scheme only broke down once. After Melbourne the company were due to play for a week in Hobart, Tasmania. Unfortunately the chartered Dakotas were too small for even the Sherdian scenery, and the difficulty was only overcome by Roger Ramsdell, the master painter, working for two days and nights repainting Beaton's designs on smaller cloths which could be carried in the planes.

March 31*st*. Adelaide. Arrived at 8 quite exhausted after a really deadly night. Straight to South Australian Hotel. Breakfast, unpacking; popped over to the Theatre Royal which is quite divine. Pretty old, lovely atmosphere, holds 1,450. Very much wished we were doing "School." Came back to Press Conference at 12.0. When I talk slowly to the press I'm inclined to get very pompous, and I am apt to lose the trend which is faithfully quoted; when quickly, then fairly intelligently and am wildly misquoted. After lunch went to call at Government House. Sir Willoughby and Lady Norrie both charming—also the house. Dread news that "Skin" must open Monday, May 12th, instead of Tuesday.

April 4th. Sunday. Lighting for "Skin"—worth describing. Stage ready by 5. Quite confident all cues just had to be run through. First cue came up quite wrong with a lot of pinks in it. Thought at first colour wrong, but no. Cues came at right times but wrong things happened. I really thought my time had come. This was the *only* day when lighting could be done, so it was no use my going home and working out a new plot all night even if I had the energy. Then Bill Bunday said something about having a vague memory that at the Piccadilly Theatre, whose lighting plot we were working from, numbering went from Prompt Side to O.P. We tried plugging in all spots in reverse—it worked! We nearly died of relief. Could it be H. M. Tennent's spite against the Old Vic!

April 12th. Dress Rehearsal "Skin." Opening performance 8.o. It really went wonderfully and Vivien made a *very* good *long* speech. Elsie [Byer] and all stage management to supper. The end of a really hectic fortnight.

April 13th. Rather a bemused notice in the paper quoting desperately from the foreword.

April 14th. Rude letters about "Skin" in the press. After lunch to our great joy we were taken to a private collection of white kangaroos. They are Albinos. Vivien had seen kangaroos in Perth, but these were my first and I was ravished. People pointed out joeys that had just at that moment—if only we hadn't missed—jumped from the does' pouches. Just like Ruth Draper's garden. I took photos desperately but I know the light too bad for my sort of photography.

April 16th. Sir William Mitchell (Stephen's uncle) took us round the university, 4,000 students. Very impressive. Talked and answered questions to the Students' Theatre Group for about ½ hour. After lunch to Stony Fells Vineyard. Saw the crushings and had a great deal explained to us. We sampled all and sundry and thought the sherry very good. It was all delightful but we dared not enjoy it as we should have liked. Tearing ourselves away we dutifully went to Art Gallery. We flung open the door on our arrival forgetful of the flagon of sherry we had been given which was on the floor of the car and which shattered itself in the gutter directly opposite the entrance to the noble edifice. We could not face the disgrace and had to drive on several yards. The car behind was very angry. Correspondence has raged over "Skin" in the papers. Those in favour being rather pushed into the background by the *Advertiser*. It has gone really wonderfully generally. I am not at all happy about Antrobus * yet, feel very uneven and unfinished. The whole show makes me excessively nervous and I frankly dislike the break up bits. I've wanted to play the part so often I hate to be disappointing myself in it. V. is wonderful—better than ever.

April 17th. Two last shows and farewell to Adelaide. Vivien insisted that I make the speech—quite long. "A picture gallery must have its Rembrandts *and* its Henry Moores"—an allusion as to why a play like "Skin" was in our repertory. Threw a party afterwards. His Excellency [Sir Willoughby Norrie] came and was most charming and kind, saying jolly nice things about our being good ambassadors. His small son asked why Lady Olivier called herself "Miss Vitamin B". 400 other people also turned up. The front of house girls gave us an enormous box of chocolates and the staff a remarkable inkwell made of Burraburraburra wood or something. Waltzing Matilda was sung.

Adelaide gave the Old Vic the finest reception of the tour—the only comparable reception was at Melbourne—preceded by all the advance enthusiasm which was to be repeated everywhere the company went. Queues started at the theatre two days before the box-office opened; more than a hundred people slept the night on the pavement through a bad storm, and on the actual morning that the seats were on sale there was a queue of over 1,000. A woman flew 2,000 miles from Darwin to see one of the plays.

It was not to be expected, however, that *The Skin of Our Teeth* would be an unqualified success. As in London, there were a great many people who found that it produced an impression which Olivier in his foreword called "somewhat haphazard." In Adelaide there was no lack of people eager to show their downright commonsense and, like Hans Andersen's little boy, confess their perplexity when they could not see what others admired. "Quite frankly," wrote one, "what the play was about or what idea was intended I have not the faintest conception. To say that I was bored almost to tears would be to put it mildly." Had it not been for Vivien Leigh's

* Olivier's part in *Skin of Our Teeth*.

performance it might well have been an unwise choice for a company abroad to include "a Henry Moore" in its repertory.

April 18th. Excerpt from Vivien's letter to Binkie [Hugh Beaumont]: "We drove . . . through the most wonderful country imaginable, the first bit so Dali-esque as to be incredible—great shallow blue lakes surrounded by glistening white sand, black and white branches of trees sticking up out of the water and birds of every kind and description everywhere. Then through great forests to Mount Gambier where we spent the night in a very strange hotel. The midnight clock struck eighteen and the fire alarm was sent off every two hours just to see if the poor old thing was all right (and that we knew it). A lot of Marsupials tramped about in the roof and all the inhabitants seemed to get up at six to whistle and sing and bang on each others' doors. Not very restful, but different."

April 19th. Up to Mount Gambier and the (not) Blue Lake. Took photos of the distance where Bobbie [Helpmann] was born and the house where he spent his boyhood. Then on through really wonderful pasture country, brown hills of dry grass cut by cypress windbreaks. Always high mountains in the distance and always cream, dirty ochre and black dairy cattle in foreground. But never never no kangaroos. Arrived Melbourne at 4 p.m. Bathed and changed and got to the Menzies Hotel for press conference at 5.0. V. carried the wretched thing off with superlative charm, starting by breaking up the formality of the arranged chairs and making us all mill round. A wearing hour and a half. Questions ranging from fairly sensible to entrapping headline stuff. "Tell me, Sir L., about your *stoop*, was it a childhood accident?" "Now that England is finished, Sir L., what do you think about . . ."

April 20th. Managed to beat a barrage of coughing for last night's first night. Notices good on the whole with reservations from people who seemed to know a great deal. Sheridan is old-fashioned! Melbourne being "fobbed-off" with something taken out of a drawer. British Council reception in afternoon. Quite harmless. Just shaking hands.

April 24th. Anzac Day. Got plane at 10.30 which dropped us obligingly at Canberra at 12.0. "Honoured to be here," over the microphone. To Gov. House. Mr. McKell very affable in a manner rather resembling a Peter Ustinov impersonation; Mrs. McKell

gracious and friendly. Mr. Chiffley, the Prime Minister, amiable
very, if protected by an armour plating of political mysterioso.
After lunch to War Memorial for service to the dead. Tea with
Chiffley who introduced a lot of Cabinet and their wives. He made
a speech. So did I. Back to Gov. House, V. and I now getting
thoroughly scared about our speeches for this evening [for a nation-
wide Food for Britain appeal]—no time to think about them. Car
to the Capitol Cinema. We were taken round from our seats and
on to the stage during a turn. Seats immediately in front of the
screen so close to the four Hitlerite mikes that the back of the broad-
caster's legs touched the knees of the person behind. I have never
known a more alarming set-up including the Albert Hall wartime
stuff. Arc lights, two movie news cameras, four microphones, 2,000
people. Vivien looked wonderful in pale lime green and a blood
red rose at her waist. Half way through she hesitated, but went on,
finishing with Sonnet 116. Then my turn—oh it was really horrid.*
I left out a wodge but got through. Back to Gov. House. Lovely
view from our room.

April 25th. We left Gov. House at 8.30. The kind official secretary to Mr. Chiffley who had looked after us so beautifully throughout murmured that we had "a well-earned day of rest" ahead of us.
We put him wise that we had a dress-rehearsal and a heavy opening
awaiting us that evening. He hastily said, "Oh yes, of course,
'George III'." In the aeroplane we heard we had been cut off the
air in the middle of last night's programme. Full run through
"Richard" (not George) in afternoon. Opening the flattest I have
ever known—very depressed.

Here the diary petered out. The strain, which was to mount
steadily, was becoming too great to make it any pleasure to sit down
at the end of a heavy day to record events.

The Old Vic was in Melbourne for two months, alternating the
three plays and, in contrast to Adelaide, having more success with
The Skin of Our Teeth, which was, in fact, the most popular of the
three. Away from the theatre public engagements kept them as
busy as ever, and while experience imposed its own discipline, Olivier was to see how easy it was to make a slip. In Perth he had caused

---

* Olivier is here perhaps a little too deprecating. Newsreels of his speech
which were shown in England produced a shoal of letters congratulating him.

raised eyebrows by calling on the Governor in sandals and a blazer, and in Melbourne he brought down an avalanche of criticism by an attempted pleasantry.

After a lunch given in their honour he, Vivien, and the whole company were invited by the Premier of Victoria to see the local House of Representatives. On entering the Assembly Hall, Olivier found that a crowd was waiting and a speech was expected of him. As he had only just finished making a speech at the lunch, and many of his listeners were the same, he felt rather at a loss for words and fell back on a joke which he knew lacked brilliance but never dreamt would offend. After a few sentences he dropped into Australian slang, referred to his listeners as "beauts" and ended by saying, "We want you to know that we're having a bonzer time." This was greeted with laughter, but when reported in the press it became the subject of an icy correspondence from readers who chose to interpret it as a reflection on Commonwealth culture. Melbourne's disapproval, however, had evaporated by the end of the two months there, and the last night produced the usual display of almost hysterical enthusiasm. At the final curtain the company was bombarded from the stalls with streamers, and this prompted Olivier to step forward and say: "Ladies and gentlemen, our ship hasn't sailed yet!"

III

After Melbourne and Tasmania the Oliviers felt that if they were to have any strength for what remained of the tour they must have a break, and they flew north to a coastal resort with the idyllic name of Surfers' Paradise. Here they hoped to have a week's holiday and enjoy a little peace. But by now their legend and the magic of their names had spread all over Australia, and they aroused so much curiosity wherever they went that privacy was impossible. From the moment of their arrival there was trouble in Paradise; a crowd of at least three hundred had collected outside their hotel and greeted them whenever they appeared with a ripple of nervous cheering and outstretched autograph books. "This is too much!" Vivien Leigh said desperately. "We must get some peace—even if we have to go back to Tasmania or right up to Darwin!"

This remark, carried by the manager to the crowds and reporters, had some slight effect. Even the most persistent pressmen started to show sympathy, and a cautionary cartoon appeared in a Sydney paper. Two monkeys surrounded by crowds of onlookers who were peering into the cage were telling each other how much they sympathized with the Oliviers. It became impossible, however, to stay at the hotel, and they moved into a remote little bungalow which had been lent to Dan Cunningham. Roger Ramsdell came up from Brisbane to cook for them, and there with Cecil Tennant, the managing director of Laurence Olivier Productions, Ltd., who had just flown to Australia with the finished film of *Hamlet*, they were able to relax for the few days that remained before they were due in Sydney.

During the eight weeks' season in Sydney there was the same frantic demand for seats (£70,000-worth of advance bookings had to be returned), the same hectic receptions, the same speeches, light-hearted but inspiring, to be addressed to youth at the university. But two things helped to impress Sydney on Olivier's memory. It was there that he slipped a cartilage in one leg during the duel in *Richard III*, developed a slight thrombosis in the other, and in consequence had to play on crutches for several performances. It was there, too, that he received a letter from Lord Esher. Vaguely expecting to hear the reaction in London to the success of the tour, he read the letter with growing bewilderment. The Chairman of the Old Vic Governors said plans were being made for the reorganization of the Old Vic and its administration in 1949. After going into a few details, the letter slowly and politely came to the point. Lord Esher said that he and the other Governors had decided that the valuable services of Olivier and his fellow-directors, Richardson and Burrell, would not be required after the coming season. At the end of their five-year term of office their appointments would not be renewed.

In any circumstances such news would have come as a serious blow. In the middle of an exacting tour, conducted on behalf of the Old Vic, it seemed incredible. What politics had been at work in London, he wondered, to bring about such a decision? After four years, in which the three of them had worked so hard, the Old Vic had taken on new life and its prestige was high. In the first two seasons considerable profits had been made; during the third they had broken rather better than even. Why, then, were they being dropped, and how had it come about that the announcement was so ineptly timed?

His first thought was to consult his fellow-directors and his cable

to John Burrell in London started with a quotation from *Richard III:*
"O me, I see the ending of our house!" Another went to Richardson and was addressed to Hollywood where his friend was filming
in *The Heiress.* Hollywood . . . in this address, could Olivier have
detected it, was probably the vital clue to the mystery of the Governors' decision. At a moment when the Old Vic was suffering
severe financial losses at the New Theatre and the standard of productions was under fire, two of the three directors were out of the
country. There had been an understanding that during their five
years as directors both Olivier and Richardson should be allowed a
period of absence to make a film. It had been agreed with the Governors that while a film would interfere with their duties this would
be more than compensated by the amount of indirect publicity that
it would bring to the Old Vic. Olivier had made his film the previous year; Richardson was making his now. It was just an unfortunate coincidence that Richardson's plans for *The Heiress* had
coincided with Olivier's Australian tour. Neither was to blame, but
the Governors, looking ahead, were perhaps wondering if it was
wise for the interests of the theatre to be in the hands of two men
who had such considerable activities outside the Old Vic. In the
next five years, they may well have thought, it was quite possible
that both would again be absent in a crisis.

But this argument would only have been valid if the Governors
had been in any doubt about their directors' intentions. Olivier and
Richardson had not only clearly defined their responsibilities to the
Old Vic, but had even drawn up plans which stretched as far as
twelve years ahead—to the time when it was hoped the Old Vic
would merge into the National Theatre. The most ambitious of
these Olivier was actually carrying out at that moment. Part of the
purpose of going to Australia was to create a second Old Vic company so that within a few years there would be two separate companies which, alternately, could play in London and in the provinces
or abroad. Quite apart from their own wishes they had also seen
that it would be a great mistake for them to continue at the Old Vic
playing all the leads over a period of years. Their idea had been to
foster young actors, build them up slowly, and then let them take
over when they had proved their quality and popularity at the box-
office. To this end they had sponsored the initiation of the Old Vic

Theatre School, the Young Vic Company, and—a provincial tributary, as well as a theatre in its own right—the Bristol Old Vic.

These plans seemed so obviously sensible and straightforward that it was difficult to escape the suspicion that something else besides fears for the future had helped to dictate this sudden decision. Although they were to get no hint of it until much later, there was a small body of influential opinion against Richardson and Olivier.

Impressive though the record of the Old Vic had been under the three directors, there were those who disapproved, not of John Burrell, but of the two actors whom they referred to slightly disparagingly as "the Knights." They chose to believe that "the Knights" were using the Old Vic as a vehicle for themselves, and that the ideals of the theatre were being sacrificed to the star system. It was argued that there were too many white ties in the stalls, and that Emma Cons' theatre for the poor was becoming too luxurious; commercial success suggested vulgarity, and, so the argument went, would lead inevitably to a lowering of the standards of integrity. A press report from Australia referring to "Sir Laurence Olivier's Old Vic Company" had produced a single, brief comment from an English theatrical columnist; "*Whose* Old Vic?" This was the sort of small barb which had a lethal effect. None of this was ever admitted, of course; and as prejudice never came out into the open and no public statement was ever made about the Governors' decision, "the Knights" had to remain, visors down, in dignified silence.

To make matters more frustrating the official announcement was not to appear until the New Year, so that Olivier had to continue with the rest of the Australian and New Zealand tour as though nothing had happened, and even go on making arrangements for the Old Vic autumn season in London. It cast a shadow over the tour, and quite suddenly he and Vivien began to share a feeling which was general throughout the company. They were homesick. Because, however, of pressing invitations from New Zealand, it had been agreed that they should finish the tour there, and they flew from Brisbane to Auckland during the first week in September. But New Zealand was not given the chance of providing an enjoyable climax. What should have been a leisurely visit, with the opportunity of seeing the beautiful country, developed into a whirlwind tour during which they travelled over a thousand miles and gave forty-four performances in four different cities in just under six

332

weeks. Their eyes were now firmly set on the *Corinthic*, which was sailing for home from Wellington in the middle of October.

Only the ease with which they could carry *The School for Scandal* made it possible to evolve an elaborate jigsaw of alternating performances, so that they could present all three plays in so short a time. In eleven days in Auckland they gave nine performances of *The School for Scandal*, four of *The Skin of Our Teeth*, and three of *Richard III*. They closed on the Saturday night, flew five hundred miles south to Christchurch on the Sunday with Sheridan virtually in their pockets, and opened with him there on the Monday.

The last of twelve performances at Christchurch took place on their eighth day there. This was a Tuesday. On the Wednesday morning they flew a hundred miles to Dunedin, and gave the first of six performances of Sheridan that same night. During four days at Dunedin the other two plays were shipped north to Wellington, ready for fourteen performances with all three in the eleven days left before they sailed. It was a wearying schedule, and not without some justification the Oliviers told a startled reporter in Dunedin: "You may not know it, but you are talking to two walking corpses." Sadly they admitted that New Zealand had become just a succession of theatre dressing-rooms and hotel bedrooms. When asked if they had seen anything of the country, Olivier thought for a moment and then announced that on their flight from Christchurch they had come sufficiently low to see some Canterbury lambs—"quite distinctly."

During a performance in Christchurch Olivier's knee, which he had injured in Sydney, gave out again. He struggled on with his performances for another week using a crutch, but for the last three performances of the tour was forced to hand over his part of Sir Peter to Derrick Penley, his understudy. He had been told that unless he had it operated on the knee would give him constant trouble, so he went into hospital to have the cartilage removed.

It was a sad ending to a tour which had been so successful, and, in contrast to the crowds which had cheered them on the brilliant March morning when they had arrived in Perth seven months before, there was only a small group of people at Glasgow Wharf in Wellington to see them off. It was pouring with rain, and a few soaked streamers lying on deck made a pathetic attempt at gaiety.

Vivien Leigh and the rest of the company had gone aboard overnight, and shortly before seven o'clock an ambulance drove on to the quayside. Olivier, who had been brought from the nursing home, was lifted out. The stretcher was placed in a canvas sling, and while it was being adjusted a girl in the crowd stepped forward and reverently held an umbrella over his head. With two ambulance men standing on the stretcher, one on either end to balance it like a seesaw, a crane swung him aboard. He had had a bad night and was taken straight down to his cabin.

The last that New Zealand saw of the Old Vic company was Vivien Leigh, the hood of a mackintosh pulled over her head, waving through the rain as the ship pulled out into the harbour.

CHAPTER 3

Tradition at the St. James's
1948-1953

I

THE LITTLE TUGS which had joined the ship in the Estuary
worried the *Corinthic* into her berth, and looking out of their
porthole the Oliviers saw the bleak and rainswept Essex
shore. Tilbury docks, outlined against the grey November sky,
offered their sombre welcome. After the ten months abroad this
was their first view of England, and suddenly they realized how
grateful and pleased they were to be home. There was no need to
assume false smiles for the photographers who swarmed on board;
they were genuinely happy, and friends who had come from London to meet them thought both of them had seldom looked fitter.
Olivier, still forced to walk with a stick, talked with enthusiasm of
the tour, and had figures to support his traveller's tales. They had
covered thirty thousand miles, given 179 performances and played
to over 300,000 people. After all expenses were paid, they had
brought home about £40,000 for the British Council. Reporters
were eager to know of their plans, and while he had to keep the
news of his retirement from the administration of the Old Vic a
secret, Olivier was able to tell them they would be opening at the
New Theatre in January. They would play *The School for Scandal,*
revive *Richard III*, and also produce Jean Anouilh's modern version
of *Antigone* in place of *The Skin of Our Teeth.*

In their car, which was waiting on the dockside, they drove up to London and through the wet and gleaming streets of Chelsea to Durham Cottage. Another car followed with a trunk-load of clothes which they had bought in Australia and in the back was piled a mixed assortment of boomerangs, aborigines' knives, stuffed koala bears, woven rugs, stone hammers, emu-tail brooches, and chewed-wood loin cloths. A number of fine Australian paintings completed the list of the trophies gathered on a safari the memory of which was already rapidly fading into the past.

It might be a wretched night, but it was wonderful to be in London again, and, as she stood for a moment in the entrance to the little sitting-room at Durham Cottage, Vivien felt the special sense of warmth and security which is the greatest joy of homecoming. Except for a new Siamese cat, which Larry had arranged to be awaiting her and which replaced New who had been run over while they were abroad, everything was familiar. And yet—another pleasure of homecoming after a long time away—it was possible to see the house with fresh eyes. There were new pleasures to be found in the Sickert over the fireplace, and in the uniform editions of Thackeray and Jane Austen on the shelves. While they had gone far and seen so much their home had not changed its gentle and comfortable expression. And when at last she and Larry were alone and sat before a blazing fire with the curtains drawn across the winter night it was a pleasure to glance round at the trivia collected over a life-time . . . the china cats . . . the enamelled snuff and patch boxes . . . the photograph of the Lunts in the garden of the house in Wisconsin inscribed, "Darling V. and L. hurry up and come to tea . . ." These, they decided, were personal and precious things for which they would willingly barter all the sunshine of Australia.

II

A week later there was a rather uncomfortable meeting with Lord Esher. It was a paradox, which strengthened Olivier's position, that the public, who knew nothing of the impending change, were clamouring to buy seats for the coming cycle of the three plays at the New and advance bookings already amounted to £10,000. Lord Esher went over, in more detail, all that he had said in his letter; but there was really nothing that could be added, and in the middle of November an official announcement was made by the Old Vic that, as a further step towards preparing the way for a National Theatre, certain changes were to be made in administration. Gratitude and admiration were expressed for "the work of the three retiring directors." Thus, obliquely, the bombshell was dropped. No one was deceived that this was anything but a dismissal, and, although he would not make any public statement, Olivier told all his friends who rang up to ask incredulously if it were true: "Yes, old boy, fired! Left without a job."

There was much buzzing and paragraphing, but as Olivier, Richardson and Burrell could not comment without being disloyal and Lord Esher declined to elaborate on the bare announcement, little fuel was added to the controversy. Perhaps the wisest and most far-sighted comment came from Stephen Mitchell. In a letter which he wrote to *The Daily Telegraph* he reviewed the whole question of state aid for the Old Vic.

"Three years ago," he wrote, "the Old Vic had reached a national position due to the work of Sir Ralph Richardson and Sir Laurence Olivier. Accordingly one would have supposed that the ardent co-operation of and continuation of these two gentlemen as directors would have been a *sine qua non* of the Governors' policy.

"It must accordingly be a surprise that, at this vital moment in the life of the Old Vic, Sir Laurence Olivier, who has just completed a great tour of Australia in which he did so much for the British theatre, and Sir Ralph Richardson, who absented himself from the Old Vic but for one season, have been summarily dropped —politely called resigning. In their places, and presumably to make up for them, have come £30,000 of public money and the bountiful and industrious secretary of the Arts Council. If Olivier and Richardson did wonders without that sum, what, it will surely occur to the theatregoer, could they not have done with it?"

But at the time the news broke the Oliviers were not so concerned with Theatre politics as with their opening in *The School for Scandal*. It was an important moment in both their careers; they had suddenly realized that they would be acting together on the English stage for the first time in their lives. They had made three films together, and had played together on the stage at Elsinore, in America, and on the recent tour; but the night of January 20th, 1949, was the first time that they bowed together to the cheers of a London audience. It was a first night for which three hundred people slept on the pavement in St. Martin's Lane (although Olivier went round personally telling them it wasn't worth it); it was a night when the cheering at the end meant that London had truly taken them to its heart.

Perversely—for it would seem a part for which she was ideally suited—Vivien Leigh did not care much for Lady Teazle, but Olivier had always loved Sir Peter, and, like Beerbohm Tree, considered *The School for Scandal* the most brilliant comedy ever given to the world. Undoubtedly part of the play's appeal for him lay in the fact that it belongs to a period which has a style and atmosphere in which he is particularly comfortable. "I feel," he wrote in an introduction to the Folio Society's edition of the play, "that I understand instinctively the spirit of Sheridan, and am more drawn to it than that of anyone else in the eighteenth century except, possibly, Handel!" It was therefore the play in which he was delighted for Vivien and himself to make their London debut together and their first appearance on the London stage since they had become Sir Laurence and Lady Olivier.

He appreciated Vivien's reaction against the "pretty-pretty" quality of her part, but considered that she was potentially the perfect Lady Teazle, and that one day she would enjoy the part as much as he did Sir Peter. Time alone, he knew, could make her love a character which she then considered shallow and uninteresting. A real appreciation of the pleasures of the part, he would tell her, would only come with the years. First she would have to test her strength in big parts and accept all the challenges of ambition . . . and then, when she had a better idea of the range of her capabilities, she would be able to relax and enjoy rôles for which she was naturally suited. "When you are at the height of your career," he said, "I believe you'll enjoy acting Lady Teazle." Vivien Leigh argued with him, but, despite her dislike of a part which she thought provided her with few opportunities (except in the screen scene), she succeeded in giving a completely disarming performance. It was greeted by the critics with frail pale-pink adjectives such as "bewitching," "exquisite," and "enchanting." Her own sense of frustration in the part, however, was probably best conveyed by the critic who described her briefly as "negatively perfect."

With infinitely more zest she bit deep into *Antigone*, in the modern version of Sophocles' tragedy, to which Anouilh had added

overtones of wartime France. This play born out of suffering—it
was first put on in Paris during the German occupation—made a
far greater appeal to her imagination. The curtain went up on a
Thebes where all the characters stood or sat in motionless silence
while the Chorus (Olivier in evening dress) outlined the plot in easy
colloquial phrases. At the back of the stage, her arms clasped on her
crossed knees, sat Antigone. The eye travelled at once to this pale,
dark-eyed creature, whose whole appearance of sullen misery
marked her as the tragic target of the gods. It was a performance
far beyond any that Vivien Leigh had hitherto given in a serious
part; it had strength and a taut, emotional power. Her voice had
lost nearly all trace of its usual silky undulations—the "tricks of
vocal singsong" for which she had been criticized when playing
Lady Teazle—and had somehow become deeper; it had about it from
the first a ring of authority and passion. A previously unsuspected
tragic actress had appeared. Olivier, who had feared that the young
Antigone would not be sufficiently challenging for her, was delighted, and watching her from the wings, he realized that he had
made a mistake in trying to dissuade her from playing the part.

III

It was with this new confidence in Vivien's abilities as a tragic
actress that, two months after the end of the Old Vic season at the
New, Olivier started rehearsals for *A Streetcar Named Desire*. As
soon as she had read the play early in 1948, Vivien Leigh had been
fascinated by the character of Blanche Du Bois, and had quickly
developed the same single-mindedness about playing her that she had
felt about Scarlett and Sabina. She had told Hugh Beaumont of
H. M. Tennent's, who owned the English rights, how anxious she
was to do the play, but, as she had pointed out, the Australian tour
would mean that she could not hope to be available for over a year.
Beaumont had said that he was quite prepared to wait.

Beaumont had first heard of the play while in America in the
autumn of 1947. On the day he was due to sail from New York
back to England he had been told by a friend that a play had opened
in New Haven the previous night which was destined to be an
enormous success. It was written by a comparatively new playwright with the unusual name of Tennessee Williams. Whatever he
did, the friend had insisted, he must see the play and acquire the

English rights before he left for home. Beaumont, who as the managing director of one of London's most important managements had heard such enthusiasm for out-of-town masterpieces before, had not cancelled his passage. But he had taken the precaution before leaving of writing a letter to Irene Selznick, who was putting on the play, saying that he hoped she would get in touch with him if and when the play was to be done in London.

A *Streetcar Named Desire* proved the success on Broadway which Beaumont's friend had predicted. It won the Drama Critics' Circle Award and the Pulitzer Prize and made Tennessee Williams famous. It was destined to run for three years. Beaumont's foresight in writing to Mrs. Selznick had paid dividends, for when she came to London to arrange the disposal of the English rights she had got in touch with him, and at their first meeting had announced crisply that the play was his if he wanted it. And now, two years after it had originally opened in America, Vivien was available, and *Streetcar*, with Olivier as producer, went into rehearsal in London at the end of August, 1949.

Many managers who present a play on both sides of the Atlantic make it a rule not to have any say or exert their influence over the second production for which they are responsible. They know how difficult it is to shake off preconceptions and fear that any advice they give may be unduly prejudiced by the original. Although she was not presenting *Streetcar* in London Irene Selznick retained considerable personal interest in the play which she had first presented, and shortly after the London rehearsals had started she arrived, full of enthusiasm. She asked if she might attend rehearsals, and would be very happy, she told Olivier, to give him her advice, based on the New York and other productions which she had sponsored.

Her first surprise came when she discovered how much more free a producer seemed to be in England to make what cuts or changes he liked to the text of a play, whereas in America the full approval of the author had to be obtained. She found that Olivier had not hesitated to make alterations, and she did not object when these were to allow for differences between English and American audiences. But she felt she had a responsibility to Tennessee Williams in trying to prevent cuts which, in her view, meant the loss of any overtones and nuances. Olivier was equally determined to make cuts where his judgment insisted they were necessary, and there were many sug-

gestions made by Mrs. Selznick which he was not prepared to accept.
In the same way Vivien Leigh was also unwilling to follow her advice about the way to play Blanche. She realized how difficult it
must be for Irene Selznick, having seen the play countless times in
New York, and having been responsible for more than one production, to accept her reading, which in certain scenes was different
from that of the American Blanches. But she maintained that it was
wrong, if not impossible, to interpret a part in the same way as
another actress.

This conflict about changes in the script complicated Olivier's
task, but there was a larger and more fundamental principle involved
which made *Streetcar*, he would sometimes say, the most painful
undertaking of his career. He wanted to produce the play along
original lines, but, try as he would, he could not completely discard
the ideas invented by Elia Kazan. His personal pride demanded
that, whatever happened, the London version must not be a copy of
the one on Broadway, but, having decided that he would use the
set designed by Jo Mielziner—which had in some degree been
planned in collaboration with the producer—it was impossible to
avoid adopting a great deal of what Kazan had in his mind. As a
matter of course, he had received the prompt script from New York
with all the business and moves written in detail. This he would try
to ignore, but during his "plotting" of the play prior to rehearsals
he would decide, after working for half an hour or so on his own
script, that it was simply perverse and unintelligent not to study the
methods of a producer from whom he could probably learn. He
would then pick up Kazan's script . . . only to throw it aside after
a while with the feeling that he was being hopelessly unenterprising.

During rehearsals Kazan arrived in London to produce *Death of
a Salesman*, and while there was no opportunity for them to meet,
Olivier felt he had to phone him and apologize for copying so many
of his ideas. "For goodness sake don't worry," Kazan told him.
"Why, I bet by the time you're through with the play you won't
know what moves are yours and what mine. In fact when the play
opens there won't be a thing that is exactly the same—except of
course the light. You can't change the light!" * Despite this reas-
surance Olivier did not feel justified in claiming that he was entirely

---

* This was a reference to the naked electric light bulb which at the climax
of the play Mitch shines mercilessly in Blanche's face to show up her age.

responsible, and on the programme insisted that there should be a credit line saying that he had produced it "After the New York production."

In October *A Streetcar Named Desire* opened at the Aldwych, a theatre which is still so much associated with the farces of Ben Travers that someone was moved to remark that Tennessee Williams' play was "a very different cup of tea to *Rookery Nook*." In the same vein of understatement Vivien Leigh said that she "wouldn't exactly call it a drawing-room comedy," but she was surprised at the extraordinary amount of abuse that was hurled at it as soon as it opened.

It was, in essence, a tragic study of a faded, unbalanced woman who pretends to the gentility of her girlhood while staying with her sister in the slums of New Orleans, is raped by her brother-in-law, and finally goes out of her mind. It was not a pretty theme, but the author's intentions were serious, and it was a mystery to Vivien why the play was labelled as salacious and pornographic, attacked as "low and repugnant" in the House of Commons, and condemned by the Public Morality Council. The reason was probably that most of the audience regarded Blanche as either a nymphomaniac or a prostitute, and many of the critics referred to her in these terms. Vivien Leigh did not consider her as such; she saw Blanche as a sensitive woman who had never recovered from a tragic early marriage to a homosexual, and whose loneliness may have led her, eventually, to decadence. This idea about Blanche's morals possibly arose from what Vivien held to be a misinterpretation of one of the speeches in the play. The main reason for imagining that Blanche's past was particularly sordid was the description (given by her brother-in-law when in a vindictive mood) of some gossip he had heard from commercial travellers who had been in her home town. Vivien had always regarded this as malicious and unfounded, yet because in the theatre that particular speech carried a force which made it sound authentic it was possibly misleading. There was certainly no evidence in the dialogue that Blanche had accepted money from men.

A section of the press, which makes a good thing out of a combination of emphatic denunciation and detailed description, turned on the play rather as critics at the beginning of the century had turned on Ibsen and Brieux. It provoked what C. E. Montague long ago termed "the vocabulary . . . of Medical Officers of Health." With righteous relish words like "cesspool" were used, and one journalist claimed that after sitting through the play he felt as if he had crawled through a garbage heap.

There were, of course, many critics whose concern was not with sanitary or moral values, but with the play's dramatic qualities. By this standard there were some strictures that the play was over-melodramatic. Blanche was a marathon performance for Vivien Leigh, who was on the stage, or speaking just off-stage, for the whole of two hours, and her wide emotional range and understanding of the part finally disposed of the criticisms (untenable since her Antigone) that she was just a beautiful woman and not an actress. She suggested with a quite horrible intensity the mind of the desperately unhappy woman who was losing her reason. It was only surprising that she did not win more pity for her unhappy heroine.

Fanned by abuse, *Streetcar* settled down to a secure success. It was a success summed up in the classic, apocryphal comment of the foyer: "It should never have been allowed. It gets worse and worse every time I see it." For the eight months that Vivien Leigh played her long exhausting part the theatre was packed to capacity.

IV

From the moment he had received Lord Esher's letter in Sydney, Olivier had started to make some far-reaching plans for the future; these culminated soon after the end of his last season at the Old Vic in the realization of his lifelong ambition to "open his own shop." For many years the leasing of theatres whenever he wanted to put on a play had dissatisfied him, and he decided to become an actor-manager and acquire a theatre of his own.

This meant the immediate expansion of Laurence Olivier Productions, Ltd., the private company which he had been nursing since 1947. His solicitor, his stockbroker, his old friend Anthony Bushell, Roger Furse, the scenic designer, and Sir Alexander Korda all joined the board of directors. Vivien Leigh, also made a director, protested that she knew nothing about business, but was informed that her function was to be "decorative" and to cheer up the meetings if they threatened to get dreary.

If they were going to have a theatre they would need practical theatre men to run it, and Olivier had no compunction in robbing the Old Vic of Lovat Fraser, who became his general manager, and David Kentish, his general stage director. Herbert Menges, who was to arrange most of the music for future productions, was also a friend with whom he had worked at the Old Vic and had known since Menges was leader of the little orchestra at the Royalty during the run of *Bird in Hand* in 1928. With Olivier himself as chairman, and his agent and friend, Cecil Tennant, as managing director, the company was now complete.

As good fortune would have it, just as they were looking round for a theatre, the St. James's became available. It had disadvantages, as Olivier was to discover, but it was a beautiful early Victorian theatre, with an intimate red-plush-and-gold atmosphere which he loved, and also possessed a great actor-manager tradition. Sir George Alexander had made the St. James's famous in the 'nineties, and it was there that he had presented Oscar Wilde's greatest successes. It had been built in 1835 for £26,000, and during the course of its history it had been in the hands of the Kendalls and John Hare; Rachel had once brought a French company over from Paris to the St. James's for a season, and for a short time it had even been under the management of Barnum, the circus king.

There was also a trivial, half-remembered occurrence of boyhood which gave Olivier a sentimental reason for wanting to take the St. James's. As a rather nervous boy, he had gone round to the stage door of the theatre one afternoon to see Sybil Thorndike. It was after a matinée, and as he had waited to be taken to her dressing-room he had seen Franklin Dyall in the passage. He had noted something he had not seen from the audience—the join of his wig. It was his initiation into this particular mystery of his future profession. Here a few years later, as a young actor of seventeen, he had come to see Sir Gerald du Maurier about a job; and here too, on one never-to-be-forgotten evening during the run of *The Mask of Virtue*, he had first set eyes on Vivien Leigh. Now, if he went back as Manager, the pattern of life would be revealed, the cycle completed. On November 14th, 1949, he took over the lease of the St. James's from Gilbert Miller for four years.

His first play there was one which he had asked Christopher Fry to write for him while he had still been in Australia. As terms of reference he had simply said that he wanted a play in verse which would provide suitable parts for Vivien Leigh, George Relph, certain other members of the company, and himself. This was, perhaps, rather slender inspiration for a poet even with as fertile an imagination as Fry, for it took him a very long time to finish *Venus Observed*. He wrote the first act and then got stuck, and had to lay the manuscript aside for several months. When at last it was completed, however, Olivier was charmed by it, and decided that it was the perfect play with which to open his management of the St. James's. By then, unfortunately, Vivien Leigh was no longer available; *Streetcar* had opened two months previously. She had warned Fry latterly that she might not be able to be in his play, and when she had read the final script she had felt sure that the part of Perpetua called for an actress, not only younger than herself, but completely fresh and unknown to the public.

An actress who fulfilled these requirements was found at the Windsor Repertory Theatre, and just before the end of the year *Venus Observed*, a play of strange, autumnal sadness and dazzling, exasperating poetry, went into rehearsal with Heather Stannard, as Perpetua. Olivier produced it as well as playing the Duke of Altair, and he was sometimes to wonder if this was wise. Perhaps he could have done even more to bring out the fragile, elusive quality of the play if he had been outside its framework. From the start he found it difficult to shape the part of the Duke, a middle-aged, highly-cultivated man who decides to marry one of the three women he loved when he was younger. His problem was to find a consistent angle of approach. For an actor who is at all versatile there are half-a-dozen or more ways he can play most characters. Somehow he must make a choice, and, as in the past, Olivier had searched for "the green umbrella" * that gives an actor a clue—however slight—to character and a method of approach. It was provided by the Œdipus-complex theory for *Hamlet;* Laughton's exclamation of "You're England!" for *Henry V;* Sir Maurice Bowra's advice just before he appeared as Œdipus—"Just feel *doomed*"*;* the stammer on the "w" as Hotspur; and often by details of make-up. Sometimes he had had to wait a long time for inspiration. For *Uncle Vanya* it

---

* The origin of "the green umbrella" is half lost in theatrical legend, but it is believed that it was carried by a German actor, possibly in a Reinhardt production. For weeks the actor had been groping hopelessly for an interpretation of a part, and then one day, to the producer's surprise, he appeared at rehearsal carrying a green umbrella. From that moment the part came right. He had discovered the one prop he required.

had not come until the first night; his whole interpretation of a complex character was unified when he first put on the beard and, tilting his head slightly backward, peered with half-closed eyes through pince-nez. At once and with extraordinary clarity, as he told Vivien Leigh, he had visualized the part of Astrov as a whole. She had said that she thought it a ridiculous assertion and that she simply did not believe he could have possibly reached so mature a characterization suddenly and at the last moment; while agreeing that it might sound unlikely, Olivier had insisted that it was so.

It was Vivien Leigh who gave him his "green umbrella" for the Duke. She noticed at an early rehearsal how much gesture he was working into the part. Because he always enjoyed inventing "business" it was all far too busy. She suggested that he should play the whole part without any "illustrative" gestures. The only exception should be in the second act, on the line, "We know . . . How the indolent fish waves its tail in time with the waving weed," when he should mime the movement with his hand. It might seem a negative and artificial restriction, but Olivier found it a valuable discipline on which to build his characterization of the Duke.

The first night of *Venus Observed* at the St. James's Theatre on January 18th, 1950, was an occasion for which Olivier had prepared with loving care. He was determined that his entry into theatrical management should mean the restoration of all the old values for which the St. James's had stood in its heyday. Theatres enjoy vogues, and the St. James's, a little distance from the centre of the West End, had for some years previously been rather in eclipse. Olivier wanted to restore its prestige, and bring back its popularity to the peak which in his lifetime it had only enjoyed during the management of Sir Gerald du Maurier. In his more wishful daydreams he would often imagine elderly ladies gossiping over their tea and saying of his new regime: "My dear, you only get the very best at the St. James's!"

To this end he poured a large, quite uneconomical amount of money into this first play. His cast, which included Valerie Taylor, Rachel Kempson, George Relph and Denholm Elliott, was not a cheap one; Roger Furse's sets were built without thought of cost, for he was determined on realism and would have nothing slipshod on the stage; actors had their shoes made to measure and were sent

to the best tailors for their suits; the dresses of the women were all
changed after the first night; a hairdresser came to the theatre twice
a week to ensure that all hair-styles were immaculate. And in the
orchestra pit a six-piece orchestra costing £100 a week was employed because Olivier could not bear to think of the audience—
his audience at the St. James's—sitting in the dark during a scene
change and being forced to listen to "canned" music.

Venus Observed was not only Olivier's first play as an actor-manager; it was also Christopher Fry's first play since *The Lady's Not
for Burning*. Both of them were on trial. In one way Olivier felt
extremely unprepared to face it. He was used to the emotional
excitement of first nights, and the added responsibility of being a
producer as well as a star was not new. But he experienced the
nightmare that every actor knows if he is at all shaky on his lines.
Because he had divided his interest between acting and producing,
and because the imagery and metre of Christopher Fry's verse possessed an often rococo complexity, he had found great difficulty in
learning it. All would be well, he believed, if he could get through
the important speech which contained the "waving weed" and went
on to explore even more involved imagery about a toad petrified in
stone. This speech, he considered, would be the key to the evening
—the point from which his performance would either take wings or
crash. No toad was ever so petrified as Olivier at the prospect of
"drying" on his much-heralded debut as an actor-manager.

The first act went without a hitch. There was a sense of high
excitement in the theatre as the lights dimmed for the second. A
round of applause greeted Roger Furse's set of a classical temple set
beside a lake in the Duke's park. Knowing nothing of Olivier's
fears, that very accomplished actress, Brenda De Banzie, who played
Jessie Dill, sat in the temple writing a letter while Laurence Olivier,
the Duke, started the speech, which was made to Denholm Elliott,
the Duke's son. The first half of the speech went well. He began
to build up slowly in the second, reaching a climax with his one
permitted gesture of the evening, and then, in a moment's pause
exactly when he had reached the perilous lines

> *If a pulse was in the stone,*
> *And the stone grew moist, and the toad petrified,*
> *Patience would still be as patient as the sun.*

he heard behind him an unmistakable noise. With a natural but over-zealous gesture Brenda De Banzie had torn a piece of paper off her writing-pad. She could not possibly have foreseen the consequence, and the noise itself was not serious, but, coming as it did at such a critical moment, it suddenly eclipsed everything else. He dried, floundered for a few seconds paraphrasing wildly, and then got back on text.

The audience was not aware of what had happened, and it was a triviality which could not be seriously considered against the success of the play, the cheers of the first-night audience, and the almost unanimous praise of the critics for his acting and production. But because his performance had fallen below his own exacting standards the incident slightly marred the glory of this, one of the most important nights of his career.

v

Venus Observed was to run for seven months and, except financially, was the complete fulfilment of his hopes for his new management at the St. James's.

The problem of making the business as well as the artistic side of the theatre a success is one which has been confronting Laurence Olivier with particular insistence since 1947 when he first formed a small company to put on *Born Yesterday*. Garson Kanin's comedy had run for eleven months at the Garrick, and this had encouraged him to present more plays even though it had shown surprisingly little profit.

Between then and *The Happy Time*, presented at the St. James's at the beginning of 1952, Laurence Olivier Productions Ltd. has presented twelve plays. They are *Daphne Laureola* (Edith Evans), *Fading Mansion* (Siobhan McKenna), *Venus Observed, Captain Carvallo* (Diana Wynyard), *Top of the Ladder* (John Mills), *The Consul, Cæsar and Cleopatra, Antony and Cleopatra*, the Jean Louis Barrault Company in a short season of French plays, and *Othello* (Orson Welles). In variance with the usual practice of actor-managers and their wives, the Oliviers have appeared in only a few of their own productions. Olivier has been in three and Vivien Leigh in two.

On paper these would seem to be an enterprising selection with a number of notable productions and long runs among them, yet on balance they have not proved financially successful. James Bridie's comedy *Daphne Laureola* with Edith Evans at Wyndham's in 1949 ran for nearly a year, but its success at the box-office was quickly offset by *Fading Mansion* which closed after a fortnight. *Captain Carvallo*, a modern comedy by Dennis Cannan, which Olivier put on the following year, and which had a good run at the St. James's and the Garrick, did not show a profit. Though it was written by Tyrone Guthrie and had John Mills as its star, *Top of the Ladder* taught him how tricky was the unpredictable business of play-fancying. But the most expensive gamble of all was in bringing Menotti's opera *The Consul* to London. He had thought it magnificent in New York, but its intensely tragic middle-European setting, curiously blended with opera, was not to the public taste.

To those who consider it strange that, with his long experience, he cannot always pick winners, Olivier points out that the life of a theatrical manager is one in which hope is constantly at odds with better judgment. He knows that if he finds a really great play once in a lifetime he will be lucky; he will also be lucky if he comes across a play with enough merit to pass for great once in five years. For the rest of the time, and with eight plays out of ten, he is trying to get the best out of material which he knows is not the best. He is simply taking a gamble with a play because it has good parts for actors, or an original idea, or some other quality that will make for success. Like a wine merchant, he cannot wait for a vintage year before laying in a stock. And like the wine merchant he often has no illusions about what he offers; it is simply the best available at the time.

Olivier often complains that he is being turned into a complete illiterate because he spends all his spare time reading plays, most of which are hopeless, that pour into the company's office in St. James's Street. Impatience and his theory about the rarity of great plays has sometimes led impulse to outweigh careful judgment. A line, a single speech, or a situation has been enough to persuade him that a particular play is worth producing.

He read no further than the moment in *Daphne Laureola* when the tipsy woman in the restaurant breaks raucously into, "Pull for the Shore, Sailor!"; he didn't bother to go on; he simply rang up and bought it. He saw *Fading Mansion* first in Anouilh's French version, *Romeo et Jeanette*, in Paris, and was partly influenced by

Vivien Leigh's enthusiasm. His understanding of colloquial French, however, was not good enough to allow him to follow it completely; but in the adaptation by Donagh MacDonagh two good "curtains" and some dialogue in the second act were enough to decide him. The drunken, rapscallion Irish father (to be played by George Relph) is talking to his son:

"I had my rules of courtship to which I rigidly adhered," says Cormac Joyce. "I always made it a rule to break off the affair first. Never more than three months. On the last day I raised the siege and nothing would turn me. I have had them on their knees before me, had them run in their night attire after me down the street. But I was implacable . . ."

"But if you were unhappy," asks his son, "what did you do?"

"But that is just it," he replies, "that is what I am trying to tell you. I was never unhappy. It is necessary to live by rules . . ." (and here came the line which so caught Olivier's imagination, ". . . a gentleman is *never* unhappy!"

These decisions were not fool-proof—he never expected that they would be—and, when the plays were presented at his own theatre, difficulties were aggravated. With only about two hundred and fifty expensive seats at the St. James's and with a total capacity of under a thousand, it was difficult with high entertainment tax and rising costs to show a profit.

So that he should not be unduly worried by personal financial problems and to prevent his and Vivien's annual income fluctuating between extremes according to whether he was in a Hollywood film or a London play showing no profit, it was decided that they should become the main capital "assets" of their own limited company. This was a stabilizer and a safety valve. Now every penny which they earn belongs to the company and this extends from the sale of cabbages from the market garden at Notley to their salaries for films and plays. In return for this somewhat drastic self-sacrifice, an almost mystical abnegation of worldly rights, they are paid a fixed and regular salary not above that of a cabinet minister. Olivier calls it a "modest stipend" without noticeably blushing. He also fails to specify which cabinet minister.

Venus Observed had only two sets and ten characters, but, even so, a long run could not compensate for the large production and running costs. Olivier also made a mistake in cancelling Monday

night performances so that he should have one weekday free to look
after his other managerial responsibilities. He gave an extra matinée,
but matinées at the St. James's he soon found belonged to the dear,
dead days which it was beyond even him to recall, and Cecil Tennant soon began to wear the expression of a man who might at any
moment produce a balance sheet which was not going to be the
least bit favourable. What was the way out? Once again the Oliviers fell back on their age-old solution. In June, in the middle of
the two successful runs, it was announced from Hollywood that
Vivien Leigh was going to make the film of *Streetcar*, and that
Olivier would also be there at the same time for a film of Theodore
Dreiser's *Sister Carrie*. Tactfully, and with no skin off anybody's
nose, Hollywood was once again being made to subsidize the London theatre.

VI

Vivien Leigh flew ahead of Olivier to America so that she could
spend a few days in Connecticut with Elia Kazan, who was to direct
the film of *Streetcar*, before she and Kazan went out to the West
Coast to start rehearsals and shooting. They had decided that it
would save time on the set if each knew the other's ideas about the
character of Blanche and were in complete agreement on the way
certain scenes were to be played.

Although Kazan was a film director of long experience, the theatre
was his first love and his values were not those of Hollywood, so
that Vivien Leigh found she had an immediate ally in what threatened to be a serious battle ahead of them. *Streetcar* had to be filmed
in a way which would be acceptable to the Hays Office and yet it
must still keep the most important factors in the play. They were
both agreed that somehow the reason for Blanche's unstable and
neurotic personality must be conveyed to the audience. It must be
made clear that the shock in her youth had been so great that it had
altered her entire life and character. The difficulty was to say
frankly what the shock had been.

Kazan told her that on Broadway it had been possible to mention
perversion unmistakably. Blanche had been able to give an account
of her first tragic marriage without any censor to forbid the line:
"I came into a room and found my young husband with an older
man who had been his friend for years." The implications were

obvious, and, because of her reaction, the husband had committed suicide. The sense of guilt had never left her. At once the pattern of Blanche's life clicked into place for the audience. The past explained the present with sudden clarity, in the same way that audiences learn for the first time the nature of the ghosts which haunt Mrs. Alving.

It had always seemed to Vivien Leigh that Blanche's life and behaviour could only be interesting provided this was understood. Before the London production of the play she had personally pleaded for the line to be kept in unaltered, but while the Lord Chamberlain's reader agreed about its importance, he considered it would give too much offence. So, Vivien explained to Kazan, the line had been modified. Blanche said: "I came into a room and there was my husband and . . ." here she broke down and the rest of the line was lost in sobbing.

If they had hoped this compromise would satisfy the Hays Office, they were soon to be disillusioned. To convey any such reason for Blanche's character was ruled right out of the question, and it was not until Vivien Leigh and Kazan began to talk of calling the film off that Warner Brothers really awakened to the seriousness with which they regarded this aspect of the film. Accustomed as the studio executives were to dealing in surface values readily understandable to a world audience, they were surprised to find a star and a director so deeply concerned about the psychological background of a screen heroine. The offending speech was rewritten several times, and when these versions were in turn frowned on by the Hays Office the studio, at the request of Kazan and Vivien Leigh, called in the author.

Tennessee Williams was flown to Hollywood, heard the difficulty, examined the rejected dialogue and went into retreat. He emerged with a completely new speech, which satisfied the Hays Office and produced smiles of gratitude round Warner Brothers. To Williams it must have seemed a poor compromise. For millions who would go to see *Streetcar* on the screen, Blanche's marriage would remain a mystery and her behaviour unexplained; only a few people who knew the play well would be able to place the right interpretation on a line foggy with equivocation. Blanche would simply say of her husband: "He wasn't like other people."

When the idea of making the film had first been suggested, Vivien

Leigh had been very doubtful if she wanted to act Blanche on the screen. She had found that the play took a great deal out of her emotionally, and by the time she had handed over her part to Betty Ann Davies at the Aldwych she felt she had played it quite long enough. She would probably never have accepted had it not coincided with Paramount's offer to Olivier for *Carrie;* but once shooting started she was glad that she had. She found it a great help to be playing a character, in front of the cameras, which she had already studied in such detail and knew so intimately. The lack of coherence and logical development, inevitable when filming (which had made Scarlett so difficult ten years before) did not worry her now.

Ten years had also made a difference in the conditions which she found in the Hollywood studios. At the risk of upsetting the touchy English film unions she was quite forthright in saying that she found the American technicians far more efficient and generally more cooperative and interested in the film than British technicians. To meet the threat of television, all the old extravagance had disappeared and schedules were planned to the last degree. The waits caused while the right union man was sent for to move an ornament or knock in a nail, which still hampered British production, had gone overboard in a gesture of self-preservation.

In the middle of August Olivier arrived in Hollywood with Suzanne, Vivien's daughter, who was now seventeen and was training at the Royal Academy of Dramatic Art. It was his first time in the United States since his knighthood and a certain amount of confusion was created by his simple request that he should not be called *Sir* Laurence Olivier on posters or on the credit titles of the film. It led to the assumption by a number of people in Hollywood that, making a concession to republican sentiment, he wished to be known as *Mr.* Olivier at all times. At least one other actor at Paramount had no time for such humility and ordered a notice to be fixed on his dressing-room door which read "Sir Robert Hope—peasants keep out."

William Wyler, who was directing him and Jennifer Jones in *Carrie* at Paramount, noted with a good deal of quiet amusement Olivier's new interest in the cinema. He made friends with all the production crew, carefully studied all the new production methods with a retentive eye, and was continually picking the brains of engineers on various technical advances in the studios. It was a far cry, Wyler thought, from the days of *Wuthering Heights*.

When the day's shooting was over neither Olivier nor Vivien Leigh could completely relax; there was a great deal to be thought about. The Festival of Britain lay ahead the moment they got back from Hollywood, and they had decided that they must have one first-rate production, if not two, at the St. James's. Rather half-hearted attempts by the Theatrical Managers' Association to persuade the leaders of the profession to make a concerted plan for the Festival had broken down, and the coming summer looked like developing into a free-for-all with each management and star vying with the others. Olivier had more or less staked a claim by tentatively announcing *Cæsar and Cleopatra*, but this was not finally settled.

"What we want," he kept saying, "is an idea—a really exciting *idea*."

Rather forlornly he and Vivien were ploughing their way through the plays of Barrie, Pinero, and half-a-dozen other dramatists. With the whole world of drama and two thousand years of plays to choose from, nothing seemed to force itself to the front and demand production.

Their quandary had been precipitated by a long, apologetic letter in John Gielgud's minute handwriting saying that he was very sorry but he wouldn't be able to manage the all-star *School for Scandal* which he and Olivier had been considering. The letter was written from New York where he was playing in *The Lady's Not for Burning*, and it meant the end of one of Olivier's most cherished hopes. It had been Gielgud's suggestion that Olivier should put on *The School* with himself as Joseph and Olivier as Charles Surface. This had set Olivier dreaming of an all-star production of Sheridan—a production "to knock their eyes out," as he put it—which would also have Ralph Richardson as Sir Peter and Vivien Leigh as Lady Teazle.

To avoid the crowds and to give themselves the chance of a holiday, they sailed home on a small French cargo boat when their two films were finished. The *Wyoming* carried fruit, timber, and only six other passengers, and during the weeks out of San Francisco and travelling slowly homeward by way of the Panama Canal they read more plays and played canasta. But the month at sea produced no

inspiration, and they had few suggestions to make when, two days
after their arrival in London, they came face-to-face across the conference table with their fellow-members on the board of Laurence
Olivier Productions, Ltd.

During the Oliviers' absence in Hollywood Anthony Bushell,
Roger Furse and the other directors had also been supposed to think
of ideas, but they, too, had got nowhere. Olivier's suggestion of
Mary Rose met a rather bleak reception, and the idea of *Othello* was
discussed. Then Roger Furse, absently scribbling, said what about
doing *Antony* as well as *Cæsar and Cleopatra?* At least they'd halve
their advertising costs; they need put the name Cleopatra only once
on the posters. Everyone laughed and Furse was reminded that he
must be serious; there was very little time left for planning. It was
now January and the Festival opened in May.

Five days later the Oliviers sought inspiration in Paris, an expedi-
tion which ended with Olivier being ill and having to retire to bed
in his hotel. While he was lying there he suddenly told Vivien that
he had found the missing idea. *Antony was* the answer. She reminded him that they had talked it over many times before and they
had decided that neither of them was ready for it . . . that it was a
play they didn't want to consider for about five or ten years. With
this she went out to do some shopping. The moment she left the
room Olivier phoned through to London and arranged to present
the two Cleopatra plays. The idea which everyone was to greet as
a considered master-stroke by a shrewd man of the theatre was really
the outcome of casual pleasantry.

The decision was made in the middle of January, and the two
plays opened in Manchester before coming to London, at the end of
April. It meant two months of intense activity, but, although he
was worn out by the end of them, Olivier welcomed the rush. Most
of his productions were carefully planned months in advance, but he
believed that sometimes spontaneity was an advantage. Ideas would
come out of the air at the last minute; their realization would be
spurred by necessity.

But this idea, happy though it was as a superficial *coup de théâtre*,
had practical limitations of which the Oliviers very soon became
aware. The plays *as a pair* were tremendously successful throughout
the London season, and were to repeat that success in New York,
but it was really a marriage of incompatibles. Even Michael Bent-

hall's production, and Roger Furse's sets, all of which were designed to fuse them into a whole, could not disguise the fact that Shaw's comedy was a weak partner. During rehearsals Olivier found himself more and more annoyed with Shaw for his construction of the play because he considered it left Cleopatra in mid-air half-way through, and because of his insistence that there was no liaison between Cleopatra and Cæsar. The weakness of construction could be overcome if the audience had the theatrically interesting idea of a romance between the ageing general and the young queen. History gave them a child, and, disregarding Shaw's preface, Olivier was determined that Vivien should suggest, from the start of Act II, that the relationship had ceased to be platonic. Shavians might disapprove of this but he didn't care. He was almost certain from the first brilliant scene at the Sphinx that Shaw had intended to write a love story—what other interpretation could there be of the prophetic line, "You'll be the most dangerous of all Cæsar's conquests"? —and then, perversely, had preferred the usual Shavian anti-romantic paradox. It seemed to Olivier he became so interested in Cæsar as the pacifist general that the rest of the play suffered badly. Much of the action was illogical; there were weaknesses in construction (only partly disguised by brilliant "curtains"); there was not one line written for a laugh after the middle of the play. "This is Shaw at his most impish and schoolmasterish," he would complain to Michael Benthall, the producer, as they discussed ways of trying to restore the balance—anyway as far as the romance was concerned.

But to suggest the romance posed a difficulty as it meant acting against the lines, and Vivien Leigh was only prepared to go so far in changing what Shaw had meant. It would have been easy to have put a particular emphasis on Cleopatra's bearing and behaviour to hint at the start of a love affair, but she resisted this as dishonest to the dramatist's intention. Her only concession was to assume, at Olivier's insistence, a far greater maturity in Act IV, and even this she did not really regard as a concession because the part was written much more incisively for this act.

Olivier, superbly made-up as the ageing Cæsar,* instilled a won-

---

* To obtain the best possible likeness he went to the trouble of having a cast taken from the head of Julius Cæsar in the British Museum, and, until he had perfected his make-up, worked with this on the dressing-table in front of him. He knew that modern authorities do not accept this head as absolutely authentic, but as the most familiar portrait it seemed the most suitable.

derful sense of world-weariness into his performance, but after a few weeks of the run, he himself found the illogicalities of the play very annoying and the part uninspiring. Once he thought he had the measure of the character it seemed to offer no challenge. Free-wheeling as an actor never appeals to him.

He was almost equally unhappy as Antony for exactly the opposite reason. He was continually beating at his own performance in an attempt to better it and always complaining that it was an impossible part. The problem, as he saw it, was that if the fall of a Tragic Hero was to have poignancy there must be heights to fall from, yet right from the start of the play Shakespeare made Antony a weak character; he was the "strumpet's fool" and a man run to seed even before the curtain went up. It seemed to Olivier that Antony only half believes that he can reclaim his lost dignity and is too quickly set on his own destruction. Audiences, judging his performance on a gossip level, were inclined to say that he was "playing down" in order to give Vivien Leigh more limelight as Cleopatra; what he was really doing was to present Antony, as Shakespeare wrote him, the weaker of the two characters with only occasional flashes of the great man that had been.

This reconciling of strength and weakness was Olivier's constant problem, and everyone was appealed to for a solution. How much of Antony's nobility should he show, and how? Dr. Dover Wilson, faced suddenly with the question in a car between the St. James's Theatre, where he had just seen the performance, and Durham Cottage, where he was to sup, turned it over carefully in his mind for a month before writing to say:

"Antony's nobility? I think it's more important to make him 'terrific'; that's what the man was whom Cleopatra saw in her vision of him after his death and that, I believe, is what Shakespeare wished us to think of him. Everything Philo says about him before his entry bears this out—a terrific man, the triple pillar of the world and looking like it, a plated Mars. And it's only a terrific spirit that could love as 'Let Rome in Tiber melt,' etc., tells us he did. I don't think you can possibly overdo this, especially as the audience gets its first impression of him. And I do think that certain things in the production as I (twice) saw it militate against it. The lion's skin, for instance, was a mistake. It was all right for the Elizabethans as it at once suggested Hercules to them, but to a modern audience it merely suggests mental effeminacy. No: enter as a 'plated Mars' (just back from a little field practice if you like) and *dominate* the stage, with Cleopatra to boot."

Turning to an earlier scholar, Vivien Leigh was given her first glimpse of the tremendous task of playing Shakespeare's Cleopatra by Professor Bradley. In his famous lecture, delivered at Oxford and published in 1909, he had said that Cleopatra's wiles, taunts, furies and meltings, her laughter and tears all bewitched Antony. "She loves what he loves, and she surpasses him. She can drink him to his bed, out-jest his practical jokes, out-act the best actress who ever amused him, out-dazzle his own magnificence. She is his play-fellow, and yet a great queen. Angling in the river, playing billiards, flourishing the sword he used at Philippi, hopping forty paces in the public street, she remains an enchantress. Her spirit is made of wind and flame, and the poet in him worships her no less than the man." This, added to the description by Enobarbus, and the ideas she received from Plutarch and Emil Ludwig's biography, was enough to overawe any actress.

At first she felt too slight and young for Cleopatra and found herself inclined to play the part a little too heavily by way of compensation. To convey the idea of dignity and greatness and still keep a lightness of touch in the less emotional scenes was a problem which, while it never came over the footlights, worried her a good deal. Like most actresses she experienced difficulty in her first scene because Shakespeare provides Cleopatra with so little opportunity to show her full character or suggest that she is a genius. But it was a relief, after playing Shaw, to find the part growing as the play progressed and to build up a performance to the magnificent climax in the speech just before her death.

By almost unanimous consent in London and with only a little dissension in New York, Vivien Leigh's Cleopatra was accepted as one of the best performances of her career. "The challenge is to Cleopatra," wrote Ivor Brown, "and Vivien Leigh takes it not only with the necessary beauty which was certain anyway, but with a technical skill, a range of voice, and an emotional power that are a revelation of developed artistry." The most difficult of all the boy-player parts had at last been turned to verity and to glory by a woman. "Here," he concluded with Charmian's phrase, "is the seemingly unattainable, 'the lass unparalleled'." "Miss Leigh's Cleopatra is superb," concurred Brooks Atkinson seven months later in New York. ". . . She is sensual, wily and treacherous, but she is also intelligent, audacious, and courageous." Despite Vivien Leigh's very natural fears, the "infinite variety" had not escaped her.

Although he, too, was praised for his Antony, Olivier was not happy in the part. Even Dover Wilson's advice could not provide the whole answer to his problem. The trouble went deeper. It was the almost permanent dissatisfaction that an actor, like any other artist, always feels—the sense of shortcoming, the disparity between the ideal conceived in the mind's eye, and its realization. Alternating with *Cæsar*, *Antony* ran for five months in London and four in New York, yet on only one occasion, and for no reason on earth, during an evening in June, did he give a performance that came within measurable distance of the standard he set himself. "Enjoyed Antony to-night," Olivier wrote in his pocket diary. It meant more to be able to say that than all the praise of friends or critics. For one performance he had pleased himself.

VII

The present crowds the past. All that has been written may well be the opening chapters for the biography of the future. The Oliviers both consider they have much to achieve; neither has any intention of resting on successes in the past.

Both decline to shape their careers too far ahead; impulse remains the motto. But impulse, of course, is apt to be tempered by necessity, and Vivien Leigh often wonders if they are becoming too hedged in by material responsibilities. She is torn between a love of their two homes, Durham Cottage and Notley, and a suspicion that actors should really have no property and should resemble vagabonds. Shouldn't she and Larry really be free to go anywhere and everywhere and to take any interesting work that turns up? If salary, standards of living or personal comfort are allowed to dominate their choice of parts or plays they run the risk of losing their integrity, and of their work becoming stereotyped; they may cease from what should be the artist's perpetual quest for the true and the original.

They see another possible danger. If they are ever tempted to stand on false dignity or lose the ability to laugh at themselves, they know their work will suffer. For this reason, while in their hearts they probably both want to be considered as great tragedians, they are not afraid of the frivolous. They do not mind being accused of playing the fool. They will dress up as Victorian children and prance around the stage as they did with Danny Kaye at the Sid Field Memorial performance. If they thought it justified they would probably not be above going into white-face or throwing a custard-pie. They will not devote themselves to a heavy succession of classical tragedy, although a now highly-developed interest in the cinema has decided Olivier to film more Shakespeare plays. In a love of doing the unexpected he will secretly train his voice while playing Shakespeare's Antony so that he can follow it by singing Macheath in *The Beggar's Opera*. And this last decision shows a trend which is peculiarly Olivier's own. He has a sense of showmanship which insists that if there is one thing of which audiences shall have no cause to accuse Vivien or himself, it is of the crime of being monotonous.

When they are working—and it sometimes seems to them that they never do anything else—they have insufficient time to see friends and keep abreast of everyday affairs. There seems no time to read much except plays, and this particularly concerns Vivien Leigh, who believes that actors should not live so completely in a world of their own that they eventually have no interest in anything outside their sphere of work. She is sure that they must really understand the people who make up their audiences and must not be theatrically or socially rarefied and so lose touch with simple, un-affected sentiments and everyday humour.

This would not, however, seem to be a danger that theatens too ominously. On one recent occasion Olivier showed, by his choice of phrase and wide, imaginative breadth of allusion, that his sympathies are very far from being limited or confined. It was at the time of King George VI's death in February last year when he and Vivien Leigh were playing on Broadway in the Cleopatra plays. The English theatrical colony in New York held a memorial service in the Church of the Transfiguration in down-town New York, and to Sir Laurence Olivier, as the senior member of the profession there, fell the honour of giving the address. As he planned his speech he recalled the cry that rose in Westminster Abbey at the King's coronation: "God save the King! May the King live for ever!" It had seemed to him, when he heard it over the radio in 1937, the most dramatic phrase in the whole service, and its mystical implications had stirred his imagination. Fifteen years later in his address to his fellow-countrymen in the tightly-packed church 5,000 miles from home, he tried to convey what the phrase meant to him.

"The words," he said, "are like a banner into which are woven all the mixed fabrics, adopted and native, of legend and fact that are for ever fermenting in our national consciousness. It has the thrill of Angel Trumpets and a glint of jewels on an Eastern Tent, the dim grandeur of a Saxon Chapel and the evening light on a soft green hill, the dark stain of blood, the cavernous blackness of coal-mines, salt spray and steamship funnels, the crash of industry and the glowing majesty of William Shakespeare, cool country lanes, alehouse laughter, oysters, whelks, firesides large and small, and the ink-stained dustiness of commercial life."

In these words an actor spoke, not for the stage or for any special section of society, but for England.

INDEX

Index

Wilmot, Charles, 320
Wilson, Beatrice, 39
Wilson, Dr. Dover, 356, 358
Wilson, John C., 82, 207
Winter, Cecil, 292
Winter, Keith, 74, 85, 86
Wolfit, Donald, 277
Wong, Anna May, 60
Wood, Sam, 189
Woolland, Norman, 303
Woollcott, Alexander, 61, 177, 205, 215, 216, 233
Worthy Down, 229, 233, 236, 237

Wray, Maxwell, 120, 122-124, 127
Wren, P. C., 53
Wuthering Heights, 170-178, 186, 192, 201, 353
Wyler, William, 171-179, 191, 239, 352
Wyndham, Howard, 83
Wynyard, Diana, 347

Yank at Oxford, A, 103
Yeats, W. B., 284
Yellow Ticket, The, 69
Young Woodley, 59
Young, Terence, 240

141
194